ONLY ONE YEAR

Svetlana Alliluyeva

ONLY ONE YEAR

Translated from the Russian by Paul Chavchavadze

HARPER & ROW, PUBLISHERS

NEW YORK AND EVANSTON

1817

Grateful acknowledgment is made for permission to reprint the following: "Graze on, ye peaceful sheep and cattle," on page 175, from *Poems of Pushkin*, selected and interpreted by Henry Jones. Copyright © 1965 by Henry Jones. Reprinted by permission of Citadel Press, Inc. Lines from "To the Sea," on pages 343–344, from *Pushkin*, introduced and edited by John Fennell. Copyright © by John Fennell, 1964. Reprinted by permission of Penguin Books, Inc.

FIRST EDITION

LIBRARY OF CONGRESS CATALOG CARD NUMBER: 79–81883

TO ALL NEW FRIENDS,

TO WHOM I OWE MY LIFE IN FREEDOM

Contents

I. THE DECISION

Last Day in the U.S.S.R.

Iт NEVER crossed my mind on December 19, 1966, that it was to be my last day in Moscow and in Russia. Still less could others around me have imagined anything of the kind—my son Joseph, his wife Helen, my daughter Katie, and many friends who dropped in that day.

A very cold day—a frosty five degrees (Fahrenheit), reaching four below by nightfall. Snow kept falling, threatening to turn into a regular storm. My plane was due to leave the Sheremetyevo Airport at one o'clock at night, but no matter how often I called the dispatcher's office, no one there could tell me whether a flight would be possible in such weather. It seemed as if Moscow was determined not to let me go. Friends and acquaintances kept calling up—"Is it true? Are you really flying away today?"—and for the hundredth time I had to repeat the same thing. It was indeed extraordinary that I should have been given permission to take my late husband's ashes to India, and people just couldn't believe that I would actually leave that evening.

This was to be my first journey abroad, not counting the ten days during the summer of 1947 that I had spent with my brother in East Germany, where he was stationed at the time with an air corps. The whole thing seemed strange even to me, and although the permit had been granted a month before and I had had ample time to get ready for the trip, I still had not packed the big suitcase, borrowed from a friend, having no clear idea what Delhi's climate was like and what I should take with me in the way of clothing. The second, smaller suitcase stood ready. It contained numerous presents for Indian relatives, without which, I had been told, I could not go; as well as presents from the Indian philologist, Dr. Bahri, to his family in Allahabad.

My greatest concern was an overnight bag into which I had put a smaller white bag containing a porcelain urn with the ashes. I had racked my brains for a long time, not knowing how to carry the urn. Much advice was given me, but there was only one thing I knew for certain: I must keep it near me, very close. It was something almost alive, which seemed very heavy to me. A sort of mysterious part of my own self.

My old school friend, Alya, had been with me since the morning. We had finished school together, and together had entered the university and had graduated from it, both of us majoring in the modern history of the United States. Even the choice of this subject was made for both of us, in part, by Alya, or rather by her mother, who had served for many years in the foreign department of *Pravda* as senior reader of reports from the United States. Alya's mother spoke English well, and had a sister who had been living for years in Detroit.

Alya was a quiet, blue-eyed girl, one of the top students both at school and at the university. She didn't know how to be angry or irritated, nor did she ever raise her voice. Yet she was firm about her principles, which were kindness, honesty, and work. And just like her were her three daughters, whose friend and pal she was, an equal among equals.

It was easy to talk to Alya about anything: she knew how to listen and always tried to understand. The only time she

failed to understand me was when I told her that I had
had myself baptized. She could understand my religious feeling—she had something of the kind, too—but she was distrustful of the Church as a social force.

Her whole family had known Brajesh Singh. Her daughter
Tanya and her husband, a student of mathematics, had for
several months occupied Singh's apartment, placed at his
disposal by the publishers; he himself was then living with
us. Alya knew many Indians in Moscow—she worked as an
editor for the Publishers of Oriental Literature.

Now she had come to me, quiet and sweet as always, and
we drank coffee in the kitchen, the chief room in my apartment, where our best friends were always entertained. On
that day two other former schoolmates also dropped in to
see me—Misha and Vera.

Misha and I had been at school together since the age of
eight. Like me he was redheaded, freckled, and read more
than anyone else in the class. We used to discuss Jules Verne,
Fenimore Cooper, and modern science fiction. At the age of
eleven we became completely engrossed in Maupassant—
in both our homes there were large libraries. It was at this
time, too, that we began writing notes to each other on
blotting paper—"I love you"—and would then kiss on the
rare occasions the opportunity to do so presented itself. But
soon Misha's parents were arrested (they worked for the
State Publishers), and later his aunt, a doctor of medicine,
was sent to prison, too. My governess insisted that Misha be
transferred to another class, having presented the school's
principal with the damning evidence—those love notes on
blotting paper. Our friendship was cut short; we met only
once again, briefly, during the war. But after the Twentieth
Party Congress (at which Khrushchev denounced the cult of
personality), Misha found my telephone number and called
me up: he was anxious about me. I immediately recognized
his voice—while in school we had called each other up almost every day—and from then on we became friends once

more. By now he was a construction engineer, although from childhood he had loved literature and the humanities and, as before, continued to read a great deal. Kind and considerate, he knew everything about his former classmates: who was working where, who had married, who had children. He managed not to lose sight of any of his old friends and had kept up close contacts with many. He used to come and see me about once every six months and we would discuss our problems as parents. His younger son, who sang all day long like a nightingale, he had sent to a music school, dreaming that someday he might become a second Caruso. His older daughter, pretty and high-strung, caused him some anxiety. She was finishing school and, quite unexpectedly, developed a great interest in the history of the Far East and India; so I gave her my favorite books about India: the *Autobiography* and *The Discovery of India* by Jawaharlal Nehru.

Vera I had known since my earliest childhood, as our mothers had been friends. They were also on friendly terms with Regina Glass, the gifted teacher; it was her educational ideas that were practiced in my home, and it was to her, in essence, that I owed my interesting early childhood. Regina Glass had been educated in Switzerland. In Russia she had worked with Shatsky.* My mother, who had such faith in *enlightenment*, was greatly influenced by Regina, with whom no one else in our family had any rapport: Father could not stand her and her "pedagogical tricks," and soon insisted that she no longer frequent our home. But in Vera's family Regina was loved.

Vera, since way back when Mama was still alive, used to be brought to us at Zubalovo—her family usually spent their

---

* Well-known Russian pedagogue, follower of Tolstoy's "free school." He organized a school for poor peasant children and taught them art. He corresponded with Rabindranath Tagore, borrowing a great deal from the latter's pedagogical experience.

summers in the country not far away. Sometimes my nurse would take me to see them, or we might meet in a fragrant pine grove nearby. Later, Vera studied with me in the same school and in the same class, but here each one of us, having different interests, found her own friends. Vera was a born naturalist and, after graduating from school, entered the Biology Faculty at the university. I, on the other hand, always loved literature and the humanities.

Not an easy life fell to Vera's share, but then from childhood she had been trained to give all of herself to her work, to persevere and be selfless. She took up genetics with her usual dedication. But in 1949, when she was graduating and could have started some research work on her own, this science had been declared "idealistic" and was forbidden in the U.S.S.R. Vera, like many geneticists who did not wish to renounce their vocation, had to continue her researches "under cover." At present the chromosome theory has been "rehabilitated," so that, after all, those years of clandestine work were not wasted. Vera is now one of the leading geneticists in the country. When I was leaving, she was completing her thesis (by now, doubtless, she has become a Doctor of Biology).

Vera never had a family of her own, but no one could be more full of love and care for others. Every day she carried dinner to the nonagenarian Regina, who lived not far from her. We had tried to place the lonely, half-blind Regina in a home for old people, but this proved to be difficult: Regina refused to give up her independence. Furthermore, she could not live without concerts and the Conservatory, where she always managed, somehow, to obtain tickets to the most exclusive and rare recitals.

During our student days Vera and I used to see one another at recitals when there were no other occasions to meet. But of late those faraway years of our childhood had once more become meaningful to us, and we again became drawn to one another. My children fell in love with her the very first time she came to see them.

She had a wonderful gift for creating close relations with people, though not with everyone: she meant nothing to those of superficial judgments, and they were of no interest to her. You couldn't call her pretty or well dressed. She was not very "Western" in appearance, yet in Paris, where she gave a report in French on her work, she charmed everyone. In looks she belonged to the classical type of Russian intellectual of the last century—the face of a peasant, illuminated from within by the light of intellect. Her long fair hair lay in a braid around her head; her features were large and not very regular; her body was stocky, big-boned, conditioned for work in the fields. But what eyes! Enormous, sad, gray, like a bleak Russian sky, and like that sky, unforgettable. And when she spoke, everything became significant and important, even the stories about her cat and canary, which she used to tell my Katie.

It was always sad to part with Vera. Her life of a solitary ascetic carried within itself a reflection of pure and high tragedy. Under no circumstances could one call her unhappy or helpless, yet one's soul constantly grieved for her as for a priceless diamond unnoticed among the cobblestones by passers-by.

Many of those with whom I had worked in the Institute of World Literature called me up that day. Liza merely asked, "Is it true?" and then a long pause. Lena wanted to know every detail: Was it possible that I would be allowed to go alone? Would I be able to travel in India? What would I take with me? Such questioning was distasteful, and unpleasant was her having apparently forgotten the sad reason for my journey, my dolorous mission so unlike any sightseeing trip.

Anna Andreyevna and Marina called up; these two understood everything and did not ask foolish questions. And how could it have been otherwise? Although we had known each other for but a few years, these older friends, who had seen much in life, had become very close to me, as though we had spent all our lives together. Furthermore, it was second nature to Marina, and to her husband Nathan, to take people under their wing, and they protected me with their love. Among Marina's "wards" was Igor—she had introduced us—who also dropped in that day to say good-bye and convince himself that I was really leaving.

Igor was a connoisseur of Indian and Indonesian art. He wrote about it, but was not allowed to go to those countries, even though the Institute of the History of Art, in which he worked, had requested that he be granted a permit.

Under the same interdiction lived my sweet Bertha, the greatest expert in Moscow on African music and art, who dropped in later that day. Apparently we were all considered "unreliable." Bertha had been Singh's favorite: alone of all my friends to speak fluent English, she also had a merry disposition. She would regale us with all the news and gossip of Moscow, her loud peals of laughter ringing through our apartment.

Bertha was the daughter of an American Negro and a Jewish woman, who had come to the U.S.S.R. in the thirties and remained there for good. She was born and brought up in Tashkent, where her parents had settled down. Bureaucratic formalities have no limits in the U.S.S.R., and when Bertha, having come of age, received a Soviet passport, the police insisted on describing her nationality as "Uzbek" or "Russian."

"But look at me!" cried Bertha, who was the spit and image of her father. "Look at me! What kind of Uzbek or Russian am I? I am a Negro and I want to remain a Negro!"

The point was conceded in view of her being the sole "Soviet Negro" in Uzbekistan, and that Republic's tennis champion to boot. But later it would be raised again and again, and questions asked, whenever she had dealings with Soviet officialdom.

This big, noisy, jolly woman, who was not afraid of having her own opinion and arguing her point with the authorities, who wore bright colors, still brighter costume jewelry, and was always surrounded by lively companions, aroused silent shudders of fury in the colorless Party functionaries in the Institute in which she worked. They could not stand her laughter, her black skin, her red manicure, her independence. She was the one who spoke English and knew African art, but it was they, the ignoramuses, who went to Africa, because they held Party cards and had proletarian-peasant ancestors. Bertha, like Igor, could only envy me my thirty days during which I would be able, if not to see the whole world, then at least to get a glimpse of it through a narrow window.

Bertha remained with us that day in order to accompany me to the airport. She kept smoking cigarette after cigarette. The weather grew steadily worse, a blizzard was now sweeping over Moscow, and it was still not clear whether the plane would leave on schedule.

Later Murad Ghaleb, Ambassador of the United Arab Republic, paid us a call with his charming wife. They had been in Moscow for twelve years, their youngest daughter had been born there, and everyone in their family spoke a little Russian. Besides the Indian Ambassador, this was my only contact in the diplomatic world of Moscow, and it had come about through the personal friendship of the two ambassadors and their fondness for the late Brajesh Singh. Murad and Shoushou, his wife, had witnessed Singh's grave illness and all that we had gone through. Murad was worried and kept repeating, "Don't stay there too long, come back soon. Would you like to make a stop in Cairo on your way back? Shoushou could meet you there and spend a week with you in our house. You would get a rest after all you've been through. . . ."

"No," I said. "Some other time, Murad. Now I am not going in order to rest."

He had no grounds to worry about my return, but he knew well what was being thought in the "upper spheres" about my trip, and he was anxious about his own reputation and Soviet-Egyptian friendship. He and Shoushou had sensed what few people understood: the extremes of despair, grief, and resentment to which Singh's death had driven me—a condition that makes one capable of anything.

They tried to persuade me not to go to the airport until the hour of the flight had been established. But I was firm about leaving home at ten, so as to reach the airport ahead of time and wait there, if necessary, until morning. A superstitious fear was beginning to take hold of me. It seemed to me that all the elements had united against me, that something would happen and the plane would not leave—no, no, I was determined to wait at the airport.

At last Mrs. Kassirova arrived, an official of the Ministry of Foreign Affairs who, at Gromyko's insistence, had been appointed to accompany me as a "person in attendance." In vain were my efforts to explain that I would not need an interpreter in the narrow circle of relatives, in vain were Kassirova's tears, whose mission seemed to her nonsensical; in the end we both had to submit to the decision of the government. They were putting my journey to India on a grand state footing in order to compensate for their rude proscription of our marriage, and to smooth over the unpleasant impression created by Singh's death.

From the very beginning this "in attendance" drove me to despair; a tragic denouement was being made to serve the interests of two governments. And here I had been naïvely wondering why the permission for my trip had been granted so quickly. Why had the former Indian Ambassador,

T. N. Kaul, now Secretary of the Ministry of Foreign Affairs in Delhi, sent me several letters? Why had my husband's nephew, Dinesh Singh, a State Minister, asked me to delay my arrival until the session of their Parliament had come to an end and he could go with me to the country? Why so much sudden attention and fuss after a man's death? And Kheval Singh, the new Indian Ambassador in Moscow, was full of attentions, pulling a mournful face every time he entered my apartment.

State interests, in superimposed layers, were piling up around my journey, which to me had been dictated by purely personal motives. But this was not surprising—my whole life had been spent under pressure of "State interests," and no matter how much I had tried to become just an ordinary human being, rather than "government property," I never succeeded in doing so.

But now unpleasant "layers" were my last concern, absorbed as I was by the thought, which even to me began to appear miraculous, that I was really leaving that night and in some eight hours or so would be in another country—a thing which for me was like suddenly finding myself on another planet.

I don't know why, but I was certain that I would easily establish a sympathetic understanding with my late husband's brother and relatives, although I had written them only once. My soul longed to find rest in the village of which I had heard so much; I wanted to sit on the terrace and see the sun setting over the Ganges. I knew that there was peace and quiet there, that every little village boy had known and loved Singh, and that perhaps I would rest at last after the daily strain of the past three years. The thought of not returning in a month never crossed my mind. Or rather, to be exact, I had no thoughts at all about what might happen in a month—I felt all spent and drained. All I wanted was to reach the smooth surface of the Ganges, to see that eternal, peaceful stream, to which every Hindu returns. There

—I was convinced of it—my unshed tears would at last "melt and flow."

My journey appeared to me as a triumph of justice, a crowning of three years of vain struggles for human dignity and the elementary rights of a human being.

Already it was time to leave for Sheremetyevo. The blizzard was raging, the road might be bad. It was still not known whether the plane would leave on time. Bertha and my son decided to come with me to the airport, even though it meant returning home late at night. Sorrowful Mrs. Kassirova was going with us.

And now at last my bags were packed. In my haste I forgot to take with me photographs of my children and my mother. I was in a hurry, I was agitated and not fully aware of what I was doing.

The First Secretary of the Indian Embassy came to escort us. The presence of an official person deprived me of the possibility of bidding a proper farewell to my children. I entered my room for the last time and stood there for a while. . . .

Here Brajesh had lived for only a year and a half. We had had a difficult, distressing time, yet being together had been so good, so peaceful. Here, only a month and a half ago, he had died in my arms, and later the little urn had stood here. His presence was still in this room. He continued to take a part in my life. There, on the night table, were his spectacles; his pen and paper were on the desk; his books were on the shelves. During the month and a half that had gone by since the cremation, every time I entered the room I felt that I was not alone in it. A slightly weird feeling, yet at the same time a pleasant one. The room had not become empty and uninhabited. A kind spirit hovered in it, caressing with a gentle look these walls and windows, stroking the table and books with a small, weak hand, which had patted my cheek only a few moments before the heart had stopped beating.

But a good heart never stops. A small, weak hand caresses

my cheek, as before, to encourage me, and a serene smile watches over me from far, far away. . . .

*

In the car we were all silent, each preoccupied with his own thoughts. I felt vexed with myself for having only hurriedly kissed Katie, who had stood near the door to her room, upset by an unpleasant incident that had just taken place, distressing us all, though no one had been actually to blame for it: we were already in our overcoats when Helen, my daughter-in-law, grabbed my overnight bag to be of help; but I grew frightened—it contained the urn (Helen didn't even know this)—and said sharply, "Leave it alone! Don't touch it!" Joseph, his eyes furious, rushed to the support of his beloved, while Helen looked offended. And indeed, there was so little time left us in which to be of service to one another. Everyone that day was irritable and tense, and the tension did not subside in the car. My son sat gloomily in his corner. Mrs. Kassirova looked despondent, and only Bertha, as always, talked and laughed.

The airport had its own regulations. I had hoped that before the plane's departure, which had been postponed for an hour on account of the weather, I would be able to sit quietly in the waiting room with Bertha and my son. But as a "passenger leaving for foreign parts" I was already considered a menace to other citizens and was, therefore, immediately segregated from them behind a glass partition. The only thing left was to bid each other a hasty farewell amid heaps of baggage and with other passengers pressing from behind.

I kissed Joseph (his eyes were still angry on Helen's account), I kissed Bertha; rather absurdly we said to each other, "Write"—"I shall," and I remained with Mrs. Kassirova, who had now become my shadow and followed me beyond any and all partitions. We checked our luggage, relinquished our Soviet currency, had our passports examined, and only once was I able to catch, beyond the glass partition, a glimpse of Bertha, no longer laughing, and of Joseph, sad and no longer angry. I could only wave to them, and they waved back. . . .

That was all.

Brajesh Singh in Moscow

Only eight hours of flight separated the icy
storms of Moscow from the warmth of Delhi, where December is like our May—so much sunshine and so many
flowers.

In my case those eight hours proved to be fateful. They,
and the mileage they covered, severed me from everything
to which I thought I had been tied, chained, sentenced, to
which I had seemed to belong. But then, we all imagine
that we belong to something or someone. . . .

That night in the plane I was unable to sleep. We were
flying east. Morning here came upon us earlier. Very soon
day began to break and stars were extinguished in the lilac
sky. I gazed at that sky, at the high ridges and passes of the
Hindu Kush below us, all pink now in the sunrise, little
dreaming that soon those mountains would rise, an unscalable barrier, between me and my past life.

Mrs. Kassirova slept. Even in her sleep her face looked
unhappy, her eyelids reddened by many tears. Beside her
stood a suitcase containing presents for her colleagues at the
embassy: she was bringing them loaves of rye bread and a
Moscow smoked sausage.

We were flying fast and the morning was rushing toward us. Somewhere ahead the sun had already risen, but all I could see was the sky, blinding at this altitude and ever more ablaze with light. The window was on my left. Between the window and me lay my precious overnight bag. I kept my hand on it all the time.

And so here we are, flying to India, you and I, Brajesh Singh. You longed so for this, you promised me this trip, and you always kept your word. I am not alone; I'm not afraid of leaving the city in which until now my whole life has been spent. My passport, my ticket, my papers are in your wallet, which was with you when you came to Moscow. I have kept it as a remembrance. And here at last is the sun! The air is full of it, the shadows cast by the mountain ranges grow sharper. We are flying to your home, together. At last we have been allowed to do it.

*

We met in Moscow in October 1963, having by chance found ourselves on the same day in the same hospital. He had had his nasal polyps removed, I had been shorn of my tonsils. In the corridor outside our wards our small dinner tables stood next to each other. For several days we silently walked the corridor in pajamas and hospital robes that looked like prison wear. I was told that this short, stooping, gray-haired man in glasses, with cotton tampons in his nostrils, was a Communist from India, and I observed him unobtrusively. He spoke English to a girl from Canada, French to a young Italian, he tried to explain something in sign language to the dietitian, and all of it with a polite, endearing smile. He glanced my way once or twice without much interest; the scarf wound round my neck, the hospital clothing, and my sickly appearance hardly encouraged anything else. My throat was terribly sore, I could not speak.

In those days of Khrushchev's liberalism one could find in

this suburban government hospital at Kuntsevo people from all over the world, all of them Communists of course, or particularly outstanding "fighters for peace throughout the world." They were even placed in wards together with Soviet citizens, where they could talk to them without interpreters or other mediators—something that ordinarily hardly ever happened. In our corridor one could see guests from Italy, India, Canada, Indonesia; and the young man with a Malayan face, who spoke French, turned out to be from the Isle of Réunion. But, naturally, the Indian interested me most of all.

This was not fortuitous. An interest in India had been aroused in the U.S.S.R. by Jawaharlal Nehru, that brilliant man and outstanding political leader, whose recent visit to the Soviet Union had been a great event. An interest in Indian philosophy and culture had always existed in Russia. Nehru rekindled it, not only with his book *The Discovery of India*, but in a much stronger sense through his personality, in which the East and the West found themselves combined. I was far more taken with the India described by Nehru the realistic politician, the aesthete, the connoisseur of art, the historian with a wide field of vision, than by Indian philosophy. The mystico-religious elements in Indian culture didn't interest me much. About Ramakrishna and Vivekananda I knew little, and that only from the books of Romain Rolland. The moral teachings of early Buddhism, the personality of the Buddha, the great ascetic life of Mahatma Gandhi, who blended ancient philosophies so harmoniously with modern conditions, fascinated me far more. I had even brought with me to the hospital Namboodiripad's book about Gandhi, and I wanted very much to know what this Indian thought of it. I wanted to go up to him, start talking, ask questions, but couldn't bring myself to do it. I was still very unpracticed in English, and in general, the idea of making the first advance to a stranger, and what's more a foreigner, was utterly beyond my imagining.

Once, seeing him coming along the corridor toward me, I nerved myself and, having prepared in my mind a few English sentences, was about to approach him. But very politely he stepped aside to let me pass. I grew embarrassed and went my way in silence.

It was a couple of days before I could bring myself to try again. I went to the hospital library to see what they had on India: not much, just a few books by Nehru and by Rabindranath Tagore. Might they not have *Gitanjali*, songs I had read when still at school? No, I could not find them. But wait, what was this phrase?

> Today for some reason my heart opened up,
> Peace entered and embraced me.
> ("Morning Songs")

I wrote the lines down on a piece of paper and went back to our floor, repeating them to myself. Singh came out of his room just as I was approaching his door, and suddenly I ceased to be afraid. I said: "I believe you are from India—?"

"Yes, yes." His smile was friendly.

"Then may I ask you—?" I went on, gathering courage.

We sat down on a sofa in the corridor and talked for almost an hour about Gandhi, Nehru, the Indian caste system. Singh, already familiar with the fact that here everyone spoke in the name of some collective, asked me what organization I represented. When he heard that I was "on my own," he beamed. Dinner cut our conversation short, but now we could speak easily and freely whenever we met.

It soon transpired that although Singh had been a Communist for twenty-eight years (he became one in London), he did not share his colleague Namboodiripad's views on Gandhi. When I asked him about Namboodiripad's book, he merely waved the subject away.

"Namboodiripad is one of our leftists," he said with a disdainful shrug.

To Singh Communism was an ideal of brotherhood,

founded on humaneness and justice. He did not want to shed blood in order to attain an ideal, nor could he have ever done so. He believed in reforms and in peaceful, democratic struggles. In the London group of young Indians who had embraced Communism, no one had seriously studied Marxist theory; after reading a few popular brochures, the young protesting enthusiasts had "decided to become Communists."

After that, Singh, the son of a rich raja, lived for a long time in Germany, England, France, Austria. He helped European Communists whenever he could. For many years he was a close friend and follower of M. N. Roy.

In the late twenties and early thirties Communism was fashionable throughout the world and attracted many intellectuals. In India, at that time, only people belonging to the highest castes were exposed to European education and European social teachings, and of such consisted the London group. It was not the Marxist class struggle but the struggle for India's independence that remained the chief concern in the lives of these educated, liberal intellectuals.

With the attainment of India's independence they supported peaceful parliamentarianism and differed more and more with the left wing of the Party. From Singh's very first words one could easily conclude that, no matter how great the cause, he would never kill, not just a human being but even a fly.

To my delight, it also soon transpired that my interlocutor had no idea who I was. On the second day he began asking me questions about the U.S.S.R., wanting to know "if life had greatly changed in the Soviet Union since Stalin's death." I said that of course it had, but that I didn't think the changes were deep or fundamental. Then I decided that the time had come to introduce myself.

Singh looked at me through his thick lenses, then over their rims, and said, "Oh!"—that inimitable English "Oh!" that can have so many inflections. He said nothing more; and never once—not even when we lived together—did he

question me about my father. He was neither his admirer
nor one of those to whom the Soviet Union represented the
embodiment of justice on earth. He knew Europe well, and
his friends were European Communists. Socialist Poland and
especially Yugoslavia were closer to his heart than Russia.
And in general he was old and ill, tired of the useless
shedding of blood on earth, of the fruitless quarrels within
the Party, of the empty clash of ambitions.

That is why he said only, "Oh!" later adding some philo-
sophical remark like, "Times change, new people appear,
new policies. . . ." But to him all this was nonessential. The
one thing that mattered was that unexpectedly he had met
in Moscow a human being independent of any organization,
who spoke to him in English and in a human way. For him
I was just a human being. What's more, he belonged to a
family which had known Gandhi, Nehru, and other famous
men of India. In his life he had seen a great deal and had
known many people, and his "Oh!" therefore was not overly
surprised. In other words, I couldn't have found a better
conversational companion.

During our remaining days in the hospital we spent every
free minute together and told each other the stories of our
lives. I cannot explain why I had such absolute confidence
in this stranger from another world. Neither do I know why
he believed my every word.

My extensive but dead stock of English words suddenly
came to life. Never before had I had the opportunity of talking English to anyone, yet now I spoke it without trouble
and understood every word that was said. Singh had a good,
pure English intonation, learned from a Scottish tutor and
English teachers at the College at Lucknow. All his manners
and behavior were European. Only his gentle calm, and the
constant serene smile, betrayed the traditional Hindu virtues
of nonviolence and spiritual equilibrium.

In his appearance there was no exotic colorfulness of the
East. When he put on his beret and scarf to go for a walk,

he looked like an elderly Italian or a quiet, sorrowful Jew.

We either sat in the hospital corridors or wandered through them in our hospital robes, never stopping talking, so that other patients were already beginning to glance at us askance. It should be borne in mind that all the patients in this hospital were high Party and government officials, famous actors or members of the government and their families: in other words, the "high society" of Moscow. In the eyes of these people (with maybe a few rare exceptions) I was behaving provocatively by obviously preferring the company of a foreigner to that of the Soviet elite. But I was used to breaking the rules of that elite, which, in turn, considered me a sort of freak in its midst.

The conservative Party members who filled the wards of this hospital, built to serve the needs of the Kremlin, had long been indignant at Khrushchev for encouraging contacts with foreign lands. Displeased with everything that had happened in the country since 1953, banished from their "lucrative places," grown obese and apoplectic on vodka, resentment, and enforced inaction, they gathered around the television sets and gambled the time away over games of dominoes.

Whenever these ponderous carcasses in pajamas loomed up in the corridor coming toward us, I felt afraid for my frail, nearsighted Singh. Talking loudly in English, he would laugh without constraint, unaware of the Soviet habit of conversing in undertones. And they, in their indignation, would fall silent at such "indecent behavior" within these walls which had been built especially for them and had once belonged to them exclusively.

Singh was incurably ill. More than twenty years of bronchiectasis, contracted in England, and emphysema had brought on a hopeless deterioration of the lungs. Antibiotics gave temporary relief, but the freezing climate and colds quickly knocked him out again.

Like all Hindus, he was patient, never complained, was

not afraid of death, and spoke humorously of his illness, turning everything into a joke. He no longer actually worked for the Party and wished only to end his life in peace, earning a living by doing translations somewhere in Poland, Germany, or Yugoslavia—he had friends everywhere. To the U.S.S.R. he had come for the first time and quite by chance: every Communist Party receives from Moscow a certain number of invitations for medical care and rest. He had been offered one and decided to take advantage of it to get a rest, receive medical treatment, and take a look at that "Communist Mecca"—Moscow.

He had already been in this hospital for a month and a half; soon he would be sent to Sochi, on the Black Sea; after that, on his way back to India, he would be shown Tbilisi and Tashkent—the usual program for foreigners. So far nothing he had seen of the U.S.S.R. had delighted him; he was convinced that this trip to Russia would be his first and last.

The chain of fortunate circumstances that had brought us together continued to work in our favor. The doctors recommended a postoperative rest in the South to both him and me. We had the same doctors, we were in the same hospital under the same state system of medical care, in which every patient was given a place according to his social standing. And this system called for a month's trip to Sochi in November for both of us.

In Moscow there was snow and sleet. In Sochi, in that November of 1963, the weather was unusually warm and sunny, roses bloomed everywhere. The House of Rest, built in the early fifties in that pseudo-classical style of "Socialist realism," with columns, frescoes, and statues at every step, was a miracle of bad taste and pretentiousness. Only Party members stayed here. They had gathered beside the warm sea from all over Russia, members of district, regional, and territorial Party committees. Muscovites were few; November in Moscow is a month full of responsibilities—a grand parade, festivities, the entire government is out on Red Square—no time for rest. The Party's entire leadership is in Moscow at that time, at its post, while provincials go on leave. In Sochi those from Siberia delighted in the warm sun and the sea. But Uzbeks, Tajiks, and Azerbaijani felt frozen: there was one who never took his *papakha* (fur cap) off, even in the dining room; another shivered in his warm jacket and heavy felt boots. Russia is immense, you cannot please everyone.

There were also some Communists "from way beyond the seas," as they say in Russian: two from Greece, several Africans, and two Indians: Brajesh Singh and Somnath Lahri of Bengal. The House of Rest had an interpreter on its staff, but the Indians declined her services; they preferred taking walks in town with me. The three of us would sit by the sea or stroll along the Sochi quay, spending entire days together. This was a grave violation of rules on their part and on mine, which was noted by the Party people.

Although these were liberal times, most of the old dogmas continued to hold sway, especially in such Party circles as were to be found here. One such axiom is that every foreigner in the U.S.S.R. is a potential spy; more than one sharp eye must therefore be kept on him, and he must never be trusted. In accordance with this, a separate table was set in a corner of the dining room for "foreign guests," with an abundance of bottles and caviar on it. This elicited murmurs of discontent from the rank-and-file "inmates." Of course, they could have joined the foreigners, who would have been glad to have them, but the precepts taught them since their earliest schooldays kept them away.

The two Indians were ignorant of these axioms and invited me at once to join them for tea at their table. This was a serious breach of the rules, and we paid for it. The very next day the table for "foreign guests" was set in a separate room, which was kept locked between meals. The Chief Doctor explained to the Indians through an interpreter that now they could invite me to their table to their heart's content. Baffled, they turned to me for an explanation, and I told Singh what I thought of the whole matter. He just smiled and dismissed it with a wave of his hand.

During those November days the three of us heard on the radio of President Kennedy's assassination. The Indians were terribly shaken by it. But the Party members in the Rest House did not know how to react until the Moscow newspapers published the telegram of condolence sent by the Soviet Government to the United States.

A "show" of the country was always made for foreign Communists. Now the Indians were taken to the office of the Chief Architect of Sochi, where they were made to listen to a report on a prospective plan for the development of this resort during the next twenty years. The report was translated by an interpreter. Smilingly, the Indians expressed their thanks, remarking that in twenty years they would not be alive. The authorities then took them to a tea sovkhoz, thinking that this would be of interest to them: everyone in the U.S.S.R. drinks tea imported from India. But on the way the Indians confessed to one another that they had never seen how tea was grown. In their respective provinces it wasn't cultivated.

In the sovkhoz they were taken first into the fields and told about the crops, then to a children's garden, where children tied red Pioneers' ties around their necks; after which, exhausted, they were made to listen to a report on the development of the tea industry in that region. The interpreter translated. They waited patiently, hoping that at last they would be allowed to talk to the peasants who worked in the sovkhoz—they so wanted to learn something about Soviet rural life. But the program did not call for such an occasion, and they were taken back to Sochi. Somnath Lahri slept all the way; Singh carried in his hand a tea branch in blossom, which he brought to me.

As they were telling me all this, I seethed with indignation,

with shame, incensed by my total inability to do anything
to change or alter this bureaucratic order of things. They
agreed with me, but laughingly, without rancor. They did
not know how to be nasty, they were entirely incapable of
getting angry. There was a certain majesty about their serenity and calm. They saw and understood everything, but
nothing ever seemed to upset their equanimity. They laughed
at our soulless red tape. They were above it.

I, too, showed them Sochi, though in a very different way.
During the day, when few people were around, we used to
go to a seaside restaurant and sit on the terrace, looking out
to sea. Singh wanted to see a Russian Orthodox service, and
I took him to a church. He remarked in astonishment that the
service in the Orthodox church reminded him of a Hindu
temple—something he had never felt in the West.

We used to go to the market, where we would inquire
about the price of grapes, quince, pears, fresh fish. We
walked along the quay, and in contrast to Singh, Somnath
Lahri, who was a member of the Bengal Parliament, tortured
me with questions about my father and his policies.

The Indians longed for free and easy intercourse with
Soviet citizens, but felt that people here were not accustomed
to it, and that Party members were simply scared. This depressed them. They had seen Czechoslovakia, Poland—the
atmosphere there was different. I explained that they had
found themselves in the worst possible milieu: Party members in the U.S.S.R., as a rule, are the most inert and conservative people; I told them that among intellectuals they
would have felt differently. This, however, depressed them
even more; Soviet Communists were idealized in India.

Many in our House of Rest tried to "divert" me from the
foreigners. A few people told me straight out: "It isn't seemly;
you should spend more time with your own people." An
amiable invitation was given me by an elderly couple: "Join
us others from Rostov. There are many of us here, we'll all
go for an evening's walk together." It was difficult to refuse;

I went, and all evening was obliged to listen to hackneyed jokes about Party life.

Quite often people would come up to me, lead me aside, and, glancing over their shoulders, would say in a half-whisper, "Your father was a great man! You wait, the time will come when he will be remembered!" And invariably they would add, "But do chuck those Indians!"

Sometimes strangers would approach me, press my hand, and ask to be photographed with me. All my life I had been shamed and embarrassed by this sort of thing, not knowing how to rid myself of these "loyal-subject" effusions. Now they were being expressed by people who did not know that since 1953 my life, like that of the whole country, had become easier and better.

Those who hadn't accepted Khrushchev's new direction and the decisions of the Twentieth Congress felt that I was "disparaging my father's memory," and expressed surprise at my bearing my mother's name instead of the "great name."

Doctors, nurses, and servants had apparently been instructed never to leave us without surveillance. If the three of us played cards in Singh's room, someone would enter it every other minute, either to bring in fruit, or do some dusting, or suddenly start changing the bed linen in the middle of the day.

A roommate was installed in my room, although I had begged to be left alone. They dared not plant anyone on the Indians—they were guests after all and might put in a complaint with the Foreign Division of the Central Committee. The Indians were much too good-natured to complain to anyone. But a report about the three of us and our inadmissible behavior had undoubtedly been sent to Moscow. At the time we didn't pay much attention to these reverberations from the past, but unfortunately only a year later Khrushchev fell, and many things began to change, turning back toward that ugly past. It was then that I remembered Sochi and its vacationing Party members. . . .

That warm November in Sochi, with its roses, its orange sunsets, its chirp of cicadas under a starlit sky, had brought us close together and much had been decided. Brajesh Singh, who was scheduled to return to India in December, changed his plans for the future. He firmly decided to return to Moscow no later than in six months to work with the publishers there as a translator, and to be with me.

Like me, he was lonely. His first wife, a Hindu, and their two daughters had dwelt apart from him for twenty years and had become total strangers. It had been a traditional Hindu marriage, arranged by the parents without the young people knowing or caring for one another. In Vienna, when the Germans occupied it in 1940, he met a Jewish girl, who was seeking to escape from the Nazis. She went with him to India and they lived together for sixteen years. But after that she decided to live in England in order to give their son a better education. Singh, unable to find employment in England, returned to India, although he dearly loved his son, a talented photographer, and missed him greatly.

Singh could live in any country. Moscow, at this point, seemed to offer the best chances for a quiet life. He knew many Indians in Moscow; he had known the Indian Ambassador, T. N. Kaul, since his youth. And last but not least, he knew that my heart and home were his.

He believed in me and felt sorry for me. "To live all one's life in one town!" he would exclaim in horror. "I will show you India, Europe; we shall travel together. I can renew my contract every three years, and we can spend all my vacations with friends in different countries. You Russians live such a locked-in life! It's dreadful!"

Poor innocent, he didn't know that for fifty years Russians had been forced to lead this sort of life. My generation had grown up in complete isolation from the world. But all of us hoped that now life would improve, that it would become at least as free as, say, in Socialist Yugoslavia or Czechoslovakia, that at last people would start traveling. Everyone should see something of the world. All this we hoped for. But we were mistaken. . . .

He left for India in December 1963, and I settled down to await his return. My children had met him and knew of our intentions. As usual, I had discussed them with my son, who was then eighteen. We always talked everything over as equals, as two adult friends.

To me Singh was someone from another world, spiritually far richer and more interesting than the one I had been brought up in. The dissimilarity of our lives, the differences in our backgrounds, tongues, experience, ages never stood in our way—Singh was older than I by seventeen years. On the contrary, these differences seemed to draw us to a reciprocal understanding, compassion, love: we loved and completely trusted one another from the very first moment.

On his last day in Moscow he came to see me. In my room he suddenly covered his eyes with his hand to hide his tears.

"Sveta," he said, "what if I should never see you again?" But he added instantly, with an effort at a smile, "No, no, everything will be all right. In a few months I will be back."

He found it easier to call me "Sveta" rather than "Svetlana." The name "Sveta" exists in Sanskrit. It means "white" (in Russian "*svet*" means "light"). He knew no other words in Russian.

Not until a year and a half later was he able to return. Letters came seldom and only when sent by hand—the Soviet postal service was most unreliable. Singh used to write through an Indian biology student in Moscow. The young man would bring me the letters and take mine, which, like his own, he sent through the Indian diplomatic pouch. We became friends, and I translated his thesis on genetics from English into Russian; a little later he got his master's degree.

A year and a half were spent in obtaining a contract and invitation from the Soviet publishers, and in overcoming the opposition of two Central Committees: Indian and Soviet.

We had failed to take into consideration how swiftly the political climate of Moscow could change, and how Communist parties in other countries, like weathervanes in the wind, instantly turned in the same direction. Besides, how could we have foreseen Khrushchev's downfall at the height of his world popularity? Or that our destinies would depend on it?

Obtaining from the Soviet publishers an official invitation for a foreign translator to come and work in the Soviet Union is a long procedure. But Singh was an old Communist, recommended by S. A. Dange, Secretary General of the Indian Communist Party, and seconded by T. N. Kaul, Indian Ambassador in Moscow. Insofar as formalities were concerned, nothing could have been better. But in the final analysis everything depended on the Moscow Central Committee and its Foreign Division.

At first everything went smoothly. Singh wrote me that Dange had sent his recommendation to Moscow. We waited patiently.

In 1964 the Soviet Union's friendship with India was growing stronger by the day. In September the Indian President, Radhakrishnan, was to arrive on a state visit to Moscow. Dinesh Singh, at that time Deputy Minister of Foreign Affairs, arrived in Moscow to make final arrangements for the visit. He was a young man my age, a nephew of Brajesh Singh.

He, of course, knew of his uncle's plans. He called me up from his hotel, was very amiable, and came to see how I lived. I never expected so much attention on the part of this brilliant young diplomat. He wore European clothes as impeccably as his uncle did, and his English was as flawless. He gave an interview on Moscow TV, speaking about Socialism and the Indian Five-Year Plan, and charmed everybody. He assured me that Brajesh would soon be here and that he and his family hoped to see me someday in Delhi.

I kept waiting to hear that the official invitation had been extended. Singh expected it from day to day and couldn't understand why it hadn't come. He was unable to undertake any work in India, knowing that he would be going to Moscow; he made fruitless trips through dust and heat from the country to Delhi and, judging by his letters, was often indisposed.

I remembered now the oblique glances of Party bureaucrats in Sochi and in the hospital. I knew from the bitter experience of my whole life that they would not leave us in peace and were merely biding their time. I also knew that the group of Indian Communists in Moscow (all formalities concerning Singh's case had to go through them) were under leftist influence. To them Brajesh Singh was "not a Communist at all but a raja," as Chandra Shekhar, secretary of the group, had laughingly said when, together with Singh, he had come to see me shortly before Singh's departure from Moscow.

Chandra had come to Moscow in 1949 from the southern state of Kerala after an unsuccessful attempt at establishing a commune in that state. He had rejected his Indian citizenship, had married a Russian, and had become a true "Soviet man," speaking Russian fluently. In Moscow he was recognized as an expert on the Indian labor movement, although in India he would hardly have been accepted as such. He wrote works about the "Indian proletariat," which earned him a master's degree in history, supplied the Central Committee of the Soviet Communist Party and its Foreign Division with information on India, and was the sole announcer in the Malayalam tongue on Radio Moscow. He cherished the hope of a revolution in India, as did his fellow countryman Namboodiripad, leader of the leftist Communists, whose book on Gandhi Singh and I had so disliked. And it was in the hands of this man that Singh's fate now lay.

I called on Chandra and asked him point-blank if he had

any knowledge of Dange's letter, reminding him that it should have been submitted to the Central Committee long ago. Chandra, with his usual smirk, glanced up at the ceiling, then to right and left, trying to avoid my eyes. "I don't remember what I did with it," he said at length. "Can't imagine where I could have put it!"

During the summer of that same year I saw A. I. Mikoyan, who was always thoughtful and kind to me. I told him all about Brajesh Singh and our plans, and he expressed great sympathy. However, in order to have the backing of someone "higher up" than himself, he related the whole story to Khrushchev. According to Mikoyan, Khrushchev had been very pleased and had said, "Splendid! Let her go and have a look at India—it does one good to see other countries!"

I told Mikoyan that the procedure for the official invitation had not yet been started.

"Ach, these *apparatchiki!*" he exclaimed in irritation. "Always scared of something! But when your Singh gets here, bring him to see me and I'll give you my 'blessing.'"

In March 1965 the invitation was at last received, and Singh was able to come to Moscow to sign his contract with the publishers.

On April 7 my son Joseph and I went to meet him at the Sheremetyevo Airport and, stationing ourselves behind the glass partition, searched the faces of the passengers from Delhi. How could I have guessed at the time that in a year and eight months I would again be in this waiting room, carrying my husband's ashes back to India, and that I would be seeing my son for the last time behind this same glass wall? . . .

All the passengers from Delhi had disembarked and still no sign of Singh! We pressed our faces against the glass. Sensing my agitation, my son grew agitated, too.

At last I caught sight of Singh, moving very slowly and carrying a heavy bag. Even at a distance one could see that he was breathing with difficulty, and I realized that this was why he had been the last to get off the plane. He smiled at us, waved his hand, coughing all the time. It was clear to me that during his year and a half's absence his condition had worsened; he had aged, his face had grown puffy. But he had the same heavy coat, beret, and warm scarf; the same kind, nearsighted eyes behind thick lenses, the same serene smile.

We were not the only ones there to meet him. The publishers had sent two representatives: a Russian and an Indian, an old-time resident of Moscow and Singh's personal friend, who had been the first to suggest his working with the Soviet publishers. They took him to the apartment which the publishers, in accordance with Singh's contract, had placed at his disposal. We agreed that I would meet him there later; in the meantime, my son and I went home. My son, always understanding, said to me, "Oh, come now, Mama, bring him over to our place. Sooner or later that's how it's going to end anyhow, so why not now!"

And now at long last Singh and I were able to talk. It was hard to believe that after a year and a half of uncertainty and anxious waiting we were actually together again. But wait! Before saying anything he fastened a small watch around my wrist, the gift he had brought me (Singh is no more, but that watch is still with me, alive, ticking . . .). Then he said, "Listen, Sveta, I'm not feeling well, as you can see. I need antibiotics, maybe two or three weeks in a hospital. I hope I'll be better, I got very tired in India— that uncertainty was dreadful! But I beg you, think carefully before it's too late. I haven't yet signed the contract. I could join some friends in Yugoslavia and work there. It's going to be hard on you, I don't want to be a burden. I won't live much longer. . . ." I could hear the wheezing and rattling in his lungs.

No! How could we separate now that everything had

been attained after so many difficulties? I said, "Nonsense! Come to our place. You can't live alone in this empty apartment anyway. Let's go home!"

We did, and he began to unpack. First of all he took out the presents he had brought for my children—no one had been forgotten. Later we all went into our kitchen for supper. And everything seemed so normal, so habitual— just a man come home after a long absence in a distant land.

＊

We had waited for one another a year and a half, and for only another year and a half were we able to be together. He might have lived longer if we hadn't met with unexpected obstacles, which could have undermined a more robust constitution.

While Singh had been waiting for an invitation from Moscow, in our country there had been a change of Premiers. In October 1964, using the well-tested method of "palace revolution," conservative elements deposed Khrushchev, who exasperated them, and placed Kosygin on the throne. The so-called "collective leadership" of the Triumvirate—Kosygin, Brezhnev, Mikoyan—meant, in essence, that the power was now in the hands of the Party conservatives, with Mikhail Suslov at their head. The first great act of this new leadership was Kosygin's trip to China, when the entire world saw a photograph of Chairman Mao sprawling in an armchair and Kosygin bending his head before him in a servile attitude.

But who could have thought that these "great" changes would be of significance to us in our private lives?

The laws of the U.S.S.R. recognize only civil marriages; a church marriage has no legal status. A well-known precedent was the case of the composer Sergei Prokofiev's widow. The Prokofievs had been married in the Roman Catholic Church abroad, when they had been political émigrés, and, as is well known, Catholics do not recognize divorce. After his death in the U.S.S.R. his widow was unable to establish her rights as his heir because, while she had been serving a term in prison, he had concluded a civil marriage with another woman, a Soviet citizen. As a result, according to Soviet law, this other woman became his sole heiress, in spite of the fact that she had no children by him, while from the first marriage there were two grown sons. In any other country the first marriage would have remained in force, but not in the U.S.S.R. This precedent had a direct bearing on our case, inasmuch as Singh would not need to get a divorce from his first wife, since their marriage had been a religious one. This we knew. But we also knew that laws in the U.S.S.R. could be interpreted in any way that best served the interests of the State, and in this lies concealed the danger of total lawlessness.

All we had time to do was make inquiries at the Moscow office for the registration of marriages with foreigners.

The very next day I received a call from the Premier's office summoning me to an "audience." This was a surprise to me; I did not know what to expect. I was so happy to have been a more or less "forgotten" person in the days of Khrushchev. The government had shown no interest in me or in how I lived. Now what was to happen?

The fourth of May, 1965, was a cold and windy day. I entered the Kremlin through the Spassky Gate. I hadn't been inside the Kremlin for many years, and an unpleasant feeling took possession of me.

The day was so cold, so dreary, it seemed as if it might start snowing any moment. I walked toward the old build-ing of the Kazakov Senate, on the first floor of which we had lived for twenty years. The second floor was occupied by the reception rooms, offices, and personal office of the Chairman of the Council of Ministers. Khrushchev, in his day, spoke to me twice in his office in the Central Commit-tee of the CPSU (Communist Party of the Soviet Union) on Old Square. But Kosygin was receiving me in my father's former office.

I sat waiting in the reception room, my heart heavy with forebodings. Again those dismal paneled walls, so familiar to me. Again those standard government carpets running the full length of every corridor in the Kremlin, those green cloths on empty tables . . . Why was I here? What for? How depressing this wait. How chilly those walls, those old vaulted ceilings. The primitive electric clock on the wall kept clicking as it jumped from minute to minute. Exactly the same kind of clock made the same sound in every room in our apartment on the floor below. How I had forgotten these cheerless Kremlin interiors during my years of ordinary life.

I had never met Kosygin before, never spoken to him. His face did not inspire optimism. He stood up, gave me a limp, humid hand, and screwed up his mouth into a semblance of a smile. He seemed to find it difficult to start the conversation, and I just couldn't imagine how this man spoke.

"Well, how are you?" he began at last, painfully. "How is everything, materially?"

"Thank you, I have everything I need. Everything is all right."

"Are you working?"

"No, at present I'm at home—children, a family, you know. Sometimes I do translations, but seldom."

"Why did you leave your former work?"

"I quit because of my health, and there was no one to help at home with the children. I felt that my children and my home were more important. As you know, we receive a pension—"

"I understand . . . you found the conditions difficult in the collective at the time. But we don't intend following Khrushchev's rotten line! We are going to make a few decisions of our own. And you must rejoin the collective, occupy your rightful place. We'll help you if need be. . . ."

"But no, that's not why I left. Everyone was always kind to me," I began, but suddenly felt the futility of saying anything to this man. It would have been useless to try and explain to him that for me, since the Twentieth Congress, life had become far easier than before.

"No, everyone was very kind to me," I repeated. "Now I'm no longer working simply because I have much to do at home and because my husband is a very sick man."

At the word "husband" an electric current seemed to shoot through the Premier. He began to speak easily, freely, with natural indignation:

"What have you cooked up? You, a young healthy woman, a sportswoman, couldn't you have found someone here, I mean someone young and strong? What do you want with this old sick Hindu? No, we are all positively against it, positively against it!"

At first I was so staggered I was unable to answer or think clearly.

"But—but how . . . ? What do you mean, 'against'? I know that my plans aroused no objections—" (Oh God, I had forgotten that we had a different Premier now, that everything was different, the Party line was different. . . .) "A sick man came here to work for my sake," I continued. "So what is he to do now—go back?" I said this, wanting to forestall any untoward possibilities.

"Oh no, that would be tactless. But we do not advise you to register your marriage. No, we do not advise it. What's more, we won't allow it. He would then have the legal right to take you to India, a poverty-stricken, backward country! I was there, I know. Besides, Hindus treat women badly. He'll take you there and abandon you. We have many such cases—they go, then beg to come back. . . ."

Slowly something began to turn in me.

"First of all, we didn't intend going to India," I said, commencing to reason things out soberly. "He came to work here, in Moscow. Naturally, sometime we would like to make a trip, see India and other countries—"

But the Premier had no use for these details. He wanted to impress upon me what he had in mind:

"Forget it. What you've got to do is work, return to the collective. No one's going to touch him. Let him work. The terms of his contract are excellent. But all this is not for you."

"It's too late," I said sharply. "The man came here, he is living with us, and he shall continue to do so. I will not leave him. He came only for my sake. This is my responsibility."

"That's your business," the Premier said dryly. "Lead your own life. But we won't let you register your marriage."

The audience was over. He rose and offered me his hand.

"All right," I said coldly. "Thank you. Good-bye."

I could find no support anywhere in this room, formerly my father's official office, known to the entire world. These walls seemed to crush me on all sides. Even the same Arsenal, built by Bazhenov, was looking in at the windows. For so many years, through the windows of my own room, it had looked in on me, yellow and white, with rows of cannon along its façade. And for so many years I saw nothing else but that Arsenal and the blue spruce trees of the Kremlin. All those shadows of the past were closing in on me, pressing, strangling. . . . Those empty corridors, those carpets, those vaulted ceilings . . . Away, away!

Yes, away from here as fast as I could run. Accursed Kremlin! Accursed prison! There was no escape from you anywhere, and now again you are dogging my every step. . . . Home, home, as quick as possible, where normal people lived, where my children expected me and a poor, unfortunate, naïve man awaited my return.

On my way home I tried to calm myself and reason out what was to be done. I stopped to buy some pastry, a cake, and candy, for this was my Katie's birthday and Singh's, and they both had a sweet tooth. I carefully selected the pastry, trying to dispel the somber impressions of the Kremlin, the worst of which was the Premier himself.

When I told everything to Singh, he couldn't bring himself to believe it. "But why, why—?" he kept asking in dismay. Something had taken place totally beyond the grasp of a man from the free world. He simply couldn't understand it. And I suddenly sensed all the strength that lay in this quiet, gentle man, as he shook his head and said, "No, I don't like this life. It's like being in a military barracks all the time. I'm not a criminal. I must explain it to them."

Together that same day we composed a letter to Kosygin. Singh expected to get an answer. He thought that he, a man of fifty-seven, would be given a human explanation. He didn't understand that as a man, as a personality, he did not exist here.

Unexpectedly we had collided with the State. That "Bronze Horseman,"* swaying heavily around, had suddenly rushed at a quiet man in horn-rimmed glasses, and there was no escape from the heavy hoofs.

Singh never got a reply. The "Bronze Horseman" has no time to dismount and sit down with a man. He gallops on, knocking off their feet all those who get in his way.

*

Singh lived in Moscow only a year and a half. His condition grew worse with every day. The cold Moscow climate contributed to this, of course. But I think that the political climate of our country proved to be far more destructive to him, a climate that had turned from Khrushchev's thaw to chilly blasts and hoarfrosts. The whole atmosphere changed sharply in the ideological institutions, in the publishing divisions, in literary journals, in all circles of the artistic, learned, and political intelligentsia to which I had close ties through my education and personal friendships.

In September 1965, the arrest of the writers Andrei Sinyavsky and Yuli Daniel started a shameless series of repressions,

* Title of a poem by Pushkin.

giving birth to a wave of protests all over the world. Singh was shaken by the cruelty of the sentences.

"Seven years of prison for writing books? Just because a writer writes books?"

When I told him about the meetings that had taken place in our Institute of World Literature, at which, even before the case had come to court, all those present had been made to judge, to condemn their former colleague Andrei Sinyavsky, who hadn't even admitted any guilt, and at which, by order of the Party bosses, the outcome of the whole case had been, *de facto*, predetermined, he just dropped his hands and shook his head sadly.

He had heard from me that in the U.S.S.R. there existed a vast literature that on account of the censorship did not get published, and that many people wrote "for the drawer," as they said. He knew that I also had a manuscript—the story of my family. He was not very interested in the contents of my *Twenty Letters;* he knew all my thoughts and convictions and didn't give his mind to the details. Sometime during that winter he advised me to send my manuscript to India through his friend Ambassador Kaul; and that's what we did. In the U.S.S.R. one could expect anything: the search of one's home by warrant, the confiscation of books from one's shelves, of manuscripts from one's desk. In this way the government had confiscated the second part of Vasily Grossman's novel *For the Right Cause,* Alexander Solzhenitsyn's archives and his novel *The First Circle.*

My sole wish at that time was to save at least one copy of my manuscript; I could think of nothing else. Ambassador Kaul took the manuscript with him in January 1966 during one of his trips to India. He seemed a reliable friend to me then. He often came to see us. We—my children, Singh, and I—frequently visited the embassy. For us it was a pleasant breath of fresh air. We spoke English, saw foreign newspapers and magazines. Kaul, as well as his friend Murad Ghaleb, Ambassador of the United Arab Republic, liked to attend my children's student parties, enjoyed their songs to the strumming of guitars, danced with the girl students. The young people loved Kaul; he used to come to our dacha, bringing with him rice and curry, gin and whiskey, and would sing Russian songs.

Singh's old friends—the Indian Communists—turned away from him as soon as they heard that the Soviet Government was displeased with him. Dr. Ahmad, Hajra Begum, Litto Ghosh (the widow of Ajoy Ghosh), all of them gradually disappeared. The Secretary General of the Communist Party of India, S. A. Dange, came to Moscow several times but found no time to see Singh, although the latter tried hard to obtain an appointment with him. Dinesh Singh, who with the advent of Indira Gandhi to power had become State Minister of Foreign Affairs, stopped writing, though he knew that his uncle was dangerously ill. Only Singh's brother, Suresh, who had always lived in the village of Kalakankar, wrote regularly every week.

A. I. Mikoyan, who by now was no longer President of the U.S.S.R., continued to be amiable, but had no longer any wish to "bless" us. Now the line he took with me was: "Formal marriage has no significance in love. I and my wife have lived together for forty years without registering our marriage and no one has ever said that our five sons were illegitimate."

Poor Mikoyan, about whose wiliness so many jokes have been made! We understood that he was no longer able to help us. There was a joke current about Mikoyan's long and cloudless career under different regimes: "Have you heard? Mikoyan is writing his memoirs, entitled 'From Ilyich to Ilyich* without thrombosis or *paralich.'"† Another story proclaimed the restoration of the Romanov monarchy in Russia, and when Khrushchev petitioned the Czar, the latter asked his minister—Mikoyan—"What shall we do about this

---

* From Vladimir *Ilyich* Lenin to Leonid *Ilyich* Brezhnev.
† Paralytic stroke.

Khrushchev?" and the Czar's Minister Mikoyan replied, "Never heard of him. Who is he?"

Mikoyan was now warning me against "close friendships" with foreign ambassadors. "This Kaul is very pushy," he would say. "Not at all like other Indians. Keep away, keep away from him."

In the end I stopped visiting the Mikoyans. Their eldest daughter-in-law, an old friend of mine, actually "ceased to know me."

The Soviet Union became split into liberals and conservatives right down the line, and the struggle between them was reflected in everything. The argument arose in every category of endeavor and thought: Should we maintain the old order or unequivocally reject it? Continue along the line taken by the Twentieth Congress or return to "Stalinism"? Chart our course toward international contacts or to narrow Russian nationalism? Accept modern art and experimentation or stick to the conservative "classical tradition"? Breathe the fresh air of the times, always brought in by younger generations, or continue to inhale the "heavy" Leninism of old-time Party members? These contradictory tendencies collided everywhere. Dissent penetrated into families, broke into long-standing friendships, into personal relations.

I might call it the struggle between the Party of Memory and the Party of Hope, using the terminology of a book I have read here in the United States. It is Emerson's terminology, but it is applicable in any country. And nowhere more so than in Soviet Russia, an immense country in which seemingly everything happens according to the dictates of a single party. But don't believe it! At present in the U.S.S.R. there is a constant life-and-death struggle between the Party of Memory and the Party of Hope, the Party of the Past and the Party of the Future.

This collision was acutely felt when the new regime of Suslov-Kosygin tried to turn history back and return to old methods. Memory pushed them to what had been. Hope forced others to resist in everything, wherever possible.

At Progress, the publishers where Singh translated English texts into Hindi, this struggle existed also. The Chief Editor of the English Division was V. N. Pavlov, my father's erstwhile personal interpreter (he had interpreted at Teheran, Yalta, and Potsdam, and had handled all the correspondence with Roosevelt and Churchill during the war). The women editors in the division adored Singh and praised his style in Hindi—they were young girl graduates from the university. The Chief Editor of the Hindi Division, on the other hand, who under Khrushchev had been transferred to the publishing office from the Central Committee—a slight which he could not forget—complained that Singh did not fulfill his norm and translated badly.

Singh, in his astonishment, would ask, "Whose native tongue is it? His or mine? Why does he correct me?" He did not understand that they were trying to get rid of him; the only way to accomplish this was by proving his incompetence as a translator. His work at the publishers was the sole formal grounds for his residence in Moscow; if he lost it he would have to return to India.

Had we been able to register our marriage, the law would have protected Singh and his health. But this we couldn't do. His work was becoming more and more of a burden. All that was left to him was to work beyond his strength, even when hospitalized. He was loved and respected by his co-workers, but all the time he sensed the secret ill will of his superiors. V. N. Pavlov was unable to accept the fact that Singh, a mere translator, was my husband, just as he could not stomach all that had happened in the U.S.S.R. since the death of my father, whom he worshiped.

Even medicine didn't remain inactive and objective, although medicine, at least, should have been above Party interests. At first they tried to put Singh into a hospital for tuberculosis. I threw myself into his defense like a tigress fighting for her cub.

I refused to let Singh go to that hospital. We spent a month and a half proving to the Intourist Polyclinic, through X-rays and diagnostic records, that the diagnosis had been wrong, that his case was one of bronchiectasis, that the patient didn't have to be isolated and could work. Why should this have been necessary when a year and a half before the Kuntsevo hospital had confirmed the diagnosis of bronchiectasis and had treated him for that ailment? But then, of course, those were the days of Khrushchev. Now one had to prove it all over again, to other doctors, in another polyclinic, to other bosses. We succeeded in this. But a lot of time was wasted in doing so, and a lot of strength, of which there remained little.

During that year and a half Singh went three more times to the hospital in Kuntsevo. There people knew him, remembered him, liked him. On the ninth of October, 1966, doctors and nurses came to congratulate us—they knew that we had met in that hospital three years before, and the ward was filled with flowers that day. . . .

I cannot accuse anyone of intentionally prescribing the wrong treatment. But under the Soviet system of free medical care you are denied the possibility of choosing your doctor, or going to another if you are displeased with the one you have. You are sentenced to one doctor once and for all. It seemed to me that the treatment was too exhausting, that in taking too many different medicines the patient was poisoning himself; I could see the man growing weaker by the day. And by the time his heart began to fail, there was nothing left to do but keep the heart going with intravenous injections.

During the last months Singh was under the care of a woman doctor, a blue-eyed Georgian. Every time she entered his ward he gave her the same assurance: "I am much better today." She spoke a little English, her whole personality breathed friendliness, and she was a wizard at administering injections intravenously, always finding his thin

weak vein right away. She would leave the ward with
tears in her eyes, telling me that the situation was hopeless
and that I must be prepared for the worst at any time. Whenever his heart began to give out, or he had an attack of
asthma, only an injection would help.

That charming young woman always entered a ward with
a smile, and no one could have guessed that at times a
stomach ulcer gave her acute trouble, that she was over-
worked and had hardly time to eat.

"And if you only knew how much of a doctor's time is
wasted on Party meetings," she would say. "How much unnecessary chatter, papers, lists, reports! We are supposed to
treat the sick; it would be better to spend an extra hour
at a patient's side."

In the hospital Singh used to be visited by his Indian
friends and by two ambassadors—Kaul and Murad Ghaleb.
Every time passes had to be obtained the day before. At the
gates, at the entrance, doormen had difficulty in reading
the names of foreign visitors. Passes to the Kremlin had been
abolished long ago, but every institution had reserved for itself the right to its own bureaucratic regulations. In the case
of ambassadors these regulations were even stricter; a special pass had to be issued every time. Yet they continued to
come all the same, and Shoushou Ghaleb always brought
Singh his favorite caramel custard.

The hospital had new rules now: all foreigners had been
moved to one floor, so as to isolate them from "native" patients. Only those who went for walks in the garden could
exchange a few words with Russians. This annoyed the
foreigners, who got tired of each other's company. Three
years earlier the situation had been much simpler. Then
Singh and I could talk together for hours in the corridors.

In the middle of October 1966, hospitalized again, Singh
of a sudden told me one day that he would like to die in
India, after seeing at least some of his old friends. He felt
that his days were numbered. He was tired of these endless

drugs, this diet, these passes. He liked to cook and now, in the hospital, spent his time reading English cookbooks and copying out recipes. He wanted to live. We had been making plans for the future, trying to convince one another that we still had years ahead of us! Now he seriously began to tell me that ahead lay not years but perhaps only weeks.

I used to spend all my days with him, leaving home for the out-of-town hospital in the morning and returning in the evening to my children, who understood everything. Joseph, by now a medical student, would ask me, "How are things?" and, having consulted his textbooks, would explain that the condition was bad.

Singh was allowed to walk a little in the corridors. We roamed them together, but he soon got out of breath. On warm days I took im out into the garden in a wheelchair. He spoke mostly of his youth, of the years he had spent in Europe, of the past in general. The present held no solace. He criticized the Communist Party of India for splitting into rightists and leftists; laughed at the Chinese reports about "Chairman Mao swimming across a river." When he heard of the "Cultural Revolution" in China, he said sadly that it reminded him of the pogroms during the first days of Nazism in Germany—he had seen them. One day he told me very gravely: "If I return to India alive, my first action will be to quit the Communist Party."

He often spoke about Indian history, told me about Buddha, repeated the legends about Krishna. He suddenly felt himself a true Hindu once more. He longed to be in touch with his own roots, drink of the eternal spring. He had no one to listen to him but me. I used to sit down on the ground at his feet, or on the small bench in the ward, while he, with his weak hand on my head, would talk with his eyes closed. It was easier for him that way, and so blissful for me. . . .

I was in despair: his life was fading away, nothing could be done to help him, and I felt responsible for it, I felt I was to blame. In my despair I wrote a letter to Brezhnev, begging to be allowed to take Singh to India, telling him that Singh's days were numbered and that he was asking me to do this. I explained that it was a question of an indefinite but short stay in India on my part, Singh could not live long. I pleaded with him because I was afraid of facing this death alone—he was so completely in my hands.

Instead of a reply I was summoned a few days later to the Central Committee, to see not Brezhnev but Suslov. This was the very worst that could have happened to me: an interview with the leader of the Party's conservatives.

I went to the Old Square, expecting no good. When my father had been alive, I had seen Suslov several times but had never spoken to him. He began in exactly the same way as Premier Kosygin had done: "How are you? How is everything, materially? Why aren't you working?"

But I allowed myself to remind him of my letter: "Will I be granted the permission I'm asking for? We are both asking for it. Is it possible that a man's last wish cannot be granted?"

Suslov moved nervously in his chair behind his desk. His pale hands, with thick sclerotic veins, weren't quiet for a single moment. He was thin, tall, with the face of a fanatic. The thick lenses of his glasses did not soften the manic look with which he pierced me.

"Your father was very much against marriages with foreigners, we even used to have a law about it!" he said, relishing every word.

"So what?" I replied as politely as I could. "He was mistaken. Now such marriages are allowed everyone but me."

Suslov's whole frame gave a jerk and he almost choked. His fingers began to twist a pencil furiously.

"We shall not let you go abroad!" he said with great precision. "As for Singh, he may go, if he wants. No one is holding him back."

"He will die!" I exclaimed, feeling that the time had come

to speak plainly. "He will die here and very soon. His death will be on our consciences, on my conscience! I cannot allow it. It will be a great shame, a disgrace to us all."

"Why a disgrace? He received treatment, is still getting it. No one can reproach us with not having given help. If he dies, well, all right, so he dies. He's a sick man. But you can't go abroad. There'll be provocations."

"What provocations? What have provocations got to do with this?"

"You know nothing," he cried. "When I went to England soon after the war, our plane was met right at the airport by a crowd carrying banners—'Give us back our wives!' D'you get me?"

"I don't understand—in what way is that a provocation? And I don't understand why everyone is so afraid for me. I'm perfectly capable of answering questions if need be."

"You'll be instantly surrounded by newsmen. You don't know what it's like. In short, there will be political provocations at every step. We want to save you from it."

It was like beating the air: we spoke of different things from different points of view. To continue the conversation would have been useless. Like the Premier before him, Suslov was much more concerned about my "taking my proper place in the collective"—a place suitable to my famous name.

"Why are you so anxious to go abroad?" he asked at the end of our interview, as if I were asking to be allowed to go on a tourist trip. "Take my family and my children—they never go abroad, don't even want to. Not interested!" he concluded, proud of his family's "patriotism."

I left, carrying away with me a grim impression of this fossilized Communist, who lived entirely in the past, yet at present was directing the Party. . . .

Next day I went to the hospital and told Singh about my interview. His sense of humor never failed him. He laughed over Suslov's "patriotism," shaking his head: "To think that we in the Communist Party consider Suslov an internationalist, the most up-to-date Marxist!" And with a quick gesture of his hand, he waved away the whole absurdity.

He had been seriously upset by something else that day. In the morning they had applied leeches and, as is always done in Soviet hospitals, had thrown the leeches into a jar with a liquid in which they died. This distressed Singh; in India leeches were not destroyed, they were kept in water to be used again.

"If I had known they would do this, I would have refused to have them applied," he said. In the ward he didn't let me kill even a fly buzzing at a window; I had to open the window and let the fly out.

That day he looked sadder than ever. Suddenly he said to me: "Sveta, take me home. I'm fed up with these white walls and robes, these visitor's passes, all this gruel! I will make an omelet myself—they don't know how to cook here. Let's go home. Tomorrow!"

They let him go, knowing that he was tired and that it was not for long.

He spent a week at home. The local doctor—a morose, elderly woman—was polite, but nervous; doctors in Moscow are afraid of treating foreigners and bearing the responsibility for their lives. Injections were given by another doctor, a man—she could not find the vein. But all this didn't worry Singh—he was at home, felt blissfully happy in an armchair in our big living room. Indians came to see him.

His last day—Sunday, October 30—was marked by a great event in the family: Joseph and Helen announced that at last they had decided to get married and the date for the registration of their marriage had been set for the end of November. We all drank a toast to their happiness.

Later, R. Jaipal, Chargé d'Affaires at the Indian Embassy, and his wife came to say good-bye—they were leaving for England. In the evening Naresh Vedi, who worked at the publishers with Singh, dropped in and brought him a letter from his brother. Singh felt very tired that evening, and Naresh soon left, saying to me, "How badly he looks today."

When he had left, Singh, sitting in his armchair, read and reread his brother's letter for a long time. Then he called me. As usual, I sat down beside him and took his hand.

"Sveta," he said very softly. "This is my last day. I feel cold. I'll go and lie down."

I wanted to make light of it, but he was in dead earnest. He was tired and soon began to lose his breath, as so often happened. The doctor had to be called to give him an injection. There was no time for words. I just did my best to try and reassure him, and myself.

One attack of asthmatic suffocation followed the other, together with a weakening of the heart. I called for a doctor a second time during the night, and a third time toward morning. The injections brought relief and Singh would doze away, but not for long. Different doctors came; every time I called, a new one would appear, whoever happened to be on duty during those Sunday-night hours. Every time the doctor got frightened, suggesting taking Singh to the hospital, and every time Singh shook his head, repeating, "Leave me here." I had to tell every new doctor the history of Singh's illness and what treatment he had been given in the hospital. Every time, when the doctor had left, Singh would ask me to sit beside him, would caress my cheek and assure me that he felt better.

His attacks were so much like his ordinary ones that I could not bring myself to believe it when he told me early in the morning, "Sveta, I know that I will die today." He said it very calmly, softly, he didn't complain, he wasn't nervous, and I didn't believe him. . . .

Toward morning they gave him an injection of strophanthin, which in the hospital had been replaced by some milder drug. But it was impossible to argue with the doctors—they did what was usually done in such cases.

Five minutes after the injection he said he felt better. "But

I feel something throbbing here"—he pointed to his heart. "Now here—higher—here!" He pointed to his throat and fell back on his pillow—the heart had stopped beating.

I rushed to get Joseph, woke him up; together we ran back to my room. Doctors were applying artificial respiration. The body was lying on the floor. "Why? What for?" I asked Joseph. "It's right. They are doing the right thing," he kept repeating, standing beside me. We held on to one another. Everything in me was trembling. My son was very pale.

"Dead," said an unknown young doctor, glancing at me desperately. It was seven in the morning. Hindus say that righteous men die in the morning when it is light. Then, they say, death comes more easily and it is easier for the soul. This death was an easy and quick one.

Until that day I had seen only one death—my father's. The two deaths were just as unlike as the lives had been.

The doctors left, having laid out the body on the bed. They said they would call to tell me what to do next.

Afraid of bureaucratic formalities and delays, which would have been an outrage to so peaceful a death, I called up our Indian friends, who knew what should be done. The Ambassador was informed, a wire sent to Singh's son in London. After that everything was done and organized by the Indians, quietly, calmly, with dignity. And it was all done in the nick of time, for the medical authorities wished to make their own arrangements: take the body to the morgue, perform an autopsy. I was averse to this last twenty-four-hour separation, while autopsies were contrary to Indian custom.

I sat quietly in our bedroom. Our Indian friends came one after the other. They all moved about smoothly, softly, spoke in low voices. They brought peace with them. This was what I had loved most of all in Singh: an inner peace and equilibrium under any circumstances.

My two friends Bertha and Tamara also came. The latter worked in the Indian Division of Radio Moscow. They remained with me all day, saw to it that my children got fed, carried tea and coffee into the living room, did everything that was necessary; they were at home in my home.

I sat on a small sofa in the bedroom, unable to leave. I didn't cry, but something inside me had been severed. Something had been irreparably torn and lay dead in me. I was forty years old. Something was left behind—some inner line of demarcation. I sat and looked at what was happening in the room as though from somewhere else. . . .

I was not afraid of death or of this dead body, whose sufferings were at an end. I slept soundly in the next room, although I had never before spent a night in an apartment with a deceased person. My children were a bit nervous; Bertha remained with us for the night. But a kind, gentle, benevolent soul was hovering here, and there was nothing to be afraid of. I calmly entered the bedroom in the morning and laid my hand on the cold, waxen forehead. It was a frosty day outside. The room was already filled with sunshine.

In the afternoon, before the bearing out of the body, all the Indians gathered here together, the Ambassador came, also my own best friends and the sweet woman doctor from the hospital, all in tears. One of the Indians read in Sanskrit some verses from the Bhagavad-Gita about the immortality of the Spirit. Small sticks of sandalwood were burned in the room. Women editors from the publishing office brought flowers and wept. Our apartment was full of people, and soon everyone followed the coffin to the door. Only Katie and Helen remained at home. They were afraid of the crematorium.

It was a sunny, frosty day, this first of November. Only a few small boys stood gathered in the yard. Neighbors had hidden, afraid of foreigners and embassy cars. I was surprised to find at the crematorium entrance my friend Marina and her husband (in spite of her trouble breathing in cold weather), and also my friends from IMLI (Institute of World Literature). They had all come to take leave of

Singh, although they had never actually met him. I hadn't expected this. It warmed my heart.

Nor did I expect my son to kiss the forehead of the departed during the final farewell. He did it on the spur of the moment, obeying an impulse. I hadn't realized at the time that a man who harbored no ill will toward others aroused in other men, if not actual love, then at least a sincere respect.

Three years before, I had read in Singh's notebook: "In case of my death, let my body be cremated and the ashes thrown into the river. No religious ceremony is necessary." I remember remarking to him at the time that after all the Hindu religious ceremony consisted of casting the ashes into a river, but what river had he in mind—the Ganges? He smiled and said, "Yes, the Ganges. But I might die abroad, and who's going to think of going all that way? All rivers are the same, they all flow into the same ocean."

Now I remembered that conversation. In the last three years he had changed a great deal, had moved away from Communism. Sometimes he would read aloud to me the Vedic mantras. He had met death as a Hindu should, and now he should return to the Ganges. But who was going to arrange this?

I couldn't bring myself to trust anyone with the small urn, which now stood in my bedroom. I seemed to be tied to it by invisible threads. I couldn't part with it. It called and drew me to itself with all the strength of attachment and devotion, heretofore unknown to me.

"You must go yourself. Don't ask anyone else to do it. You must go yourself." Shoushou Ghaleb was the first to express this thought aloud. Bertha supported her. I didn't believe I would be permitted to go. Hadn't I been told, clearly and concisely, that they wouldn't let me out of the country? Nevertheless, I wrote again, to both Kosygin and Brezhnev this time. Obviously no time was lost in coming to a decision, for I was summoned the very next morning.

This time something had changed in the expression of

Kosygin's face. Did he feel ashamed? I wouldn't be the one to judge. The audience was over in five minutes: I was allowed to go on condition that I would avoid contacts with the press. The conversation was unpleasant for both of us, and we quickly ended it.

The governmental machine in Moscow works swiftly and methodically. By evening all my papers had been taken and a promise given to issue my foreign passport as soon as I supplied the photographs. In the consular division of MID (Ministry of Foreign Affairs) I was met with politely frozen faces. No one expressed surprise; here they had long ago ceased being surprised at anything. No questions were asked. Since everything had been decided "up above," all responsibility lay with those in higher echelons.

My passport was issued on November 11, 1966. It bore an Indian visa good for a month from the date of my arrival in Delhi. But my departure was delayed until the twentieth of December, in accordance with a request from Dinesh Singh. Now at long last he sent me a polite letter, inviting me to stay in his home.

For a month and a half I hardly left my apartment. I feared leaving my room and the urn in it unguarded. Old schoolmates and former fellow students at the university, as well as friends from the Institute of World Literature, were with me constantly. They kept calling me up to make sure that I was not left alone.

At the end of November my son got married. Helen came to live with us. The young couple, very much in love, was a happy sight to see. Life went on. Singh had loved life, had loved good food and good wine, and the last thing he would have wanted was to be mourned for a long time. His kind, cheerful soul was with us, warming us. It would have shunned darkness and gloom. Darkness and rancor were alien to it.

. . . And now here is the dry, dusty grass of the Palam Airport near Delhi, covered with crude oil and strewn with scraps of paper. A colorless whitish sky, a blinding sun. Bearded technicians in turbans stand near the hangars, toward which our plane is cruising.

And so, Brajesh Singh, we have come home. Your beautiful soul has overcome so many obstacles. Before it, even the "Bronze Horseman" has been forced to retreat.

Delhi

STUMBLING OVER the dry grass in my fur-lined snow boots, blinded by the sun, I take my first steps on Indian soil. But I do not feel like a stranger on another planet; the small airport of Palam reminds me of an airport in some southern resort on the Black Sea, somewhere near Simferopol (in the Crimea) or Adler (in the Caucasus): the same small white building, the same burned-out plain, and everywhere those scraps of paper which no one bothers to clear away. Among the people meeting the plane I recognize two women in saris—Naggu (Dinesh Singh's wife) and Preeti (Kaul's daughter). They are waving to me.

I had expected to go straight from the airport to Dinesh's house—officially I was his guest. But now I saw three figures in gray suits coming toward us across the field, where others were not allowed. I heard Mrs. Kassirova's joyful cry, "Those are our boys, from the embassy!"

For some reason or other we instantly began to hurry. I hardly had time to exchange two words with Naggu. It appeared that I was expected first at our embassy, that later we would call each other up and make further arrangements. Surov, Second Secretary of the Soviet Embassy, hurried me along, anxious to get through customs as quickly as possible, and I followed him with a vague feeling of annoyance. We got into his car. I had already lost sight of Naggu and Preeti, and I felt that the first meeting had been irreparably marred.

Instead of Dinesh's home with his six daughters, I found myself in the Soviet Hostel, situated on Soviet colony territory, where everything was all too familiar, as though I hadn't left Moscow. A nurse-hostess with a strong Ukrainian accent handed me a key to my room. My eyes searched for a telephone and didn't find one. No, I was informed, the telephone was in the other building—to which Surov added politely, "You can make calls from any room you like in the embassy. Now Nikolai Ivanovich is expecting us for breakfast."

Ambassador I. A. Benediktov was not in Delhi at the time. Nikolai Ivanovich Smirnov, the Chargé d'Affaires, turned out to be a tall and flustered man, whose nervousness instantly communicated itself to me. We sat down with him at a small table in the living room—Mrs. Kassirova, I, Surov, and a portly, dark-haired man with a round, impenetrable face. Although just a breakfast, the table was laden with food, with a whole battery of bottles full of cognac. Smirnov poured some out, and with a tortured smile, raised a toast to "Mr. Brajesh Singh, who was loved and respected by all who knew him." The three men made sad faces, but drank with gusto. Having swallowed a couple of mouthfuls and trying hard to sound amiable, Smirnov turned to me, coming straight to the point.

According to him, I had chosen the worst possible time for a trip to India. The country was on the eve of general elections, which would take place in February, and the political situation was extremely tense. The opposition to the governing party was very strong, and no one could tell what road India would choose to follow.

"The threat of Fascism is real," the portly man of the imperturbable face said weightily. "The reactionary Jan Sangh and the pro-American Swatantra want to lead the country away from Socialism."

"In other words, the situation is very, very tense and therefore—" here Smirnov took a deep breath—"we strongly recommend that you remain in our hostel. In fact, it would be well if you gave up altogether the idea of going to that village. We can easily arrange for the transfer of the urn with the ashes to take place right here—we are in constant touch with Dinesh Singh. They will fall in with our suggestions. We'll arrange a ceremony in the embassy, everything as it should be, flowers, et cetera. It will be solemn and dignified. Afterward you can see something of Delhi, go to Agra and have a look at the Taj Mahal; there is a lot that is of interest around Delhi. And it so happens that one of our Aeroflot planes is scheduled to leave on January 4. That'll bring you back to Moscow right on time—your permit is for two weeks. Of course, in the meantime, we will assist you in your shopping. Comrade Kassirova knows all the shops in Delhi. It's extremely important, though, that no mention be made in the press of your presence in India. We do not advise you to stay in the home of Dinesh Singh. He and former Ambassador Kaul, of course, are friendly to us, but you'll have greater peace and quiet here."

"We do not trust either Dinesh or Kaul!" was the portly man's categorical comment, although his face remained as imperturbable as ever.

I felt dizzy after a sleepless night and the drastic change of climate. I hadn't eaten anything, nor did I feel like touching the food in front of me. Everything I heard was unexpected, but then I was used to unpleasant surprises. Only why these dates, why two weeks?

"My Indian visa is good for a month," I said. "This was confirmed by the consular division of MID in Moscow. I was planning to spend a month here. Why the fourth of January all of a sudden?"

"Oh, these Indians, they'll grant any kind of visa!" ex-claimed Smirnov. "But visa or no visa, a decision has been made in Moscow, a special decision. Don't you see, this is your first trip abroad—" he was sincerely trying to make me understand. "The decision in your case is two weeks. Neither I nor the Indians can change it without Moscow's authoriza-tion."

"But then why wasn't I told about it in Moscow? You know perfectly well that I'm an official guest of Dinesh Singh in Delhi and of Suresh Singh in Kalakankar. You know the reason for my trip. I didn't come here to look at the Taj Mahal! I must go to my husband's village, stay there for a certain time with his brother and family—they wrote me, they are expecting me. The elections here don't concern me in the least, nor do the political tensions in this country. I don't have to see anyone but my husband's brother and niece, whom he loved. I don't intend giving any interviews to the press. So why must that be brought up all the time? I haven't yet seen Dinesh and his family. After all, I delayed my departure from Moscow for a whole month and a half on his account—he was busy with the session of Parliament. No ceremony in the Soviet Embassy could replace what I came for. What you suggest is impossible. Otherwise why did I come here at all! I was promised one thing, now I find something very different, very unexpected!"

Smirnov was having a hard time of it; to a certain degree he understood my position. We were unable, though, to come to an agreement that morning and decided to discuss the matter further the next day. In the meantime, I was to see Dinesh and Kaul.

I could hardly stand on my feet. I desperately wanted to take a nap. But since there was no telephone in the hostel, I had to make my calls and arrange those evening engage-ments over an embassy telephone, with an unknown em-bassy official sitting beside me at the desk, his face a stone mask.

Later I tried to rest but was unable to sleep. So I went to the house of Raja Dinesh Singh. Naggu, who had put on some weight since I saw her in Moscow in 1964, was very gracious, asking me about their uncle's last illness and death. Her six daughters, ranging from six to twenty-two, looked modern, and if it hadn't been for their antique jewelry, might have passed for schoolgirls and collegians in any country.

They showed a certain amount of curiosity about me, but not for long, and soon returned to their various occupations: a game of lotto, American magazines, a miniature Japanese TV set. In the big modern drawing room an electric fire was lit in the open fireplace, three dogs were lying on the thick rugs. The big family discussed its own affairs: the forthcoming marriage of Reva, the eldest daughter, her trousseau; also plans for building a house of their own in Delhi—this handsome residence with its big garden had been placed at Dinesh's disposal by the government.

All of them were full of rosy dreams for the future, for in the coming spring Dinesh hoped to get the portfolio of Foreign Affairs in the new cabinet. Soon he himself made an appearance and was as amiable and nice as he had been in Moscow. But he didn't know if he could go to Kalakankar at the present time, he would do his best. . . . His family would be leaving in two days, he planned to fly there on the twenty-fifth and could take me with him.

I told him of the surprises I had met with at the Soviet Embassy. He laughed, seemingly in sympathy with me, then said: "I think you had better not argue with Smirnov. After all, he doesn't make the decisions, you know. Remain at the hostel since that's what they want. In Kalakankar you will stay with us. I'm sure they will agree to your going there."

"But they don't even want to let me stay here a month," I expostulated. "Even though my visa is good for a month!"

Smilingly Dinesh dismissed the matter with a wave of his

hand, just as his uncle used to dismiss anything unpleasant.

"In our Ministry of Foreign Affairs," he said, "the question of visas is decided by my Naggu's brother. If Moscow allowed you to stay longer, we would renew your visa for any length of time."

He showed me old photographs, brought out family albums and colored slides. He seemed full of concern and sympathy. But he wanted no conflicts. Also, he was anxious to become Minister of Foreign Affairs. His successful diplomatic career, which he had been advised to follow by his Uncle Brajesh, led toward it, as well as a long friendship with the Nehru family and with Prime Minister Indira Gandhi. And next summer, he said, when he had attained what he was reaching for, he would come to Moscow and would certainly visit me and my children. . . .

Dinesh's whole manner was simple and democratic. He had served for a long time as secretary at the Indian embassies in London and Paris and had learned long ago that to belong to the highest caste was not always and everywhere helpful. In sum, he was a subtle, reserved, successful diplomat.

Kaul, the former Indian Ambassador in Moscow, with whom I dined that same evening, was a diplomat of quite another feather. Even in Moscow he never hesitated to criticize—something that delighted the young generation. He had many Russian friends—poets, artists, young movie actors. He visited Bella Akhmadulina and Yevgeny Yevtushenko. He liked student parties, danced the fox trot and a dance called *Tsyganochka* (Little Gypsy). He often brought his son and daughter to our house.

This noisy Kashmiri spoke Russian and loved *gorilka*—a Ukrainian vodka with pepper—two qualities that won him the hearts of many Moscow generals and marshals. He was outraged that diplomats were not permitted to go beyond twenty-five miles from Moscow and often broke this rule. He used to go with friends to previews of new films to which foreigners were not admitted; and used to take visiting foreigners to Pasternak's grave in Peredelkino. Now he was loudly indignant about the conditions laid upon me; but at the same time he advised me not to linger too long in Kalakankar, where, he said, there was little of interest. He suggested that I return to Delhi and spend the following week with him and his children touring the country in an automobile. He would show me some remarkable places! The Taj Mahal, he said, was shown only to tourists who knew nothing about the history of India.

We dined in a free and easy atmosphere, *en famille*. The food had been prepared by Kaul's wife, a handsome middle-aged Kashmiri with a very white skin and European features. Their son, who had recently graduated from a university in England, was there, too, and so was Preeti, their daughter, who had attended Russian courses in Moscow and was longing to enter Moscow University. At the head of the table sat Kaul's nonagenarian father, a sturdy old man with a very lively look in his sly eyes. After dinner, he lit a cigar, and Kaul said, "You naughty boy!" After that the old man settled down on a rug near the open fireplace and became engrossed in reading the Gita.

In the drawing room, in which we now sat, the old man alone was happy and at peace. Preeti was aching to go to Moscow. She had fallen deeply in love with Russia and did not want to marry in India a man chosen for her by her parents. The son wrote poetry in English and dreamed of a literary career instead of joining the Diplomatic Corps, as his father wanted him to. Nor did he wish to marry a girl of his mother's choice. The parents understood the futility of struggling with their children. But the mother grumbled against the children and Kaul, displeased with them all. Kaul complained that he "felt stifled in this vegetarian country, where one couldn't get a proper drink," and said that he longed to go away again as ambassador somewhere. How delighted he was with the vodka I had brought him from his Moscow friends!

Kaul was dissatisfied with everything he had found on his return to India—everywhere corruption and decay. He had been Ambassador to China, Ambassador to the U.S.S.R.; he was accustomed to a wide range of activity, to exercising personal initiative. He claimed now to miss Moscow. . . .

No one here had any real interest in me and my sorrows. Kaul was of the opinion that I would have to go back to Moscow in two weeks. He casually criticized everyone, including Dinesh, whose loud talk about Socialism, he said, was nothing but affectation: in reality he was gathering around himself rajas and maharajas and would most certainly lose the next election. I returned to my room depressed by the sudden discovery that among my Indian "friends" I would find no support of any kind.

Next day another long talk with Smirnov. This time we argued and bargained. They gave in: "All right, go to the country, but accompanied by Kassirova and for only one week. After that you may make a tour by car with Kaul. But on January 4 you shall return home!" (The Aeroflot plane flew only once a week.)

This was something new again: Why Kassirova? I was told in Moscow that she would wait for me in Delhi and would accompany me only on the plane. What would she do in the country? What would she have to say to the relations of a man she had never seen?

"All right, don't get excited," said Smirnov. "She knows this country—she accompanied Valentina Tereshkova on her tour of India. She will find something to do, she knows how to behave."

It was useless explaining that my journey differed from that of the first woman cosmonaut. Something blew up in me. I was about to exclaim that I would give up the whole idea of going to the country. But a certain quiet voice restrained me. I had come all this way with the express purpose of reaching the Ganges—all right then, let them do what they liked, so long as I got there. . . .

I kept my temper; I agreed. Smirnov was even more nervous than on the previous day. Apparently, our authorities were most unwilling to let me go to the country—a remote region far from Delhi, where there were no telephones, no Soviet representatives. I was fed up with these useless arguments; and realizing that my every move depended on Moscow's changing moods, I could hardly bring myself to talk quietly.

Oh, those ever-changing moods of Moscow! How swiftly they go from black to white, from one extreme to another, from friendship to accusations, from adoration to hatred, from the permissive *"da"* to that annihilating *"nyet."* Those eternal swings from a thaw to a freeze, whims that disregard their own rules, norms, and regulations! Unhappy land, unhappy people, who instead of promised freedoms got nothing but whims—whims far worse than those of any emperor, upon whose will everything in the country had depended.

I didn't even notice how I got out into the street. I walked under a hot sun without knowing where I was going. My head swam, my heart ached after the strain of these last months and days. Oh, how I hate you all, my whole being seemed to cry out—it was more of a sensation than a thought—as I kept on walking just for the sake of moving, of getting somewhere, anywhere. To remain sitting in my room with Mrs. Kassirova would have been intolerable.

I was walking along a sidewalk. To my right was a boulevard, to my left some buildings. I saw a wall and an entrance gate, a small crowd, a few snake charmers on the sidewalk, in front of them cobras in baskets. I didn't stop to watch. I turned a corner, rounded the wall of a tall building with a wide flight of front steps and a big Christmas tree near the door. The Embassy of the United States—I could see the coat of arms on the façade. Yes, of course, they were about to celebrate Christmas! We were only allowed to celebrate New Year's. How merry it would be in there . . . presents for children. . . . The whole world led a uniformly normal life. We alone were a strange species: oddities, scared of everything. . . . "Provocation!" they had said. What provocation? "Threat of Fascism!" . . . Fascism my hat! No Fascism here! They judged everything by criteria over twenty years old. Such obtuseness! How I hated all those bureaucrats. Jailers, you don't let people live normally, don't let them breathe!

A dark-skinned man in a white dhoti was carrying a big basket of sweetmeats on his head. He smiled at me. I don't like sweet things, but his smile acted on me soothingly, and I bought some honeyed nuts, which stuck in my mouth like putty. I knew I had paid too much, being unfamiliar with rupees, but that didn't matter, so long as he was pleased! Kassirova had warned me never to buy anything in the street—everything, she said, was covered with flies and germs. Oh, go to blazes, all of you! You despise this country; I love it. You are scared of everything; to me this sun-filled air is like sweet nectar. How warm it is! What a tender breeze, how bright those red creepers!

I went down a narrow lane and turned back. After all, I didn't know the streets of Delhi. Now, as I retraced my steps, I felt a little calmer. I passed by the U.S. Embassy again and examined it—no thought of ever entering it, simply noting that it was a handsome building, located not far from the Soviet Embassy and the hostel, to which I was now returning.

And so, my first twenty-four hours in India slipped by. They had proved to be tempestuous. What lay ahead? There was nothing to do about it, I would have to humble myself and do my duty. That was what I had come here for. I returned to the hostel, where Mrs. Kassirova had already laid out some Moscow pastries on the table and had brewed some tea. She, too, was disgruntled. She wanted to stay in Delhi, do some shopping, instead of accompanying me to the country. In her own way she tried to comfort me: "When I get back to Moscow I'll tell my superiors in no uncertain terms how wretchedly this whole trip has been organized."

✳

During the next three days Preeti Kaul showed me around Delhi. She skillfully drove her father's red Mercedes, which I had known in Moscow, maneuvering it deftly through masses of rickshas and cyclists, all of whom remained unperturbed, as did the pedestrians. I could only wonder that in this dense undirected traffic no one got crushed. It was warm and sunny. We sat on the grass in the park, strolled about the Red Fort, drove out to the mausoleums in the old Moslem capital not far from present-day Delhi. It was good to be with this sweet girl, head over heels in love with everything Russian. Under her guidance Mrs. Kassirova had "trusted" me on my own and hadn't accompanied us.

During those days I got some definite impressions of Delhi. This, my first "feel" of India, didn't alter during subsequent days. Around me I saw a variety of different eras, countries, influences. Lovely women in saris, like Preeti, driving cars of the latest make; a yogi standing on his head right in the middle of the park; beggar children surrounding us in droves as we passed by the shops of the Red Fort; Hotel Oberoy, where we ate ice creams, as luxurious and comfortable as any first-class hotel in Europe; beggars and half-naked men moving through the streets of Old Delhi like ants; dozens of little shops looking like honeycombs, with men and women swarming around them; many-storied department stores rising nearby, large posters announcing American films displayed everywhere in the streets—*Doctor Zhivago, The Sound of Music*, detective movies; young men dressed in Western style, elderly ones in pajamas and kurtas, in long white shirts hanging loose, or in black achkans, from which the Nehru jacket was derived; Indian women in saris, young girls and schoolgirls in dresses with long wide shalwars or *churidars*. European clothes were to be seen only on women from the West—there were many of them here.

The roads around Delhi were lined with beautiful old shady trees with wide-flung branches. On their thick, knotted roots sat monkeys picking fleas off their offspring. Strangely enough, I felt that all this was familiar. It was as if I had already seen somewhere those trees, those monkeys, those tiny shops. I seemed to know it all so well—perhaps from stories I had heard?

In the stores my eyes ran wild, my head almost swam— so bright, so inimitable were the saris, the Kashmir shawls, the sandals, the bracelets. But I saved my American dollars, exchanged in Moscow for the hundred rubles I had been allowed to take out with me, remembering the tips I would have to give in Kalakankar, the gifts I wanted to get for my children.

Again I dined and lunched at Kaul's. Everything here was simpler, more friendly than in Dinesh's house, although actually it was the latter's family who were supposed to concern themselves with me. But the maharanees and maharajas, Naggu's brothers and sisters, whom Preeti and I met during one of our visits, instantly made us feel that we belonged to a lower caste. Preeti, ordinarily so lively and gay, grew very quiet, seemed to wither in their presence, for she knew this difference well. And I, too, felt ill at ease.

For the first time in my life I had come up against that invisible barrier which aristocrats raise between themselves and others. The maharajas and maharanees continued to converse in our presence as though there was nothing in the room but furniture. They were not exactly rude; they just made you feel that you were not there at all, or that at best you were like one of those three dogs on the carpet, to whom no one paid any attention. The six daughters of the house would occasionally ask me a question for the sake of good manners, but even then it was as if they had patted a dog.

In Kaul's house everything was informal and pleasant. His wife, forever carrying a bunch of keys at her waist, asked me no questions; she would scold her children and retire to her room to pray. In her ears she wore heavy silver earrings suspended by long red silk threads. She never accompanied Kaul abroad, never left India, remaining an old-fashioned Hindu; the outside world was unknown to her and did not interest her. The old man—Kaul's father—would warm himself by the fireplace, sitting on his small rug and always giving me a friendly smile.

"Your manuscript is here with me in a safe place," Kaul told me. "Preeti read me the first pages."

"Good," I said somewhat absently. I didn't need it and had no intention of taking it. My mind was set on other matters. All I could think of was how to get to the country without further complications and surprises.

But surprises didn't fail to come thick and fast.

＊

On the twenty-fifth of December Mrs. Kassirova and I got up at six to meet Dinesh and go with him to the airport. For a long time we waited in vain at the gates to the Soviet colony, where we had agreed to meet him. He never showed up. Perplexed, I returned to my room. There being no telephone in the hostel, I couldn't even call up! At last Surov appeared in his car, offering to take me to the airport— maybe Dinesh was waiting for us there? We went, but found no Dinesh. What's more, the flight to Lucknow, we were informed, had been postponed and no one knew when it would leave.

I said to Surov, "Please take me to Thyagaraja Marg, to Dinesh. I want to find out what happened."

Surov, confused, did not know what to do.

"Let's go, please," I insisted. In the end we went back to town; but halfway there we met Smirnov's limousine traveling at full speed. The two cars stopped on the road. After a brief consultation with Surov, Smirnov came to me:

"Dinesh's secretary just called—he cannot go to Lucknow today. I think you had better return to your room. We will call him up later."

"No, I'll go to him myself. There's no telephone at the hostel, it's all very inconvenient. I wish to clear this up myself."

It was eight in the morning, but for Indians that was not too early. Dinesh received me, wearing a fine European dressing gown, and took me to his study.

"Have breakfast with me?" he asked. "Only Reva is here, you can fly with her at noon. Everyone else went by train, but I can't go. I must be at the Prime Minister's in an hour, and this evening I have to go to Sikkim. I was unable to let you know. We called the embassy, but there was no one there. Then we called Smirnov at his apartment. But don't worry, you'll be in Kalakankar today."

He spoke soothingly, trying to soften all these vexations, although he himself had managed to wriggle out of going to the country. No wonder his uncle had recommended the diplomatic service for him!

Dinesh was particularly amiable that morning: "Stay here, take a rest. You can go to the airport in my car with Reva. I'll tell Smirnov to have Kassirova meet you at the plane. So they forced her on you after all, eh?" he added with a deprecating smile. "But that's all right. You will be met at Lucknow and can have a bite to eat there. It's another three hours by automobile from there to Kalakankar."

Indeed, he was most attentive. Perhaps he felt badly that after making me wait a month and a half in Moscow, he still found himself unable to go with me; or perhaps he had remembered the urn and felt embarrassed that I had been forced to carry it around with me all over the place that morning.

For breakfast he had scrambled eggs and toast in the English fashion, then changed into a Nehru jacket and said, "I am going to the Prime Minister. She knows you are here and has expressed her sympathy. Would you care to come with me and see her?"

"No, this is not the time. I'm not prepared for such an interview—" I began and paused. Then, of a sudden, unexpectedly even to myself, I obeyed an impulse that came from the very depths of my being: "Dinesh, tell her—I would like to stay in India. Is—is that possible?"

He seemed to look deep into me. "Come with me," he said. "I can call up and say I'm bringing you."

"No, no! Not today, I couldn't—but would you speak to her, put in a word for me?"

"Yes," he said, "I will. And I'll be in Kalakankar soon—it's my constituency, you know. The Prime Minister's constituency is next to it. So we'll see each other there." As he left, he shot me an unexpectedly kind, reassuring glance. I retired to a guest room, where I stretched myself out on a bed and shut my eyes.

What had I said? What had I asked for? How could such a thing have escaped me? And how relieved I now felt! Yes, yes, yes, I wanted to remain! I longed for a no-return to the past! All this went through me as a sensation. Oh yes, I could adapt myself to anything, give anything not to return to that terrifying world of Kosygins and Suslovs.

I felt tired; there was no strength in me to think things through, to argue the point. Soon I would be taking a plane. I had a week in the country ahead of me—only a week. . . . Well, maybe something would work itself out. . . . Might be well to sleep for half an hour, and still reach the Ganges that day. . . . I couldn't stand these people another minute, couldn't bear to see them. . . .

The Banks of the Ganges

THE SMALL PLANE flew over square fields, all of them flooded—it had been raining here recently. Reva, long-nosed and sulky, sat silent. She was thinking of her forthcoming marriage to a very rich and illustrious young man, whom she had met only once; thinking perhaps, too, of the emeralds and rubies she would be getting for her wedding. Our conversation lagged. We were preoccupied with such different things.

Later we traveled for three hours over a dusty dirt road. A strange emotion took possession of me, growing ever stronger as we neared the objective of my long journey. Why was this scorched plain with its round, sparsely scattered trees so familiar? Where had I seen this dusty road before?

We were six hundred miles from Delhi, in a remote countryside where I knew no one, about to visit a family I had never met, yet it seemed as if I were returning home. I pressed the overnight bag closer to me. You are happy, Brajesh Singh, to be coming home. Your soul is rejoicing, and we are flying as on wings. Very soon now, very soon, just wait.

. . . We have turned off onto a side road. Dry, scorched

fields on either side, trees with faded, dust-covered foliage. And now a narrow village street, which is also still part of the road. Women with babies in their arms, men—they have all come out into the street, they are waiting for us, falling in on foot behind our car, which is wending its way through this dense crowd to the gates of a big white house, beyond which a peaceful stretch of water glistens in the sun.

So many people on all sides! Some of them must have come from other villages. Look, Brajesh, they have come to meet you and see you off. Here, at last, I see kind human faces, human eyes and tears. . . .

We stopped, and a number of people surrounded us. Two men, barefoot, in white clothes, took from me at last my precious burden: It's your brother, Brajesh, you are now at home. And here is your kind friend Prakashvati, your brother's wife, and your favorite niece, Dadu; and here's a nephew, Sirish, a chubby young man in a white shirt. He is neither a raja nor a minister of state, but his face is bathed in tears. I am giving you over into good hands. Now at last I am at peace.

There was no question of resting after the trip; all these people had been waiting here for hours. The men now moved toward boats, in which to row out into the middle of the great stream and cast the ashes into the Ganges. Women were not allowed to participate in these rites. We all stood on the large terrace of the house, Naggu and her six daughters among us.

We looked closely at the sandy shore of the Ganges, toward which the procession was wending its way. The entire beach became crowded, small boys ran about raising clouds of sandy dust. The procession moved down the shore farther and farther, to where boats lay anchored in deeper water: Good-bye, Brajesh! Good-bye.

Suddenly I began to weep. I shook all over, unable to control myself. Someone laid a hand on my shoulder, gave me a handkerchief—it was Prakashvati. And thus she remained standing beside me, her arm around my shoulders. We stood there for a long time, until the boats reached the middle of the river and the men stood up in them, remaining standing for a long time, heads bent.

From the terrace we could see far down the river, with all its twists and bends, its sandy shores and sandbanks. After a while we could see the boats turning slowly back and returning to the shore.

"They threw flowers into the water," Prakash explained. "The flowers will float for a long time downstream. See? Children are running along the shore, watching them. They always do that."

Everyone began to leave the terrace. I couldn't tear myself away from Prakash, this tall graceful woman.

"So many friends wanted to come from Lucknow and Allahabad," she said with a sigh. "But for almost two months we had no news of you. It was only today that we heard from Dinesh that you were on your way. So we quickly sent word to everyone in the neighborhood. Brajesh, you know, was loved in all the villages around here—you can see for yourself how many people came! We waited all day, fearing that again you might not come. But we had no time to let those in the cities know about it. Now they will probably be offended."

"What?" I cried. "Is it possible that you were not informed? But it was Dinesh himself who had asked me to delay my departure from Moscow. And he knew all along that I would arrive in Delhi on the twentieth of December. It was he, too, who set this particular date; only at the last minute he himself was unable to come. I thought you knew it all along, that all your friends knew it—believe me, it was no fault of mine!" I was burning with shame. I knew all too well whose fault it was. *They* had decided to prevent me from going to the country and failed to tell Brajesh's brother. It was *they* who were afraid of informing his friends, having decided to keep this great "state secret" under lock and key.

And Dinesh, of course, had assisted and helped the Soviet Embassy in every way.

"Oh, I know it's not your fault," sighed Prakash. "We are so glad to see you, though! Let's go to our house, everyone will join us there. This is the *raj-bhavan*, the palace of the Raja. The villagers are afraid of Naggu, but to us they will come."

I was made to sit down on a bed in a small room in which Brajesh had lived during the last years after his return from England. At one time this whole house had belonged to him, but he had given it to his brother. Poor, simple villagers came in and sat on the floor, their legs crossed. Suresh also returned with his son, both of them still in tears. Everyone told me something about Brajesh Singh, how he had helped the peasants, donated money, assisted those in trouble, and given good advice. They spoke Hindi, with a member of the family translating what they said. They asked me about Brajesh's last illness. None of them seemed able to believe that his heart could have given out so quickly. He had left here so full of vigor, they would exclaim.

Dr. Nagar came. He had worked in the small local clinic for forty years. Brajesh had told me all about him. Altogether, it was marvelous how much I knew about Kalakankar. Brajesh used to describe everything to me in such detail. And now at every step I saw how true his every word had been. How blissful I felt here after those five days of lies and strain in Delhi. No wonder I had so longed to get here!

"This will always be your room now," I was told. "Come here and stay as long as you like."

In the evening everyone went to the *raj-bhavan* for dinner. Rooms had been prepared for me and Mrs. Kassirova in this huge white house that looked like a fortress with its thick stone walls. The house had been built by Raja Rampal Singh at the end of last century. He himself had spent most of his life in England and had brought back an Englishwoman as his wife. He was the most remarkable of all the Singh ancestors: he had always worn European clothes, I was told, had founded the first local newspaper in the Hindi language, and had had a wide canal dug for the irrigation of the entire region. In the house they still kept a pair of immense dumb-bells with which he had exercised every morning.

Naggu described it all like a first-rate guide, while Mrs. Kassirova and I sat listening like tourists. Undoubtedly she had a great deal to take pride in, but in this big house Brajesh Singh had been forgotten.

Later I went out again on the terrace and sat there for a long time, unable to tear my eyes from that majestic, peaceful river.

It grew dark. The cicadas were chirping. One by one big, luminous stars appeared in the sky. Tall old eucalyptus trees rustled gently. Later there were the calls of night birds soaring over the river, like the cries of sea gulls. Peace and quiet reigned around me, almost incredible after the frenzy of the morning and the pain of the day.

Everything in me quieted down and lay hushed. The night was balmy. And the longer I sat there alone, the clearer one thing stood out in my mind: I would not return to Delhi in a week. It meant putting up a fight with my embassy. So what? Near this river I felt invulnerable. Yes, I would remain here. My Indian visa was good until the twentieth of January, I wouldn't be breaking any laws. As to what would happen after that—time would show.

The night grew cooler and I went to bed in the white, fortress-like house.

*

Next morning I wrote a letter to Smirnov and Ambassador Benediktov informing them that I intended to remain in the country until the eighteenth of January, since my visa was valid for a month; that Kassirova could return to Moscow whenever they wanted her to and that at Kalakankar I could be Suresh Singh's guest, if Dinesh's family left.

I then went on to tell them what I thought of the inadmissible way in which the Soviet Embassy brought pressure to bear upon private lives in India. I pointed out that Dinesh, who in a personal letter had invited me to Delhi, had been forced by them to go back on his invitation; and inasmuch as they had decided not to let me get through to Kalakankar, he had been unable to give his Uncle Suresh any date for my arrival. As a result, relatives and friends had been kept in darkness. Fortunately, they all understood that I, if I had had my say, would have arranged things differently. I ended by saying that all this did no honor to my country or its embassy and that I felt ashamed of both.

I gave the letter to Mrs. Kassirova to be handed to the Ambassador. Having told her of its contents, I asked her to return to Delhi and thence to Moscow.

She was stunned; but coming to, tried to reason with me, then began to plead. Finally, taking it as a personal affront, she flew into a rage. I stood my ground firmly: I would remain here as long as my visa was valid. It was my legal right. In the end there was nothing left for her to do but leave. Naggu ordered a plane ticket for her from Lucknow to Delhi and, accompanied by her six daughters, all of them secretly snickering, saw her off as far as the jeep at the gates.

I remained in the country and sank into Indian life as into a warm, fragrant bath, enjoying every moment of it. Life in Kalakankar was in every way different, unlike the life I had led until then. This total change proved as indispensable to me as air. I was exhausted by the last few days in Delhi, the last months in Moscow, the last difficult three years, and in general by all the forty years of my unnatural dual life. I felt that I had reached a limit, beyond which an inner turning point would occur.

I wasn't able yet to come to any clear or concise decisions, longing only for a change. I didn't know whether I could remain in India, though this was what I was hoping for, without any clear idea as to *how* I would live. I was waiting for Dinesh's arrival and for a possible meeting with Indira Gandhi, who was expected at Kalakankar in the middle of January. For hours I sat gazing at the Ganges, feeling only how much I needed this peace, that fresh breeze from the river.

Life in Kalakankar was not altogether harmonious. From what Brajesh had told me, I already knew there existed here a sharp rivalry of long standing between the two families, two different modes of life. It poisoned the atmosphere of this otherwise beautiful and peaceful little corner of the earth. I was glad to have been warned about it.

The *raj-bhavan*, which belonged to Dinesh and his family, resembled a large white steamer docked near the shore. From its flat roof, much like an upper deck, a grand view opened up across the full expanse of the Ganges and the entire neighborhood. It took one's breath away. When the river rose, the waters flooded the basement and reached to the very edge of the terrace. Old Raja Rampal Singh had known how to choose his location. His house had as its foundation a rocky ledge bathed by the river on three sides. But this handsome house, with its big library, was cold. A superficial layer of Western influences—the bobbed hair and contact lenses of the girls, English breakfasts and American magazines—lived here side by side with an ingrained sense of superiority, of belonging to the highest caste.

Everyone entering this house felt its aristocratic aloofness. Even Dadu, Dinesh's sister, who once upon a time had broken the laws of caste and had married for love, had been rejected and deprived not only of consideration but even of private property. For many years she had not been allowed to come to the *raj-bhavan*, in which she had been born. At present she was staying there as a guest. The others were friendly to her on my account, and Prakash told me how happy this had made Dadu.

Small and round like a ball, Dadu delighted in spending

the day on the terrace chatting with the girls. Brajesh had loved her, had helped her in every way he could, sending her money from Moscow. He had been her defender in the family. But even he had been powerless in the face of traditions centuries old, which in India to this day are stronger than the law: Dadu was never able to get even her mother's jewelry, which Dinesh had placed in a bank. She had sad eyes and a kind smile. She looked a bit like Brajesh. I enjoyed it when she dropped into my room of an evening and settled down on my bed. We would talk together like two old friends.

It was obvious that in this house Dadu felt like a poor relation, and so did I. A shyness overcame other visitors, too: relatives, neighbors, guests from the village, who came to see Naggu, always found her sitting with her daughters on an immense ottoman in the drawing room, knitting. Only before older women of the family would Naggu humble herself: she would rise from the ottoman, approach her guest, and bow very low, touching her hand to her forehead and then the floor at the feet of the older woman. After that she would return to her ottoman and continue talking to her daughters as though no one else were there. Guests left their shoes at the door and entered barefoot as a sign of respect.

The inaccessibility of the *raj-bhavan* was further emphasized by a hefty Punjab guard, who stood in the yard, holding a long wooden spear with a steel point. He always locked the gates and threatened the hungry village dogs with this spear. I might add that aside from the dogs, I don't think anyone from the village ever approached those gates.

The doors of the other house, in which Suresh's family lived, were always wide open. It was an old house that had been reconstructed. Covered with vines in bloom, it looked like a modern villa. It had been a pretty house once upon a time, and well cared for. There were still some traces left of the days when both brothers had been rich landlords.

The independence of India and agrarian reforms had left them but a small farm, an immense mango garden, and, of course, a grand old name.

Now this house, which Brajesh had given long ago to his brother, had fallen into neglect, half of it turned into store-rooms. The other half, with all its windows looking out on the Ganges, was inhabited and cozy; but everywhere one sensed impoverishment, that life was pressing so hard on its owners that they had let things go. In the rooms, furnished in unpretentious European style, one found many English books, portraits of Mahatma Gandhi, and good water colors by a modern Indian painter. The stone floor in the drawing room was covered by a large frayed rug. The village elder, the clerk with a typewriter, women with babies, and the many other callers always settled down on it; while Dr. Nagar, the President of the College, the schoolteacher, as well as any guests from the city, occupied armchairs.

Suresh Singh, an educated liberal landowner, was in constant residence at Kalakankar. He and Brajesh, after graduating from the best college in Lucknow, had given themselves completely to the struggle for independence, as all the best people in India had done. After the establishment of independence, Suresh had served for many years as a member of the Legislative Assembly of Uttar Pradesh, his state.

In his spare time he wrote short humorous stories in Hindi about village life; he also wrote a book for teen-agers about Indian birds and plants, which had won a national prize. He loved plants, collected and grew them in his small garden, where he made a close study of them. A quiet, mild man, profoundly peace-loving and impractical, he couldn't boast of wealth or of any success in farming. Besides, half his strength and energy was consumed by a constant conflict with his own nephew—a conflict of interests and ambitions.

According to tradition, in an Indian family the title of raja, together with the house, the wealth, and high social standing, was inherited by the eldest son alone, and his own brothers were no longer considered his equals.

Traditions of caste, evolved throughout several millennia, couldn't die away in twenty-five years or so, especially in remote rural districts. In Kalakankar the forty-year-old Dinesh was the Raja and factual ruler of the little kingdom. It was also his constituency, and the peasants of the neighborhood would never have dared elect anyone but their "Raja-Sahib" to the national Parliament. Furthermore, Dinesh was head of a family trust that supported two colleges in Kalakankar, a small clinic, several temples, a school of Sanskrit, and in general underwrote all local undertakings.

Dinesh's two uncles enjoyed a high reputation and esteem far beyond the borders of Kalakankar, but here they were almost nothing next to their young nephew, the Raja. It is a very usual situation in Eastern countries, which Western minds often have difficulty in grasping.

In this fight between the two families Brajesh Singh had played the role of peacemaker. In his youth he had broken with the traditions and rules of his family. Later he had become a Communist. But the predominant drive in him had always been to do good to his neighbors and make sacrifices for his fellow men, in accordance with a commandment found in all religions in India. Having followed these precepts all his life, he found himself in the end without property, house, or land, and with none of the means of subsistence usual in his class. It was then that he had sold the little that was left and had gone with his wife and son to London. And when a few years later he returned to India, he had been obliged to ask his brother for a room in the house that had formerly been his own, and he was often left with no money at all. During the last years of his life his entire mind had been turned toward giving help and counsel to those around him. That is why he was loved everywhere. To his brother he had been a real support, a protector to the wronged, commencing with Dadu, deprived of all her rights. As a result, he became a thorn in the side of the Raja. He always told me that life in Kalakankar was full of difficulties, similar to those known to every large Indian family. Now I could see how right he had been.

Near the room in which Brajesh had lived there was a small terrace looking out on the sandy shore of the Ganges. It was sheltered from the sun by thick, dark-green ashoka trees and edged by cactuses ten feet high. Grass sprouted between its large stone slabs. It was wonderfully quiet here. I used to sit on that terrace by the hour gazing at the Ganges, admiring its varied moods that changed at different times of the day. I felt so peaceful, so utterly well. To me this was the most perfect spot on earth. A sense of bliss so unexpected, so fragile and fleeting, that I drank in every moment of it.

Between the two houses there was a small platform with an old Hindu temple on it, filled with painted statues of different gods, so numerous in Hindu mythology. I had to pass every day between the temple and a shed, under which —almost under the open sky—lived Pundit Chakra, a bent old priest of ninety, with his wife and small granddaughter. Every time I went by, the little girl would call out a greeting to me—"*namasté*"—and I had to stop and return the "*namasté*" to each one of them in turn.

I was soon asked how I would feel about a "service for the repose of the soul," to use Christian terminology. But it's all the same: to him who believes in the immortality of the soul it matters not through what religious ceremony or in what tongue a prayer is raised for its rest and peace. I suggested that the relatives themselves decide what to do— whatever they considered necessary. This, however, proved to be not so easy, as Dinesh's and Suresh's families belonged to two different branches of Hinduism.

At first Naggu arranged a ceremony in an orthodox Hindu temple. Pundit Chakra (whom, incidentally, Brajesh had always called a "cheat and a bastard") rang a small bell, circled the temple several times, lit small oil lamps, sprinkled everything with "holy water" taken from the Ganges, and told his beads at length, mumbling prayers. The ceremony was a long one and seemed endless. I sat in a white sari, my legs folded under me and growing numb; I lit my oil lamp, in short did everything that was proper.

Next day Suresh, somewhat excited, explained to me that Brajesh, like himself and his family, had belonged to Arya Samaj, a Protestant branch of Hinduism, based on the Vedas. It didn't recognize polytheism, temples, sacred statues, long ceremonies. Now, he said, they would like to pray for the repose of Brajesh's soul in their way. I agreed. It was all so fascinating to me. Another pundit came, more pleasant and attractive in appearance, and the sole ritual in the ceremony was a lighted bonfire under the open sky. They threw fragrant resin into the fire while reading prayers in Sanskrit. Everything was simpler, lovelier, more comprehensible somehow. The meaning of the Hindu prayer for the repose of the soul sounded very familiar: "May this soul from now on find peace and rest." The only thing the two ceremonies had in common was that money had to be given to the pundits and their disciples, who sat with crossed legs, murmuring prayers.

From Prakash I learned all the interrelationships in this place. Although Naggu bore the title of Ranee of Kalakankar, she showed little interest in the life of the big village. Prakash, on the other hand, was recognized by the community as its moral leader.

From early morning she would sit on a small terrace near the entrance to the house, shading her eyes from the sun and discussing all kinds of household problems and affairs. The village was next door, just beyond a brick wall. One could hear the monotonous singing in the Sanskrit school, as its pupils learned their prayers. Everyone who wished to have a talk with Prakash came here in the morning. Women came in search of advice and medicines; Prakash was also an authoritative proponent of planned parenthood. It was she, too, who arbitrated in family quarrels and gave the peasants detailed information about the elections.

With a general election so close at hand, there were heated discussions about political parties and struggles, in which the inhabitants of Kalakankar took a lively part. Dinesh belonged to the ruling National Congress Party. So did Suresh. But the latter's sympathies leaned toward the Socialists, who were influential in his state. Prakash leaned toward the young procapitalist party of Swatantra. Both she and her husband secretly hoped that Dinesh would lose, but out of loyalty to the family and its honor they worked for him in the pre-election campaign. Prakash often drove in a jeep to neighboring villages, called meetings, spoke to the women. Naggu, of course, never did anything of the sort. These days her one wish was to go to Benares to buy wedding saris for Reva and then return to Delhi.

One day, as I sat with Prakash on her morning terrace, I saw two young men, one black, the other white, in European clothes, wearing sandals and bush shirts. They were coming toward us, but Prakash said something in Hindi to her son, and he led them away.

"Who was that?" I asked.

"Americans from the Peace Corps." Prakash looked slightly embarrassed. "Nice good boys, working all day in our agricultural center. They are so young and all alone here. They come to see Sirish. I often invite them in for tea. But Dinesh said they were 'American spies' and ordered me never to let them come near you. I really don't know what to do. They are accustomed to coming and going at will. Miller, the Negro, always says he feels at home in our house. They know a little Hindi—"

"Oh, what nonsense! Forget it!" I cried, blushing once more for my embassy. "Besides, do they know where I am from?"

Prakash shrugged helplessly: "They never ask questions. Such really nice boys, working all day, teaching the peasants.

Though our peasants are not easily taught. For you know, no matter how hard we work, we depend in the end entirely on the rains."

It was so good being with Prakash. So relaxing! I was so tired of high-ranking officials, of ministers and prime ministers, ambassadors and aristocrats, in whose hands lay the destinies of nations and individuals. With what pleasure I forgot them all, sitting here on a mat, beside Prakash on the stone floor, which also served her as a kitchen table. On it she sliced vegetables and cooked them on a small kerosene stove—something extremely good, consisting of kidney beans, potatoes, onions, tomatoes, and cauliflower. They called it "winter vegetables." In summer there would be mangoes, papayas, and other summer produce.

The vegetable garden near the house was a small green oasis, constantly watered from the well, as was the small flower garden, in which Prakash and I gathered flowers in the morning. Mignonette, stock, sweet peas would be blooming in a month's time. But how many plants were growing and blossoming here now which were totally unknown to me.

❋

Brought up in the country, it was second nature for me to observe closely the awakening in the spring and the death in the fall of the green world around me. Trees and flowers were often more meaningful to me than people. They always helped me, consoled me, giving the soul a chance to believe once more that the world was beautiful and sensible, that the mad absurdities and cruelties of men were *against* the laws of Nature and the Universal Mind; that sooner or later violence would suffer utter defeat on this Earth. No words collected in books were more effectively convincing to me than foliage, clouds, rippling waters, rain. That's why now, transported to a warm climate straight from Moscow's winter, I again listened avidly and again heard Nature speaking to me.

The way I met the New Year—1967—in that Indian village was most unusual. With Indians the thirty-first of December goes by unnoticed because in rural districts they continue living by the Hindu calendar. Therefore, all I could do was go to bed early. And yet I wanted so much to mark in some way the coming of the New Year, for at home I had always been accustomed to meeting it with my children and with a few choice friends. And so I left the *raj-bhavan* to spend the night in the small room in which Brajesh had lived.

It had old white furniture, no doubt brought from England at the end of the last century, together with his English wife, by that same eccentric ancestor. The old-fashioned wooden bed stood near a window that looked out on the river.

For a long time I lay in bed without falling asleep, gazing at the sand, pure white under the bright moon, trying to visualize the deep snowdrifts around Moscow and the sharp pinching frost. It had been a great joy in my life to go to Zhukovka on New Year's Eve and wander through the snow-covered woods by moonlight. . . .

Now just outside my window lay the terrace with its big stone slabs and row of cactuses tall as trees, and beyond it the sandy shore. Farther still, but no more than a hundred yards from me, the quiet smooth surface of the Ganges. The night was cool and very quiet. The only sound—a chirping of cicadas. But then Pundit Chakra appeared on the shore, bent almost in two and limping toward the river. With one hand he was leaning on a stick, in the other he carried a brass pot with which to get water from the river. The brass glistened in the moonlight. . . . On that I fell asleep.

According to an old belief, one can tell by New Year's

Eve what the year itself will be like. The coming year promised to be quite unlike any that had gone before it.

In the early morning hours, before dawn, I went bathing
in the Ganges. I wasn't prompted by any mystical or religious motivations. An agitation, nevertheless, took possession
of me, partly because Brajesh's ashes had been cast into
this water, partly because to me the Ganges represented
an image of eternity, a symbol of wisdom and serenity, of
everything that was dear to me in India. There is about this
river something inexplicable: every time the eye meets its
watery surface, the heart skips a beat.

Dadu, and a maidservant, went bathing with me. Dadu
had explained that it was customary to do so before sunrise,
usually under a full moon. We walked along the sand to a
boat, barefoot; and a boy, using a pole, ferried us across
to an island in the middle of the river.

People in India enter the Ganges as they do a temple.
First they throw flowers into the river, then with their hands
cupped they moisten their mouth and brow. Only after this
do they step into the water, saying a prayer. Dadu observed
all these rites meticulously. She bathed in her sari, as all
Indian women do. Prakash had advised me not to undress,
suggesting that I bathe in my pajamas. I followed her advice and I went to the river barefoot, having thrown a coat
over my shoulders.

At first the cold water burned me, but then I experienced
a tingling sensation all over, and the water seemed warm. I
didn't want to get out. For centuries it has been said that
the waters of the Ganges have curative qualities. Perhaps it
is naturally radioactive. It contains many natural salts and
smells of sulphur. In any case, it is most refreshing, and
one's skin, after bathing, stings as after a light sunburn.

With quiet splashes the boat returned to our shore. The
sky had grown bright red, the water pink; a light breeze,
forerunner of sunrise, blew gently. The boy with the punt,
Dadu, her maid, were all smiling at me. I felt rejuvenated,

happy, my heart as peaceful as the quiet rosy waters around me.

The Ganges changes many times during the day, and one is never tired of watching it. Its shores are sandy, one higher than the other, and there the winds sweep the sands of the dunes along with them. Farther down the river there are sandbanks on which, resting during their migrations, birds of the north settle down: wild ducks, herons, gray cranes. . . .

One day as I was strolling along the shore, I heard a familiar gabble high above. I wouldn't have believed my own ears if I hadn't caught sight of a triangle of cranes up in the sky. There they were, my cranes, out of Russia and over Kalakankar, lucky birds who knew nothing of visas, passports, and other foolishness invented by man. But they did know that the Ganges was not an ordinary river, and from high above in the vast expanse of sky and earth they stuck to it as to a path. Now and then they might alight on a sandbank, move about the sand. . . . And so they went, flying south, returning north, at will.

In Kalakankar the sun rose behind the village. Around noon the sparkle on the ripples of the brown muddy waters became almost unbearable. During the day, though, there was always a fresh breeze, sometimes a strong gust. The village boats would spread their sails. There were no bridges anywhere for hundreds of miles. People, bales, cattle had to be ferried across by boats. Kalakankar was just such a ferrying point.

In the daytime its shore was lively and crowded: dogs running about; dust hanging in the air; people coming after water; people washing saris and dhotis, mercilessly thrashing them against the surface of the water, then spreading them on the sand to dry; people rubbing kitchen utensils of brass with sand to clean them; and still others sailing across to the island in the middle of the river, where watermelons had been sown and were already sprouting. They would ripen in time to be plucked before the rainy season set in, when the river would rise and flood the island. Until then, however, the watermelons had to be watered and protected at night against rodents. Village boys were in command over there, tending the watermelons, putting up scarecrows to chase the birds away. Occasionally camels would appear on the opposite shore. There was a village there, too.

Toward evening the noise and bustle on the shore subside, the dust and the wind die down, the water becomes dark, heavy like oil, and the sun now doesn't leave its smooth surface until sunset. This is the beginning of the sun's death. It no longer burns, no longer blinds, suffusing, instead, the sky, the earth, the water with an orange light—the national color of India. The color deepens, not out there somewhere on the horizon, but right here, all around you. It's as if one were breathing this fading light. . . .

And now, beyond the opposite shore, the orange globe sinks under the earth. And darkness falls very suddenly, as though everything had sunk into the black density of night. While the river, benumbed, lies very still until morning, reflecting unbelievably large stars.

This solitude was always complete. Kalakankar lay far away from any cities; forty miles from Allahabad, ninety from Lucknow. It was in the very heart of India, known in the ancient days as Aryavarta; and these sandy shores had not changed since then, and the river still washed on three sides the rocky ledge, to which now a big white house had attached itself. The name itself—Kalakankar—meant "Black Stones."

Twenty generations of Singhs had lived here, all of them gone into the Ganges, some of them performing great religious rites: after a long fast, bodies emaciated, they would cross on a raft to the middle of the stream, and to the roll of many drums, plunge into the river forever. The river accepted them all, carried all of them into eternity; and every winter, as now, it fell shallow, to disclose islands and hidden shoals.

There were no famous temples here, no historical monuments; no rare sights in this lonely land, with its scorched
earth and dirty village. The colors were not bright, the
peasants wore nothing but plain white, the dusty foliage
of the trees was dull. There was nothing exotic about the
place, none of the fairy-tale quality that tourists sought in
India. But instead, present in everything, permeating everything, there was an imperceptible deep sound, like that of
an organ. If you remained very quiet, if you sat very still
gazing at the river, you too would hear it. You would sense
it coming as a slow, reverberating gong, as the quietly
breathing heart of a mighty, eternal life, in which everything—the earth, the river, the sky, the birds, and man—
found itself blended. Even he who knows not God, who does
not believe in Him, would, without knowing it, thank Him
for the peace that filled his soul, and involuntarily, as though
against his will, the words would escape him: "Lord, what
bliss!"

Delays and Efforts

THESE CONTEMPLATIONS and this rest were brought
to a rude end, cut short as by an electric shock. One morning, as Dadu and I sat after breakfast on the terrace of the
raj-bhavan, we heard a commotion in the yard. A servant
came running to us. Hardly able to believe my eyes, I saw
Surov, the Second Secretary of the Soviet Embassy in Delhi,
coming toward me. In his light trousers and brightly colored
shirt, he looked like a visitor to a summer resort.

Naggu appeared with her six daughters, showed him the
house and the glorious view. Surov exclaimed in amazement
and admiration. Naggu grew visibly animated, while the
eyes of the girls sparkled with curiosity. Surov was asked to
stay for lunch. After that the others retired, leaving us alone.

Surov looked disconcerted. He lit a cigarette and informed
me that my permit had been extended a week, that, instead
of January 4, my return ticket would be good for the plane
on January 11. Kassirova would wait for me in Delhi. He
himself had traveled twelve hours by car and had spent the
night in a hotel in Lucknow, where he could stay for another
day or two, waiting for me, and then take me back to Delhi.

"Your wishes have been met halfway," he declared, not

without a certain pride in his embassy's action.

"But," I said, "I wrote Smirnov and the Ambassador that I would stay here as long as my visa was valid. It's good until the twentieth of January. I won't leave sooner. Give me a chance to stay a little longer with these people, whom I may never see again. Why should that be so difficult?"

"I will transmit your reply," was his rejoinder. "But it seems to me you have already had a rest. You look very well."

"I can't add anything to what I told the Ambassador. Let Kassirova go home. I'll send a letter to my children with her. There was no need for her to come here in the first place. You can see for yourself, this is an out-of-the-way spot, no newsmen. That's all I have to say."

A little later we joined the others for lunch. As always, Indian dishes were served (breakfasts in the morning were served English style). The girls kept exchanging glances; the situation was becoming intriguing: the embassy had sent to fetch me, and I wanted to stay.

Naggu again told the old story how Raja Rampal Singh had built this house. Surov ate his curry without much appetite. At last he got into his car at the gate, and I hurried to Prakash's house, where the whole family had gathered, waiting anxiously: "We were afraid he would carry you off!"

Surov's visit left an unpleasant aftermath. I wondered what the Soviet Embassy would think up next. My thoughts involuntarily turned to Moscow, giving me shivers of anxiety and dread. I didn't want to think of our apartment, of my room, where death had paid a call. But my children were waiting for me there. I wrote them a letter. I tried to think of what I could bring them as presents. Prakash was already knitting a sweater for Katie. My children were all that drew and called me back to Moscow. I was beginning to miss them badly. Our life had been so close for so many years. And yet, at the same time, my aversion to returning grew in intensity. . . .

This division in me became sharper. It compelled me to be calm and consider soberly the whole situation, weighing all conceivable contingencies. The thought of being obliged again to attend Party meetings, of "re-entering the collective," as Kosygin and Suslov had said, was intolerable. For the last ten years I had lived quietly with my children, unnoticed, attending to my household duties, doing translations. What business was it of theirs what I did with my time? No, they would never let me lead the life of a normal, ordinary person. . . .

Surov's visit had an entirely opposite effect to what he had hoped to achieve. Now I awaited with impatience the arrival of Dinesh, so as to have another talk with him about the possibility of my remaining in India. It seemed to me that he wanted to help. At any rate, our first talk in Delhi had been encouraging.

*

To satisfy the Soviet Embassy, Dinesh had instructed everyone here never to let me roam through the village. But during his absence I, of course, had walked all over it.

There had been no winter rains that year. Everything was utterly dry. The slightest breeze raised clouds of dust. Hungry dogs roamed the narrow, dirty lanes, and in the same lanes vegetables, fruit, and spices were displayed in open stalls. From one of the wells water was drawn, as in Russian villages, with a bucket at the end of a rope; here women always gathered, carrying brass pitchers. The other well was large and ancient; a leather receptacle full of water was drawn up by a creaky contraption, put into motion by a bullock, whom a boy led to and fro. At certain intervals another boy emptied the leather pail down a wooden scupper, and the water flowed along wooden troughs into the fields. This "perpetuum mobile" functioned with a slow rhythm, at once creaky and soporific; but the water flowed.

A few electric wells lay idle, as the nearest power station had gone on strike, hoping to get a raise in salaries before the elections.

For the same reason, the bus to town wasn't running, and in town the Court of Justice and government offices were closed. In order to let the electric wells function at least part time, the power station supplied current for a short while every day, closing down again in the evening; and kerosene lamps would then be lit in the house.

In spite of the closeness of a great river, the fields around the village looked as after a long drought. A deep well, constructed especially for the irrigation of the fields, was inactive; an electric pump had proved too expensive to buy. A sad spirit of desolation and inertness hung over everything. The deep wide canal, dug in the days of Rampal Singh, could have transformed this whole region into a lush garden. At one time fairly sizable boats had sailed through it. But the canal had dried up long ago. Its bottom was now sparsely overgrown with trees and shrubs. Goats grazed there.

Another sad memorial to benevolent landlordism was the broken-down printing press of the first Hindi-language paper, established by the same Rampal Singh, who had also been one of the founders of the National Congress Party. Near the overgrown remnants of the canal, on a pretty hillock, stood the ruins of a house once upon a time inhabited by a well-known poet, Sumitra Nandan Pant, an old friend of the family.

These mournful remains of a lordly existence, as well as the mode of life led by Suresh's family, repeatedly brought to mind Chekhov's *Cherry Orchard*. Here, too, there was a garden—in this case a mango garden. Huge, beautiful, evergreen mango trees stood neglected, and the earth around them was as hard as rock. True, no one here threatened to cut down the symbolic garden. But neither did anything come to take its place, nor was anything forcing this slow extinction. Kalakankar had had only one important, impressive reformer—Raja Rampal Singh—but those were other times. Now life dragged itself along in hopeful expectation of rain. And this, evidently, was but one example of conditions prevailing in all rural districts of India.

The independence of India and the agrarian reforms had dealt a death blow to the feudal tenure of land and to the old culture, but what was to take its place? Experiments in the spirit of Socialism cannot solve the problems of peasant India, and do not arouse enthusiasm in the masses. Nehru's idealistic partiality to Socialism had been left as his legacy to the country. But when Dinesh spoke about their "Five-Year Plan," I simply felt that he wanted to pay another visit to Moscow and create a good impression there. One couldn't accuse him of idealistic delusions.

How I used to laugh to myself when Naggu—this maharanee with a diamond in her nose, to whom life hardly existed beyond the consciousness of her high caste—tried to explain to me the advantages of Socialism and governmental control. To me! As if we in the U.S.S.R. didn't know better what it meant when put into practice.

The only Communist in Kalakankar, a poor old peasant called Ram Din, also tried to prove to me these "advantages," holding in his hand a Communist brochure in Hindi. But the moment I told him that in the U.S.S.R. the peasant didn't own the land but worked in the fields as workers do in factories, he became downcast and sad. Poor Ram Din couldn't speak English, couldn't read anything but Hindi, and he believed in Communism and Socialism simply by virtue of his love and devotion to Brajesh. As for enlightened rajas and maharajas, they were simply being hypocritical. Actually Dinesh and Naggu would have infinitely preferred the old order. Their big farms and several houses with land were managed by a steward, known in Kalakankar as Manager-Sahib. The peasants were more afraid of him than of the raja and ranee.

True, following the spirit of the times, Dinesh had given the old palace of his ancestors to the government, and in it was now located the Agricultural Training Center of the region. In front of the handsome white palace, built in the style of the Rajputs of northern India, youngsters raised clouds of dust on the volleyball field. But the peasants reacted to these "new methods" passively. To them the answer to it all lay in a good downpour of rain. The two American boys from the Peace Corps complained to Prakash that they had difficulty in getting the peasants out into the fields because the peasants followed numerous superstitious Hindu signs and omens, were afraid of evil influences, and preferred prayers for a good harvest to steady work.

I saw two other old palaces not far away, belonging to distant relatives of the Singh family. Prakash once took me with her to pay our respects to the oldest woman of the clan. I put on my white sari and did everything Prakash told me to do. Upon entering a large open inner court paved with stones, we took off our shoes as a sign of respect. Near a small open fire squatted a thin woman in a rough homespun sari. She looked like an old sick bird. Her eyes, with red eyelids, were fixed on the fire and she kept stirring the coals with a stick. Imitating everything done by Prakash, I bowed low and, repeating Prakash's gesture, touched with my hand the woman's bare foot. But I soon learned that I had committed a grave error: I should have touched only the ground near her foot. As a result, before long she got up and went to wash herself, for I had soiled her with my touch. She never returned to us. Prakash, laughingly, patted my shoulder: "She is very religious and is getting ready to die. She has never left this yard. Even now the young women here go out of the house only after having covered their heads and faces with their saris, and always with downcast eyes. We gave all that up long ago!" Prakash and I, pulling up our saris, climbed back into our jeep and went home, to where people led a normal life. . . .

In Prakash's home everything was simple, but to clear a place of the caste atmosphere took a long time. They had to have a number of servants in the house, as each one could only do a certain kind of work. When Prakash wasn't cooking, the food could only be prepared by a cook of Brahman origin; another servant brought everything to the cook and washed the dishes, but had no right to do the actual cooking. There were two house servants who cleaned the rooms and served at meals, but could not eat the same food. They were always ready to answer a call, even if only to bring a glass of water. Both of them—one quite a young man and the other a bit older—did splendid laundry work and ironed with an electric iron, though always on the floor, never on a table. These two were not of Brahman origin, but neither were they of the lowest caste.

The stone floors in the house were washed by a woman who was an untouchable. According to law, untouchables did not exist any more, but all the same, no one else had the right to wash the floors and clean the bathroom. Oh, that bathroom!

Fortunately, the modern toilet in the house functioned perfectly; a miracle in so remote a place, which bespoke the high cultural level of the owners. In general, toilets were unknown in rural districts. As in many Russian villages, when the need was upon them, people just went out into the yard. In Kalakankar peasants went to the shore of the Ganges and squatted there, which did not add to the beauty of the landscape. As for sanitation, it was left to the hot rays of the sun and to a herd of black shaggy swine, who daily passed along the shore.

The house had running water, but none of the faucets worked. Water to wash with was brought every morning by a *panivala*, an aged water-carrier, whose legs were bowed and back bent from carrying water all his life. Ordinarily he got the water from one of the electric wells, but when the power failed, he went with two large buckets on a crossbar to the Ganges. The same system was in effect at the *raj-bhavan*, where lovely modern furniture stood in the drawing room, but water for washing—both hot and cold—was brought by water-carriers. In the *raj-bhavan* they had even more servants than at Prakash's, most of whom worked in the kitchen and never appeared in the house. The house servants in both families wore tennis sneakers and long homespun dhotis with a loose European shirt or jacket.

I very soon betrayed my plebeian origin by washing my own clothes and then asking for an iron. But to do one's ironing on the floor, if one is not accustomed to it, is well-nigh impossible; and to wash one's European clothes without a plentiful supply of hot water is equally hopeless. So as not to ruin the few dresses I had brought with me, I took to wearing saris, which I found very comfortable. These I gave to the servants to wash and press. But all the same, the servants considered me of "common origin" and were therefore always friendly.

All the housework could have been done by one Western woman supplied with modern appliances. Here a servant would do the dusting with a towel, swinging it in his hand. Dust, nonetheless, covered everything in layers, and all the corners in a room were thick with cobwebs. But I gladly put up with it, for the warm friendliness of my hosts and their servants, their kind smiles, their sincere sympathy were far more important to me.

I encountered warmth and friendliness at every step; as for the living conditions, I quickly got used to them and found them agreeable and healthy. What could be more salubrious than cold ablutions in the morning with water from the Ganges, a plain fare of rice, vegetables, and fruit, pure spring water from the well instead of wine, and strong Himalayan tea instead of coffee? After spending two months in the country I felt healthier and stronger, with no ill effects either from the unboiled water or from the kitchen, where the stone floor served as a kitchen table on which to prepare food. I never dreamed of boiling the water or washing the fruit, cups, and plates, as I had been strictly instructed to do by my embassy. I simply loved everything I saw around me, and everything here repaid me in kind.

The poverty everywhere was all too obvious, although Kalakankar did not represent the utmost in hunger and need. It was a comparatively fortunate district, if one considers that in neighboring Bihar, in this year of drought, people were dying of starvation. And yet even here one felt distressed every time one walked through the village. No matter how friendly and endearing the villagers might be, one couldn't help seeing that their faces were haggard, their half-clothed bodies skin and bones.

One day Suresh told me that he would have liked to do something in Kalakankar in memory of Brajesh. He had asked Dinesh to consent to the establishment of at least a Brajesh Singh Memorial Room in the college. But Dinesh, who disposed of all public funds in the village, did not support him in this.

"We would have done it ourselves, but we have no money," Suresh and Prakash concluded sadly.

It was then that an idea struck me, inspired by them. If I remained in India, I would write; my first manuscript might be published somewhere abroad. Then I would be a burden to no one and might be in a position to help all these people. How nice it would be to build a small hospital in memory of Brajesh; there was nothing in Kalakankar but a small clinic, in which Dr. Nagar gave first aid and indispensable help in two dirty rooms. Yes, I must take my manuscript from Kaul as soon as possible and send it to Paris to d'Astier, the only man known to me beyond the borders of the U.S.S.R., who, it so happened, was a writer himself.

I never considered that my *Twenty Letters* could offer any political revelations to a reader in the West. They were written as a family chronicle and not as historical memoirs. But I also knew that a family chronicle so unusual and tragic as

ours would perforce bring the reader to some political conclusions.

I wrote Louba Krassin, Emmanuel d'Astier's wife, in Paris.
I had met him three times in Moscow. To Louba I wrote in
Russian, telling her that I was in India and didn't want to
return to the U.S.S.R., at the same time asking if it would
be possible to publish my book abroad with the understanding that all royalties would go to Kalakankar.

A few days later I received a short telegram: "Yes, possible." Later a letter came. In it Louba, also writing in Russian, told me that she fully understood my feelings. But
she offered no practical suggestions.

Was I right in so trusting people I hardly knew? It seemed
to me that under the circumstances it was safer to address
myself to d'Astier than to ask help in India. Louba, his wife,
was a Russian, daughter of L. B. Krassin, first Soviet Ambassador to England, who in her childhood had known my
mother. My grandfather, Sergei Alliluyev, had known the
Krassins in his youth. It was pleasant to think of this in the
desperate situation I now found myself in. That is why I
wrote to Louba, whom I had never actually met.

As for her husband, I first met him in Moscow when my
doorbell had rung one day in July 1962. It turned out to be
Emmanuel d'Astier, come to pay me an unexpected visit.
He introduced himself, explaining that he was writing an
article about my father and was anxious to check with me
certain biographical data. By all the rules and regulations of
Soviet life I should have politely shown him the door, or at
any rate have first found out from official quarters whether
I had their permission to receive a foreigner. But these
"rules" were so repulsive that I decided to ignore them and
invited him in. We talked for several hours.

D'Astier's name was known in Moscow's intellectual circles: he was considered a liberal, a pacifist, a pro-Communist,
and a fighter for peace. In the preface to the Russian translation of his novel about the French Resistance, Ilya Ehren-

burg had referred to him in a friendly way as a "dilettante in art and politics" and a "Don Quixote."

At the very start d'Astier informed me that Ilya Ehrenburg had dissuaded him from coming to see me, but that he, nevertheless, had obtained my address from some Moscow acquaintances. He then showed me the brochure he had written about my father and the photographs he had collected for it. I was obliged to tell him that half of those photographs, obtained from European sources, were fakes. In their place he took a score of photographs from my albums. He just couldn't believe me when I told him that such a "source" as Budu Svanidze's book *My Uncle Joe* was entirely fake. Only the son of A. S. Svanidze, whom I tracked down and invited to meet d'Astier, was able to convince him that "Budu" Svanidze never existed at all. D'Astier, at the time, made notes of many things I told him and kept repeating that I myself should write a book about my life. His book, *Sur Staline*, appeared a year later. In it I found, without reference to their source of origin, my photographs and stories, with all the dates, names, and facts confused and mixed up.

Soon after this interview Mikoyan suddenly invited me to his house in the country. Strolling in the garden, he remarked that of course I wasn't forbidden to meet progressive foreign notables, but "better not." Then, of a sudden, he asked me: "Did you ever feel like writing your memoirs? Write them, if you want to. Only don't give them to foreigners. They'll start hounding you."

My answer was that I didn't intend writing anything. Yet this conversation stuck in my mind, and that is why, when a year later I wrote my *Twenty Letters*, I concealed them carefully from all official circles. I knew that they would instantly confiscate the manuscript, or make me change it in the spirit of whatever Party line happened to be in effect at the time.

After that first meeting, d'Astier returned to Moscow two

or three times and always came to see me. Every time after
his visit I would be summoned to the Central Committee
of the Communist Party and asked politely, "What did that
Frenchman want?" They didn't believe me when I told them
that he had simply brought me a letter from Louba or some
French perfume.

It is a fact that in not notifying them of these visits I
was breaking "Party rules." But I had no intention of following those rules. To us recluses, fenced in in the U.S.S.R. from
the rest of the world—and especially to me—such an unexpected opportunity to commune with an outsider was a
precious event. I valued it and believed in the sympathy of
this French writer and his Russian wife, although, by and
large, I knew little about them. And so now I wrote Kaul
in Delhi, asking him to send my manuscript to Kalakankar,
where I would be staying longer than originally planned.
Falling back in thought on that forgotten manuscript, I
began experiencing a strong desire to write more, tell more.

If I had stayed in India, I couldn't have found a better
place for working than this quiet village.

❋

In the meantime Kalakankar and the entire region were
heatedly discussing the forthcoming February elections to
Parliament. Dinesh was the local candidate for the governing party, National Congress, and in obedience to traditional
vassal loyalties, many local peasants voted for him, often
simply out of fear. This somehow reminded me of elections
in the U.S.S.R. But in contrast to the U.S.S.R., the voters
here had a choice of candidates from seven different
parties.

I hadn't expected to find in this village so much activity
and interest in politics. Half-clothed, hungry peasants, who
were to elect their state and central parliaments, discussed
in detail all the news reaching them through local papers and

the radio. Many of them had cheap little Indian transistors. Suresh Singh and his family, Dr. Nagar, the President of the College, a local college teacher, all of them participated in the pre-election campaign—they, too, following tradition, in favor of Dinesh. But in reality their hearts were often far from him and even from his party.

In this state there were three strong opposition parties: the parties of Swatantra and Jan Sangh, and the Socialist Party. Congress, the party in power, had disappointed many, and in Lucknow there was a possibility that an opposition government might be elected. Communists were not popular in this province, and in Kalakankar only poor Ram Din campaigned for them and therefore was called "Tovarishch."

Indira Gandhi was expected in Kalakankar on the sixteenth of January, during her tour of the neighboring district. It was laughingly said that at all meetings at which Indira spoke there would first appear about six hundred security men dressed as peasants who would occupy the first rows. At any moment they were expected to descend upon Kalakankar. Suresh's house was like a club: doors were open wide and visitors squatted on the floor, discussing the news and listening to the radio.

Many expressed displeasure with the governing party and the Prime Minister. They asked me how it was in the U.S.S.R. When I described what elections were like under a one-party system, they shook their heads in dismay. These peasants, barefoot and with transistor radios, couldn't believe that there could be only *one* candidate on a ballot and laughed merrily at such an absurdity.

At last Dinesh himself arrived from Delhi, surrounded by a suite of assistants, secretaries, and electioneers. His democratic Western ways had disappeared. Here he was never addressed in any other way but "Maharaj." He had exchanged his Western clothes for cotton *churidars* and a blue achkan, and received everyone sitting with his bare feet crossed on an ottoman under the portrait of his father, represented in all the regalia of a Raja of Kalakankar.

To approach him and have a personal talk with him was now impossible. When guests left, instantly his six daughters would surround him. He pretended to have forgotten our talk in Delhi. He was friendly, entertained me at meals, but told me I should return to Delhi, as "the embassy was most anxious." He gave me a letter from Kaul, also calling me back to Delhi. About my manuscript not a word in this letter.

I understood one thing: I was being called back to Delhi so as to prevent my meeting the Prime Minister. Whether Dinesh had spoken to her about me I couldn't tell. What alarmed me, though, was that Kaul had not returned the manuscript. Instead, he had written that he must soon be leaving Delhi for a while but would delay his departure especially on my account, as he earnestly hoped that I would take his advice and return to Delhi soon. I wrote back, asking that my manuscript be dispatched to Kalakankar and adding, pointedly: "Maybe the manuscript is no longer in your hands? Maybe you have given it to the Soviet Embassy?"

There was only one thing left for me to do: try and have a talk with the Prime Minister here in Kalakankar. I therefore flatly refused to return to Delhi at present, explaining once more to Dinesh that my visa was good until the twentieth of January and since the next Aeroflot plane did not leave until the twenty-sixth, I would linger on here. Dinesh heaved a sigh, but the laws of hospitality obliged him to respect my wishes.

"Oh well," said he, "my family and I are leaving here on the twenty-fifth; you can come with us then."

Soon all those rumors about the security men were confirmed—there was, indeed, a regular invasion of them in Kalakankar. They inspected the two houses and the river front. Accommodations had to be found for them, and a great hurry and bustle ensued. Dinesh, with his suite, kept traveling through the district, sometimes staying away for several days at a time. Naggu prepared her house for the reception of the Prime Minister and her suite. I was freed of my room at the *raj-bhavan* and moved to Brajesh's little room.

In Suresh's house everyone was happy that I was staying on; Naggu, on the other hand, grew visibly nervous, doubtless anxious on her husband's behalf. Sweet Dadu plied between the two houses, carrying gossip back and forth. My tug of war with the Soviet Embassy intrigued and interested everyone. Nor had the telegram and letter from Paris escaped attention.

Besides, I wasn't concealing anything. In general, in an Indian family there never can be any secrets; for members of a family to read each other's private correspondence is considered perfectly in order. Anyone wishing to participate in discussions of family problems is welcome to do so, sitting either on an ottoman or on the floor. In Kalakankar it soon became common knowledge that Mem-Sahib did not wish to return to Moscow. Visitors never failed to ask me, "You like it here? Would you like to stay in India?" And I, having nothing to hide, always replied, "Yes, I would like to very much."

This engendered a feeling of sympathy toward me. The teacher, the College President, the doctor, the servants, all sympathized with me, at the same time knowing full well that neither the Raja-Sahib nor the government would jeopardize their relationship with the U.S.S.R. on my account. The teacher, however, went so far as to give me lessons in Hindi, a language I had already made a slight study of in Moscow.

At last the day came when the entire village was summoned to a meeting outside the college building, where Indira Gandhi was scheduled to speak. We went there in our jeep. Dinesh's family was already there, waiting near the entrance. The seven-year-old Ratna, in an orange dress, held a garland of orange flowers in readiness. I was surprised to learn that

Dinesh hadn't returned from one of his trips that day.

Soon the Prime Minister's limousine drove up in clouds of dust. A woman in a sari quickly got out and was already coming toward us, greeting everyone right and left with a "*namasté.*" Ratna rushed forward and flung the garland of flowers round her neck. All of us greeted her, folding our hands in a "*namasté,*" and she, as she passed by, responded in kind to each one of us. She had known the Singh family for a long time, knew all their faces well. For just an instant her attentive glance rested on me and my white sari (Ambassador Kaul had presented me to her in the summer of 1965 when Indira, not yet Prime Minister, had visited Moscow). Then we all hurried after her to the college's open gallery, where a microphone had been installed and, instead of a "table of honor," an ottoman covered with a rug, on which Suresh, Prakash, and Naggu settled down. I sat with all the others on the floor at one side.

Indira Gandhi wore a dark sari of checked homespun cotton. Being a widow, she wore neither jewelry nor adornments of any kind. She had an intelligent, inspired face and sharp eyes. She spoke at length and with fervor in Hindi, probably something about progress that offered hope. Who would say anything else on the eve of an election? Her audience, sitting on the ground in front of her, seemed somewhat inattentive to what she said, but they scrutinized her closely. If these were security men and not peasants, they must have heard it all many times before. . . . When she got through, she was presented with more garlands of flowers, and Dr. Nagar, nervous and stuttering, greeted her inaudibly in the name of Kalakankar, completely forgetting about the microphone.

The meeting was over. As hurriedly as she had come, she now returned to her limousine, while we, holding up our saris, ran to our jeep, for we were all going to the *raj-bhavan* for dinner. The Prime Minister hadn't deigned to address either the doctor, or the college teacher, or any of those present. Perhaps, I thought, she would invite them in the evening to the dinner table?

Before dinner, in the drawing room, which was full of people, the Prime Minister amiably asked me how I liked Kalakankar. Looking straight into her eyes, I said that I liked it very much indeed and would like to stay here as long as possible. Indira, rather naïvely, asked, "And you're not being allowed to?" Here Prakash, very resolutely, sat down on the ottoman beside her and started whispering something in Hindi right into her ear. Indira listened, nodding from time to time and glancing at me out of the corner of her eye. The Raja and Ranee of Bhadri, who had come especially to see the Prime Minister, were exchanging impatient glances. Naggu summoned everyone to dinner. My audience with the Prime Minister was over.

Tables were set in the big dining room under the frescoed ceiling depicting the exploits of Rama and in a small adjoining room. There were floral decorations everywhere, and that evening even the electricity was not on strike. At the Prime Minister's table, in the small room, sat Naggu, Suresh, and Prakash, the Raja and Ranee of Bhadri, and a few chosen people from the suite. Those entertained in the big dining room consisted chiefly of members of the numerous suites and a few people from Kalakankar, who were not admitted into Indira's closer presence. The girls, Dadu, and I were also put beyond "the pale," so to speak; which, incidentally, didn't surprise me: I understood that Dinesh had probably said nothing to the Prime Minister about me. Perhaps that was why he had kept away that day, having given Naggu instructions not to let me get near Indira. All right then, I was with Dadu, who had not been placed at the Prime Minister's table either, even though she had been born in this house. Poor Dadu was sadly picking at her curry. The food, however, was wonderful—curry, rice, spices, fruit—an abundance and a plenty! Did the Prime Minister know how people lived outside the walls of this *raj-bhavan*? I wondered.

There was nothing more for me to do. I soon took my leave and went to bed. The Prime Minister was leaving in the morning after breakfast.

Early next morning Prakash entered my room. "I spoke to Indira yesterday, as you saw," she said. "We have known each other for a long time. I can discuss anything with her. All these others are scared, and of course it is a bad time right now before the elections. But I think that if you stayed here until the spring and she became Prime Minister again, she and Dinesh could easily help you. Come now! They are having breakfast on the upper terrace. Dinesh returned late last night."

"Oh, what's the use?" said I. But Prakash helped me on with my sari and went ahead, saying, "Come with me!" I followed, feeling depressed and disgusted.

On the upper terrace, flooded in morning sunshine, Dinesh sat with Indira, drinking orange juice. He pulled a long face when he saw me and for the first time looked at me with undisguised hostility. Prakash and I sat down, drank some orange juice. "Well," said the head of 400 million people, "I must be going!"

Everybody stood up. Dinesh took a snapshot of a family group with Indira, inviting me to join. After that we all descended into the yard to see the Prime Minister off.

Just as everyone was giving her a farewell "namasté," she suddenly came up to me, stretched out both her hands, and said with real feeling, "I wish you luck!"

"And I wish *you* luck," I replied, touched by her sudden warmheartedness.

Then everyone left.

We went back to the small terrace near my room. Prakash was fuming with anger:

"Dinesh doesn't want it! All of them just can't wait for you to leave. Naggu is furious—oh, if only the late Premier Shastri were alive! What a man that was! So kind. I could always speak to him or his wife. They were always so out-

going. But Indira didn't even speak to anyone! Nothing but
security men around her! Oh, how everything has changed in
this country! Would Gandhiji have treated people like that?
Now they want to lean on rajas and maharajas, but Gandhiji
spoke to untouchables. To him there were no untouchables.
Oh, what our Congress Party has come to!" She sorrowfully
shook her head, repeating what everyone else here was saying: "What our Congress Party has come to!"

We sat on the terrace near the ashoka trees. Servants were
bringing back the furniture, which had been borrowed by
the *raj-bhavan* for the Prime Minister's suite. The servants
told me that my room there was free again.

"It won't be long now," said Prakash. "At the end of the
month Naggu and the girls will leave for Delhi, and you can
move over to us." She never doubted that I would stay on.
How grateful I was to her and Suresh. They offered me their
hospitality, so that I could make an effort to prolong my
visit by two or three months as their guest. According to
Soviet law, those who are visiting relatives abroad can always
prolong their visas for two or three months, providing the
Soviet Embassy does not incur any expenses on their behalf.
So, why not try? It would be another effort at any rate. I
may really have come at a bad time, and if the elections went
her way, the Prime Minister might become a little bolder. . . .

It was disquieting that nothing had been heard as yet
from my children in Moscow. I had sent Bertha a telegram
asking for news of them. I had sent a telegram to my children, too, and was waiting for an answer from day to day.
Suddenly one day Naggu said to me very casually, "Why
didn't they give you the telegram that came from your son?
It came to our Delhi address. Dinesh told me about it. He
saw it. There was nothing particular in it, just your son saying
that everything was all right."

I all but jumped! This sort of thing was habitual here:
Dinesh had read my telegram, had told his wife, but they had
all forgotten to tell me! And Naggu, needless to say, had dis-

cussed this bit of news with everyone, sitting on her ottoman.

Oh, that big ottoman in her drawing room! It was a regular women's club, a rostrum, a presidium. Nothing ever escaped the attention of the women, always knitting with great speed and never holding their tongues except to stick a fresh betel leaf into their mouths.

And now, in the last few days, a new topic for discussion and speculation had cropped up among them.

"American Theme"

IN DINESH'S HOUSE there was a big English library.
In the drawing room one found numerous magazines: the
Ladies' Home Journal, Time, Life, Newsweek. The girls read
nothing but English.

During my stay there I read *Lessons in World History* by
Nehru, the autobiography of the Duchess of Windsor, a
book by the former U.S. Ambassador Joseph Davies, and
leafed through Churchill's memoirs. Finally I became
thoroughly engrossed in *Ambassador's Report* by Chester
Bowles, then the American Ambassador to India.

It was a captivating, lively book. The Ambassador knew
his India and loved it—every page spoke of this. At one point
I came across a remarkable saying by Mahatma Gandhi,
which meant so much to me at the time that I couldn't resist
my old habit of writing it down:

> *It is possible for a single individual to defy the whole
> might of an unjust empire to save his honor, his religion,
> his soul, and lay the foundation for that empire's fall or its
> regeneration.* *

* Chester Bowles, *Ambassador's Report*, first edition, New York, 1954,
p. 74.

For some reason or other people usually think that "the East attaches no importance to the individual." This is a grave mistake, and Gandhi's words, as well as his whole life, go to prove the contrary. I pondered a great deal over those words of his—in Kalakankar one had plenty of time to think. And for many days I never separated myself from this book, a thing that didn't escape the attention of the older daughters.

And now, like a bright butterfly, a new subject of conversation hovered over the ottoman: Why shouldn't "she" ask the American Embassy for refuge and later return to India with an American passport? This new idea was excitedly discussed on the ottoman and just as excitedly reported to me by Dadu:

"They say it's the best way for you. What do you think? Have you had any further news from your friends in Paris?"

No, my Paris friends were silent. But I began to give serious thought to this Ambassador, Chester Bowles, feeling that if I could tell him about myself, he would understand. I kept this to myself, however, and said nothing. It was not yet *my idea*. I was still very far from taking any such decision. I simply went on reading the book with a feeling of sympathy for its author and unable to resist making comparisons between him and the ignoramuses at the Soviet Embassy. But all I told Dadu was that I would try to get permission to stay here until May.

This "American Theme" seemed somehow to have sprung into being of its own accord, just as no one knows whence a butterfly appears in the air. And like a butterfly it hovered, reappearing again and again, recalling itself to me with unexpected tenacity.

In Suresh's family they often spoke of the United States, not on my account but because their eldest son, Ashok, had been living in America for the last seven years. After graduating as an engineer from the University of Washington in Seattle, he began working as designer for the Boeing Company. Ashok, like his younger brother Sirish, was born and grew up in Kalakankar. But Sirish, like his parents, never left India, while Ashok felt drawn to the West. His work had tied him firmly to the United States. What's more, in Seattle he had married a fellow student, a Dutch girl, and now they made their home there with their two children. Two years before my arrival the young family had paid a visit to Kalakankar. To everyone's sorrow it transpired that India had no need for designers of jet planes, and the orderly young Dutch woman had no use for a home without running water and electric kitchen appliances.

So they went back. But the young couple's visit was still talked about in Kalakankar, where they had left behind them a few "traces of civilization": radio antennas in some of the rooms, and an electric stove, on which only a teapot was still warmed up now and then. Prakash preferred a kerosene stove, sitting on the stone floor.

All the same, her greatest treasures were in "Ashok's room," the key to which she always wore on her belt. In this room one found wooden bookshelves made by Ashok, full of his technical books and journals. Here, too, were sets of the *National Geographic Magazine* and *Life*, subscribed to by Ashok for Kalakankar. The sight of these magazines here, in this remote village of India, involuntarily brought to mind how impossible it had been for me in Moscow to subscribe to the *National Geographic Magazine* for my children; only the Soviet Academy of Sciences received a few copies. As for political magazines such as *Life* and *Time*, they could only be found in special libraries, and could never be taken out.

In Ashok's room there still remained some bright-colored wicker furniture, a discarded radio, records, and a few discarded toys. Prakash treasured them all. Ashok, apparently a talented young man, was the favorite son, a leaf blown far from its tree.

In Seattle Ashok's family now had its own house, two automobiles, good employment, a hectic but comfortable life, which he described in his letters. The parents lived by these letters, retelling daily what he had said on every possible occasion. Sometimes Ashok sent colored slides to show how fast the children were growing or how beautifully the flowers were blooming in his garden. He loved gardening. But all this was far, far away from here, somewhere at the other end of the earth.

To his parents, who had never seen any country but India, life in America appeared too tense, too accelerated, though they gave credit to its industriousness and the resulting wealth of the United States. It pleased them to know that everyone there worked hard, that work brought comforts and freedom, that good things were inexpensive, that the people were enterprising yet simple in their ways. They were endlessly proud of their son, who lived so successfully and so well in that distant land. And every time they spoke of it they would say, doubtless repeating his words, that India also needed private initiative, free enterprise, small industries in town and country, and modern mechanized farms. Everything "Ashok said" was taken by them as incontrovertible truth.

The idea of my turning to the American Embassy didn't seem unthinkable or extraordinary to anyone in Kalakankar. The whole world knows that Soviet citizens often resort to this. But all the women here spoke of such a step for me with a naïve lack of understanding of its political implications. They simply believed in the God-given truth that every man should choose for himself where he wants to live.

I, however, had grown wise to their chatter, their reading of other people's letters, their discussing other people's problems, and so I just kept saying that "this step was not for me," that "the plan was not suitable." I knew all too well what such a step would mean—even the mention of it— if it ever reached the Soviet Embassy.

It is hard to say when the whole idea presented itself to me as a concrete possibility. One thing I'm certain of—it was after I had read Chester Bowles' book. In this the girls had sensed something, intuitively. I secreted in the very

depths of my consciousness the thought that perhaps Ambassador Bowles might understand me, allowing myself to peek
at it only when I was alone; and only in silence, when no
witnesses were present, did I begin to toy with the idea
more frequently, trying to visualize once more the building
of the American Embassy I had passed in Delhi.

Actually, I knew more about the United States than about
any other country. It so happened that from childhood I had
been taught English, and at an early age had begun reading
Wilde, Galsworthy, Steinbeck, and Hemingway. An acquaintance with American films, and through them with
American life, had been made possible for me, as they were
always shown during weekends at the governmental dachas,
where foreign movies were presented which were not
exhibited in the theaters of the U.S.S.R. And naturally
at these dachas the audience consisted mostly of young
people studying foreign languages. In this way Greta
Garbo and Shirley Temple, Bette Davis and Deanna Durbin,
Katharine Hepburn and Spencer Tracy, Myrna Loy and
Clark Gable, Barbara Stanwyck and Robert Taylor, were all
familiar to me even before the war. Later Ingrid Bergman
became my favorite movie actress for a long time. I was able
to profit by this "private movie screen" until 1949, when
I finally left forever the old dacha in Zubalovo I had lived
in since my childhood.

As a student of history at Moscow University I chose to
major in the history of the United States, prompted by the
general enthusiasm and interest in America during the war
and for a few years after it. The spirit of friendship toward
our American allies was very strong, and everyone strove to
learn more about that great democracy beyond the ocean.

My first husband, then a student at the Diplomatic Institute, and I read together Frederick Schuman's *History of
Russian-American Relations*. In the course of my university
studies I wrote reports on the establishment in 1933 of
diplomatic relations between the U.S.A. and the U.S.S.R., on

Roosevelt's New Deal, on American trade unions. My old friend Alya wrote about the establishment of the United Nations Organization. Our entire university group studied the history, economics, and geography of the U.S.A. and its foreign policies in South America and Europe.

Not much American literature was translated in the U.S.S.R., but what there was we read avidly. During the war years I was sometimes able to see the *Illustrated London News*, and also *Life, Time,* and *Fortune,* which always contained a lot of interesting news about the allies, about the conferences in Teheran, Yalta, and Potsdam.

Only once—it was in 1942—in our apartment in the Kremlin, did my father summon me: to present me to Winston Churchill. I had time to say "How do you do," and was sent away. Even this brief appearance was an exception to the rule set by my father never to take me out into the "official world." Not only did the idea of taking me to some international conference never cross his mind; he considered my presence at any diplomatic dinner in Moscow inadmissible, although he knew that I spoke English.

These rules were strictly adhered to even after his death. That is why in Moscow I never had access to diplomatic circles, nor to foreign correspondents. The only exception had been an interview in 1955 with William Randolph Hearst, Jr., and Kingsbury Smith, arranged at their request and with the permission of the government. But first I was briefed at length by Molotov, while at the interview itself an interpreter from MID was present, although there was no need for his services.

Molotov's briefing consisted of a lot of prohibitions: I was not to discuss either internal political problems or my father's political views; I was not to tell them that my brother Vasily was in prison—illness was to be given as an excuse for his absence; in general I was forbidden to touch on any political subject and was told to terminate the interview as quickly as possible. I tried to get out of it altogether, but

Molotov said, "Out of the question! They would then say that we were hiding you, or that you were no longer in Moscow!" And so I went through with it, following Molotov's instructions to the letter in the presence of a silent interpreter. This was my only contact with foreigners. And, of course, my meetings with Emmanuel d'Astier . . .

In spite of such immurement, I had a pretty good idea of what the United States was like from books, films, and stories. Fairly recently Alya's aunt had come to visit her from Detroit, bringing with her her son, a young doctor, and his whole family. She stayed with her sister—Alya's mother—whom she hadn't seen since the day she had left Russia forty years before. She was shocked by the sight of so many women in the streets carrying heavy bundles, sometimes two bundles at a time.

"Poor women," she would say. "We are never burdened like that. We carry our purchases in our cars, or else make arrangements with the store to have them delivered."

Her son, a pediatrician, supported a large family on his earnings and had even paid for all the tickets on this expensive trip to the U.S.S.R.

Bertha, too, had had visiting relatives from the United States, who hadn't seen her mother in many years. They were an elderly couple traveling on a tour around the world. How Bertha and all of us envied them!

But far more vital than tales, exhibits, performances, and films was the old deep feeling of sympathy for America, which had been born long ago in Russia. A feeling shared by everyone in the U.S.S.R. today, commencing with schoolchildren, university students, intellectuals, down to the simplest folk, acquainted with American technical achievements rather than with American history. It is not surprising that such friendliness and sympathy should exist toward a country so like Russia in its vastness, mixture of cultures, tongues, and climates, a country, what's more, that has never been at war with Russia. The only ones not to share in such sentiments are the Party itself, lagging far behind the times, and the Soviet Government.

The famous Russian surgeon, A. A. Vishnevsky, who had traveled all over the world, told me after his visit to the U.S.A. that nowhere had he met with such cordiality and warmth. "They want to be our friends, they like us, they are wonderful people!" he kept repeating. I heard the same from athletes, musicians, writers, who had been given the opportunity of visiting the United States. Now, remembering all this, it seemed to me that if I did make up my mind to turn to the U.S. Embassy, I would find there a sympathetic response and understanding.

I had never met any Americans in Moscow, but my friendship there with Indians had done a lot for me: I could now speak fluent English. Brajesh and his friends had helped me to really feel that the world didn't end with the borders of the Soviet Union. Brajesh Singh brought me out into the world, as he had promised to do. It was through him that I became capable of free and easy intercourse with strangers, a thing that had been so difficult for me before, shackled as I had been by an ingrained shyness and inarticulateness.

Now, to my surprise, I felt thoroughly at home in a strange land far away from my compatriots. Self-assurance, calm, and tranquillity, so alien to my nature before, now seemed to blossom. Where did it all come from? I was sure none of my Moscow friends would ever believe that I enjoyed being here alone and feared nothing.

In India I gathered new strength with every day. Heavy chains, which in the U.S.S.R. had always crushed my entire being, now fell away. In Moscow the thought of going to the American Embassy would never have crossed my mind. There I had been always passive, as though paralyzed, as though there were nothing left in life but to exist, tend grandchildren—the young, not I, would *live*. Now I suddenly felt in myself the strength to start a new life of my own.

But I needed time to make up my mind to act. I wasn't

yet ready to take such a step, say, tomorrow. Meanwhile, my only anxiety was that no one should guess my innermost thought.

One day as I sat on my small terrace with the teacher from the local college, who was writing in Hindi on a slate, Surov suddenly appeared, as if sprouting out of the ground. The teacher sprang to his feet and tactfully withdrew. I braced myself for an unpleasant conversation.

Dinesh and Kaul, it seems, had informed the Soviet Embassy that I intended remaining in Kalakankar until the twenty-fifth of January, until the next plane for Moscow. This the embassy had unwillingly agreed to. But when I told Surov that I intended asking permission of Moscow to stay on here another three months, he remained silent for a long time.

"So? And then what, Svetlana?" he cautiously ventured at length.

"Then I will return home." I had to make an effort to say this. "After all, I have the right to visit relatives, haven't I?"

Surov nodded in agreement, but he looked perplexed. At last he said, finding it hard to get used to my sari, "I see you have thoroughly adapted yourself. You are even learning the language!"

Outside of Kosygin, who had given me permission to go to India, no one in Moscow would ever take it upon himself to prolong my permit. There was, therefore, only one thing to do: write and ask him for it. I gave the letter to Surov. He shook his head dubiously, cogitating over what would happen next. I knew that it would take some time for my letter to reach Moscow and be discussed there. But even if my request were turned down—and of this I had not the slightest doubt—I would still have gained time. Surov, by now thoroughly gloomy, left, carrying with him my letter to the Premier.

A few days later Kaul at last sent me my manuscript with an offended note: "How could you have thought that I might give your manuscript to the Soviet Embassy? If that is your true opinion of me, then our friendship is at an end."

Dinesh handed me the manuscript. Needless to say, he had already heard from Naggu that I had written to Paris. He tried to question me carefully about the contents of the manuscript, written three years before. So curious was he about it that he found time to speak to me alone. Apparently he felt a bit stung by the discovery of how close Kaul had been to us in Moscow. As a result, I saw before me again the charming, democratic Dinesh. And I told him that the manuscript contained no political "revelations" or "secrets," that it was the story of my family.

"Do you intend sending it to Paris?" was his next question, to which I replied evasively that I didn't know—perhaps. I was determined not to tell him anything definite, although I had already firmly made up my mind not to send the manuscript to d'Astier. To Dinesh all I said at the time was that if Soviet officialdom ever got wind of the manuscript, they would instantly confiscate it.

"But are you sure they don't already know about it?" he asked.

"Quite. In any case Kaul hasn't said a word to anyone for a whole year."

Dinesh changed the subject to something that weighed heavily on his mind:

"I don't think the Americans could help you. Of course, they would publish your book, make a movie of it. You would become a sort of movie star. But all that hullabaloo is not for you. As far as I know, all you want is a quiet life, with no reporters and TV cameras."

"Yes, yes," I hurried to agree. "That's not for me. No! I don't intend turning to the Americans."

"I know Ambassador Chester Bowles well," Dinesh persevered. "He is liked and respected in India. He's a very charming man. But I think that's not the road for you."

"No," I said again. "Oh no! But I am asking for an extension of my visit to India. I have sent a request to Moscow. Maybe they'll let me stay until summer. If not, I'll have to return home."

"They might possibly assent," Dinesh said, visibly relieved.

For several days he was very attentive to me, asked me about my children and, of course, about the manuscript; introduced me to his guests, entertained me at table, invited me for a trip in his boat along the shore, crowded that day with people. He became more amiable with Suresh's family, paying a call on them; and Prakash laughed, saying that such a thing hadn't happened in a long time. But seeing the modest, dusty rooms, the "Maharaj" was unable to conceal a sarcastic smile, and when he caught sight of a large picture of Gandhi in a dhoti and with an immense watch at his belt, he failed to hold back a disrespectful laugh.

He invited me to accompany him on one of his pre-election tours of the constituency and to be present at the polls on election day, but I declined the honor. Now I kept my mouth tightly shut, concerned only with one thing—that Dinesh should not guess my true thoughts.

I locked my manuscript in my suitcase, which was under my bed, and always carried the key with me. At times I went into the empty rooms on the upper floor and reread my own, half-forgotten pages. Much of what I had written three years before appeared to me now as naïve and vague. These, after all, were letters, not a book, and my first effort at writing, if one didn't count a short story about a girl friend of mine, written several years earlier. Friends in Moscow, who read it at the time, advised me to go on writing, not to give it up. How many times I heard them say, "Write about your life, you tell a story well."

And so I wrote these twenty letters, addressing them to one of my Moscow friends, a man of literary taste, though not a writer. He was pleased, saying when he had read them, "God, what gloom! Such darkness, such tragedies, so many deaths! Dreadful, dreadful! But I would like to see sharper, more definite conclusions. They seem to be begging to come out. If you would make them stronger, everything would instantly acquire greater significance. Unfortunate land! To think who's governing us!"

Other friends in the Soviet Union, who had read the manuscript, expressed themselves in the same vein.

And now I sat and pondered over what could be changed in it. Yet to me it was clear that changes would only spoil it. The only thing to do was to go on writing—writing differently. I didn't feel like changing what had already been written. There was a certain completeness of form in this story of a family, expressed in lyrical letters to a friend. In 1963 I wasn't really writing a book. I worked on it with no thought of possible publication, no thought of prospective readers. These letters, needless to say, did not pretend to unfold a picture of life in the U.S.S.R. or explain my father's historical and political role. Lyrical letters differ in dimension from historical memoirs: they come closer to poetry than to history.

Dinesh and his family were leaving for Delhi at the end of January. Everybody seemed to have yielded to the idea that I was remaining for a while at Kalakankar. Before his departure Dinesh had another talk with me in his big cool library. This time he was outspoken:

"I think you understand that the Prime Minister is unable to help you. Even after the elections, which I hope will result in her favor, nothing will change as far as you are concerned. You yourself will have to obtain the permission of your government to live in India. If you succeed, then, of course, all of us will help you to get settled. But this thing cannot be turned into a conflict between India and the U.S.S.R."

There was nothing else left for me to do but listen in silence and tell him that I understood.

Everyone left. The *raj-bhavan* became empty until the elections. The tall guard with his spear continued to march to and fro in front of the gates.

✱

Whenever Dinesh left, everyone in Kalakankar felt more at ease. And so long as he and his suite were absent and the answer hadn't come from Moscow, I decided to have a look at Lucknow.

The coughing jeep carried Sirish and me to the station three miles away. We took third-class tickets—Suresh Singh and his family always traveled third. The train was late. The evening was upon us, it grew dark. I was told that trains were habitually late, but that this particular one, coming from Allahabad, was probably carrying numerous pilgrims returning from the yearly *mela*—a ritual bathing in the Ganges, which takes place at the beginning of February.

At long last the train arrived, so crowded that it seemed impossible to get in. We ran from door to door and finally managed to squeeze ourselves into a car. Needless to say, we had to stand. There was no light. Sirish said that it would take three or four hours to Lucknow, but that sometimes it took even longer: railway schedules existed only in theory.

We stood for a long time. A small lamp was lit at one end of the car. Standing under it, leaning on a stick, I saw an old man with long gray hair and beard. His face was strikingly beautiful. Swaying and shutting his eyes, he kept singing in a clear young voice something fluent and endless. This was a pilgrim from Allahabad, singing religious hymns in Sanskrit. The melody had a quiet cadence to it.

Everywhere the baggage racks were crowded. In the upper berths people either sat or lay all curled up. Indians know how to occupy very little space, folding themselves in such a way as to appear boneless. Although the car was overcrowded, no one either pushed or was rude. It was almost unbearably close; a breeze, coming from a door, only brought smells from the toilet. But soon some young men, who were sitting on a bench, managed somehow to compress themselves, and invited me to join them. I squeezed myself in and sat there for several hours, until we reached Lucknow after endless lengthy stops.

In Lucknow we stayed in the house of Prakash's relatives. It was a big old house with a well in the yard, from which water was carried in buckets. The house was known as a palace, but its conveniences were on a par with those in the "palaces" of Kalakankar.

In Lucknow, as in Delhi, there is an old town and a town of modern streets with expensive modern stores and banks. Modern streets are very much alike the world over. But old Nazir-Abad and Amin-Abad in Lucknow, which abounds in little narrow streets, were uniquely Indian, with wonderful, cheap little shops, far more within my means than the big stores. In Moscow I had been allowed to change a hundred rubles into American dollars, and in India my 110 dollars became 770 rupees. This, however, was not much, considering that I had already given half of it away to the servants in Kalakankar and had also lent some money to Prakash.

Lucknow is the center of northern India's industries. Here handicrafts are to be found at very low prices; the same marvelous embroideries, for instance, cost twice as much in Delhi, where tourists buy them in a big department store. I bought myself a pale-gray cotton sari, embroidered all over with *shikan*, on which Moslem girls spend a whole year. Yet the sari is sold almost for a song. I tried to find something fascinating for my children: gold-embroidered slippers with turned-up noses, jingling silver bracelets, cheap Indian knickknacks. I could just see how these bright things would delight them. . . .

In Nazir-Abad there were a lot of small eating places, where the food was cooked outside in the street on charcoal grills. The food was very good, but it was better not to look around too closely: the walls, the floor, the tables were incredibly filthy. People here were probably so used to dirt that they didn't notice it. I, too, tried not to notice, but that was impossible. In the center of town we found some fine restaurants, clean and in good order, but all the same the food was best in those dirty little streets of Nazir-Abad.

We rode through town in rickshas, driven by bicycles. It was the best and cheapest mode of transportation in town. A ricksha passed easily through the milling crowds, whereas automobiles had to signal and wait for a long time. In rickshas we got to see the whole city.

Remains of the Moslem middle ages, the architectural lacework of the Imambara, mosques and minarets in the midst of lush gardens, were all typical of the "city of roses"—Lucknow. I was impressed by the size of the university. Somehow I hadn't expected to find here so many modern buildings occupying so vast a space, the Tagore Library, the numerous students, many of whom were Europeans and Africans. The city appeared at once thriving and poverty-stricken: wherever my eye fell it seemed to me that only one push was needed for sleep to be dispelled and for life to bubble up.

In one of the streets we came upon a small temple with a painted statue of Hanuman in regal robes. I knew that Hanuman was a monkey king-hero of Hindu mythology, a faithful friend of Rama and companion of his glorious exploits. But it seemed to strike a profoundly sarcastic note for people in a modern city to be worshiping a monkey king. Even Ghanesh, the wise elephant, looks somewhat better. But when I told this to Sirish, he merely remarked that Hanuman was a good god who brought luck; that was why people laid so many flowers at his feet.

We paid a call on Dadu, who lived on the outskirts of Lucknow. Even though I had expected to find poverty there, I was shocked by this dwelling with peeling walls and a small dirty yard. Her children looked unhappy and sad. I just couldn't take it in that the Raja of Kalakankar, Dadu's own brother, couldn't help his only sister. Dadu herself was friendly as always. She took us to see her neighbor, an Irish-woman called Peggy, who had been born in India and had married an Indian.

Peggy, a blue-eyed, rosy-cheeked woman, wore a printed-cotton dressing gown, while her children looked Indian. Her small house was a mixture of East and West. Peggy herself, talkative and jolly, told us how much her parents had loved India and how much she herself loved it; and almost in the same breath asked me, "Could you live in India?"

Dadu hurriedly explained that I would have liked to, but was not permitted to do so.

"Go to the American Embassy," exclaimed Peggy enthu-siastically. "Ask them for asylum and an American passport. Then come back to India!"

I said nothing, but the idea was no longer strange to me.

In the evening we went for a stroll in the streets. The pre-election campaigning here was something to see—more like a show or a fair. Several corner buildings faced a square, in which thousands were milling around. Loudspeakers stood on the balconies of each of these buildings. There were no speeches; by then people were fed up with them. Instead, whatever the various parties promised was sung in gay musi-cal verses. It was noisy but drew far more attention than speeches. The crowds listened with interest. At times one heard laughter. The party of Jan Sangh, in particular, mocked the Congress Party with a good deal of wit. The public promenaded in the streets and bought sweets to the accompaniment of loud music.

Next day Dadu saw us off at the station. The train was late as usual. Again we had to wait a whole hour and a half. Only this time it wasn't as crowded, and I dozed all the way on a wooden bench, with my handbag for a pillow.

During February I also had a chance to see Allahabad and Benares. This trip I owed to my acquaintance with Dr. Bahri, the philologist from Allahabad who was compiling in

Moscow a Hindi-Russian dictionary. His son, a lawyer, came to Kalakankar in his own car, with his wife, his small son, a friend—owner of an automobile repair shop—and the friend's wife. I gave him the many greetings and presents I had brought with me from his father, and Bahri instantly invited me to return with them to Allahabad and be their guest there. I agreed and got into the back seat with the two wives, while the young men clowned a good deal in front, trying to outshout the radio.

Young Bahri in no way resembled his father, the sixty-year-old vegetarian and ascetic. He was slightly overweight for his years, spoke in a matter-of-fact voice, and liked a drink. He and Bir, his friend, enterprising and energetic young men from Punjab, as well as their wives, were totally unlike the Singh family—this was the new middle class of India.

Needless to say, in Kalakankar they were immediately informed that I would like to remain in India but that the two governments wouldn't permit it. All the way to Allahabad the two friends discussed this. Bahri suggested that I meet one of the leaders of the opposition, the Socialist Ram Manohar Lohia, who at that time was in Allahabad. I had seen Lohia once in Moscow, when Brajesh was still living. Brajesh had said he was a good fellow but somewhat of a crank, and my impression of the man then confirmed Brajesh's words.

Bahri and Bir were really nice fellows. They were so taken with the idea of helping me stay in India that one couldn't get them off the subject. The time spent with them in Allahabad was hectic and exhausting, but thanks to these "guides" I carried away with me a lot of new impressions.

Near a certain park, where a pre-election meeting was being held, Bahri found Ram Manohar Lohia. The leader of the Socialists remembered our meeting in Moscow. He said a few heartfelt words about Singh. Very volubly, Bahri explained to him my "problem."

"What cowards!" cried Lohia, his eyes ablaze. "I will fight for you in Parliament!"

"Don't do it, don't do it," I hurried to interject. "It would be useless."

Lohia's face saddened. He pressed my hand with feeling. There was no time for further conversation; we were surrounded by people on all sides and he was already being called away.

The two friends were determined to introduce me to all the influential people in Allahabad. In the evening we made a stop at the Cosmopolitan Club, where I was introduced to a well-known lawyer and to the Chief of Police. It was crowded and stifling in the club; the people there had obviously been drinking. Indians, when they are in their cups, look slovenly somehow. This is probably due to the fact that alcohol is actually alien to their habits and traditions. The well-known lawyer kept laying his hand on my shoulder and humming something. I was obliged to put a stop to it. He then began to insult the Prime Minister in a loud voice, hinting obscenities about her. With great trouble his wife took him home. Others at the table were already discussing how to help me. The Chief of Police said that in his town no one would dare touch me, if I decided to stay. Bahri and Bir had imbibed a good deal of whiskey. The time had come to go.

In the morning we had a light breakfast with Bahri's two younger brothers, and Bahri begged me not to tell his father in Moscow that he drank whiskey. . . .

Later I was taken to meet Judge Dhavan, President of the local Society for Indo-Soviet Friendship. Bahri thought that Dhavan might be able to offer some good advice. Dhavan, an elderly dandy who much preferred listening to himself than to others, told us of the impressions he had had on his visit to the U.S.S.R. He, however, realized at once how delicate my "problem" was and that it was dangerous even to talk about it; nevertheless, he tried to be amiable, inviting me to his home, where he tried to learn more about me. There I met his wife and grown-up son. They asked me about my father, my mother, about Khrushchev. When I said that I fully realized the futility of trying to remain in India, Dhavan heaved a sigh of relief, and in parting paid me a compliment in true Oriental style: "You are as intelligent as you are charming."

Later still, in Bahri's house, a representative from the local newspaper appeared, endeavoring, while Bahri carried on excitedly, to ask me a few questions and write everything down. By now all this was becoming alarming, and I longed to be back in my quiet Kalakankar. But it wasn't so easy to get away.

I was taken on another visit, this time to a rich local industrialist, who manufactured small flashlights for the whole of India. He had just built himself a modern villa, comfortable, lovely, and with a swimming pool. The Western interiors were in good taste. His pretty, amiable wife took pleasure in showing me all the rooms. I don't know who the guests were at tea, but the conversation turned to agriculture and I described with satisfaction the failure of collective farming in the U.S.S.R. One of the guests turned out to be a Communist and argued heatedly with me; obviously he had never been to the U.S.S.R. and had only read a few brochures. . . .

In Allahabad I had the good fortune to hear an improvisation on a sitar. There was something absolutely enchanting about this instrument, and Bengal people are particularly adept at playing it.

Even after all the guests had left I sat on, unable to move; and the improviser himself, with eyes closed, seemed to have forgotten everything on earth, while melodies flowed one after the other, like babbling waters in a brook. I never had any other opportunity in India to come in touch with art, but this music late at night remained one of my best memories.

I saw the University of Allahabad, which, like the University of Lucknow, spread over a large area. We went to the Sangam, where the Ganges and the Jumna converged and where a fair was still going on after the recent *mela*. The thousands of pilgrims who had come here on foot from distant provinces were not in a hurry to leave. They slowly trod their way back, leaning on their sticks. How insuperable was the force of tradition that had drawn them here for hundreds of miles to plunge into the holy waters at this confluence of the two rivers!

Toward the end Bahri and Bir made me go with them to a gathering of the local Lions International, to which they both belonged. I had never heard of this world-wide organization of "lions and lionesses," and I was examining with interest all the well-dressed Indian and Western women, when to my horror I heard my name pronounced by the chairman. I had to stand up and tell them how much I liked India; here again my "guides" had been unable to hold their tongues. I firmly said that I was going back to Kalakankar; but, they argued, we could still see the holy city of Benares by going only a hundred miles out of our way. I just couldn't resist the temptation.

One can always see a country better from an automobile, and the roads of India, lined with huge trees, though dusty, are full of interest. How many villages we traveled through, how many country fairs, and how many chapatties we ate on the road, prepared with peppered vegetables right in front of you on a charcoal grill. The food burned your mouth, but it was very good, especially if you drank it down with a hot cup of tea and milk, which was poured out right there and then. Gradually I got used to the dust and dirt, and the street food did me no harm.

The "holy city" of Benares thoroughly depressed me, first of all by its stench and dirt, comparable to nothing on earth. Mangy cows wandered along the streets leading to the Ganges, cow dung lay everywhere underfoot; and beggars, cripples, dying pilgrims sat in all this filth. It horrified me to look at them.

Along the waterfront, with its numberless temples, people prayed, bathed, washed their saris and dhotis. On the steps of one of the temples sat a long-haired old man in a red robe and sang in the same way as the pilgrim had done on the train. This old man alone was beautiful; everything else repelled me. Boatmen offered us a ride on the river, but I refused. The quiet lonely Ganges at Kalakankar was far more beautiful and impressive than here, in the "Heart of Hinduism."

I wanted to be back in Kalakankar. I had had enough of my traveling companions, who even in the car carried a bottle of wine with them; the constant tumult which they created around them irritated me. They were good, kind fellows, sincerely anxious to help me, but the talk they had spread all over Allahabad could only spoil everything. This they did not understand. I, on the other hand, told them nothing about my plans. At last they brought me back to Kalakankar and, after a last "stirrup cup," drove away.

Alone in my room, I looked under my bed—was my manuscript safe? No one had shown any curiosity about it here— so much the better! A telegram from Louba d'Astier awaited me: "We shall be glad to see you in Paris." I laughed when I read it; at that point I could have been invited just as plausibly to the moon. . . .

Near the river next morning I noticed a group of peasants and a few men in shorts and white Western shirts.

"These are also Americans from the Peace Corps," Prakash explained. "They are teaching our men to make maps of our locality."

Inquisitive little village boys ran around the group. Suddenly I felt a strong desire to speak to these young men, just to get the feel of what sort of people they were, these Americans. They turned out to be very friendly, and asked me where I was from. When I told them I was from Moscow, one of them remarked that he had relatives in Latvia. I stood and watched them for a few minutes, then returned to my room. And they, being very busy, asked me no more questions.

When I returned home, Prakash laughed: "Well, now that you yourself have made the acquaintance of Americans, I can at last ask those other two, who work in our Agricultural Center, for tea. Let Dinesh fume, I'm not to blame!"

She arranged a tea with Indian sweets, and Sirish brought his two American friends, the black boy, Miller, and the blue-eyed Schmidt. They were both clean-shaven and freshly scrubbed, in clean shirts, their young faces beaming—they were so happy to be invited here again. Miller told us that at last they had found themselves a man to cook their food and that now they were quite happy.

"What a cook!" Miller kept exclaiming. "How I love that cook!"

The discomforts of Indian village life, it seems, did not in the least bother these strong, joyful lads. Prakash asked them whether letters from their parents reached them, whether their work was very hard. Nothing was hard, they said, as long as they had a cook! It was a nice meeting and an important one for me: I was strengthened in my surmise that if I made up my mind to turn to the Americans, I would find a rapport with them.

Election Day—February 17—was fast approaching. Suresh became upset by the discovery that the names of several score dead voters had been included on the lists. Prakash grew indignant. She said that at pre-election meetings supporters of the Congress Party had threatened those who were not going to vote for their party, and had beaten up Socialist campaign workers.

"Such a thing has never happened before," she exclaimed. "They are intimidating the peasants, who don't understand that the elections are secret. They think they *have* to vote for Dinesh."

The ballots didn't actually carry the names of candidates. Instead, they had symbols of the seven competing parties: a bullock for the Congress Party, a sickle and sheaf for Communists, and so on. The voter had to select a similar seal and place it on the ballot opposite its counterpart. This could be done by illiterate old men and women in the remotest villages, but they didn't know which party to give preference to.

In different provinces the elections took place on different dates. The radio in Suresh's house was never silent. Those were critical days for the Congress Party. In several states its success hung by a thread.

In the district to which Kalakankar belonged the elections didn't pass without violence. Opponents of the Congress Party got beaten up. The peasants were not given time to think. They were shoved along, hurriedly told where to place the seal. These outrages were discussed by everyone who during those days entered the hospitable doors of Suresh's house. In the end Dinesh won, of course, but by a very narrow margin. Now he was going back to Delhi and would forget about his little kingdom.

*

Soon after this Surov again paid a visit to Kalakankar, bringing with him Moscow's unequivocal answer to my request: "Since the purpose of the trip has been accomplished, a further stay in India is unnecessary."

I had already overstayed my Indian visa by a month. The Indian Ministry of Foreign Affairs prolonged it until the fifteenth of March. I had no choice but to return to Delhi. The airplane for Moscow left on March 1 and 8.

I wanted, at any rate, to gain an extra week in this village in which to gather all my strength. I therefore asked Dinesh to reserve me a plane ticket from Lucknow to Delhi for the fifth. The Soviet Embassy was informed accordingly. I wrote

Bahri and Bir in Allahabad that unfortunately I had to leave.

During those last days in Kalakankar I roamed the now deserted place, or else sat on the terrace gazing at the Ganges. I had been pushed against a wall. All my senses were sharpened, strained. This, perhaps, was the only chance life would give me to get away from my past.

Would I have the strength to take advantage of it, or would I return to the old familiar path of my Moscow existence? Did I have the strength in me to venture on a new road? One moment my determination grew, in the next it would ebb away. During those last days I never ceased thinking about it. My manuscript, that ticket into another life, scorched my fingers. But even if there had been no manuscript, I would still be facing the same dilemma.

My last day in Kalakankar was a sad one. Prakash had been weeping since morning. I felt crushed by the hopelessness of my situation: it was as if I were going of my own free choice to prison.

At the very end I set fresh flowers in every room—let them remember me here for a few days. My things were packed into the jeep, in which I would be shaken for three hours. There was a crowd in the yard—people had come from the village to see me off.

Sirish was accompanying me as far as Lucknow. I longed to kiss my dear hosts, with whom I had been so happy, but in India it was not customary to kiss. We could only give each other a farewell "namasté."

"I shall return," I kept saying, knowing that it could only be if I didn't go to Moscow. But this they didn't understand.

And now our jeep has left the yard. The silver ripples of the Ganges lie hidden behind the brick wall. We travel slowly up a narrow little street, uphill.

I see the old well, the college, and then Kalakankar vanishes from sight. For long? Forever? Who knows? . . .

There Can Be No Return

I SPENT MARCH 3 and 4 in Lucknow in the home of Aruna Singh, Prakash's niece. I didn't feel like going shopping again in Amin-Abad. I forced myself to chat with Aruna. We frequented a restaurant, clean, expensive, not at all cozy. Aruna's husband spoke of his trip to Japan, admiring Japan's new methods in agriculture. He himself owned a large farm, which he had mechanized as far as it was possible to do so in India, and he knew what a good harvest meant. Sitting in their small yard in the evening, we discussed at length the uselessness of "Socialist" experiments in India's rural districts.

I had a pleasant and agreeable time with these young people, but my thoughts, as in an enchanted circle, kept returning to the same thing. And I could speak of it to no one. . . .

I was thinking of my home in Moscow, where my children were waiting.

For fourteen years I had lived with them in the apartment on the embankment. It had been my first real home. I moved into it in 1952. That was before my father's death, when I had been separated from Zhdanov—Katie's father—and didn't want to return to the Kremlin. From this apartment my seven-year-old son first went to school, which Katie also attended later. At first we had had a servant and a nurse for the children; later, as the children grew up, we did our own simple housework. Here I learned to use a gas stove, to cook, sew, do the washing—until then everything had been done by others. My old nurse, considering books and learning of the utmost importance, had never taught me any household chores. I had to catch up with it all, and it took me some time to master the intricacies of "household science." I was so happy to be able to pay for my own light, my own gas, my own apartment. After so many State residences, this was at last a home.

My children had two rooms to themselves. In my bedroom I had my writing desk. We seldom used the living room; we loved to entertain close friends, but seldom invited guests. Our chief room was really the kitchen, with its table near a window looking out into a yard, in which, by some miracle, there still stood a small sixteenth-century church, all carved and painted white. In this kitchen we used to receive our friends, eat lunch and dinner, and drink our evening tea. The children came home from school at different hours, each having his own schedule, but we always tried to gather together near the kitchen stove. Here we prepared our simple lunches and suppers. We brought ready-cooked dinners from a communal kitchen.

In fourteen years we slowly made our home very livable. Each one of us had his corner for work and rest, his own books, his own plain comfortable furniture. We had moved into an empty apartment. I didn't want to take anything from the Kremlin, which I had never loved. And so we gradually bought what we needed. Only once, in 1955, I asked Premier Bulganin to let me have at least a part of my father's immense library, which, actually, had been started by my mother. According to all existing laws the whole library should have been given to me and the grandchildren.

But in the U.S.S.R. laws do not function. As for the Premier, he simply left my request unanswered. I didn't insist. I gradually began to collect my own small library. It was much better that way.

Each one of us lived according to his tastes. The walls in Katie's room were hung with photographs of horses and horsemen. There was a picture of Jackie Kennedy on horseback with little John, and Caroline on a pony beside them. She had cut it out of a magazine.

Joseph had a Vietnamese mat in his room, silver-inlaid horns on the wall, some black Georgian ceramics. My son is both artistic and conservative. Knowing my passion for moving furniture about, he wouldn't let me touch his old, torn armchair, teasing me: "You have already moved everything. What next? Going to break a door through the wall and wall up all the others?"

In his childhood he didn't kick a ball, didn't tear or dirty his clothes, and never played at "war," as other boys did. Maybe this was the result of the first seven years of his life, before his school days, when he had lived like a hermit in a dacha in the woods, unaccustomed to what was known as a "collective." He was always lazy about sports, although he skied and swam very well. On the other hand, he began reading at an early age and at fourteen had devoured Tolstoy.

I never taught him music; I thought English lessons would be more useful to him. But he had a good ear and good taste, and very soon he grew deeply attached to serious music. Together we used to go to chamber music recitals and symphony concerts at the Conservatory. He liked Handel, Haydn, Vivaldi; we both loved organ recitals of Bach, especially when given by Germans. He knew how to listen, his company was enjoyable, and I always glanced around with pleasure at the young faces of his contemporaries. When I had been a student, only elderly people attended organ recitals; we, the young, could be counted on the fingers of one hand. Times and tastes have changed. My son danced all the newest dances well but, in contrast to his generation, he didn't like modern trends in art.

He drew nicely and could have become a professional artist-animator: he drew expressive little animals in the style of Walt Disney, also caricatures. He and I used to have great fun in summer in the country, editing a humorous wall-newspaper and competing with a similar house organ edited by our neighbors.

Liking the humanities and foreign languages, he nonetheless chose medicine, in order that politics should not interfere with his work and life. He wanted to deal in permanent values, uninfluenced by the changing whims of politics. He followed politics, as I did; but just as with me, they were not an essential part of his life. He loved work and knew how to work; he will make a good doctor. He is a quiet, peaceful builder, born after the Second World War and victory, in May 1945. All my friends are very fond of him, and he has always enjoyed the company of older people.

He was seven, and Katie only two, when we moved into our apartment. I bought his first books, taught him to swim, to ski, to take snapshots. With me he danced his first fox trot. Later my old writing desk was passed on to him, my books, my love of Bach, my enchantment with India, and, in the end, my bed, when he married the girl with whom he had been going and quarreling four whole years.

At present the hard but gratifying life of a doctor lies ahead of him; he has a sweet, hard-working wife, and he is the apple of his father's eye. He misses me less than Katie does, and he no longer needs me; all I could do I have done for him.

Katie was born in 1950. She grew up playing with a group of children in that same gray stone yard, and sociability is perhaps her outstanding characteristic. She is a gay, open, artless young creature, with bright red cheeks and always surrounded by a noisy gang of playmates. She loves skiing, ping-pong, basketball—she is all movement. She dropped her music lessons at the age of twelve, saying it was better to spend the time horseback riding, of which she has been passionately fond ever since. During the summer, in a sports camp, she played football with other equally daring girls.

She was never able to get halfway through *War and Peace*. Novels bored her; she never analyzed herself or others. In her childhood she had loved fairy tales and all kinds of fantastic whimseys, which she thought up herself. Later this brought her to science fiction. Like my son, she wrote the best compositions in her class at school and very lively letters, but literature and art in general were not in her line. Physics, chemistry, mathematics, astronomy, mineralogy were of far greater importance to her.

It is a pity that artistic feelings are so weakly developed in her. Maybe they will come later. But at sixteen she still found no enjoyment in form and color—movement, action were much too essential to her. She has no flair for clothes. Joseph and I always had to give her hints, and Helen would do her hair in a becoming style.

In some ways she lagged behind girls of her own age, who often fell in love. With boys she was either good pals or she fought with them. She is an unselfish, kind, true friend, and that is why all the young love her so. She would approach the fiercest dog with no fear at all, and always chose the most recalcitrant horse; if she fell, she would jump back into the saddle. She would even bring the horses our fresh fruit, vegetables, and sugar.

She was affectionate and easy to please. A box of chocolates would send her into transports of joy, as though half the treasures of the world had been given her. Chocolate and books were the material things she valued. Dresses meant nothing to her, which always shocked my son, who was very particular about his appearance. Katie loved blue jeans and sweaters best of all.

When I think of her future, her impracticality sometimes

frightens me: she knows neither how to sew, nor iron, nor cook, all of which my son does beautifully. But on the other hand, she can solve mathematical exercises and knows what she wants. Brother and sister are very different. But they are very close and miss one another when parted.

Both of them are "Mama's children." For a long time I was the sole authority in the house. We were a closely knit family, all three of us great friends; later Helen joined us. It was so good to have young lives around one, hear young voices, like the chirping of birds.

Whenever they threw a party, they would dance the twist, rock and roll, shake, performing it all with grace. But ordinarily our home was very quiet. The children went to school early. When they came home, each one would heat up his own ready-cooked dinner and retire to his room. There they spent many hours, each at his own desk with his own books. They grew up in a quiet, loving atmosphere, and they loved peace and work. Theirs were neither belligerent nor destructive natures, but they had a good deal of critical common sense, so often to be found in their generation all over the world.

Lies are keenly felt by this generation; it does not tolerate them. It wants a truthful, natural, free life. It believes in reality, not in philosophy. Marxism and all other "isms" do not attract these young minds; "isms" have outlived their day.

If I never return to the U.S.S.R., the life of my children will not be changed; it is too well established, they are such close friends, they will carry on with their work. They are surrounded by loving friends. Their fathers will do everything in their power to be of help to them. Joseph's father is a well-known Moscow specialist in international law and foreign policy. Ever since we separated he had longed to take part in his son's life; he has no other children. Katie's father is the president of one of the largest universities in the U.S.S.R. and a doctor of biochemistry. Katie is on very close terms with him, although he lives in Rostov, where he has another family and a small son. This, however, does not in any way disturb their common interest in the sciences. Undoubtedly he will help her with her further education. In fine, it is good for the children to spread their own wings. My heart will always miss them, but I am not indispensable to them. Yet it's they alone who draw me back. . . .

When I was still at Kalakankar I received a letter from my son, tender and friendly as always:

Mama, my dear, hello! I received your letter and telegram. I'm so surprised that you didn't get the telegram I sent you. It must have gotten lost somewhere. Here everything is in good shape. With the documents you sent us, we obtained coupons for ready-cooked dinners. Everything is well, except that Katie misses you terribly. I, too, miss you very much and want to see you. Otherwise everything in our lives is fine. . . .

This is how we have been living: Katie spent her vacation in the country with Tanya. And we, during our vacation, took a trip to Tbilisi to I.M.'s cousin. During our absence O.S. was here to take care of Katie. In general, everything goes very well, with one exception: we miss you so very much. We feel very badly being without you. Come back, please! May God give health to Sri Suresh Singh and his whole family. I kiss you lovingly and I am waiting for you. I kiss you.

Joseph

Apart from my love for my children and attachment to close friends there was nothing to call me back.

My whole life had been but a withering away of shallow, unreal roots. I felt no attachment either to my blood relatives, or to Moscow where I had been born and had lived all my life, or to any of the things that had surrounded me since my childhood.

I was forty years old. Twenty-seven of those years I had lived under a heavy weight, the next thirteen had been spent in gradually liberating myself from it. In the U.S.S.R. those twenty-seven years (1926-1953) have been named by historians the "Period of Stalinism"—a time of singlehanded despotism, bloody terror, economic hardships, the cruelest of wars, and an ideological reaction.

After 1953 the whole country gradually began to come to itself, began to revive. The terror, it seemed, had vanished into the past. But that which had taken years to build up as an economic, social, and political system proved tenacious and clinging within the Party itself and in the consciousness of enslaved, blinded millions.

And although I lived "at the very top of the pyramid," where truth hardly reached one at all, my whole life, like that of the entire nation, became divided into two periods: before 1953 and after.

My own process of liberation, however, went its own way, different from that of others; but it moved on unerringly, and drop by drop truth seeped through the granite.

"*Gutta cavat lapidem, non vi sed saepe cadendo* (A drop furrows a stone not by force but by continually falling)." This Latin saying we learned by heart at the university. And if this saying had not been true, I should not be sitting now in Lucknow, pondering over what to do; I would have been living quietly in Georgia, where my father's name was still respected, and would be conducting tourists through the Stalin Museum in Gori, recounting his "great deeds" and "achievements."

In the family in which I was born and bred nothing was normal, everything was oppressive, and my mother's suicide was most eloquent testimony to the hopelessness of the situation.* Kremlin walls all around me, secret police in the house, in the kitchen, at school. And over it all a wasted,

---

* Returning to the past, to my life in the U.S.S.R. and the relationships in the family, it is impossible to avoid repeating certain facts already told in *Twenty Letters*, my first book, written in August 1963. I was then writing a history of my family, never thinking that someday it would be possible for me to leave my country. But all those events of the past served as a foundation for future decisions and unfolding events, which cannot be foreseen either in a book or in life.

obdurate man, fenced in from his former colleagues, his
old friends, from all those who had been close to him, in
fact from the entire world, who with his accomplices had
turned the country into a prison, in which everyone with a
breath of spirit and mind was being extinguished; a man
who aroused fear and hatred in millions of men—this was
my father. . . .

If only fate had let me be born in the hovel of some unknown Georgian cobbler! How natural and easy it would
have been for me to hate that distant tyrant, his Party, his
words and deeds. Wouldn't it have been all too clear then
where things were black and where they were white?

But no, I was born his daughter, beloved in my childhood.
My adolescence was spent under the sign of his irrefutable
authority; everything taught and forced me to believe in this
authority, and if there was so much grief around us, I could
only conclude that others must have been at fault. For
twenty-seven years I was witness to the spiritual deterioration of my own father, watching day after day how everything human in him left him and how gradually he turned
into a grim monument to his own self. . . . But my generation
was trained to think that this monument was the embodiment of all that was most beautiful in the ideals of Communism, its living personification.

We were trained in Communism almost from our diapers
—at home, at school, at the university. At first we were
"*oktyabryata* (Little Octobers)," then Pioneers, then Komsomols. After that we were accepted into the Party. And
even if (like many others) I did not work for the Party
and only (like everyone else) paid my dues, all the same I
had to vote for any decisions of the Party, even if they
seemed wrong to me. Lenin was our icon, Marx and Engels
our apostles—their every word Gospel truth. And my father's
every word, either spoken or written, was accepted as a
revelation from on High.

To me, in my early years, Communism was an unshakable

stronghold. Unshakable remained my father's authority and the belief that he was right in everything without exception. But later I began to doubt that he was always right; I became more and more convinced of his senseless cruelty. The theories and dogmas of Marxism-Leninism began to wither away and fade in front of my eyes. The Party lost its heroic revolutionary halo of righteousness. And when after 1953 the Party endeavored clumsily and hopelessly to dissociate itself from its former Leader, it only convinced me of the inner unity between the Party and the "cult of personality," which it had supported for over twenty years.

Little by little, it became more than obvious not only that my father had been a despot and had brought about a bloody terror, destroying millions of innocent people, but that the whole system *which had made it possible* was profoundly corrupt; that all its participants could not escape responsibility, no matter how hard they tried. And it was then that the whole edifice, whose foundation rested on a lie, crumbled from top to bottom.

When you have once gained sight, it is impossible to feign blindness. To me this process came neither easily nor quickly. It is still evolving. My generation was far too ignorant of its country's history in general, of the history of the Revolution, of the Party. Truth had been concealed from us too long.

I knew my father at home, in the circle of his family, with whom he was contradictory and changeable. But for a long time I was unable to know the history of the political struggle for supreme power, which he had waged in the Party against all his former comrades. And the more I learned about it—sometimes from the most unexpected sources—the more my heart sank, numbed with horror. I felt like fleeing without a backward glance—where to I did not know. . . . So this was my father! And the fact that he was my father made the truth all the more terrifying.

The official unmasking of the "cult of personality" ex-

plained nothing to me. The illiterate phrase itself only bespoke the Party's inability and unwillingness to disclose the
corrupt foundations of the whole system, so contrary and inimical to democracy. Not political interpretations but life itself, with its unexpected paradoxes, helped me to understand
the truth. And although my mother had long since been dead,
I must first and foremost render her memory its due.

Only my first six and a half years had been warmed by
Mama's presence, but they remained in my memory as a
childhood filled with sunshine. I remember Mama as a very
beautiful, graceful woman, smelling of perfume. I was completely entrusted to the hands of my nurse and a governess,
but Mama's presence expressed itself in the whole tenor of
my childhood life. She considered most important our education and ethical upbringing. Honesty, labor, truth were to
her more important than anything else. The hard, sharp
crystal of Truth lay as a cornerstone to her nature, the kind
that demands to live "not by bread alone." Mama was not
yet thirty, she was studying for a degree in engineering
in the textile industry, wishing to be independent of her
"high position," which oppressed her.

Mama was an idealist; toward Revolution she had the
romantic approach of poets. She believed in a better future
brought about by people who had first improved themselves.
That is what her old friends told me about her—Paulina
Molotov, Dora Andreyev, Maria Kaganovich, Catherine Voroshilov, Ashkhen Mikoyan. She had other friends, much
closer to her in their interests, friends from her school days,
but I never had the opportunity of meeting them after her
death. I only knew her former music teacher, A. V. Pukhlya-
kova, a gifted, interesting woman. Much later she gave me
music lessons too, and always spoke of Mama as a sensitive,
artistic nature.

Grandmama, Mama's mother, who even in her old age
remained temperamental, with an uncurbed tongue, often
said, "Your mother was a fool!" From the very first she had

disapproved of my mother's marriage to my father, and her sharp appraisal was a reflection of the habitual attitude of realists toward romanticists and poets. According to my aunts, Mama was very reserved, always very correct, and somewhat melancholy, in contrast to Grandmama's hot nature. The aunts considered Mama too "severe and serious," too "highly disciplined" for her age. And everyone who knew her unanimously confirmed that in her last years she had been unhappy, disillusioned, and depressed.

She was only sixteen when my father took shape in her eyes as a Hero of the Revolution. When she matured, she understood how mistaken she had been. Her own principles ran afoul of his political cynicism and savagery. Everything around her followed what she felt was the wrong road, and my father was no longer the ideal she had pictured to herself, but rather the contrary. . . .

Her life, according to her sister, became unbearable. At one time she left for Leningrad, taking us children with her, intending never to return—but she did. Later she wanted to go to the Ukraine, to her sister, and work there. She argued with Father, protesting against his reprisals, but it didn't help: she could change nothing. When she was only thirty-one she took her own life, driven to despair by a profound disillusionment and the impossibility of changing anything.

This was in 1932, the frightful year of hunger, of the struggles of the Five-Year Plan, of enforced collectivization; a year in which even within the ranks of the Party itself loud demands had been heard for the removal of my father from the post of Secretary General.

Before her death Mama left Father a letter full of political accusations. Only a few very close intimates were ever able to read that letter, which was quickly destroyed. Because of its political implications her suicide would have been of too great significance for the Party itself.

My aunts, who returned from prison in 1954, told me

about this letter. My father was dead, I was grown up, my aunts would not have lied to me after all they had been through. They told me that the event had so shaken everyone that people lost their heads, thinking only how best to conceal what had happened. For that reason, doctors had not been permitted to examine the body, there had been no medical verdict, and obituaries had mysteriously spoken of an "unexpected death on the night of November 9." It had even been forbidden to embalm the body prior to the funeral; no one had been allowed to enter the house.

Aversion, fear, hatred of my father ran so strong that year that murder was instantly suspected. To many this seemed more plausible than the suicide of a young healthy woman, who had held everybody's sympathy. I had occasion to hear many different versions of the supposed murder, some very conflicting, but always coming to the same conclusion: the murder had been committed by my father's own hands.

And yet, according to my aunts (my mother's sister, Anna Redens, and her brother's wife, Yevgenia Alliluyeva), Father was more shattered than anyone else, for he fully realized that this was a challenge and a protest against him. He couldn't even force himself to go to the funeral. He was a broken, drained man. He had considered Mama his most faithful, devoted friend. Her evaluations and opinions, which differed from his, he had underestimated and ignored for the simple reason that his whole attitude to his wife and family had always been Asiatic in the most banal sense of the word. When he finally came to, he had grown even more obdurate. And in 1948 he didn't hesitate to send the two aunts to prison for ten years, simply because they "knew too much." As for the Party, in latter years an official version of the event had become firmly established—that my mother had been a "neurotic" and it was very bad form even to mention her name. I heard this version in 1948-1950 from the Zhdanovs, my second husband's family.

Everyone who knew Mama had loved her. Among her

closest friends had been Bukharin and Kirov. Indubitably their liberal and democratic views were closer to hers than my father's intolerance. Bukharin and Kirov still hopefully fancied that my father could be "influenced" in a better direction. Mama had lost all such rosy optimism, and her despair broke her. She turned out to be more discerning than those two experienced politicians.

The tragic destinies of these three closely knit people—my mother, Bukharin, and Kirov—give me a deep and merciless insight into what "Stalinism" really stood for. All three had fought against it, each in his way, and had perished in the uneven struggle. What explanation could Khrushchev, Mikoyan, and other former accomplices give me, those men who were cowardly enough to support my father in everything and then tried to escape responsibility?

When my mother died, I was only six years old, and for a long time I was incapable of knowing the truth. During the following decade I could only observe how everything which she had created with her own hands and efforts was being systematically destroyed. Servants and teachers were fired. The whole system of my education broke down. And as a symbol of the happy childhood she had created for us, even our playground at the dacha in the country was done away with. Mama's simple furniture, her knickknacks disappeared. All her papers and personal belongings were taken away and put under lock and key, the key itself given into the safekeeping of the commander of the MGB. The whole household was militarized: the servants were salaried employees of the MGB, and a captain of that force was placed at their head. Our home, as it had been under Mama, ceased to exist; the Kremlin apartment, our old dacha, and my father's new one, in which he now lived, became known as numbered government "objects."

For me the ten years after my mother's death passed in monotonous isolation. I lived in the Kremlin as in a fortress, in which the only kind being near me was my nurse. I was unable then to grasp what was going on in the country, but the cruel tragedies of those years didn't spare our family. In 1937 the brother of my father's first wife, an old-time Georgian Bolshevik, A. S. Svanidze, and his wife Maria were arrested. His sister Mariko was arrested, too. After that the husband of my mother's sister was arrested—the Polish Communist Stanislav Redens. The three Svanidzes and Redens perished in prison. Mama's sister was forbidden to visit us children. Her brother Paul died of a heart attack, shaken by the arrests of his relations and numerous friends, for whom he had vainly pleaded with my father. His widow was forbidden to see us. The old people, my mother's parents, were to all intents and purposes deprived of the possibility of seeing my father: he wanted no questions about the fate of "disgraced relatives," whose destruction no one but he could have sanctioned.

It was impossible for a schoolgirl of twelve and thirteen to grasp all that was happening. At the same time it was inconceivable to think of "Uncle Alyosha," "Aunt Marusya," and "Uncle Stakh" as "enemies of the people," which is what even schoolchildren were repeatedly told by the official propaganda of the time. I could only assume that they must have become the victims of some frightful mix-up, which "even Father himself" could not disentangle. Many years had to go by before everything that had taken place, not only in our family but all over the country, could range itself in my consciousness with my father's name, before I could realize that all of it had been done by him. In those years I just couldn't conceive of his being capable of condemning to death people whose innocence and decency were well known to him. Only later, as a young adult, did several discoveries convince me of this.

I was sixteen when I learned that Mama's death had been a suicide. It was a cruel discovery. The war was on, I was in Kuibyshev that winter with my aunt and grandmother. I began questioning them at once and understood that

Mama had been very unhappy, that she and my father had had different points of view on everything, from politics to the upbringing of children. I had always loved Mama, though she had never spoiled me. And now I felt that my father had clearly been in the wrong and that he was to blame for her death. His irrefutable authority was violently shaken. . . .

I was brought up in absolute obedience and respect for him. At home, at school, everywhere, I never heard his name otherwise than with such epithets as "great" and "wise" tagged onto it. I knew that he loved me more than he did my brothers, that he was pleased that I studied well. I saw him seldom, he lived in his dacha, but all the same, after Mama's death, and right up to the war, he tried to give me as much of his attention as he could. I loved and respected him until I grew up.

But then "the time of mutinous youth" came along, when all authority is subjected to criticism, that of one's parents first and foremost. And I suddenly felt a certain absolute truth in everything I remembered of my mother and in what others had told me about her, while my father was suddenly deprived of his authority in my eyes. And this was strengthened as time went by: the more I learned about my mother, the more she grew in my eyes, while my father lost his aureole.

A year hadn't gone by before I received a new shock. I was a schoolgirl of seventeen; a man twenty years older than I fell in love with me and I with him. It was an innocent enough romance. We would stroll through the streets of Moscow, go to the theater and the movies—but this tender attachment of two individuals, very different yet completely compatible, horrified all the MGB employees around me and enraged my father.

My friend understood that for him, a full-grown, mature man, there was no future for this romantic attachment. It was so evident that he was preparing to leave Moscow for good, when suddenly he was arrested, accused of spying, and sent to the Arctic for five years, and then to a concentration camp for another five. There could be no doubt that this had been done at my father's explicit orders. I found it out: the whole initiative had come from him. It was such obvious and senseless despotism that for a long time I was unable to recover from the shock. There was no possibility of helping my friend—Father never changed his decrees.

These two revelations in one and the same year served to separate me from my father forever; and in the years to come this breach only grew wider.

After the war Father hardly ever stayed in the Kremlin apartment, preferring his dacha, and we seldom saw one another. I was no longer the beloved daughter, while my filial love and respect for him had vanished like smoke. Yet I was a long way from understanding the full purport of his "political biography." I withdrew myself from him, but it was still as from a human being.

Truth did not penetrate the high walls that shut the Kremlin off from the rest of Russia. Behind those walls I grew like a plant on a barren rock, reaching out toward the light, feeding somehow on air. My home was that rock, and I was reaching out, away from it, as far as I could. The school, the university, were breathing holes through which the light and fresh air reached me: there I had friends, but not within the walls.

All my life I was happy in the company of my friends; they definitely separated me from my name. To them I was just another student, their age, a young woman; in a word, just another human being. The friends I made at school and at the university remained with me all my life. I saw many of them on that last day before I left for India. Books, art, science were the interests that united us. Many of their parents and close relatives were under arrest, but then it was the same in our family and it changed nothing in their feelings for me. The memory of my mother, which was still alive, must have helped me.

In 1940 the father of a schoolmate of mine was arrested. The girl and I were friends, and one day she brought me a letter from her mother to my father, begging him to save her husband. I gave him the letter that evening at dinner. There were a good many people at table, and they all began discussing the case. Molotov and others remembered this man: M. M. Slavutsky, formerly Soviet Consul in Manchuria, later Ambassador of the U.S.S.R. in Japan. An extraordinary miracle occurred: he was freed and returned home a few days later. But I was strictly forbidden ever again to take such letters for transmission, and my father scolded me for it for a long time. However, the case served as a clear illustration that the life of a man depended entirely on a word from my father.

Sometimes my father would suddenly say to me, "Why do you associate with children whose parents have been arrested?" Apparently these things were reported to him. Often his displeasure would result in the school principal's transferring the children in question from the class I was in to a parallel one. But years would go by and we would meet again, and their feelings for me remained as friendly as before.

In the university the circle of my acquaintances grew larger. I often visited my friends in their homes, saw their run-down "communal" apartments. Seldom did anyone come to see me in the Kremlin, nor did I feel like inviting them in. One had to order a "pass," which was to be shown at the Kremlin gates, and I was ashamed of these rules.

In those university years the Moscow Conservatory was our "club." There I also met classmates from my school days. Music was one of our greatest "air shafts," a reminder of the existence of the beautiful and the eternal. In the years after the war the life of the intelligentsia grew more and more gloomy: all efforts at independent thought in the social sciences, literature, and the arts were mercilessly crushed. People came to the Moscow Conservatory for a breath of clean fresh air.

At the university I went through a course in history and in social science. We seriously studied Marxism, analyzed Marx, Engels, Lenin, and, of course, Stalin. The conclusion I carried away from these studies was that the theoretical Marxism and Communism we had studied had nothing whatsoever to do with actual conditions in the U.S.S.R. Economically, our Socialism was more of a state capitalism. Its social aspect was some strange hybrid: a bureaucratic, barracks-like system, in which the secret police resembled the German Gestapo, and our backward rural economy made one think of nineteenth-century villages. Marx had never dreamed of anything of the sort. Progress was forgotten. Soviet Russia broke with everything that had been revolutionary in her history and got on the well-trodden path of all-powerful imperialism, having replaced the liberal freedoms of the beginning of the twentieth century with the horrors of Ivan the Terrible. . . .

I was never on close terms with any of the young people of "my" Kremlin set, although, of course, I knew a good many of them. They, too, felt the yearning to get beyond the Kremlin walls, and all of them had friends outside—this was not an exception but rather the rule.

I was drawn to kind, gentle, intellectual people. It so happened, independent of any choice on my part, that these lovely people, who treated me with such warmth, both at school and at the university, were often Jews. We were friends and loved each other; they were talented and sincere. My father, though, was indignant about it and would say about my first husband, "The Zionists put him over on you." It was impossible to convince him that this was not so.

In the years after the war anti-Semitism became the militant official ideology, although this was concealed in every way possible. But it was known everywhere that in the enrollment at the university and in all types of employment preference was given to Russians. For the Jews a percentage quota was, in essence, reinstated. It was the resuscitation of the State chauvinism of czarist Russia, in which one's attitude toward Jews had always been the great divide between the liberal intelligentsia and the reactionary bureaucracy. In the Soviet Union only during the first decade after the Revolution was anti-Semitism dormant. But with the expulsion of Trotsky and the extermination during the years of "purges" of old Party members, many of whom were Jews, anti-Semitism was reborn on new grounds and first of all in the Party itself. To this my father not only gave his support; he even propagated a good deal of it himself. In Soviet Russia, where anti-Semitism had old roots among the middle classes and the bureaucracy, it now spread throughout the width and breadth of the land with the speed of a pestilential plague.

In 1948, quite by chance, I almost became a witness to an intentional murder. It was in the dark days of the Party's campaign against so-called "cosmopolitans" in art, when the Party would pounce upon the slightest sign of Western influence. As had happened many times before, this was merely an excuse to settle accounts with undesirables. In this instance, however, the struggle bore an openly anti-Semitic character.

The atmosphere in Moscow was very tense and oppressive in those days—arrests had started all over again. The State Jewish Theater in Moscow had been closed down, declared a "hotbed of cosmopolitanism." Solomon Mikhoels was the theater's director, a well-known actor and public figure. I heard him speak during the war after his trip to England and the United States, where he went as President of the Jewish Anti-Fascist Committee. He had brought back with him a present for my father from the furriers of America—a fur coat in which, on the reverse side of every pelt, the signature of a donor had been inscribed. (I never actually saw this coat, it was kept somewhere together with all other similar presents, but I heard about it from my father's secretary, Poskrebyshev).

One day, in father's dacha, during one of my rare meetings with him, I entered his room when he was speaking to someone on the telephone. Something was being reported to him and he was listening. Then, as a summary of the conversation, he said, "Well, it's an automobile accident." I remember so well the way he said it: not a question but an answer, an assertion. He wasn't asking; he was suggesting: "an automobile accident." When he got through, he greeted me; and a little later he said: "Mikhoels was killed in an automobile accident." But when next day I came to my classes in the university, a girl student, whose father had worked for a long time in the Jewish Theater, told me, weeping, how brutally Mikhoels had been murdered while traveling through Byelorussia in a car. The newspapers, of course, reported the event as an "automobile accident."

He had been murdered and there had been no accident. "Automobile accident" was the official version, the cover-up suggested by my father when the black deed had been reported to him. My head began to throb. I knew all too well my father's obsession with "Zionist" plots around every corner. It was not difficult to guess why this particular crime had been reported directly to him.

A few days later I learned of the arrest of my two aunts. The two elderly women had no connection at all with politics. But I knew that my father had been irritated by the memoirs of Anna Sergeyevna Redens and annoyed that my Uncle Paul's widow had remarried soon after his death an engineer, a Jew. Her second husband had been arrested with her. "They knew too much. They babbled a lot. It played into the hands of our enemies," was the way my father explained the arrests to me.

He was embittered against the entire world and no longer

believed anyone. "You, too, make anti-Soviet statements," he said to me at the time, quite seriously. It had become impossible to talk to him. I avoided meeting him, and he had no particular wish to see me. In the last years we only saw each other once every few months, even less often. I had no feeling left for my father, and after every meeting I was in a hurry to get away. During the summer of 1952 I left the Kremlin with my children for good and moved into our apartment in town, where my children, at present, were waiting for me.

During the winter of 1952-1953 the darkness thickened beyond all endurance. Already accused of "Zionist plotting," Molotov's wife Paulina had been arrested, as well as the former Deputy Minister of Foreign Affairs, Solomon Lozovsky, the Academician Lina Stern, and many others. The "Doctors' plot" was cooked up, accusing them, too, of plotting against the government. The wife of the Secretary of the Komsomols, N. A. Mikhailov, told me, "If I had my way, I'd expel all Jews from Moscow!" Her husband was obviously of the same mind. It was the official temper of the times, and its origin, as I could easily guess, stemmed from the very top of the ladder. In spite of all this, at the Nineteenth Congress of the Party, in October 1952, they continued to proclaim "internationalism."

To this madness was added the rattling of swords. Under the flimsiest of excuses the Ambassador of the United States, George Kennan, was declared *persona non grata*. A certain artillery colonel, a comrade of my brother's, said to me confidentially, "Now's the time to begin, to fight and to conquer, while your father is alive. At present we can win!" It was terrifying even to think of such things seriously, yet such tendencies apparently existed in the government itself. People were afraid to speak, everything grew very still as before a storm.

And it was then that my father died. The bolt hit the very summit of the mountain, and thunder rolled over the whole land, predicting warm showers and clear blue skies. Everything had waited so avidly for that clear sky, free of heavy leaden clouds that had hung immobile for so long overhead. People began to breathe, talk, think, walk the streets with greater ease, I among them.

I spent three days at the bedside of my dying father. I saw his death. I experienced pain and terror because this was my father. But I felt and knew that liberation would follow his death, and I understood that this liberation would be for me, too.

In those days, before the funeral, I stood near the coffin, looking at the stream of people passing through the Hall of Columns. They all behaved differently. Many wept. Some carried flowers. Others looked curiously to make sure that, indeed, he was no more. At times my eyes would encounter those of former schoolmates; many of them I hadn't seen in years. I stood aghast because my own feelings were so contradictory, I was experiencing pain and relief together, and scolded myself bitterly for being a bad daughter. At the final leave-taking, when I was supposed to kiss the forehead of the deceased and everyone there expected it and was looking at me, I couldn't bring myself to do it. And I never visited my father's grave beside the Kremlin wall.

In those days great confusion reigned in Moscow; and not in Moscow alone. Some people sincerely wept, others just as sincerely cursed him and rejoiced. I received dozens of letters and telegrams of condolence, but millions in prisons and concentration camps were shouting, "Freedom!" For they knew that the hour of freedom had struck.

The streets of Moscow leading to the Hall of Columns became so crowded that a stampede occurred. To get to the Hall of Columns I had to go through a small room in which members of the guard of honor awaited their turn to take their post near the coffin: cabinet ministers and members of the Politburo, generals and marshals. I heard one general saying to another that "the crowds had got out of hand,"

that he had just been there to "take measures." Khrushchev
was there, too, and heard what had been said. His reaction
was very different: "I'll go and talk to the people!" After all,
the "crowds," which were the "people," were paying with
their lives, and the government, always in deadly fear of
any large gatherings, lost its head and could think of nothing
better than police measures.

The police and trucks surrounded the center of town to
stop the flow in this direction. It was then that a panic and
a stampede occurred. There were casualties. The "last farewell" had turned into one more bloody nightmare. . . .

During that spring, symbolically referred to by Ilya Ehrenburg as "the thaw," everyone expected that now at last the
land would be freed of its chains and fetters. Everyone understood that changes had to come, and that they would
now come. Hopes, of course, were directed toward the one
ever-present Party, for, unfortunately, the country had nothing else to turn to.

Many within the Party, both at the top and at the bottom,
understood that instead of the worship of idols and dogmas
the country needed democratization, the release of its inner
energies, bound by a deathlike torpor. The rural population
awaited enfranchisement from the unsuccessful, disastrous
collectivization. Industry longed to be free of the bureaucratic yoke of the Center. Workers awaited the long-prom-
ised participation in production and in the revenues from
their labor. Science, lagging behind the rest of the world
because of various ideological taboos, should be participating in the international exchange of knowledge. Artists
wanted to write, sing, create openly and freely, the only
way artists can work. And the time had come for everyone
to be freed from fear for his life and that of his family and
friends.

The banner of freedom had been drawn from its shroud
and unfurled, waving above everyone's head, and the "leaders," like a bunch of small boys in the absence of their tutor,

rushed to tear it away from each other, to seize it, pushing all others away with their fists. Each one wanted to become the Great Liberator.

In this frantic struggle for power they began by shooting Beria and his minions in the MGB, having "unmasked" them as "international spies." Then they ousted Bulganin. After that, having heaped the progressive Malenkov and the conservatives, Molotov and Kaganovich, into one "anti-Party bloc," they accused them of being subversives. They nosed about, unearthing one "scapegoat" after another. For after all, no other methods were known in a country and in a party that had bred, in fifty years of totalitarianism, a whole generation to which democratic freedoms were but a legend.

And while millions all over the country waited in silence, gazing with hope at the Kremlin, inside that Kremlin, under cover of "collective rule," one palace revolution was fought after another. Everything moved in skips and thrusts: one step forward, one step back. Using a cannon to scatter sparrows. To the gallows with the "scapegoats"! But first and foremost, never let the people find out that it was time they started ruling their country. And if some upstart poets and intellectuals were whispering it into their ears, make them eat their words! Make them remember once and for all that in the U.S.S.R. the Kremlin alone had the right to think, to speak, to decide the fate of millions. The Kremlin and the Party, which, its bloodcurdling history notwithstanding, remained "wise," unsoiled, and pure as a dove. . . .

The banner of liberation fell to Khrushchev. It might just as easily have fallen into the hands of Malenkov, or Bulganin, or even Beria for that matter, because the eradicating of the long-standing system of terror was the nation's first and foremost need.

In the years following the Twentieth Congress a great deal happened: thousands of innocents returned to life from prisons and concentration camps, the terror of the secret police was abolished, a few timid contacts established with the outside world, efforts made to decentralize industry and agriculture. Tensions slackened, the threat of war moved away, and hope for a sound peace began to take root. Science, art, ideology made attempts to free themselves from dogmatism. But also, in those same years, the bloody events in Hungary took place, and the execution of university students in Georgia and of workers in Novocherkassk.

In March 1956 hundreds of Georgian students, as well as other young people and intellectuals, gathered in front of the building of the Central Committee in Tbilisi, demanding a clarification of Khrushchev's "secret" speech. Rumors of it had just reached Tbilisi and, as always in the U.S.S.R., no one knew anything about it, except that "portraits were to be taken down," this time Stalin's. The frightened secretary of the Georgian Central Committee called out the army. The demonstration was a peaceful one. As an expression of a long-standing protest against "Russian oppressors," it carried pictures of Stalin—the pictures that had been ordered taken down. All this was mostly due to a feeling of trampled national dignity, which in Georgians was strongly developed. Everything could have been settled peacefully if it hadn't been for the army's encirclement of government buildings.

When a group of students, after sending a telegram to Moscow, emerged into the street, they were seized. Comrades rushed to their defense. A scuffle resulted and the soldiers opened fire. Dozens of bodies remained lying in the street. The rest were chased away. But relatives were forbidden to carry away the dead and bury them. It was feared that the funerals might end in mass demonstrations against the Georgian Central Committee and the central government in Moscow. Bodies of dead students were dispatched somewhere under guard, arousing the indignation of the entire small nation. Students threw rocks at trains leaving for Moscow—the trains arrived with all the windows smashed. The result of it all: a growing hatred of Moscow.

The official Moscow explanation of these events—not in print, of course, but in one of the Central Committee's regular secret letters—proclaimed that in Georgia "nationalist elements" had tried to secede from the U.S.S.R. . . .

Soon after the Twentieth Congress, it transpired that the former creators and participators in the "cult of personality" did not wish to and could not tell the truth, and that they would not let anyone else tell it, be it historians or economists, artists or poets.

The Party and State apparatuses, brought into being and trained during the past decades, did not wish to make any concessions to liberalism and democratization. Khrushchev's efforts in this direction met with resistance at every step. Every "case" concerning the posthumous rehabilitation of victims of the years of 1937-1938 had to be "pushed" with immense efforts through the Central Committee. O. G. Shatunovskaya, an old Communist from Baku, spent seventeen years in prison and in exile in Siberia. When, after the Twentieth Congress, she had been freed and rehabilitated in the Party, the Control Commission of the Central Committee took her on to work on rehabilitations—mostly posthumous ones—of Party workers who had suffered in the "purges." But despite the support of Khrushchev and Mikoyan, after a few years she was squeezed out of her job by the same people who in former days had arrested and jailed many. Shatunovskaya told me that she simply could not go on; the entire apparatus of the Central Committee was muttering almost openly against de-Stalinization.

And no wonder, when one of the most reactionary men, the most devoted to the old way, M. A. Suslov, who began his career in the apparatus of the Central Committee in 1937, had remained its Secretary, gathering around him all those opposed to the "new course."

Khrushchev was unable to get his way with the Party apparatus. Too much had to be smashed. He was afraid to do it. In the end he paid for it—the *apparatchiki* got rid of him.

Khrushchev couldn't openly declare that the Party itself had supported the "cult of Stalin" and that, after yielding him the full measure of power, it had become the obedient agent of his absolute will. By fearing to admit the Party's guilt, and dumping all the blame on the terrible dead man, he had eloquently discredited not only himself but the entire Party. For this the Party could not forgive him. It became clear to the whole world that a totalitarian regime could neither accuse nor transform itself: suicide was not in its nature, it could only kill others.

Once again the well-tried method of palace revolution was successfully resorted to, and the new Premier, Kosygin, together with the new "leader," Brezhnev, swore allegiance to the same old despotic tradition: that the nation remain mute, while the Kremlin alone spoke and made decisions.

But the unrestrainable process of liberation was strong and bold in the lower echelons. While the ugly battle for power went on upstairs, progress followed its own course. It grew and spread from below, pressing like hot steam on those on top, forcing them to give in one moment and in the next to resist. There was no halting the process. Progress pushed its way through like bright grass among flagstones.

The same slow, unyielding process of inner liberation from the past went on in my soul: a liberation from my country's past and from my own.

It moved along its own line. Khrushchev's "secret" speech was of no help to me, nor did it come as a surprise. Among close friends we had often discussed the inevitability of a change.

At the end of February 1956 Mikoyan gave me the opportunity of reading the speech. He sent his car for me, asking me to come to his home. "Read this. Afterward we'll discuss it, if necessary," he said. "Don't hurry. Think it over. We shall wait for you downstairs for supper."

I spent several hours that evening in the library of his home on the Lenin Hills. The most terrifying thing was that

I believed every word I read. It was impossible not to. And as I read on, I remembered what my aunts had told me upon their return from prison. My mother's sister, Anna, had gone mad in prison and had come home a sick woman. Yevgenia Alliluyeva, the widow of Mother's brother, bore it all, but she said that she had signed all the accusations set before her: spying, poisoning her husband, contacts with foreigners. "You sign anything there," she would say, "just to be left alone and not tortured! At night no one could sleep for the shrieks of agony in the cells. Victims screamed in an unearthly way, begging to be killed, better be killed. . . ." She spent six years in solitary confinement, forbidden to correspond with her family, of whom she knew nothing during all that time. In 1954 all the accusations were admitted to be false, and she was allowed to go home.

I kept thinking of the fate of Svanidze and that of Redens, of the tragic destinies of many others I had known, and my heart continued to sink into a dreadful void. If only I could have refuted it all, not believed it; if only I could have exclaimed, "It's a lie! He didn't do it!" But I could not. I recalled certain talks with friends and the little that was accessible from unofficial sources, for official sources always presented everything in a false light. Again the postwar years and that grim winter of 1952-1953 came to mind, when with my own eyes I had seen how much was done under my father's direct orders.

At last I went into the dining room, where Mikoyan and his wife were anxiously waiting. "Unfortunately," I said, "it all looks very much like the truth." Mikoyan heaved a sigh of relief. He had probably feared that I would start weeping and disputing it all.

"I hoped you would understand," he said. "Let's go to supper. We didn't want you to hear it unexpectedly at some meeting. In a week's time this document will be read to all the Party's organizations."

I told him I was grateful. That evening we touched on

the subject no more; we kept reminiscing about my mother, with whom Ashkhen Mikoyan had been friends.

A few days later I was present at a Party meeting in the Institute of World Literature and sat listening to discussions of Khrushchev's speech. The representative of the Central Committee tried to restrain passions, but everyone spoke of changes, demanding them: changes in the life of the whole country, freedom from dogmatism—all the things the Central Committee feared most. I sat listening to what was being said and shared in the general opinion of those around me. Toward me, personally, nothing changed after Khrushchev's speech. My friends treated me as before. I never felt any animosity directed at me.

Although during the last years my father and I had grown far apart, it was only now, after his death, that my consciousness began to be cleared of myths, of idealizations, of canonized lies, of everything with which the minds of my generation had been saturated: the false image of the "wise leader," false history of the Party, false representation of the "glorious development" of the country.

Because of the general isolation of the U.S.S.R. from the rest of the world one couldn't obtain a single book published abroad on Soviet history. All approaches to such "secret sources" were strictly guarded. Such books were to be found exclusively in State libraries and handed out only to those who held special permits for research work. But even the little which we managed to read in this way was to us a revelation. Actually, the material contained nothing but historical facts; but by this same token, to me they were far more significant than the sensational and cryptic way in which the Soviet press exposed the "cult of personality."

In 1954 I was able to read two books on the history of Soviet literature published in the U.S.—one by Marc Slonim, the other by Gleb Struve. These books were issued to me by the library from its special collection solely because I was due to make a report on them to a seminar. In these books

I came across a conception of the literature of the twenties which to Soviet students was totally unexpected. Those years were called the flourishing period in Russian literature, which had blossomed freely until "Socialist realism" was proclaimed in 1934. There were such richness of style, such a variety of directions, so many new names—*The Serapion Brothers*, "The South-West School," Pilnyak, Babel, Zamyatin; a struggle with the "proletarian writers" who tried to claim a monopoly on arts; a totally new picture of Gorky's role, protesting violently against the "inhuman cruelties of the Revolution," all of it unretouched, unedited. And again, hovering over it all, the Party's Secretary General, reputedly a patron of the arts but in reality one who had chased art up the dead end where he had wanted it in the first place. In conclusion there was a list of writers arrested and destroyed, all of whom had sung praises to the Revolution, to the Red Army, to a new life, artists who had served the Party with their pens and hearts. . . .

In 1957-1958, in the Institute of World Literature, a group of junior researchers—Andrei Sinyavsky and I among them —undertook to work on a literary chronicle of the twenties and thirties. This gave us access to newspapers and magazines of that period. After looking through the back numbers of *Izvestia* for 1922 and *Pravda* for 1934, I made quite a few discoveries for myself.

Trotsky's articles, establishing the Party line on literature and art in those days, advocated the free development of styles and total independence for the creative artist. Lunacharsky wrote in the same vein. Gorky, abroad as an émigré at the time, published a series of articles entitled "On the Russian Peasantry," a virulent attack on the bloody cruelties of the Revolution (these articles are not to be found in any edition of Gorky's works published in the U.S.S.R.). In the Russia of those years action had been brought against leftist SR's (Social Revolutionaries), and these former allies of the October Revolution had been condemned, their party prohibited. On the other hand, more and more publishing houses had been founded all over the country, and the NEP (the New Economic Policy), recently proclaimed, had given a certain freedom to private initiative. The literary life of 1922 truly offered a wealth and variety of creativity. We dug out of limbo and oblivion the names and works of writers whose books had been excluded from libraries during many decades. We collected an immense amount of material, but it was cut by our Party editors and censors. Half of the facts and names were thrown out, among them Gorky's articles "On the Russian Peasantry"; it wasn't permissible to "vilify the icon."

If Stalin's name was never once to be found on the pages of the principal newspapers of 1922, in 1934 it literally never left the pages of *Pravda*.

In that same year—1934—the first Congress of Writers took place, which put an end to a variety of styles and freedom of creativity, and abstract "Socialist realism" was accepted as the only formula for writing. This, in essence, meant that literature entered the service and control of the Party, which is what the Secretary General had wanted all along. While looking through the stenographic accounts of that first Congress of Writers (until then also excluded from libraries), I first came across Bukharin's report on poetry, delivered by him at the Congress. It was a brilliant report dealing with the essence of poetical art and given by a politician who spoke to writers as an equal to equals. Next to it Zhdanov's speech appeared pale and paltry.

At the Party's Seventeenth Congress—the so-called "Congress of Victors"—which had taken place that same year, hymns of praise to Stalin had been heard every day in every speech. Everything that year had seemed to promise economic improvements, peace and democracy in the country. But on the first of December Kirov was assassinated, and instead of democracy came terror, arrests, trials, and "purges," in which the delegates to the "Congress of Victors" perished along with Bukharin and the delegates to the first Congress of Writers.

My father not only did nothing to save his old comrades from destruction, but on the contrary seemed determined to pull up by the roots everyone who was talented and capable of independence of thought in the Party, the army, the arts, so that there should remain no colorful figures capable of attracting attention and acquiring popularity.

In 1956 Khrushchev was the first to denounce this and hint at Stalin's direct participation in Kirov's murder. He hinted at it, then got scared. Having promised further investigations of the mysterious circumstances surrounding the plot, he never again permitted any spoken or written reference to it.

I kept thinking: Is it possible? Is it possible? Wasn't Kirov an old friend? Hadn't he vacationed in Sochi with my father that very year? The awful answer came of its own volition: How about Bukharin? Wasn't he an old friend, too? Hadn't he been a summer guest at our dacha back in the days when Mama was still alive? And if it was possible for my father to accuse and execute Bukharin, what was there to stop him from using the club on Kirov? All this was so terrible that I felt like howling and running away from everyone, myself included. . . .

In September 1957 I changed my name from "Stalina" to "Alliluyeva"—under Soviet law children could bear either their father's or their mother's name. I could no longer tolerate the name of Stalin: its sharp metallic sound lacerated my ears, my eyes, my heart. . . .

I addressed myself to the President—Voroshilov at the time, an old friend of the family who had greatly loved my mother. The Chancery of the Presidium could hasten the lengthy process. What's more, I wanted to know what Voroshilov himself would have to say about my decision. He was not surprised and merely said, "You have done right."

I had wanted to take my mother's name when I graduated from school and entered the university. I told my father about it at the time. "Stalin," after all, was an adopted name, his political pseudonym. He didn't say anything, but I saw by the look he gave me that he had been stung, and I didn't continue the conversation. Now I was free to do as I pleased. Many people in the U.S.S.R. criticized me for it. The first official who saw my new documents looked frightened and asked me in a tone of commiseration: "So they forced you to change your name?" and refused to believe that it had been done at my own request.

In 1966 Isaac Deutscher's *Stalin: A Political Biography*, published in England in 1949, fell into my hands. Strange as it may seem, only then was I able to visualize for the first time the long history of the struggle within the Party and of the gradual process whereby the Party of Russian Communists had been transformed into a caricature of itself. Once again, I was making discoveries. . . .

I learned of the sharp differences between my father and Lenin during the last years of Lenin's life. All Soviet sources and political propaganda presented their relationship as an ideal friendship of many years. I already knew of Lenin's "Last Testament," in which he had demanded the removal of my father from the post of Secretary General. But now it appeared that this had been preceded by a long-standing difference on national problems. It also turned out that the idea of the kolkhoz (collective farming), which my father had always associated with Lenin's "cooperative plan," in reality had nothing to do with it. On this, too, their points of view had differed. And as I read on, I learned how power had gradually been gathered into one pair of hands, how adroitly former colleagues—opponents later on—had been outflanked. I learned of the inimitable cynicism and savagery with which possible rivals had been removed, and got a clear picture of the deterioration and ruin of the Party, ending in its complete enslavement to one man by means of terror: in sum, everything about which Lenin had sounded a warning.

I understood the great role played by Trotsky in the Party and the Revolution. Knowing my father well, I could now clearly perceive the origin of his anti-Semitism. Undoubtedly it had stemmed from the years of struggle for power with Trotsky and his followers, gradually transforming itself from political hatred to a racial aversion for all Jews bar none. Just to enumerate to oneself the names of all the Party members annihilated by my father on his way to power was enough to make one go mad. . . .

It was at this same time that I read Milovan Djilas' *Conversations with Stalin.* Someone had brought to Moscow the Australian edition of this book, and it was passed from hand to hand. As in the case of Deutscher's book, I didn't get it from a library but from friends. I was struck by Djilas' lively and authentic portrait of my father. I recognized his manners, his way of speaking, the whole setting. And the more authentic the details, the more convincing became the whole outline of Stalin's political cynicism even toward "fraternal" Socialist countries: let no popular leader stand out too far, be it Dimitrov or Tito, let absolute power not slip out of our hands. To this end "fraternal internationalism" was forgotten and the Soviet Union often behaved in the same way as Imperial Russia had done. And, of course, there was, too, the eternal vigilance of the secret police over each of those "brother-leaders"!

Some time shortly after 1956, *Ten Days That Shook the World*—John Reed's book about the October Revolution—was republished in Moscow. In the twenties it had been published in a Russian translation, and in the thirties taken out of circulation, together with all books in which nothing was said of Stalin's role in the October Revolution. This new edition carried the original introductions by Lenin and

Krupskaya: they both had considered Reed's book a very authentic, exact, and lively presentation of the events. But now the publishers added still another introduction—their own—saying that there was a great deal that John Reed, an American correspondent, hadn't known about Russia, hadn't understood and hadn't seen, and that, therefore, it was impossible to depend on the authenticity of his book. . . .

And yet John Reed had objectively described all the facts: the role of Trotsky in the Revolution, the role of leftist SR's, then the allies of the Bolsheviks. This differed too much from the official version adopted in the U.S.S.R. It was, therefore, deemed necessary to "correct" Lenin's introduction . . . and this after the Twentieth Congress!

A *Brief History of the CPSU* (Communist Party of the Soviet Union), re-edited, altered, and added to by Stalin in 1938, continued to serve for many years as the standard for distorted history. (The original version had been compiled by a group of authors.) My father needed this "text-book" to throw out of history, once and for all, those who had been in his way, those who had actually founded and created the Party and had brought about the Revolution; first and foremost among them, Trotsky, his greatest rival. Also, it eliminated those who had been in the opposition or had disagreed with him. They were called "agents of foreign imperialism." And those who had not taken part in any opposition but had simply been victims of the 1937-1938 "purges" were also tagged with the same label. It was the simplest and surest way of discrediting politicians in the eyes of the people. As for A *Brief History*, it had been conceived as a credo for the nation for many decades to come. That was the reason for my father's editing and altering it with such diligence. In this history of the Party, as rewritten by him, he appeared as Lenin's true, constant friend and comrade-in-arms, and no other names could be found in it. More than ten years have gone by since Khrushchev's speech and still an objective history of the Party and the Revolution remains to be written; and it will be a long time before such a history gets written in the U.S.S.R.

However, more important than books and documents was life itself around me. In those years I made many friends among people older than myself, who had lived through the thirties as mature men and women and had "learned history" on their own backs.

They were members of several intellectual families, interconnected by blood ties and friendships of many years: literary critics, musicians, astronomers, physicists, journalists, artists, all of them united by a creative life and by Russian culture passed down to them from their fathers and grandfathers. Among them were Russians and Jews, Russified Germans, Dutch, Italians—there was a time when Russia had indeed been an open country, receiving everyone. These people were at once creators and keepers of our culture during the dreadful deterioration that had surrounded them since their youth, and had carried the light with them throughout their lives, giving light to others.

Marina had spent seventeen years in prison and exile, although she had never been in any way connected with politics. In her youth she had worked as a surgical nurse; her first husband had been an artist. This small, fragile woman, gay as a lark, was more full of the love of life than most of my own contemporaries. God alone knows what she had had to endure; she herself considered her second arrest the worst of her trials: her first, ten-year term had come to an end, and it looked as if life was to begin anew, when suddenly—prison again, then exile to Kazakhstan. There, in a small village lost in the steppes, she took care of the sick, taught, and helped others to live. She found friends there— intellectual women like herself, who had had no connection with politics; translators from English, French, Dutch, who had been exiled because of their foreign origin. None of these women ever lost courage, they all returned after the

Twentieth Congress; I met them at Marina's. They had never stopped believing in life, had not grown disillusioned with mankind, bore no resentments, and had not hardened their hearts against anyone. Looking at them, I thought to myself that human souls were not destroyed by external blows but by some inner worm, if a man had been born with it in him. These wholesome natures had tried to help in every way possible the poor Kazakhstan villagers—just like the wives of the Decembrists who had followed their husbands, exiled to Siberia by Czar Nicholas I.

But how did it happen that in Soviet Russia a medieval tyranny had been reinstated by none other than "the Leader of the International Proletariat"? Is it possible that Russia was so hopeless that every progressive beginning was inevitably doomed to become its own antithesis? No. Nobody thought this; these people believed in Russia's great supply of energy and vigor, which would yet show itself and throw off the yoke with which the nation had been burdened.

My new friends were fond of me. They never hesitated to "think aloud" in my presence. "You are from our *Profsoyuz* (Trade Union)," they would say. This was the highest praise, and I knew that in their midst I was not "the dictator's daughter," but just a human being.

Marina's husband, a journalist, who had also spent many years in prison, often traveled through the country, visiting large factories and building projects. Everywhere he had seen economic disorganization, muddleheadedness, arbitrariness, theft. Exceptionally kind and responsive to the misfortunes of others, he managed somehow to help everyone, forever tramping government offices with requests and demands on behalf of others, something that under Soviet bureaucracy is not only difficult but exhausting.

He once took me with him on a journalistic trip to the extreme north—he wanted me to see how much things had changed there. The plane flew for hours over the tundra, that desert of snow, uncrossable on foot, from which no escape was possible. Norilsk, beyond the Arctic Circle, had sprung up near the Yenisei River after 1953, when the frightful concentration camp at the coal mines, worked by prisoners, had been closed. Many of the former sufferers remained to live and work in the new town as free men—the pay in the extreme north was double what it was anywhere else in the U.S.S.R. Norilsk had grown into a modern city, with shops, theaters, hotels, a public swimming pool. New houses had been built near the coal shafts, and instead of the former prison barracks they now had a club, a theater, a movie house. But the old mine settlement had retained its name—Kayerkan—which in the native tongue meant "black death." Yes, only after my father's death had a normal, free life come here. Nowhere else was this as evident as in Norilsk.

And it was Norilsk that I was particularly anxious to see, for my mother's brother Paul had been to that region in 1922 with the Urvantsev expedition, the first to discover the immense wealth here in coal and iron ore. Could Paul and the geologist Urvantsev ever have dreamed that their discovery would be turned into a concentration camp, into a Black Death?

I also made new friends among my own generation, whose critical minds had begun functioning long before mine. These were literary critics, poets, mathematicians. My contacts with Andrei Sinyavsky, a connoisseur of Russian art, were of great importance to me. Andrei never propagandized, never tried to convince, but his whole personality couldn't fail to influence those who knew him, making them think and search after truth.

All these young people had long ago made the discoveries which I was only beginning to make for myself.

"Just you follow the whole chain of the Party's self-exposures, revealing its odious self," they would say to me. "For forty years now those beasts have been devouring each other, just as in Dostoevsky's *The Possessed*. Except for

Lenin, all the other leaders have sooner or later been accused and condemned. It turns out that for forty years the country has been governed by scoundrels! No other party in the world has ever had such a performance of self-destruction."

Dostoevsky and his *Possessed* came to mind very often. Dostoevsky had suddenly captivated the young generation with his earnest, passionate sermon on religious humility, his hatred of Socialism. And fifty years of Soviet revolution had thoroughly prepared the soil for this: the nation was so soaked in blood that as a counterbalance the Sermon on the Mount suddenly resounded with unprecedented force. Young people went to church because it was one more way of saying "No!" to the Communist State.

In May 1962 I was baptized in the Orthodox Church. My baptism was a profound, symbolic event in my life. Of importance to me were not the dogmas of Christianity, nor the ritual, but the Eternal Life, the Eternal Good. The sacrament of baptism consists in rejecting evil, the lie. I believed in "Thou shalt not kill," I believed in truth without violence and bloodshed. I believed that the Supreme Mind, not vain man, governed the world. I believed that the Spirit of Truth was stronger than material values. And when all of this had entered my heart, the shreds of Marxism-Leninism taught me since childhood vanished like smoke. Now I knew that no matter how much sinful, cruel man might strengthen his power on earth, sooner or later Truth would triumph and the past glory would turn to dust.

And it was then that my father's whole life stood out before me as a rejection of Wisdom, of Goodness, in the name of ambition, as a complete giving of oneself to Evil. For I had seen how slowly, day by day, he had been destroyed by evil, and how evil had killed all those who stood near him. He had simply sunk deeper and deeper into the black chasm of the lie, of fury and pride. And in that chasm he at last had smothered to death.

I tried to show this downward trend of his soul in my

Twenty Letters to a Friend, which had been written shortly after my baptism and under its strong influence. This, my first effort at writing, was to me like a confession, and it also served to cleanse me of the memory of what had been.

When I was writing the *Twenty Letters,* the words of the priest who had baptized me were constantly with me: "Do not judge your father. A higher Judgment has already been passed on him: during his lifetime he raised himself too high, now there's nothing left of his glory. God straightens out and corrects what is wrong. But you can't; you are the daughter."

And I tried not to *judge* but to *show* how that to which my father had given his life had destroyed him. At the peak of his glory and power he had experienced neither happiness nor satisfaction; instead, he was tormented by an eternal fear. Having created a void around himself, he then had led up a blind alley all those who had gone on blindly believing in him.

A man is judged by history, by life, and by the highest justice of all. To us the Lord gives the strength to understand and accept the justice of the sentence. But no one can take away from me the right to have my own opinion of the so-called "Epoch of Stalinism." It had come to me at too great a price, had been reached through hardship and pain, and cleansed in tears. . . .

In prisons and concentration camps many men and women preserved their integrity and survived because they were religious and were convinced that Truth would triumph in the end. Others, even in prison, continued to believe that "Stalin did err but the Party could do no wrong." I couldn't agree with Communists who, having returned from prison, still clung to their fanatical faith in the "righteousness of the Party's cause." Where was it, this "righteous cause"?

For fifty years the Party had tried to do away with all independent thought in Russia, reduce the intellectual life to nothing, bury the freedoms which had existed under the

Czars, render all political activity tasteless to the many millions who had been double-crossed, blinded, and made to slave for a piece of bread. Those half-literate millions had been trained for centuries to suffer and have faith in the justice of their "little father" the Czar, to bow their heads before the yoke and the knout. As the great poet Pushkin wrote with bitter irony in his day:

> Graze on, ye peaceful sheep and cattle.
> The call of honour cannot grip
> Or charm you into freedom's battle.
> For you—the knife, the shearer's clip!
> Your heritage—the herdsman's rattle,
> The yoke, the chain, the drover's whip!*

And another poet, Maximilian Voloshin, wrote a century later, in 1922:

> Pray and endure. Accept
> A cross round your necks, a throne on your shoulders.
> Kitezh, submerged, still rings in our souls:
> Our unattainable dream.

The Revolution, basing itself on Karl Marx, gave the nation a new cross and a new throne. When the bloodiest of wars had come to an end, my father, in all sincerity, thanked the Russian people for their *patience*.

And well he might, for what other nation would ever have stood for this new yoke, this new Czar!

"The yoke . . . the rattle": sputniks, festivals, jubilees, and consciousness drowned in vodka on every occasion: "We are the greatest!" "We are the best, the fastest, the foremost! We shall overtake and conquer everyone!"

When the Party needed an atom bomb or a sputnik, nothing was spared, and the talent, in which Russia still abounds, conjured up what was needed. In such cases everything was forgotten: Jewish, German, noble origins, all forgiven. No

---

* *Poems of Pushkin*, selected and interpreted by Henry Jones, New York, Citadel Press, 1965.

matter who the creator, the Leader showered him with dachas, automobiles, prizes. But the recipients of such generosity and munificence were obliged to live under the strictest police supervision. Their names were kept a secret from their own people as well as from the rest of the world. And these captive creators were never allowed to know the joys of a well-deserved glory.

I had known some of them. Their position never changed even after 1953. Talented, charming people, who had brought fame and might to their country, lived like recluses. Not only were they forbidden to go abroad; they were not even permitted to meet in Moscow such innocent foreigners as the Indians. No one ever heard of the numerous secret prizes and decorations they had received. The most insignificant government official high-hatted them, little suspecting that he should be bowing and taking his hat off in their presence.

The government exploited brains when it needed them. Not a single Jew worked within the apparatus of the Central Committee—those were executive jobs. But when information was required on economics, foreign policies, philosophy, then such work was done for that same Central Committee by specialists—Jews. They merely supplied the information; they were never called in to discuss and decide. Often they signed their articles in magazines with Russian pseudonyms. Of course, compared with 1952, when they were about to be exiled from Moscow, even this represented an advance. But that was about the full measure of progress in the U.S.S.R. up to this day.

And when a talented young man with a special diplomatic education had been singled out for work in the Soviet Embassy in the U.S., Minister Gromyko turned his candidacy down for one reason only: a Jew. This happened in the year 1966, not in 1952!

"The Party's righteous actions?" Oh no! I could sooner agree with those who affirmed that the events of October

1917 had been a fatal, tragic mistake. Such a conclusion was far closer to what I felt as a result of everything I had seen with my newly opened eyes, of everything in history, which I had to learn all over again from the very beginning.

My own life in the Party was unsuccessful. In general, political activities are not much in my line, and in the U.S.S.R. they amounted to just a "semblance of activities," to idle talk at meetings. I was forced to join the Party in 1951 after many reproaches that it was "unseemly for the daughter of such a man to remain outside the ranks of the CPSU." I joined and paid my dues, silently sat for hours at meetings. Only twice in all that time was I moved to stand up and speak.

The first time was in 1954 (this was still before the Twentieth Congress) when the Party's criticism had fallen on Ilya Ehrenburg for his novella, *The Thaw*, in which for the first time mention was made of repressions in the U.S.S.R. and of the thaw that had come since 1953. Ehrenburg was accused of presenting Soviet life in much too dark a color, and of imitating "Western patterns." I stood up and said that I could not understand in what way Ehrenburg was to blame, when our own Party's press admitted the mistakes of the past, and innocent people, wrongly condemned, were returning from prisons.

Professor A. S. Myasnikov, the Party's well-known exponent of Gorky's works, referred to my statement as "irresponsible and politically immature." Myasnikov's book about Gorky's writings was an example of how history was "corrected," a regular habit in the U.S.S.R.: Gorky's criticism of the Revolution, of the Bolsheviks and Lenin was not to be found in Myasnikov's book.

The second occasion on which I stood up and spoke was even less successful. It happened in 1966 (ten years after the Twentieth Congress), when a regression to former methods had become discernible. The shameful trial of Sinyavsky and Daniel had just taken place, with its sentences

of seven and five years in concentration camps. In the Institute of World Literature, the leadership and the Party
committee started a campaign, not against protesters, but
against those who had dared abstain from approving the
sentences, who in some form or other had sympathized with
the condemned, and who, knowing Sinyavsky for many years,
still considered him an outstanding literary critic. A witch-
hunt was started against all those who had refused to sign
an official letter to the *Literary Gazette* approving the court
sentences. A certain research worker in the Institute, who
had publicly expressed his gratitude to Sinyavsky for his
help, was struck off the list and eventually expelled from the
Party. Older members of the Institute said that the sickening
atmosphere reminded them too much of 1937.

I protested at a Party meeting, saying that it was shameful
to treat members of the Institute in this way; that the trial
had been a mistake; that with writers one had to speak
professionally as one of them, and how was this to be done if
we were not even allowed to read their works? We had no
right to throw groundless political accusations in the faces
of our colleagues; and in conclusion I said that everyone was
free to sign or not to sign any declaration, no matter what it
might be.

The meeting was tempestuous. It lasted two days. Many
supported me, but the Director of the Institute, Professor
I. I. Anisimov, accused us all of "political immaturity." In
literary circles the "politically mature" Ivan Ivanovich
Anisimov had been long since nicknamed "Vanka-Cain" for
his betrayal in 1937 of numerous fellow writers.

The ugliest feature of Soviet life was the endless dissimulation and double-facedness infused into the Soviet
people from their schoolroom days, so that it became almost second nature. People not belonging to the Party
were never heard, they were not called upon to express an
opinion; but Party members and Komsomols were in duty
bound to stand up and express themselves. It had become a

habit with them to express one opinion aloud while convinced of something quite different. And the same man, half
an hour later, would be telling friends in the corridors his
real opinion.

What an ominous return to the past this closed trial of
the writers had been, and all the circumstances surrounding
it! I couldn't bear to remain any longer in the Institute. In
the summer of 1966 I left it, to the delight of the directors.

Now I was at home, without a "collective," alone with my
children and with a hopelessly ill Brajesh Singh.

This man had brought into my life the real wisdom of
India, the kind I had read about. I had long ago fallen under
the spell of Mahatma Gandhi's life, for whom nonviolence
and "persistence in truth" were not only an abstract teaching
—Indian philosophy had taught it for thousands of years—
but an everyday mode of life. When living India entered my
home, I learned the real meaning of "Harm not thy neighbor." And again I thought about those two Communists—
Brajesh Singh and my father.

What two approaches to life could have differed more
drastically? The tolerance of one, the dogmatism of the
other: calm and fear, trust and suspiciousness, modesty and
ambition, forgiveness and revenge, kindness and wrath, the
strength of the spirit and the strength of arms—Singh's
character, his life, his death, were not only an antithesis
but also a challenge to the entire bureaucratic system of
the Soviet State. That is why that State rose up against this
harmless, quiet man. He died, but he won.

He vanquished them all forever in my heart, and in the
hearts of many who had known him in Moscow. No!
Khrushchev could never explain anything to me, and he
wasn't able to free me from the past. The kindly wisdom of
India liberated me from my spiritual bondage. All that was
left to do was to cut myself off from physical and formal ties.

Nothing had been more terrifying in the U.S.S.R. than
when, with the removal of Khrushchev, people sensed a

reverse movement, a rolling back toward norms more habitual and convenient to those in power. Once again I would
hear, "Your father was a great man! Just wait, he will be
remembered yet!" The government suddenly became interested in how I lived; Kosygin and Suslov insisted that I
return to the "collective," declaring that now I would be
"treated differently." But this "different treatment" was just
what I feared most, having been all too familiar with it in
the past.

Shortly before my departure for India the directress of
the Stalin Museum in Georgia came to see me, proud that
Brezhnev had sanctioned the reopening of the museum. In
the presence of this poor woman, whose joy I was unable to
share, I felt embarrassed. I understood too well that if
Brezhnev succeeded in "reinstating Stalin's merits," it would
be disastrous not just for the U.S.S.R. but for the world.

The directress continued to exult, inviting me to stay at
her house in Gori, while I vividly pictured to myself what
would be going on all around me if I did. I felt sorry for her
and for other Georgians, still drugged by the lie which at a
distance had a majestic appearance, easily acceptable to
simple souls. This was well understood by conservatives in
the Central Committee: they hoped to play on just such
feelings.

And unfortunately not conservatives alone. To my
astonishment even Mikoyan—that same Mikoyan who had
given me Khrushchev's speech to read—had now forgotten
what he himself had said at the Twentieth Congress. During
the summer of 1966 he invited me with my children to his
dacha and several times, during dinner, spoke of my father
in warm, conciliatory terms. And when we were leaving, he
brought out a large bundle and gave it to my Katie, saying,
"Here's a present for you—a rug. You can hang it up on your
wall." At home we unrolled the rug: woven into it was a
portrait of my father. Katie looked embarrassed and was glad
when I rolled it up and put it away. In her consciousness my

father existed neither as a grandfather nor a "Great Leader."
She had not been taught anything like that.

It was hard for my father's former comrades-in-arms to
forget the past. Together they had created all that later they
had called a "cult of personality." Together they had crushed
the opposition, shut their eyes when comrades were being
destroyed. They had supported the "cult" because it spelled
power for them, too. And how reluctant they were to lose
that power! Hence their inability to write an authentic history of the Party: it would have revealed their appalling
nakedness.

How unanimously they all threw themselves on Solzhenitsyn in order to silence him about his one day: *One Day in
the Life of Ivan Denisovich*! How scared they were that the
whole world would learn of the thousand days in the lives of
millions of other martyrs!

The eleven years of Khrushchev's rule will be remembered
for his effort to call things by their real names. The timid
half-efforts of this vital, jolly, pigheaded man broke the
silence of many years. The ice broke and was on the move.
No one could stop it now. More and more the angry
waters of the river could be seen through the widening
fissures. . . .

It was more difficult for me than for the rank-and-file
Stalinists to free myself of myths and lies. All that the term
implied had always been alien to me. But it was hard for
me to realize what my father had really done to Russia,
simply because such a realization was too terrifying for me.
And the deeper I saw into the truth, the more shattering it became. Even when I had already learned a good deal, it still
seemed to me for a long time that my father had been a
victim of this horror rather than its author and perpetrator.

No, others were its victims. Millions of them. My mother
among them. He gave his name to this bloodbath of absolute dictatorship. He knew what he was doing. He was
neither insane nor misled. With cold calculation he had

cemented his own power, afraid of losing it more than of anything else in the world. And so his first concentrated drive had been the liquidation of his enemies and rivals. The rest followed later. In postrevolutionary Russia he had resurrected the absolutism, terror, prisons, bureaucratic government officials and police of over a hundred years ago, and had revived the chauvinism and imperialistic foreign policy of the Imperial Government. In a country in which democracy in 1917 had turned out to be a miscarriage of history and had died at its inception, such actions only served to strengthen his power and glory. In England, France, America, nothing of the kind could ever have sprung into being. Totalitarian ideologies create totalitarian regimes, and in this sense Communism doesn't differ in any way from Fascism.

It was this kind of force that had seized power in 1917. My father was the instrument of this ideology. Lenin laid the foundation for a one-party system, for terror and the inhuman suppression of all dissenters. He was the true father of everything that Stalin later developed to its furthest limits. All efforts to whiten Lenin and make a saint of him are useless: fifty years of history tell a different story. Stalin did not discover or devise anything new. Having inherited from Lenin a totalitarian Communist regime, he became its ideal embodiment, the most complete personification of power without democracy, built on the suppression of millions of human lives. And those who managed to survive physically were reduced to slavery, deprived of the right to create and think. In this land, enslaved and half-choked to death, leaning on a cowardly and mute clique of accomplices, he created his own version of pseudo Socialism. And an old witticism of the twenties became incarnate truth: "To build Socialism—*you can*, but to live in it—*you cannot*." The construction of this half-prison, half-barracks was the sum total of my father's "great historical merits."

Once this had fully sunk in, there was no way back. It

became impossible to shut my eyes to all that went on around me. And it was not enough simply to condemn, then wash my hands and step aside. It was easy to condemn Stalinism as a political phenomenon and a period in history—it was too repulsive. No, I had to do something myself, live differently. In the U.S.S.R. shades of the past always surrounded me in a vicious circle. But here, in India, it became clear that if I found the strength not to go back, therein would lie my salvation; and only then would another life be mine for the taking. Fate itself had laid the choice before me. . . .

I fully understood that for me this meant a point of no return to Communism in general. So much the better! My position would be infinitely more honest than it could ever have been in the U.S.S.R. There, a "collective" would again be awaiting me. To go back and openly break with the Party, to criticize and protest, would only mean ruining the lives of my children. On the other hand, secret underground activities, conspiracies, cloak-and-dagger existences have always repelled me.

No, I could only live and act in the open, as a free person, and in such a way as to have my children completely separated from me, bearing no responsibility for my actions. . . .

For me all this was possible only outside the U.S.S.R.

The Only Way Out

THE SMALL PLANE flew from Lucknow to Delhi with a stop at Kanpur. The airport at Kanpur was a long way from the city itself. Passengers got out to stretch their legs, strolling along the dry, scorched field. I strolled about, too, alone, looking at the passengers and trying to imagine how I would go to the U.S. Embassy—or would I? I wasn't sure.

The plane for Moscow would be leaving on March 8. This was the fifth. Ahead of me still two days in Delhi . . . I would buy something for my children—as my return home began to shape itself into a tangible reality, I longed more than ever to see them. A whole two and a half months—never before had we been parted for so long. And yet the idea of returning to my former life, of settling down again to what had been, was appalling. These contradictory feelings seemed to grow at the same time, with equal force. I felt torn in two and partly anesthetized; though no one could ever have guessed the inner strain beneath the appearance of calm. I felt as if every muscle in me were tensed in readiness for a leap; that only a light push, a last straw, was needed to turn the scale to a final decision. . . .

The "last straw" came next day at the Soviet Embassy, when I met with representatives of the Soviet world—a world of which I had already lost the habit.

Dinesh met me at the Palam Airport. It was kind of him to do so. He was so happy about my leaving that he had cast off his unapproachable "maharaja's" mask and was again the charming young man he knew so well how to be. He tried to convince me that next year he would arrange an invitation for me to return to India with my children. Now he invited me to stay at his house until my departure, but this I refused; I needed these remaining days to myself, in some neutral spot, where I could collect myself and make up my mind—and if I decided to seek this refuge, the Soviet Hostel was close to the American Embassy. No one there would be asking me where and why I was going.

My main concern was for no one to know or suspect anything as long as possible. At present I wished to be absolutely independent, with not a soul between me and my inner voice. I had to hear it clearly. For if I did decide to seek this refuge, I knew that there would never again be a way back.

I spent the afternoon of March 5 at Dinesh's house. That evening I dined with Kaul and his family. Kaul sounded like an echo of Dinesh: I had to return to Moscow; later they would arrange an invitation for me and my children. He, too, seemed hardly able to wait for my departure and wanted to know my every step during those last two days in Delhi.

"Come again tomorrow evening," he said. "In the afternoon I'm attending a reception at the Soviet Embassy with Marshal Zakharov, but I'll be home early. Preeti will pick you up. And on the seventh—your last evening—I'll arrange a farewell dinner for you." Then, quite unexpectedly, he asked: "And your manuscript? Is it with you?"

Obeying some instinct of self-preservation, I answered, "No! I sent it to Paris."

Kaul was puffing thoughtfully on his pipe, blowing clouds of smoke, and I quickly changed the conversation. I was in deadly fear lest the Soviet Embassy should learn of the existence of my manuscript and take it from me. I also dreaded a sudden guess on Kaul's part as to what was on my mind. It seemed as if at any moment now he might give me just one look and guess. . . .

When I returned that evening to Dinesh's house, everyone had gone to bed. On the morning of the sixth, just as we got through breakfast, Surov arrived. Dinesh invited me to lunch the next day; and Surov and I left for the Soviet Hostel.

No sooner had I settled in Surov's car and we had started talking Russian than I was seized by an indescribable boredom. And there it was again—the hostel: the same hostess-nurse with a Ukrainian accent whom I had seen in December. She passed me on to another equally chubby Ukrainian woman. The dining room was in a bustle; they were preparing for a soiree that evening on the occasion of International Women's Day, as I perceived from an announcement on the wall—a lecture, an artistic program. The Soviet colony was leading its own life, separated from India by an unscalable barrier.

I had completely lost the habit of this sort of life. How dismally dull they all were, this dining room, this club, this eternal International Women's Day—just another excuse to get drunk! They would all be drunk this evening, bored to death as they were stewing in their own juice.

I stepped out into the yard. Wives and children of embassy employees sat on benches. Not one friendly face. Not a single smile. All of them fat, overfed. Dressed far better than in Moscow, though. But then, that was why they had come abroad—to buy things and then resell them on the Moscow black market, at the same time vociferously running down capitalism. Oh, you hypocrites! All of them Party members, no doubt. Naturally! Else they would never have been allowed to be here and buy their glad rags. But at night, in low whispers, from lip to ear, they would mock the Party, too.

I grew gloomier by the moment. Thoroughly depressed, I went to the Ambassador's lunch, to which Surov had also been invited with his wife. The lunch was held in Ambassador Benediktov's home. Everything in this house bore the marks of a conventional expensive lack of taste—carpets everywhere, bad pictures on the walls in heavy gilt frames. Everything was sumptuous and resplendent, but there was nothing to rest one's eyes on. Just as sumptuous and ponderous was Madame Benediktov, with her formal smile. And of course Ivan Alexandrovich Benediktov himself, tall, of immense proportions, and with a face as immobile as a monument. We had never had the occasion to meet in Moscow. We were seeing each other for the first time. Everyone was most polite. Everyone must have felt happy that at last I was returning to Moscow and the embassy could send a report on the successful conclusion of the "enterprise." With a grand sweep of his hand Benediktov gestured toward the dinner table, groaning under a mass of hors d'oeuvres, bottles—mostly cognac—and all kinds of food.

One's eyes grew dim from such abundance. For the past weeks I had been fully satisfied with the scarce but tasty Indian food, a glass of water from the well and a cup of hot Himalayan tea. I had eaten no meat. Besides, there was no meat to be had in a remote village like Kalakankar. A lenten, vegetarian diet suited me on account of my kidneys; also, I always felt better when I drank no wine and ate no meat. I do not like vodka, with its concomitant slice of herring, because my brother drank too much of it and ended up a hopeless alcoholic. I refused almost all the rich food and drinks that were being offered me. Benediktov, barely able to hide his irritation, growled, "Don't go getting too accustomed to those Indian habits! Here, have a tiny slice of herring in the good old Russian way!"

"Yes, we can't get on without our Russian food," Madame Benediktov sang out. "We do eat a great deal, a great deal, there's no gainsaying it!"

Surov and his wife were digging into their food with the utmost relish. All of them ate as though they were famished.

Surov's young wife had a pretty face, but there was something cold and metallic about her eyes, which she withdrew every time I glanced in her direction. I had lost a good deal of weight in Kalakankar and was glad of it, but to these people I doubtless appeared starved.

"But eat, eat, look how thin you are!" cried Madame Benediktov in a kind of irritated frenzy.

All I could muster was a cold and crisp "No, thank you." I wanted desperately to get away from these people.

Surov suddenly found a way of steering the conversation into other channels: "Come to our soiree at the club this evening. My wife here will be making a report on International Women's Day. Afterward there'll be a concert."

"We are full of planned entertainment here," his wife piped in, brightening visibly: a typical Party activist, this one.

Report! Planned entertainment! Couldn't they live without all those false, collective goings-on?

How completely I had lost the taste of it all, and how quickly, too! During the past two and a half months I had been myself, had breathed freely. And the people around me had not been part of a mechanism. They were poor, hungry; they had a thousand worries; but all of them were free to say and think what they wanted, free to choose what they preferred.

India had set free something in me. Here I had ceased feeling like a piece of "government property," which in the U.S.S.R. I had been all my life. And although I fully realized that in the eyes of the Indian Government I was still such a piece of property—I had no illusions on that score—inside of me I had been liberated once and for all from that eternal subjugation.

The conversation at table flagged. The Benediktovs were nothing but transients in India. In two months of life at Kalakankar I had seen and understood far more than they ever would. All they longed for was to "complete their term," buy a heap of luxuries, and return home. To Benediktov his service in India was nothing but an exile, to which Khrushchev had subjected him after demoting him from Minister of Agriculture. He had no feeling for this foreign land, in which he felt hot and bored.

After a long session at the dinner table we finally moved into the drawing room, and the Ambassador said, "Well, I think you must be pleased with your trip. As you see, concessions *were* made, you stayed longer than you were supposed to. It seems to me you have nothing to complain about." Stressing the last words, he gave me a heavy look out of a pair of sly, ill-natured eyes.

I swallowed the admonition, the look, and kept my temper. At that moment I had but one thought—to get back my passport, which had been taken from me upon my arrival in Delhi. I had no other official identification. I asked the Ambassador to return it to me now, with not much hope of it being done; according to regulations, they were supposed to return it only at the airport at the time of departure. But Ambassador Benediktov was so gladdened by my approaching departure that his joy outweighed all other considerations. In a sonorous voice he commanded Surov to bring the passport, then personally handed it to me, saying, "And we shall send a telegram to your children, so that they can meet you."

This was not welcome at all. I had purposely decided not to send them a wire, but of course there was no question of arguing the point with Benediktov.

He invited me to the soiree at the club. I refused under the pretext of a dinner with Kaul. Benediktov made a wry face.

"That Kaul! An English agent!" He dropped the words casually as something well known. I could only swallow a smile; Indian newspapers accused Kaul of being "the Soviet Embassy's right hand."

"I knew his daughter in Moscow. She is picking me up," I tried to explain, but the Ambassador only shrugged. He didn't care what I did in these last days.

Nor did I care what he and his Madame had to say. They were having trouble in hiding their irritation with my every word and action. I took my passport, bade them all farewell, and returned to the hostel. Alone at last, I stretched out on the bed and shut my eyes.

This was about three in the afternoon.

So what was I going to do?

If I were to fly to Moscow the day after tomorrow, then I should rest now, spend the evening at Kaul's as arranged, and tomorrow attend to my last shopping. If not . . . if not . . .

Suddenly I got up, began hastily repacking my things from my large suitcase to the smaller one. I couldn't really drag that big one with me to the American Embassy. Though of course I could take a taxi. Yes, that would be much better, and no one would know where I was going! Anyone could call a taxi, it looked so natural.

Of a sudden I dropped everything and went to the front gate; there was a watchman there, an Indian, he would probably know how to call a taxi. The watchman, in a turban, gave me the number—75-777—and showed me where the telephone was in a nearby building under the staircase.

I returned to my room, laid my manuscript at the very bottom of my suitcase and quickly packed everything else on top of it. First thing tomorrow after breakfast I would call a taxi. They all knew here that I was due at Dinesh's tomorrow—I could be carrying almost anything with me in a small suitcase. The large one, with half of my belongings, would remain here in the room—it would take them a long time to find out where I was. . . . And now I must rest.

But there was no rest. I got up again, switched on the electric iron, deciding suddenly, I really don't know why, to iron the green Indian kerchief I was taking with me. Prakash had given it to me. She had also knitted a sweater for Katie. All the presents for my children were packed in my big overnight bag, and this brought my thoughts back to Joseph, Katie, and Helen. Would they ever get those presents—a memory from India and from me? I doubted that the embassy would send my things back to Moscow, although by standing regulations they really were supposed to. . . .

I sat and gazed at the bag with the presents and my resolution began to fade. Those tinkling bracelets for Katie and her friend Toni, I had chosen them in Lucknow in those little shops of Nazir-Abad. Those gold-embroidered slippers, too, for Joseph and Helen—and then that funny hookah I had bought for my son in Benares . . .

I sat, my hands fallen listless at my sides. . . .

The electric iron had grown very hot and was crackling. I began ironing the silk kerchief, and this brought me back to my coat, my suitcase, figuring how I would carry these things to the taxi. The suitcase would be in my right hand, my coat over the other arm—it would come in useful, for it got cool in the evening.

Yes, it would be better to do it all in the evening. Why did I ever think of the morning? In the daytime everything could be seen; now it was getting dark, lights were few. Yes, it must happen today, at once; why was I putting it off? I must decide quickly—of what use another dinner at Kaul's? When was Preeti supposed to pick me up—at seven, at eight? I didn't remember. If she came, I would have to go with her. I must leave before she got here. How much time was there left?

It was shortly after six. Darkness had fallen. I felt I had to go now, without delay. Some inner force began hurrying me, speeding me on: quick, quick, now, today. Tomorrow nothing would come of it—you would change your mind. In the morning there were always too many people around— no, now, at once, quick!

I went out to call a taxi. It was dark in the recess under the stairs. I had trouble dialing the number. The Indian at the other end didn't understand where he was to go: "Russian Embassy?" "No, no, the Russian Residence!" I kept repeating, the way the watchman had told me to do.

I went to the gate again to ask him how long it would take the taxi to get here. He said they were nearby, it would take no time at all. I stood outside the gate, stepping from one foot to the other, pacing to and fro. Automobiles arrived, guests were gathering for the club soiree to listen to that report, partake of those "planned entertainments." No one paid the slightest attention to me—there was nothing un- usual in a person standing there, waiting.

My nerves, though, were on edge. What if Preeti should arrive first? I jumped every time the lights of a car appeared: who was it? Preeti or the taxi? The taxi didn't come.

I kept glancing at my watch; I didn't know how long, but I must have stood there for twenty minutes, maybe more. Still the taxi didn't come. Neither did Preeti. But I am stubborn by nature, thank God! I returned to the telephone, called again, and came back to the gate.

In five minutes, from around a corner on my left, ap- peared a rickety little old car—a Delhi taxi. A Sikh in a turban sat grinning at the wheel, another next to him. They opened the door. "One minute," I said, and ran to my room after my suitcase and coat.

The taxi driver hadn't cut off the motor, the door was still wide open when I returned.

"Do you know the American Embassy?"

"Why, yes, it's next door."

We turned into a dark alley—a short cut—how clever of the driver! We passed behind the Soviet Embassy, turned around a corner of the U.S. Embassy, and a minute later stood parked at its brightly lit door. I gave the Sikh a few rupees, and somewhat unsteadily climbed the long wide stairs. Only when I had crossed the threshold, something let go inside, something loosened up, and of a sudden everything became so easy and simple. . . .

Beside a small table stood a tall, young, blue-eyed Marine. At first he began to explain that no one was there, but when he saw the red cover of my Soviet passport, he must have realized that something was afoot. Quickly he led me into a small room adjoining the front hall. I sat down in a chair near a wall, put down my suitcase, laid my coat on it, and waited—I didn't know for whom, for what. Nor did I care: come what may.

Like a swimmer, I had at last reached the opposite shore, had touched bottom and could take a deep breath. It was an unknown shore, but I didn't ask myself what it held for me.

How wonderful to have reached it alive and unhurt! As for details, no need to worry: nothing would be worse than what had been. Everything that lay ahead was bound to be better than the shore I had left behind.

So all right, let us step into the next room, let us talk, let us make everything clear, let us write it down. I have nothing to hide. I came here without a shield or visor, my heart wide open. I have made my decision. Now it is up to you to choose and decide.

II. INTERLUDE

AN INTERLUDE

Encounter with the West

THE GLASS DOOR of the American Embassy in Delhi was my entrance into the Western world—a world I had never met with before. I had no idea how it would receive me. The embassy staff knew nothing about me. And on this evening of March 6 we looked at each other in surprise, at once smiling and puzzled.

The month and a half that followed was a time of mutual acquaintance. I had expected to meet with kindness and help, and I did, sensing instantly that something would be done, something would "shape itself," without my worrying about it, just trusting to the course of events. I had not been mistaken in knocking on this door. I stepped into a stream that carried me smoothly, swiftly, so that on April 21 I arrived at Kennedy Airport, having obtained in that short time well-disposed friends in the United States, a tourist visa for six months, experienced lawyers, and a publisher for the manuscript I had brought with me in that smaller suitcase of mine. After the endless proscriptions, secrecy, compulsion, and humiliation of human dignity under which I had been used to live, it now seemed as if some guardian angel were carrying me on his wings.

After reading at Kalakankar Ambassador Chester Bowles' book, *Ambassador's Report*, I imagined its author as the sort of man who would understand and do something to help me. I didn't exactly know what he could do, having no idea of the diplomatic formalities and political difficulties in which we were entangled and out of which some way had to be found. On that evening of the sixth the Ambassador was ill. He was at home and in bed when he was informed of the "Soviet defector." I never actually got to see him in Delhi. Not till four months later, in July, did we meet at his home in Essex, Connecticut. How much there was to tell each other, reminiscing about that evening, so memorable to both of us! There can be no question but that I owed my life first and foremost to the trust and kindness of Ambassador Bowles, who that evening took it on himself to make a quick decision.

He told me much later that he had been faced at the time with three alternatives: (a) to refuse me help and refuge, which he could not envisage, this being contrary to American traditions and to his own principles; (b) to grant the defector refuge in Roosevelt House in Delhi, informing the governments of India and the U.S.S.R. accordingly, and awaiting the decision of a court of justice, thereby creating a lot of noise in the press and unavoidable conflicts between the United States, the U.S.S.R., and India; and, finally, (c) to help me leave India speedily, legally, and quietly. This was what he decided on.

Due to Ambassador Benediktov's imprudence, I had my foreign passport with me, valid for two years. This simplified matters considerably. All I needed was an Indian exit visa in order to leave Delhi in any plane, in any direction. The Australian line Qantas had a flight for Rome scheduled for that same night.

Chester Bowles, from his sickbed, took counsel with his colleagues, who were with me in one of the embassy's rooms and took turns leaving it to call him up. At that moment their chief concern was my authenticity: What if this person were not who she claimed to be, perhaps a lunatic; or quite possibly some machination of Soviet Intelligence . . . ?

I am deeply grateful to all four men: George Huey, the Consul; Robert Rayle, the Second Secretary; Roger Kirk; and, needless to say, the Ambassador himself. They took a chance, they believed me, and, without waiting for an answer from Washington, whisked me out of Delhi at once. What a relief it must have been to all four to learn, when I was already in Rome, that everything I had said had been true and not a hoax.

After the Marine guard had left me in that small room adjoining the front hall, the first man I saw was George Huey—tall, stout, wearing a bright loose shirt. A little later two young men appeared: Second Secretary Rayle, in glasses, and Roger Kirk, dark-haired, wearing a light-blue jacket. To me all three looked like those typical Americans I had seen in movies.

I gave them my passport, explaining shortly who I was, how I happened to be in India, saying that I did not want to return to the U.S.S.R. and asking them to help me in this. Each one, in turn, peered into my passport, in which I was identified as "Citizeness Svetlana Iosifovna Alliluyeva"— and Consul Huey asked, "So you say your father was Stalin? *The* Stalin?" "Yes," I replied, without detecting anything special about his tone.

We spoke English. They were friendly and polite. And it never occurred to me that my appearance was somewhat like that of a visitor from Mars, or that my authenticity might be doubted.

They suggested that I write a declaration, explaining my motivations and adding a brief history of my life, commencing with the date and place of my birth. For this we all moved to the second floor and settled down in an empty study.

First of all, in order to avoid anyone's suspicions, I asked

permission to call up Preeti Kaul and give her some excuse
for not joining them that evening. Preeti had already returned home. She had been very surprised not to find me
at the hostel's gate. I gave fatigue as an excuse, promising
to spend the following evening with them, as arranged.
Everything was in order. If only Preeti had known where
I was calling from!

I wasn't in the least worried about the Soviet Embassy;
they were holding a reception for a military delegation,
everyone was drinking, no one would give me a thought.
Other embassy employees were drinking at the club in celebration of International Women's Day. To them, too, I was
of no concern. Only tomorrow would they discover my
absence, when I would no longer be here. . . .

As a result of such a happy ending to all the emotions of
that long day, I developed a splitting headache. They
brought me tea and aspirin. There was an unpleasant buzzing in the room and I asked what it was. "An air conditioner,"
they said, surprised at my ignorance.

I felt strangely calm and at home with these three nice
young men, who didn't seem at all like foreigners to me. I
dare say that during the past two and a half months in
India I had grown accustomed to accepting all people as
human beings. In these Americans, as I had with Indians, I
was looking not for what distinguished them from us Russians but rather for what we had in common. And now they
seemed to look like people I had known long ago.

Well, so what could I write for them? How was I to explain what had brought me here? After a few cups of tea
with aspirin, I wrote the following document in English:

I was born in Moscow on the 28th of February, 1926. My father
was Joseph Stalin, my mother Nadezhda Allilueva. My mother
died in November, 1932, and till I was sixteen years old I'd never
known that she had committed suicide. She was twenty-two years
younger than my father, and he knew her parents since the

nineties: her parents were also involved in a social-democratic movement. They were married after the October Revolution.

My mother was the second wife of my father; he was married firstly to Ekaterina Svanidze, a Georgian, who had soon died, and she left a son, Jacob. Though he was much older than myself, he was my greatest friend, much more than my own brother Vassily.

I graduated from the ten-year school in 1943 in Moscow and entered the Moscow University the same year. I graduated from the University in 1949 in Modern History.

As a student I married my first husband, Mr. Gregory Morosov, also a student then. In May 1945 our son Joseph was born. My husband was then a student of the Foreign Affairs Institute. We divorced in 1947, and my son stayed with me. Mr. G. Morosov is now dealing with International Law, and recently he published his book on UNO, which is known in America. He goes often abroad to meet his colleagues, he has been to Canada, to Paris, to Warsaw. My father never approved of our marriage, because Gregory Morosov was a Jew, and my father had never met him. But he never insisted on our divorce.

In 1949 I married my second husband, Mr. Yuri Zhdanov, the son of Andrey Zhdanov. My father was very much attached to him and it was his wish that we should marry. But the marriage was very unhappy, and although in May 1950 our daughter Katherine was born, we were very soon divorced.

Since then I was living with my two children. I did a little work, research work on history and on Russian philology. Also later I did translation work for the publishing house. Some of my translations were published in Moscow: (1) *The Munich Conspiracy*, by Andrew Rothstein (London); (2) *Man and Evolution*, by John Lewis (London). Also I did a little work for the Moscow Children's Literature Publishers translating from English.

The death of my father in March 1953 brought little change in my life. I lived then separately from him (he stayed for the last twenty years in his country house in Kuntsevo, near Moscow). My life was simple, as it always was. It was the same after his death.

My brother Jacob was captured by the Germans as a war

prisoner in August 1941 in Byelorussia. When my father went to Berlin in 1945, to take part in the Potsdam Conference, he had been told there that the Germans had shot Jacob before the American troops liberated the camp. Some officer from Belgium sent a letter to my father then, saying that he had been a witness of Jacob's death. There was also many years later, the article of a Scottish officer in some British magazine, about the same fact. But there has never been any official notification to Jacob's family from the army unit to which he belonged. Sometimes his daughter, his wife, and myself do believe that he might be alive somewhere; so many Russian war prisoners stayed in other countries till nowadays.

My brother Vassily was a pilot, after the Second World War he was a general and the Commander of Moscow District Air Force. After my father's death he left the army and soon he was arrested. This happened because he had threatened the government, he talked that "father was killed by his rivals" and all things like that, and always many people around him—so they decided to isolate him. He stayed in jail till 1961, when, completely sick, he was released by Khrushchev, and soon he died. The cause of his death was alcoholism, which had completely ruined his health, and of course, seven years of prison. But till now people do not believe that he is dead and often ask me whether it is true that he is in China.

Actually, nowadays I do not have any close relations, except for my two children, Joseph and Katherine.

Now about India.

In 1963, being in Kuntsevo Hospital, I met the Indian Communist Mr. Brajesh Singh who came to Moscow for treatment by invitation of the CPSU. Such invitations are given every year to all Communist Parties of the world.

Brajesh Singh belonged to the ancient aristocratic family of India. His nephew, Mr. Dinesh Singh is nowadays State Minister for the External Affairs. Mr. Brajesh Singh joined the Communist Party of India in the early thirties, in Europe. He had been many times in England, in Germany, in France, and in those days he had become a close friend and follower of M. N. Roy. Being a very educated person in Hindu and also in European ways he influenced everyone who had the chance to meet him.

He went back to India in 1963 (from Moscow), and then returned to Moscow again in 1965, to work in the Progress Publishing House as a translator. Since that time he stayed with me, in my house and we were planning to get married. We were planning also to go to India together after his contract with the publishers was over in three years.

But the Soviet Government, and Mr. Kosygin personally, strongly objected to our marriage. Although by our law marriages with foreigners are allowed in U.S.S.R.; but not for a person like myself. We were not allowed to do that because the Soviet Government had feared that one day I might go away to India with my husband and might stay there.

Mr. Brajesh Singh stayed in Moscow for one year and a half. He lived with us, we all—myself and my children—loved him very much, and he was indeed a respected and beloved member of the family. But all those troubles and obstacles were a great shock for him. His health had always been weak (he suffered from asthma for many years), and in Moscow it became worse and worse. On October 31st, 1966, he expired in Moscow. It was my duty to come to India to convey his ashes here to be immersed in the Ganges.

For coming to India with this sad mission I had to get special permission from Mr. Kosygin. He gave it, but only for two weeks. Somehow I did my best to stay longer, because in India I met my husband's relatives and friends, and I began anxiously to think about staying in India. But I found it impossible—neither the Soviet Government nor the Indian Government would allow me to do that.

I must say that there are not only these reasons why I do not want to return back to the U.S.S.R.

Since my childhood I have been taught Communism, and I did believe in it, as we all did, my generation. But slowly, with age and experience I began to think in a different way. The years of Khrushchev, some liberties, the XX Congress of the CPSU, had done much for my generation. We have begun to think, to discuss, to argue, and we were not so automatically devoted anymore to the ideas which we were taught.

Also religion had done a big change in me. I was brought up in a family where there was never any talk of God. But when I had become a grown-up person I found it impossible to exist without God in one's heart. I had come to that myself, without anybody's help or preaching. But that was a great change to me because since that moment the main dogmas of Communism had lost their significance for me.

I do believe in the power of intellect in the world—no matter in which country you live. The world is too small and the human race is too small in this universe. Instead of struggle and unnecessary bloodshed people should better work more together for the progress of humanity. This is the only thing which I can take seriously—the work of the teachers, scientists, educated priests, doctors, lawyers—their work all over the world, notwithstanding states and borders, political parties and ideologies. There are no capitalists and Communists for me—there are good people and bad people, honest and dishonest, and in whatever country they live—people are the same everywhere, and their best expectations and morals are the same. My father was a Georgian, my mother was of a very much mixed nationality—although I had lived all my life in Moscow, I believe that the home can be everywhere. True, India was my love since my youth, maybe because what Mahatma Gandhi taught is best in accordance with my beliefs—not Communism.

I hope one day I will be able to come to India again and stay here forever.

My children are in Moscow and I do understand now that I might not see them for years. But I know they will understand me. They also belong to the new generation in our country which does not want to be fooled with old ideas. They also want to make their own conclusions about life.

Let God help them. I know they will not reject me and one day we shall meet—I will wait for that.

                                        (Svetlana Allilueva)
6 March 1967, Delhi.

Having written all this in one burst, in a kind of inspiration, I felt I had said everything I could.

I asked no questions. It was clear to me that everything was being discussed with the Ambassador, and after that with whatever officials were concerned. I had sufficient life experience to understand that Washington had probably been asked for instructions, although naturally no one told me this. It was perfectly clear to all of us in the room.

We spoke about India. I told them about Kalakankar, about my wish to build a hospital there, and finally about the manuscript in my suitcase. I told them that I hoped to publish it abroad, repeating several times that I would do this no matter what fate held in store for me. I also explained that this manuscript was a history of my family and not a political document. They asked to see it, and for a while took it from me.

In the meantime Roger Kirk asked what I planned to call it, and I said: "I want something very simple, something that will express what it is—'Twenty Letters to a Friend.' Do you think I'll be able to get it published?" I asked this because to me it still seemed like an unattainable fantasy.

"Why, of course," Kirk exclaimed, and with a smile: "Will you send me an autographed copy?"

"Of course I will," I replied, amazed that, already, I was accepting it as a possibility.

At length it transpired that in order not to create complications, the best thing for me was to leave Delhi as soon as possible.

Nothing more was promised me at the time.

We were to go to the airport and take the plane to Rome. What would happen after that remained to be seen. For my part I was satisfied. And how splendid that this charming young man—the Second Secretary of the Embassy—was to accompany me and remain with me until it had been settled where I was to go. Truly splendid! Beyond that I did not try to look: "Things would shape themselves," as we Russians liked to say when we didn't know but were full of faith and hope. . . .

Bob Rayle sat down beside me, saying in great earnestness: "Do you realize that you are burning your bridges behind you? Think it over carefully. Are you prepared for such a step?"

"I have thought," I replied. "I had a lot of time to think, you know. Yes, I do realize."

We walked along corridors and down some stairs. In an elevator we descended straight into the embassy's garage. I climbed into the car with my suitcase, in my Moscow coat, with the green Indian kerchief around my head—the same which, for some unknown reason, I had ironed in the Soviet Hostel. The man who got in at the wheel smiled at me. Another settled down beside him and also smiled. Why did Americans smile so often? Was it out of politeness or because of a gay disposition? Whatever it was, I for one had never been spoiled with smiles. I found it very pleasant! We drove to the Palam Airport, where I had landed on my arrival from Moscow.

It all seemed so unreal, as in a dream; and it was late at night, too. Rayle arrived at the airport in another car. His pretty wife was waiting for him in the vestibule, her face anxious. He exchanged a few quick words with her, picked up a small suitcase, and joined me, smiling of course. I was beginning to understand that with Americans smiling was, as with healthy infants, a natural need. And my reaction was to respond in the same way.

An Indian woman in a sari took our passports. Five minutes later I had an Indian exit visa. Everything was legal now and no questions asked.

We went into the waiting room, where passengers from the Qantas plane slept in armchairs. The plane had come from Australia on a round-the-world flight through Singapore to Delhi, thence to Teheran, Rome, and London. Stewardesses in turquoise dresses and caps were strolling to and fro.

How wonderful that I should have come to the U.S. Embassy on this particular night: it was as if this night flight had been waiting specially for me! Tomorrow everything might have been far more complicated.

We had to spend an extra hour on small sofas in the waiting room. The flight had been delayed due to repairs. We drank coffee. Rayle and the two others kept glancing at the entrance door, watching out for *Sovetchiks*. But no! *Sovetchiks* that night had had plenty to drink and were fast asleep. Tomorrow they would get up with hangovers and for a long time wouldn't be able to realize what had happened. Strangely enough, I was absolutely calm. I never gave a thought to the possibility of any of them catching up with me: I was flying on the wings of success, on the wings of freedom; everything would be all right, everything would "shape itself." . . .

"Aren't you nervous?" Rayle asked in some surprise.

"Not at all." And I found myself smiling. I felt like grinning from ear to ear, and what's more, I did. What had happened to me? Only that morning I had felt crushed by a depression as heavy as a stone. Ambassador Benediktov, Surov—who would want to smile in their presence, and for what reason? I had torn myself away from those somber, heavy, gloomy people, at once oppressors and oppressed. I had stepped over the invisible boundary between the world of tyranny and the world of freedom.

And now here was our flight being announced. Rayle and I walked up the gangplank. *Namasté*, India, *namasté*! You have given me freedom.

Thank you, Brajesh! This is your gift. This is what you have done for me. How can I ever repay such love?

A Swiss Diary

Apart from my written declaration and some sketchy biographical data, the West knew nothing about me. In Moscow none of the Diplomatic Corps had known me, outside of the Ambassadors of India and the United Arab Republic, who would always support the Soviet Government. And the Soviet Government lost no time in instructing its embassies abroad what to say. Instantly the news was spread: Svetlana Alliluyeva was half insane, one couldn't believe anything she said. I learned of this a month later in Switzerland, where the Swiss officials who handled my case treated me with warmth and friendliness. But at first no one knew what to believe. George Kennan, former U.S. Ambassador to the U.S.S.R., who, altogether, had spent nine years in Moscow, was very surprised when he got a call from Washington informing him of this "defector, Svetlana Alliluyeva." "I don't know such a person," was his reply. Any other ambassador in Moscow, even one who had spent a longer time there, would have given the same answer. There was, therefore, nothing surprising in the disappointing news that awaited us in Rome.

Washington's reply was clear; a Solomon's judgment had

obviously been reached: do not hurry with the entry visa, appraise carefully her motivations and plans, in the meantime let her stay in some neutral place. Switzerland was offering me a temporary visa for three months. During that time some decision could be reached. Maybe Madame Alliluyeva, having calmed down, would change her mind and return to Moscow? . . .

It was a disappointing answer. On the other hand, I had been given no promises by the American Embassy in Delhi. Having no clear idea of the world I was about to encounter, I was prepared to go to any country, providing it wasn't in the Communist bloc or in any country dependent on it. My knowledge of Switzerland was of the vaguest, but to me anything was better than going back to what I had come from. Besides, I was given promises not to be left without support until my fate had been settled.

Bob Rayle was returning to India. I was sorry. We had become good friends during those few days in Rome. His friendliness and sense of humor had been of tremendous help to me; I, too, now tried to see the humorous side in everything that happened. Altogether, Bob Rayle's behavior during those days was the best possible illustration of the naturalness and friendliness of Americans, for whom my liking had been growing ever since I stepped into their embassy in Delhi. After all, Rayle and I were much like beings from two different planets, yet at no time did he let this be felt.

Out of my plane window I gazed wide-eyed at the Alps, pink in the rising sun. Here was another country on my journey round the world. Everything that had happened these last few days was such a novel experience in my heretofore quiet and secluded existence that at times I had an odd sense of unrelatedness, as though I were watching an adventure movie about my own self.

Sometimes the situations in it were like a detective story: the time when I got my Swiss visa in the automobile of the

Swiss Representative in Rome and our two cars had circled for a long time round a big flowerbed at the airport until we were sure of each other's identities. Then I moved into his car. The Representative was extremely nice, his secretary held a small bottle of ink and a rubber stamp in readiness. The three of us joked about it all. Then I returned to my car.

I expected to find the Alps more or less as I had seen them in Lucknow the previous week in *The Sound of Music*, starring Julie Andrews. Everywhere in the world people traveled, were accustomed to traveling; only to us Soviet recluses, a first trip abroad, a first encounter with Europe, appeared like something almost supernatural.

And this, of course, was as it should be. Everything was so completely fascinating!

❋

The month and a half spent in Switzerland proved to be a real breathing spell. But I had no intention of changing my original decision. Fortunately I had a diary with me, given me in Lucknow, into which I now began writing down my unusual "movie script." Every day it became more exciting, full of unexpected twists. I find it most entertaining today to look through this little notebook.

On March 12 I arrived in Switzerland and that same day met Antonino Janner, head of one of the sections of the Ministry of Foreign Affairs. He spoke English, French, German, and Italian equally well, and had served at one time as Swiss Representative at the Vatican. A rapport and mutual liking were instantly established between us, it was so easy to get along with him. Janner explained to me first of all that a tourist visa gave one the opportunity to rest and see the country, but precluded political activities of any kind. For the time being, this suited me perfectly. Already at the Geneva Airport I had to run from newsmen, who rushed after me shouting, "Are you going to ask for asylum in Switzerland? Will you return to the Soviet Union?" Least of all did I want to answer questions at this time, and this coincided with the wishes of the Swiss Government.

One of the first things Janner asked me was whether I wished to contact Soviet representatives. No, no! On the contrary, I wanted to avoid them at any cost. But no one was insisting on it, and I understood that I was being given complete freedom of decision and thought.

My first twenty-four hours were spent in a small mountain inn in Beatenberg. It was very cold; snow, which I hadn't seen since December, lay everywhere. From the window of my small room I could see the Jungfrau. But I have never liked mountains, I don't know how to admire them; they oppress me, I prefer wide-open spaces, plains, the sea.

It grew even colder; snow began to fall, turning into a blizzard; there was something unpleasant about this return to a cold climate. Faces in the dining room were unfriendly. During lunchtime the radio kept blaring out the news, the announcer telling in German all about my arrival in Switzerland. I stared down at my plate, totally unaccustomed as I was to hearing my name pronounced in connection with sensational news.

On this day Janner told me over the telephone that Jaipal, a representative of the Indian Foreign Ministry, had arrived from Delhi and wished to see me. This was the same Rikhi Jaipal who had come to see us in Moscow the day before Brajesh's death. But now these old acquaintances among Indian officials inspired no confidence in me, and I agreed to see him only in Janner's presence.

March 14: The three of us met in a private home on the shores of Lake Thun. Jaipal's sole object was to obtain from me an official confirmation that no one in India had helped me "flee" from the country. He had brought with him a draft of a letter from me to Dinesh—authored, I'm afraid, by Dinesh himself—in which this was stated very clearly. But it was true, the Indians hadn't helped me. Obviously, Dinesh needed this in order to clear himself before the Soviet Embassy. So I signed it.

Jaipal didn't tell me where he was going from Switzerland, but he remarked that he might deliver a letter to my children through the Indian Ambassador in Moscow. I was overjoyed and gave him a letter of fifteen pages in which I explained to my children in detail why I had decided *never to return to the U.S.S.R.* I wrote that I considered it important that the three of them should stay together, continue their studies, and try to preserve their present mode of life. I gave them detailed advice about our home, to make them understand that this was serious, that I wasn't joking, that I would not change my mind. In the papers I had seen a photograph of Katie and Joseph waiting for me in our home. Their faces were sad; I recognized our living room; my heart ached for them.

I believed that Jaipal would deliver the letter, but Janner shook his head with obvious skepticism. He proved to be right: the letter was never received. . . .

That same day I was obliged to move to a small monastery hospice in San-Antoni near Fribourg. It had been impossible to remain at the inn; newsmen were prowling all over the country. In Beatenberg I was recognized in a shop where I had bought a pair of ski pants, and reporters instantly got wind of it. I could not return there. When Janner told me that the only really quiet and unreachable spot was behind monastery walls, I couldn't help smiling: again I remembered Julie Andrews, *The Sound of Music*, monasteries, and other movie-script devices. My own adventure-script was burgeoning. All right then, a monastery it should be.

"But have they any electricity?" I asked, imagining for a moment dark monastic catacombs I had seen in Russia. Janner laughed loudly. He assured me that they had electricity, plumbing, and hot water.

We arrived in San-Antoni late in the evening. I confess my knees shook. Temples, monasteries, priests make me tremble superstitiously. Catholic nuns in black dresses and white kerchiefs showed me to a small clean room with a crucifix on the wall, a washstand, and a warm, thick eiderdown on a modern bed. If it weren't for the crucifix, one might have thought oneself in some small good modest hotel. Officially I was to be known here as Fräulein Carlen, an Irishwoman come from India.

March 15 was a quiet sunny day. The hospice stood on a low hill, from which a wonderful view opened up on a peaceful landscape of fields, a bluish forest in the distance, a chain of mountains on the horizon, small peaked chalets here and there. There were six nuns in the hospice. It was actually a sort of rest home for Catholic priests. *Schwester* Florentine, portly and cozy, called me into the dining room for breakfast. I had been taught German in my childhood; now it came back to me with a small supply of simple words sufficient for the occasion. After breakfast I cleared away my cup and plates, carrying them into the kitchen, and *Schwester* Florentine expressed her approval with a smile. Again I felt happy and at ease. Everything would "shape itself."

And it did: That evening Janner called up to tell me not to lose heart about an entry into the United States. Its State Department, he said, had issued a statement that such a possibility was not precluded. Meanwhile the Swiss Gov-

ernment announced to reporters that I did not wish to meet
the press and asked them to stop searching for me and solic-
iting interviews.

March 16: Two Fribourg Canton policemen in plain clothes
offered to take me on a sightseeing tour of the neighborhood. We went by car. It was a pleasant trip. Recalling my
university French, as well as my childhood German, I managed to explain that the cable railway at Moléson (six thousand feet above sea level), on which they gave me a ride,
made me feel dizzy, and that I would much prefer a less
sensational landscape. We laughed and joked, drank coffee
with skiers in a café; I was promised that our next excursion
would be along a flat plain. In conclusion they allowed me
to drive their small Volkswagen and we parted friends.

On returning to the hospice I found my first letters from
publishers, offering to "help" me write my memoirs about the
U.S.S.R. They didn't know that I already had a manuscript,
though not memoirs. I also received a letter from Louba
d'Astier: she had a niece in Fribourg, whom they often
visited, so that before long we would be able to see each
other.

On that same day the BBC announced that a representative
of the American State Department was intending to come
to Switzerland to see me. At the same time the Swiss Bund-
esrat was about to discuss the possibility of granting me
refuge and extending my tourist visa.

March 17: Janner called up to find out, as always, how I was,
and said that he had good news for me: George Kennan was
arriving next week. I said I didn't know who he was. Janner
sounded astonished. "Kennan lived in Moscow for a long
time," he explained. "He was the American Ambassador at
the time. It's a big honor and very lucky for you, this meet-

ing. He is one of the greatest experts on Russia. I'll bring you his books." Again I had to blush for my former existence—not knowing what went on in Moscow, right under my nose.

I began to think about this forthcoming meeting. Two days were spent in uncertainty. What would I be told, what news would I get? After the United States' unexpected refusal to grant me an entry, I didn't know what to expect. Nor did I know what I wanted. I should at least know that. Until now I had drifted with the current, giving no thought to where it would land me. Now I would be asked what I wanted, yet all I knew was that I refused to return to the U.S.S.R. At the same time I kept worrying about my children. In that photograph, taken in Moscow by the American correspondent Henry Shapiro, they had looked so sad. Why did he have to go and see them? Why question them, torment them, irritate wounds? It seemed so inhuman. I wondered, too, whether they had received my long letter sent through Jaipal.

I might have chosen to remain in Switzerland, it was so nice and quiet here. But Switzerland would never have let me publish my book, I would have been reduced to silence; it would have been impossible even to explain why I had left the U.S.S.R. because my reasons were "political." Anything I might say or write would amount to "political activities," which were forbidden. What sense was there in leaving my country in order to remain silent here, too?

March 20 was a day in which my spirit sagged. I roamed the small yard, planted with thuja trees, thinking of my children, languishing with uncertainty. I was reading Pasternak's *Doctor Zhivago* at the time, which Bob Rayle had given me on the way. This reading tore my heart to pieces. I wept over the book, mingling its words with my own, its sorrows with mine, weeping over myself, my children, over the unhappy, tortured country I had left but still loved. . . . I couldn't conceal my depression. *Schwester* Florentine became alarmed, tried to console me, promised to pray for me and my children in the chapel. Many tears were shed that day. But in the morning I felt better.

March 21 brought many letters. The Hearst Corporation offered to publish—and "help" me write—my memoirs. William Randolph Hearst, Jr. reminded me of our interview in Moscow during the winter of 1955 and sent me a clipping of the same. This was the first time I had ever seen anything in print about this interview for which Molotov had prepared me with so many instructions.

I also received many letters of sympathy, offering to help a "woman without a country." As one form of assistance it was suggested that I marry in order to obtain a passport of another country. The first such offer came from England, from a retired English naval officer, who had been in Archangel during the war. The second came from a former Soviet circus performer, an animal trainer, who had remained abroad and had become an Australian citizen. The third came from Cologne in West Germany. A very sweet letter came from the owner of a motorboat in Florida, indignant that the United States had not granted me an entry visa right away and inviting me to stay as a guest in his family's modest home. "Show this letter to the American Ambassador in Switzerland," he wrote. A rich businessman from Miami, Florida, a former Russian émigré, suggested in detail a way of obtaining an American visa as his supposed secretary. He explained that he had important connections in Switzerland and could arrange it all if I were willing.

Letters arrived with no addresses—just "Switzerland." They were all forwarded to Janner, who brought them to me, at the same time posting my mail. I sent my children a postcard asking them to write me in care of the Federal Political Department. Postcards from abroad reached the U.S.S.R.

quicker—they were easier for the censor—and I was hoping
to get a reply.

March 22: I read in a Swiss newspaper about questions
raised in the Indian Parliament regarding my "flight." Ram
Manohar Lohia, one of the most militant leaders of the opposition, accused the government of fawning on the U.S.S.R.
The Minister of Foreign Affairs, Chagla, made an official
statement to the effect that I "had never once expressed a
wish to stay in India." Lohia characterized this answer as a
"lie." When I was still in Rome I received an invitation from
the Indian Ministry of Foreign Affairs to return to India.
Of course, I had refused, knowing that this invitation must
have been inspired by Ambassador Benediktov. Now I decided to write Dr. Lohia, thanking him for challenging
their lie and telling him in detail about my talks with Dinesh
Singh regarding my unwillingness to return to the U.S.S.R.
I quoted Dinesh's statements, which to me, of course,
amounted to an informal answer from the government and
its Prime Minister. To deny our talks at this moment would
have been the height of hypocrisy and cowardice.

A few days later Dr. Lohia read my letter in Parliament.
It created an uproar in the Indian press. The facts in it
showed up Dinesh and Chagla in an unpleasant light. The
Communists, on the other hand, supported Dinesh and
mocked Lohia for his "chivalry," their papers claiming that
I had been "kidnaped by the CIA."

March 23 was spent reading Kennan's *Russia and the West
under Lenin and Stalin,* which Janner had given me. I tried
to imagine what its author was like. I was to meet him next
day, and my whole future, apparently, depended on his
opinion of me.

Judging by his book, he knew Russia well; and not only
knew it but had a profound understanding of that compli-

cated, contradictory, cruel, and unhappy land. Toward Communism he was merciless. Toward my father and his political system, the same. What would his reaction be to me? Would he be able to separate me from the "Great Shadow," which people always saw first in me—a sad fact I am doomed to live with all my life. I could only feel that the man I was going to see tomorrow was an experienced diplomat, a serious historian. According to Janner, it was very lucky for me that Kennan had been chosen to be the judge in this quandary. I waited, feeling that I was getting nervous. For I knew that a great deal would depend on his first impression, which in an instant might decide everything for me.

March 24: One of my "guardians," dressed in civilian clothes, took me in his Volkswagen to Bern. In Bern I moved into Janner's car and we drove to the small house on the Thunersee in which we had been once before. Janner was very lively and looked happy.

"I have already spoken to Kennan," he said. "He has read your manuscript and thinks it should be published. He likes it."

This was news to me. A copy of the manuscript had apparently been sent to the United States after my departure from India. But somehow it still seemed unbelievable that it should be a "finished book," as my friends in the U.S.S.R. had assured me. Did Kennan really find it interesting? This might solve half my problem, if not all of it. Was it possible that someday I would actually be able to build that hospital at Kalakankar? Only twenty days ago it seemed like an unrealizable fantasy. . . .

George Kennan was tall, thin, blue-eyed, elegant. His elegance struck one from the very start. He said a few words in Russian, but the conversation was carried on in English because of the other people present. We sat down at opposite ends of a small sofa and, together with Janner, talked for almost an hour.

That hour proved that fantasies and dreams could sometimes come true. He had, indeed, read my *Twenty Letters*. He was, indeed, of the opinion that they could and should be published. If I definitely wished to go to the United States, and not to some other country in Europe, a possible publisher there had been found. It was, however, absolutely necessary for me to have lawyers (this, at the time, I couldn't quite understand), who would make all arrangements with the publishers, as well as attend to the visa and other practical matters. He went on to explain that life in the West was very different from life in the U.S.S.R., that I would have to get used to it gradually. But wouldn't I prefer perhaps living in England or France? The book could be published there, too. No, no! I had decided, I didn't want to change my mind, if it were at all possible! Oh yes, he said he hoped that soon I would be able to enter the United States on a tourist visa. But in the meantime, I ought to meet my future lawyers and decide some practical matters with them.

Kennan was amiable, agreeable, and well disposed toward me—this I felt. I could only keep repeating, "Yes, I want to." "Yes, I agree." My head throbbed the way it had on the day I went to the U.S. Embassy in Delhi, myself not quite believing that the act had been accomplished. Now again, after an hour of this pleasant conversation, I felt that my whole nervous system was exhausted, and when Kennan suggested we go out for a stroll, I could only say, "Thank you, but I will wait here, I'll sit on the terrace."

It was a warm, sunny day, everything glistened, the last of the snow was melting away. The first narcissuses could be seen sprouting in the grass. Kennan went for a walk. He had arrived with a chill and for several days had not been out. Oberhofen clung to the side of the mountain; below it Lake Thun, surrounded by mountains, glistened blindingly. Blue shadows lay on the wooded slopes, above them summits were white with snow. The air was full of the intoxicating freshness of spring. I sat on the terrace and couldn't even think. It was so good to be sitting there, breathing, squinting at the bright sunlight. . . .

Later we had dinner with our host and hostess. Kennan returned refreshed and said that he felt first-rate. Everyone was in a fine mood, but business was no longer discussed. Only after dinner Kennan remarked that in America I would meet a circle of his friends. His two eldest daughters and their children would be glad to invite me to their farm in Pennsylvania—it was their old beloved childhood home— "Like your Zubalovo," he added, smiling. I knew then that he had read my manuscript very attentively.

Wasn't it strange, though: here was a man who recently had been a total stranger, and already he knew so much about me, had taken upon himself to settle my fate for me. Even his daughters knew about me; and somewhere far away, in the United States, there was a house "that reminded one of Zubalovo," to which I was being invited. . . .

Kennan left soon after dinner. I, too, had to return to my hospice. But we sat on in the cozy living room with a brick fireplace, listening to music. Without even consulting each other we all chose Bach. Like me, Janner loved Bach. Everyone's mood was well suited to Bach's thunderings and figurations, always finishing in harmony.

I retained that mood for the next two days.

March 26—Sunday—was Catholic Easter, and I felt like celebrating the feast, my own soul being in a festive mood.

I went to the St. Nicholas Cathedral with my "civilian" guard, who was a Catholic and sang hymns in French and Latin with the rest of the congregation. The Bishop of Fribourg delivered a sermon in French—eternal, universal words of love and brotherhood. The powerful breath of the organ rolled through the cathedral, the sounds of the choir poured in a silvery stream, there were flowers everywhere, tapers were burning; everyone knelt.

I, too, prayed; a simple prayer came gushing straight from my heart: Thank you, Lord! Thank you for everything you have given me with a generous hand. Help my children! Help them, save them, console them, strengthen them. Save and console. . . .

I knelt on a wooden stool, hands tightly pressed together, eyes shut; beside me knelt my policeman in civilian clothes. People all around me. The policeman, another human being, had six children. There was no difference, whether in an Orthodox church, on the banks of the Ganges, or in a Catholic cathedral—everywhere people prayed for love, help for one's neighbors, peace. I kept giving thanks for everything that had been given me, asking for mercy and bountiful blessings for my children. Never before, anywhere, had I prayed with such fervor as on that Easter Sunday in Fribourg. Tears choked me, there was a blackness inside my eyes, I could not stop. The Easter Mass was long, solemn, full of splendor; the congregation knelt many times, and all of it was what I needed more than anything else at that moment.

March 27: The time had come to descend to earth from my clouds and attend to business: make the acquaintance of my future lawyers—Edward Greenbaum and Alan Schwartz. I thought that I was beginning to understand a little why lawyers would be needed. But when the conversation turned to copyrights and their complications in my case, to my contract with the publishers, the large royalties the book was expected to earn, the establishment of a charity fund, and other matters, I found I had come to a big city from some remote village in the heart of a forest. I felt ill at ease, for I could hardly understand what was being said; it would have been the same even if we had spoken Russian. I felt that I was incapable of understanding most of it and would probably always be doing the wrong things. But there was nothing to be done, I would just have to try and learn as I went on, transforming myself from a village recluse into a modern urbanite. Janner, too, that day appeared preoccupied, and after the meeting we did not listen to Bach.

Skipping a day, March 29: We met again. Now two additional, Swiss lawyers were present—William Staehelin and Peter Hafter—identical with the Americans in that the first was the elderly, venerable head of the firm, the second a charming young partner. I understood the two younger ones better—Hafter and Schwartz—but even so it was all very complicated. This kind of activity didn't exist at all in the U.S.S.R., and I found it very hard to form any idea of what it was about.

This was an important business day. I signed several documents, putting in my lawyers' hands everything concerning the book's publication, the money, the visa. It was clear to me that my book would appear in many countries, that in the United States it would be published by Harper & Row. The name, as well as that of the proposed translator, meant nothing to me; but then to me any name would have been unknown. I simply put myself entirely into the hands of people who had come to my aid at a difficult moment. I was venturing on a voyage in a ship with a good, friendly crew—was it necessary to think about what the crew was doing? I could only thank them for having taken me on board.

Alan Schwartz, a young man of thirty-four with graying hair and a boyish face, showed me photographs of his sons, one of them with hair as red as a carrot. Edward Greenbaum's wife was a sculptor, she had sent me through him a catalogue of her works: thank goodness, no modernism—people looked like people, women's heads, children's figures, expressive animals. And so here were two more American families for me to know. I felt that I, for one, would be "discovering" America through people, families, children, and not by visiting sights. It is the way I would like to get to know all countries.

On this same day I learned that I would be able to go to the United States sometime in April.

The next few days passed quietly.

Everything was decided. All that remained now was to wait until that mysterious government machine had done its work and had chucked out of its depths a piece of paper on which my future depended: my visa.

I read letters arriving from every corner of the earth. It was all so strange! In the U.S.S.R. even d'Astier's letters from Paris never reached me, and a postcard from India took a month. There the censorship decided what to let through and what to hold up. Now I read letters from Russians in Australia, inviting me to come and stay with them, giving suggestions to whom to address myself at the Bureau of Emigration in Geneva. Easter cards came from West Germany, Switzerland, France, America. Kind people were wishing me success, happiness, peace. They were thinking and worrying about me.

A young man from Minnesota asked me to stay with him. He said he had completed five years of college and a commercial school, that his means were modest, and that he would be happy to have me share his three-bedroom rented house, with oil heating, a refrigerator, electricity, a radio, and a tape recorder. He had lived in forty-eight states of the Union, and in his opinion there was no more gossip in his tiny hamlet—which was not even large enough to have a post office—than anywhere else. He was convinced that we could enrich each other's political views. He added that he believed in God, that the trees in front of his house were beautiful, and that he was studying Russian but didn't know it yet.

A Swiss citizen, the owner of a store, insisted that I become a Swiss. To this end he offered marriage. "And after that," he wrote, "you will be free to go where you wish, do what you wish. Believe me, I have no other object in mind than to be of help to you. . . ."

A very warmhearted letter came from Michael Koryakov, a free-lance journalist writing in the *Novoye Russkoye Slovo,* a Russian-language newspaper in New York. He sent me the articles he had written about me—sentimental but friendly.

Finally a long-awaited letter arrived from Kalakankar. In it Suresh Singh wrote how happy he and his whole family were to know that at last my life would be free. With a good deal of humor he described how on March 10 Surov, the Second Secretary of the Soviet Embassy, had made an appearance in Kalakankar in the hope of still finding me there; how the radio at the time was announcing that I was in Rome and what a face Surov had made. He further wrote that his house was overrun by newsmen, who photographed every corner, and that now there was no peace from them and probably would not be for some time. To be able to imagine what the Swiss Alps were like, he had gone to Lucknow to see *The Sound of Music* with Julie Andrews— he had never in his life been abroad.

Janner invited me to dine with his family in Bern. Antonino Janner's mother was a Swiss Italian, his father a German, and he spoke German, French, and English equally well; but at home, with his wife Adriana and his son Marco, he spoke only Italian. For some time now eight-year-old Marco had heard from his father about an "unhappy auntie, whom no country wished to accept and who couldn't see her children." The child had been running a high fever and his father had told him this in order to be able to leave him and come and see me. Hearing so sad a story, little Marco let his father go; but then he began asking endless questions about that "poor auntie"—how was she? He was sorry for me and had already grown fond of me. When I arrived, he threw his arms around my neck and kissed me with such effusiveness that I almost began to weep. All evening he made little pencil drawings for me and wrote Russian letters, copying them out of Russian books. He gave me a box wrapped in red paper and containing his treasures: stumps of pencils and colored chalks, little pieces of chocolate, old calipers, two small coins, and a tiny marzipan elephant. Recalling my few words of Italian, I said, kissing him, "*Caro bambino, mio piccolo bambino, grazie,*" afraid of bursting into tears. . . .

Adriana was a calm and graceful woman. We ate spaghetti with tomatoes and again listened to Bach. Janner gave me a record of a Bach prelude played by a Rumanian pianist, Dino Lipatti.

April 3: I had to move from my hospice in San-Antoni to the convent proper at Fribourg, where I would have greater independence. The Sister Superior, Marguerite-Marie, handed me three keys with which I was to open three doors every time I returned home after eight in the evening. This happened often, whenever I went to Bern, and I would creep in the dark with a flashlight, afraid of getting the keys mixed up and, worse still, frightening the convent's home for old people, through whose long corridors I had to pass. During the day I went for walks in the streets of Fribourg, to the bank, to shops (I had received an advance from the publishers and had immediately refunded the money for my passage from Delhi). I took strolls in the park, situated on the steep banks of an emerald river—the Sarine. No one watched over me or dogged my steps. In my handbag I carried a piece of paper identifying me as an Irishwoman, Fräulein Carlen, newly arrived from India. India was the only country, outside of Russia, which I knew something about and could discuss.

Old Fribourg was picturesque. Narrow streets, little hunched bridges over the Sarine, a modern university, graceful, two-storied arcades spanning the river; all of this harmonized well with the Gothic cathedral, blending into an over-all picture of great charm. Here and there cozy little chapels with wide-open doors that seemed to invite one in to spend a few moments of silence. I kept thinking of my children, hoping to hear from them, and so, during my walks, I would enter one of these chapels, always with the same prayer in my heart: "Help them, save them, console them."

My room, with a window on the river and wide spaces beyond it, was quiet. I began working—I wanted so to start writing. I wrote about Pasternak, to Pasternak, the great poet; about Doctor Zhivago, and Lara's lost love, and the martyrdom of Russia, and my children. It was a "lament"— a form existing in folklore but not in literature—and nothing came of it except an unrestrainable lament. I understood at last, in all its pitiless reality, that of my own free choice I was severing forever old ties of love and attachment.

A week went by and then at last a letter came from my son:

Greetings, dear Mama!

We were very surprised when, on March 8, we went to the airport and did not find you. At first we just couldn't believe that you hadn't arrived. We stayed there, waiting for three hours. The radio being our sole source of information, for several days we simply didn't know what to think. But when Tass came out with an announcement that you had been granted permission to remain abroad as long as you wished, we more or less stopped worrying, and life returned to its normal routine; that is if one discounts that to this day Katie cannot get back on the track; and we, to tell you the truth, just don't understand anything. . . .

We were very astonished that since your departure from India we had had no news from you. I even called up the Swiss Embassy, asking them to help us in contacting you. So far I have received no reply from them. We were all the more astonished because in your last letter from India (dated February 23) you wrote that you were returning on the eighth of March.

At last we got your card, in which you said that you didn't know how to get in touch with us. Can you explain why we have to write you through a government department? We would so much like to write to you direct, or still better, talk to you on the telephone. Among other things, we would like to know your plans for the future, how long you intend staying there, and when you think you will be coming back.

Mama, all your friends are asking after you. It would be good if you wrote and told us what to say to them.

Until we see you. We kiss you.

Joseph and Katie

April 4, 1967

This made it all too clear that Jaipal had never forwarded my letter.

They knew nothing and could figure out nothing. But how could I have informed them from India of my "plans," when I myself had none until the very last moment?

I told all this to Janner. He understood what I was going through and said the best thing would be to call up Moscow.

We drove to a small hotel in Murten, not far from Fribourg, took a sitting room with a telephone, and put a call through to Moscow, giving some made-up name in Switzerland. We waited for twenty minutes, during which I got thoroughly exasperated. There was a cage in the room, with a black magpie in it, who, like a parrot, kept repeating every five minutes, *"Comment ça va?"* This became intolerable. We carried the cage out into the corridor. But even from there the same question reached us in that strange, raucous voice.

A ring at last! Moscow. My son at the telephone. "Joseph, it's me," I said as in a dream; and my son, lost, answered, "Oh, dear God . . ."

We must have spoken for half an hour. He started out by confirming that no explanatory letter from me had been received. Stammering in my confusion and emotion, I kept repeating, "I am not a tourist—do you understand? I will not return. . . ." I doubt if I ever could have given him a rational explanation, afraid as I was of being cut off at any moment. I just kept on repeating, "I am not a tourist—do you understand? It's impossible for me to go back—do you understand?" And Joseph, in a fallen voice—he had instantly caught on—kept saying, "Yes, yes, I hear you." He asked no questions, while I, still stammering, kept reiterating the same thing. I didn't even dare ask how they were. I knew too well without words how they must be feeling. . . . And I didn't tell him that I was waiting for a visa to the United States. Of what interest was it to them *where* I was going, since I was *not going to return?* Katie wasn't home—and perhaps that was just as well! I don't know how I could have stood hearing her voice. . . . Our conversation ended by being cut off.

That evening I ran a fever; I couldn't get over this talk with my son. Janner understood what I was going through and was almost as upset as I was.

It would be useless to try and describe what I felt during those days. Everything that was in my heart came pouring out in the "Lament," addressed to a poet, to Pasternak. I finished writing it that week and sent the manuscript to George Kennan, who had a fine feeling for Russian literary style. I asked only one thing: that it be translated and published somewhere in such a way as to reach Russia. . . .

April 14: I tried to call Moscow again. Again the talking magpie was banished into the corridor. My number in Moscow didn't answer, and the operator asked if I would like to call someone else. I decided on Bertha.

Talking with her was even more depressing than my conversation with Joseph.

"It will be very hard on the children," she said, and in a severe tone: "Do you understand how hard it will be?"

"I understand everything. But do you all understand me?"

Instead of answering, Bertha mentioned one of our mutual friends: "Sanya is crying. She cries all the time. About you— whom are you with, how are you?"

"I have many new friends," I said.

"What friends? What friends? What are you talking

about?" she exclaimed, at once incredulous and indignant. "What friends could you possibly have there?"

"I do though," I insisted. "Nice people. Many nice people here."

I did my best to convince her, but in vain. She didn't believe me, or perhaps didn't want to. . . .

This conversation shook me. I had considered Bertha an up-to-date, progressive woman, and here she was refusing to admit that I could have friends outside of the U.S.S.R.! Or maybe she dared not say what she wanted to? Better give up calling. It was too painful to hear loved voices and not be able to carry on an open conversation. . . .

We Shall Meet Again

Maybe i have unusual ideas about friendship. I do not set much value on meetings, parties, systematic get-togethers. There were people in my life whom I saw seldom, with whom I had time for but a brief hour's talk now and then, yet these talks remained in my heart. And a kind word said at a time of stress, how it would engrave itself in one's memory! An evening spent in the kitchen over a cup of pale Moscow tea could sometimes become a revelation, in which you told everything about yourself and in return listened to the confessions of a difficult, troubled life. But then, whose life in the U.S.S.R. was simple and easy? There was no such thing, particularly in the circle of the intelligentsia in which I had my closest ties.

There is no "social life" in the U.S.S.R.—no more or less obligatory and regular intercourse with a certain social group. We knew of such things only from Russian novels of the nineteenth century. The Revolution had destroyed social mores and had created nothing in their place. During the years of arrests and "purges" people lost the habit of contacting others—too afraid to do so. Now conditions had become somewhat better. But all the same, the basis of all social intercourse remained a friendly cup of tea or a glass of vodka, with its concomitant herring, in the close company of those who would not betray, with whom one could talk out loud and say what one thought. But a reflex, which had become second nature, still remained from darker days, and even now a man would say, "Let's go out and get a breath of fresh air!" whenever he felt like venting his spleen against the Party or the government.

This was a universal habit, irrespective of the individual's social standing, which, in the final reckoning, amounted to one and the same thing: slavery and silence, in some cases with dachas, refrigerators, and automobiles, in others without. The Soviet elite, consisting of big Party and government bosses, and those in the world of art who fawned on them, had access to representatives of the outside world, diplomatic and cultural. For others such contacts could occur but seldom, through some chance encounter. My friends and I belonged to the latter group. But in this respect again one couldn't help remembering Khrushchev's liberal decade, when everything had been so much easier, when people forgot about prisons, and wisecracks could be made even about the Premier himself, when men began to believe that the past had gone never to return. It had been easy then to meet people, easy to make friends, to find a language in common.

I met Bertha in the home of my friends, a composer called Alyosha and his wife Sanya. Sanya and Bertha had known each other since their university days in Moscow. When the new university was being erected on the Lenin Hills, the two girls worked as announcers in the construction's radio center. Bertha had then just arrived from Tashkent and was studying history. Helping others was something she had always loved to do, and so now, as soon as she came to Moscow, she became the "guardian angel" of every Negro in town. Most of them worked as extras in movies, or did translations. Seldom would any of them venture into indus-

try as had Bertha's father, who was growing cotton in
Uzbekistan. I heard of one Negro who had been lucky
enough to find employment on a large farm near Moscow, where they bred ducks. But these were exceptional
cases. Ordinarily the life of Negroes in Moscow was marked
by poverty and hardship. Girls of the second generation
sought to marry black students from abroad and return to
their homes with them. Bertha had married a student from
Africa. They had a daughter. When I made Bertha's acquaintance, she was waiting for news of her husband's return from Africa. I was waiting for Brajesh's return from
India. Thus from the very start an affinity had sprung up
between us, a mood in common.

Temperamentally we were very different though; even in
tastes we differed greatly, but this did not prevent a perfect
understanding. During the last two years I don't believe I
had a closer friend, for Bertha was a cosmopolitan and, in
contrast to most of my other acquaintances, didn't find it
odd that I and Brajesh Singh, an Indian, wanted to be
together. To her it was perfectly natural.

She was an expert on art and music in present-day Africa,
on Africa's cultural and political life. In some modern African republic she would have been a cabinet minister; her
field of vision and her energy called for social activities on
a vast scale. Yet neither the Central Committee nor MID
would let her go outside the U.S.S.R., except to Socialist
countries. A connoisseur of art who didn't belong to the
Party, half Negro, half Jew, this strange hybrid scared the
Party officials and the police, who, in the final count, made
the decision as to who could be allowed to go "beyond the
border." Bertha's husband found himself another wife in
Africa, more congenial to his Moslem habits. Bertha would
never have consented to live in purdah. Now all that was
left her was to study African music in Moscow. She wrote
a whole treatise on it with the help of records and tape
recordings. She reminded me of a flying fish: instead of liv-

ing in her own element she had to learn to fly through the air.

How that woman could dance, sing; what a sense of rhythm was hers! And how she danced the twist with my son, with whom she had become fast friends! Into my home she always brought gaiety and freshness.

In Moscow she knew all the poets, musicians, writers connected in any way with Africa. Her father was an American Negro, but the racial call came from deeper roots. Her little daughter was much blacker than she was—a real little slice of chocolate.

Bertha's daughter was the only Negro child in her kindergarten. She sang, declaimed poetry, danced on every festive occasion; everyone loved her, and she amused and entertained everybody. But one day she said, "Mama, why am I black? I want to be white, *like everyone else!*" Bertha invited a few other Negro children to play with her, so that the child shouldn't think of herself as something unusual. This helped, but not for long. "When I take her to school they shout in the street, 'Look at the Negroes!'" Bertha complained to me indignantly. She lived in a section of Moscow known as Novye Cheryomushki, inhabited by workers who had been moved there from barracks, and by a new Soviet lower middle class. To them a black skin was a wonder of nature.

The small two-room apartment in which Bertha and her family lived was cramped and uncomfortable. Bertha's mother taught English; pupils used to come in for their lessons through Bertha's room. In the kitchen one could hardly move.

Bertha used to get exasperated when American Communists—her father's old friends—came to see her and would start orating about the wonderful life in the Soviet Union.

"I keep telling them I *know* what kind of a life it is," she would explain to me, boiling with rage, "but will they believe me? They are blind, they don't see what it has become, what it has turned into! And they refuse to believe that I have to stand in line to get milk, fruit, gruel for my child! Blind and deaf dogmatists, that's what they are, yet they have the nerve to argue with me!"

During the summer of 1964, at the International Congress of Ethnographers and Anthropologists held in Moscow, Bertha read a report on African drums. This Congress was a real delight to her, she felt thoroughly in her element; other delegates mistook her for a member of the American delegation. She made friends with Swedish and German ethnographers. A Negro from the United States said to her, "Why do you people keep harping about discrimination against Negroes in our country? At home I own two houses, two automobiles. And you? How many of your books have been published?" Bertha didn't know what to say. . . .

Painstakingly she had gathered material for a book about Negroes in Russia. She had unearthed the very first written records of purchases of black slaves, who in the seventeenth century were kept at the Czar's court for amusement, as jesters. These black slaves had been brought by ship to Black Sea ports. To this day in the mountains of Abkhazia (in the Caucasus) there is a black population, descended from those slaves. Bertha went there, found the villages in question, and was horrified.

The standard of living of the Moslem blacks in those Abkhazian villages was hardly any higher than that of their distant ancestors in Africa: almost total illiteracy, dire poverty. The local population refused to mix with Negroes and had driven them back into a barren mountain fastness. The Abkhazian Communist Party authorities were scared of the black lady from Moscow, come with no one knew what powers of authority: what if she were an inspector from the Central Committee? Bertha could get nowhere. The Negroes there spoke only Abkhazian. According to the interpreter they were all perfectly happy with their life. In the village, which she visited accompanied by local officialdom—they refused to let her go alone—women began wailing: they thought that the entire population was to be transported to some unknown destination.

In the Caucasus people were all too familiar with such genocidal tragedies: it had happened to the Chechen-Ingush nation and to the Kabardians and Balkars. Horrified by the panic she had unwittingly caused, Bertha tried to question the villagers, tried to calm them; but all of it had to be done through the interpreter. Toward the end, however, very timidly a few young men who knew some Russian approached her, and only then was it explained to the villagers that she had not come there as a scourge. The young men also told her how much they longed for education, that all the women were illiterate, that the race was dying out. Bertha gave the local authorities a dressing down, making them promise to help the young, but she had no authority to issue orders or even make recommendations. She felt crushed by these impressions. To include what she had seen in her book was impossible—the censor would have thrown it out.

Eventually Bertha's book on Negroes in Russia was published for foreign consumption only, with nothing left in it but information about actors, musicians, and scientific workers, like Bertha. Bertha wasn't even shown the edited version, and she used to say that in this way she was not responsible for it, even though it bore her name. As for her book on African music, there was even less hope of its seeing the light of day: very few people in the U.S.S.R. knew anything about the subject.

In Bertha's room—the one that was used as a passageway and served her as sitting room, dining room, bedroom, and study—we often listened to music. She had a large collection of African folk melodies and songs. In this room I heard the South African opera *King Kong*, based on folk melodies (somewhat like the American *Porgy and Bess*), the spirituals of Mahalia Jackson, the songs of African natives. All these records and recordings had been obtained for her and brought by friends. Yet Bertha herself was not even permitted to attend the Congress of Culture at Dakar, although she of all people should have been the one best qualified to be there.

＊

Alyosha and Sanya, who had introduced me to Bertha, lived in Leningrad. Alyosha, a composer, a lyrical nature, should have been composing chamber music and songs. But one could not feed a large family on that, and so Alyosha wrote operas. But opera is an art that is passé, and Alyosha's family went hungry most of the time. For how was a man, a musician, to live, whose honesty and sincerity forbade him to compose panegyrics to the Party, the Red Army, and the "Wise Leader"?

Alyosha's parents had belonged to the Russian nobility and to the culture it had stood for. He had been born in Berlin, when his parents were still political émigrés. Later, unable to bear exile any longer, they had returned to a Russia become Soviet, to Tsarskoye Selo become Detskoye Selo. Alyosha had been taught German, French, music; and he had so assimilated Russian poetry since childhood that it had become an organic part of his speech. Alyosha was a huge man, clumsy, fat, and wearing glasses; infinitely kind and impractical, well read and intelligent: in sum, a perfect Pierre Bezukhov. He could have been cast in a movie of *War and Peace* without make-up, without any specially written part. Anything he would have said would have been natural and right for Pierre. Therein lies the genius of Tolstoy, that his characters go on living in Russia for centuries. And therein lies the strength of Russia, that centuries and upheavals have not the power to destroy her.

I got to know Alyosha and Sanya on the day of his mother's funeral, which became an event in Leningrad's literary life.

Elena Vassilyevna had been seldom published after the Revolution, for she could only write of what was eternal and beautiful—of love, nature, emotions. This alone could not place her in the ranks of famous Soviet poets. Literary circles, however, knew and respected her for what she was: a lovely, open, generous person, rich in spirit; and also for being, like Leningrad palaces, a living monument to Russian culture. Deserted by her husband, who had become a "well-known Soviet writer," she lived with her beloved son Alyosha, never left Leningrad, not even during the blockade, continuing even then to write poetry. She also wrote some very interesting memoirs, encompassing Russian literary life from the end of the last century, through the émigré years, and the years of return. A small section of it was published in a Leningrad literary journal. It was subjected to official disapproval, and all hope of publishing the book vanished.

She ended her life in poverty and sickness. "The well-known writer" had intentionally cut out of his will his children and grandchildren. Elena Vassilyevna, totally blind toward the end, continued to dictate her poems to her beloved granddaughters, poems that sang of the eternal beauty of life, love, and poesy.

The funeral service for Elena Vassilyevna was held in the big church on Liteiny Prospect, one of the few remaining active churches in Leningrad. Afterward there was a "civilian requiem" in the Club of the Union of Writers, where touching speeches were made. But to this day her memoirs have not been published, nor has a small volume of selected posthumous poems.

I came to the funeral from Moscow, as I had known Alyosha's half-brother before, a Moscow professor of chemistry, and had known of his and Alyosha's great love for their mother. I had also heard a great deal about her, although I had never been able to meet her. That family—complicated and interwoven by many marriages and different sets of children—was the creative milieu that had inspired and called me to lead a creative life. Alyosha's half-brother had repeatedly urged me: "Write! Write! You can do it! Start as if you were writing me a letter, the rest will come of itself. Just try it!" In this way he "dragged" out of me my *Twenty Letters,* and it was he who first read and criticized the manuscript.

Later Alyosha and Sanya introduced me to a Leningrad friend of Elena Vassilyevna, a connoisseur of literature and of Russian poetry. He typed my manuscript for me and told me that it was a "finished book." He kept one copy for himself, considering it his "foundling," and showed it to anyone he wished, without asking my permission.

He was a passionate book lover, who had bequeathed his huge library to a village school. The walls of his room, in a large communal apartment, were lined with books, and as he himself had no more space, he kept shelves with books in the big bathroom which was used by several families. An old philologist and historian of literature, he had collected material for a big work on the poet Maximilian Voloshin, but was never able to push it through the publishing offices. It was at his place that I first read the poetry of Joseph Brodsky, not yet published in the U.S.S.R. He had many fascinating books, among them the biography of Vyacheslav Ivanov, published in Oxford and sent him by Ivanov's daughter, with whom he kept up a correspondence.

One day he scrutinized the palm of my hand and said, "There will be an immense change in your life, its second half far more interesting and significant than the first." I had laughed at the time, but now I often remember those words. . . .

Alyosha was an excellent pianist; it was a delight to hear him play his "Romantic Prelude," dedicated to his mother. He wrote music to her poems. His best pieces were chamber music. Alyosha and Sanya's home was always full of people: singers, musicians, artists. It was a friendly, open home, al-

though I knew that next morning they would have nothing
but coffee and lentils for breakfast. But in the U.S.S.R. a
lack of funds made no impression on anyone. Everyone lived
that way: one suit until it almost fell off one's shoulders.
Alyosha and Sanya's telephone was often disconnected because of nonpayment of bills, but when they had money,
they could not resist long-distance talks with friends in
Moscow.

Old Russian furniture stood in their apartment, an eighteenth-century Dutch cupboard, good pictures—the property
of Alyosha's mother. But all of it in such a condition that one
feared to sit down in a chair lest it fall apart. Friends always
advised Sanya to sell the "old junk" to an antiquarian—at
least they would then have some money. But to them it
seemed too sad to part with Grandmama's bed, her armchair,
her cheval glass. Precious memories were attached to every
piece, and so everything remained in its place. And we continued to eat lentils with onions in the kitchen, sitting on a
dainty little settee with gilt legs.

I loved staying with them in Leningrad. They used to
take me to the Hermitage Museum, to the studio of some
modern artist, introduced me to their friends. And although
I had some distant relatives in Leningrad, I much preferred
staying at Alyosha's or at some friends of his—it was far
more attractive and interesting.

Alyosha and Sanya sometimes came to stay with us in
Moscow. Our apartment would immediately become very
crowded and my children would hang on Alyosha's every
word, for he had an entrancing way of telling stories. But
these visits were always connected with disappointments:
his efforts to sell some composition usually failed. Alyosha's
dream was to go to Paris someday, where his parents had
lived for many years, and meet the great musical world.
When Stravinsky visited the U.S.S.R., he was taken to see
Alyosha. Elena Vassilyevna was still alive then, and the Len-

ingrad Union of Composers decided that this was a home in which "the honor of Soviet music would not be disgraced." They therefore recommended the young composer to Stravinsky's special attention. Alyosha, however, succeeded only in going once to Bulgaria. As for Paris, it still remained beyond reach. . . .

❋

Many of my Moscow friends were connected in one way or another with the world of letters: poets, dramatists, connoisseurs of literature, philologists, journalists, publishers, movie critics, and scriptwriters. Their names were not well known— I never had any desire for the company of the famous— but all of them were professionals, who knew their business and had a keen flair for art.

Some of them worked with me in the Institute of World Literature; others belonged to the Union of Writers, where we often met for meetings and discussions. Many of them spent their summers in Zhukovka, a village near Moscow, almost next door to our dacha. There, again, we often got together. In Moscow there is only one writers' organization and few publishers; anything new—a new poem, or even a bon mot made during a discussion—became instantly known all over town, along with the Party's new decrees on art, or even just a gossipy rumor about some such decree. Moscow is like a big village. Any news spreads like fire. As for changes wrought by the Party in literature and the arts, there were so many of them in the last ten years.

Unforgettable were our walks in Zhukovka, that "literary village" of ours, along the steep banks of a river.

There were five of us: a connoisseur of German literature, an expert on American literature, two translators from Spanish, and I. Here, too, lived the editor of the only movie-review magazine in Moscow. A poet who translated from Polish and Czech would sometimes turn up as a guest. His friend translated from the Estonian. They were not, however, Bohemians. These people could hardly be called "leftists" in their literary tastes, though they were definitely leftists when it came to Party control. They had all suffered too much from that control. Now they lived in the fond hope that at last they might look forward—not to a free press, oh no!— but at least to the publication of Solzhenitsyn's and Pasternak's novels, of Anna Akhmatova's poems, and the possibility of writing in our own country about people in our own time. . . .

These people had suffered a lot. The connoisseur of German literature had spent a term in a concentration camp, where he had made the acquaintance of Solzhenitsyn. This poet published his works under a Russian nom de plume, to hide his Jewish name; otherwise they would never have been published. The fact that during the Second World War he had joined the army as a student and had fought for Russia for four years didn't seem to have convinced the publishers of his patriotism.

The expert on American literature knew full well that translations of modern American writers would never be published.

The two translators from Spanish had become convinced that they would never be permitted to see not only Spain but even Latin America. And Cuba, where they were allowed to go, had not charmed them.

And yet they were not inimical to the Soviet regime and to the Party; all they wished was to "improve" the Party and the regime, to make them conform more closely to their own ideals, to their lofty expectations of what the Party and the regime should be. They had faith and hope that this would gradually come about. Every new sign of a "thaw" strengthened their faith. Yet every time, with extraordinary obtuseness, the Party would destroy such illusions, which the Party itself had actually sown.

If the publicist Ilya Ehrenburg, or the poet Yevtushenko,

the dramatist Alexander Stein or the movie directors Schweizer, Gabay, and Tarkovsky, or the writers Victor Nekrasov and Alexander Yashin permitted themselves to unveil a bit of truth about life in the U.S.S.R. and life abroad—something which the Party itself had urged them to do—instantly there would come a dressing down, a kick in the pants, even a punch in the jaw from "above." No sooner had Konstantin Paustovsky, in a vivid speech before the Union of Writers, dared to make disclosures about the pernicious Soviet bureaucracy, and Vladimir Dudintsev dared write a novel on the subject; no sooner had Konstantin Simonov permitted himself to criticize the Party's decrees on literature and the arts, than each one of them, in turn, received a sound thrashing.

When hundreds of young people in Moscow hailed the exhibition of the sculptor Erzya, just returned from America, it was Erzya himself who got kicked. And when young artists really believed that the time had come when they could create in different styles, that the famous "Socialist realism" did not call for all their works to look alike, and creations by Falk and Neizvestny appeared at exhibitions, they, too, were instantly slapped down from "above." It made one think of serf-actors of long ago, who used to dance in front of their lord in his own private theater. . . .

The liberal Premier Nikita Khrushchev, who, through his declaration of de-Stalinization in all spheres of life, had given hope to the world of arts, now entered into single combat with the poets Margarita Aliger and Andrei Voznesensky, with the sculptor Neizvestny, and with movie director Mikhail Romm, at the so-called "receptions" and "meetings" with members of the artistic world.

Mikhail Romm said to him with a smile, "It is very difficult for me to argue with the Prime Minister and First Secretary of the Central Committee of the Communist Party of the Soviet Union!" But the sarcasm was lost on Khrushchev.

The sculptor Neizvestny reminded Khrushchev that he had fought at the front and had been in a German prisoner-of-war camp, but the Premier insisted that he was not a patriot and was even apparently a homosexual.

Margarita Aliger, a well-known poet, tried to prove to him that she "had always been with the Party," but the Premier admitted that he had never read her works and her name meant nothing to him (he had only caught on to its not being a Russian name).

Between 1957 and 1964 there were several such "meetings" with members of the artistic world. The initiative for them came from Khrushchev himself. Guests would gather at one of my father's former residences near Moscow. Tables would be set up in the park, guests would go for boat rides, or stroll about and talk with members of the government in an informal atmosphere. Wine and vodka would flow. Voroshilov and Sholokhov would sing folk songs. But after these "meetings" no decisions were ever reached—too many splitting headaches, no doubt.

Khrushchev made vain efforts to detect the trends of thought in literary and artistic circles. But with experts from the Central Committee and his own lack of knowledge, all he was able to perceive clearly was that the artistic intelligentsia was the most "restless" element in the country. Our District Party Committee in Moscow, of which the Union of Writers, the Institute of World Literature, several theaters, and the Film Actors Studio were a part, used to complain: "A difficult district ours—so many creative organizations! Much easier when it's just factories!"

Sometimes Alexander Tvardovsky, editor of *Novy Mir*, or Ilya Ehrenburg would succeed in obtaining an audience with the Central Committee or with Khrushchev himself. Then things would ease up for a while—the next number of *Novy Mir* would be quietly issued, Solzhenitsyn's *One Day in the Life of Ivan Denisovich* and other stories would be published

—but this only until the next rap on the knuckles, the next punch in the jaw.

Khrushchev had a knack of spoiling his own good beginnings. He would actually "cut the branch he was sitting on." Having first raised the hopes of the intelligentsia and thereby gained their sympathy, he then proceeded to rebuff that same intelligentsia on which he might have leaned in his struggle with the bureaucracy. But this was not surprising: after all, the bureaucracy was closer to him, he felt more at home in it. . . .

In the U.S.S.R. the press does not impart news. There are only two principal newspapers, *Pravda* and *Izvestia*, meaning "Truth" and "News" respectively. The standing joke was that "There is no truth in the *News*, and no news in the *Truth*." The Premier's encounters with writers, like all other news, were passed on from mouth to mouth over cups of tea among the currant bushes of Zhukovka or during walks along the banks of its river:

"Do you know what Ehrenburg told Khrushchev at their last meeting? His memoirs will continue to be published."

"Have you heard what Voznesensky answered back at the reception?"

"They say Margarita Aliger almost fainted and Kostya Simonov had to lead her from the table, holding her up with both arms. And do you know what happened at the next reception almost a year later? Khrushchev recognized her and said to her, 'I like obstinate people, I'm obstinate myself!'"

"Have you heard? Mikoyan's son visited Hemingway in Cuba. The Goslitizdat is at last putting into type *For Whom the Bell Tolls*. Now there's some hope of the novel being published! But be careful, don't step into something—cows go along this path every evening to the river."

"Cows? We had better go over there, across the field! Yes, yes, go on, I'm listening. I knew nothing about this. Mikoyan's son, after all, has nothing to do with literature!"

"That's of no importance. He was asked to write an article about his interview with Hemingway—you must have seen it in the *Literaturka?** The publishers are hopeful that this will help." (It didn't. The novel is still unpublished.)

"Let's sit down here, on the porch."

We sit down and stretch our legs in the dust. The little porch is part of a log hut rented by the Spanish translators. Not even a hut really, but a sort of shed; yet it does well enough for the summer. It's quiet here, one can work, electric trains run into Moscow regularly. In the tiny room a typewriter stands on a table. One of the translators is writing a book about the Spanish poet García Lorca, who perished in the Civil War.

"Do you know what Trotsky told the Mexican painter Diego Rivera? Mexico is full of memories of Trotsky, he had many friends there."

"And have you seen Emmanuel d'Astier's new book about Stalin? Interesting, but a lot in it is wrong. Svetlana, why don't you write your memoirs? You have so much to say!"

Again! They must have all got together on the subject— how many times have I heard those words! In reply I mumble something indistinct. I don't want to admit that I am in the process of writing, sitting on my terrace not far from here.

And so *García Lorca* will also be written in Zhukovka. It ought to be a good book. How alive the Spanish Civil War is among Russian writers! How many romantics rushed to Spain in those days from different countries, not only from the U.S.S.R. Many of them died there. But the Russians who died were better off: trials and imprisonment awaited those who returned.

The romantic Communism of the twenties, long dead in the U.S.S.R., had suddenly taken fire and come to life again in Spain. That was why so many rushed there. It was finally

* The colloquial Russian term for *Literaturnaya Gazeta.*

crushed in 1937-1938 and remained alive only in the depths of incorrigible hearts, which could not be subdued by prisons. Romantic Communism turned into fanaticism, for there remained no real soil in which it could have thrived. But reverberations of the Spanish Civil War continued to nourish the hearts of romantics even thirty years later. The hearts of blind romantics, for romanticism and Communism are incompatible.

"Did you know that Nazim Hikmet decided to remain in Poland? But now, they say, he wants to return. Poor Nazim, a marvelous man, one can't help feeling sorry for him!"

Nazim Hikmet, a Turkish journalist, writer, poet, and a typical representative of romantic Communism, spent ten years in an Ankara prison. Having escaped from prison, he fled to the U.S.S.R., where he lived for many years. The decisions of the Twentieth Congress raised his hopes in earnest, as they did those of many others. He wrote a wonderful satirical play called *But Was There an Ivan Ivanovich?* In it he made fun of Soviet satellites—obviously of Hungary and Rákosi. The Hungarian events of 1956 followed. Hikmet had hit the nail on the head.

The play was so unbearably real and witty that the Central Committee instantly forbade it, after its very first showing. Nazim was angered and went to Poland, which, in those early Gomulka days, seemed like a stronghold of liberal Communism. Later he returned to the U.S.S.R. Hikmet died in 1963 without having lived to see the trial of Sinyavsky and Daniel. Had he been alive, he would have most certainly been among the protesters.

"Let's go and have tea!"

We move into the other room of this very primitive but inspired abode. We drink tea, with sausage and cheese, as usual. A can of preserved fish is opened. How good! How wonderful it is to hear news. Where else could I have learned so much in one evening? A poet friend of ours said, "Zhukovka is the dwelling place of our intelligentsia—the most progressive ones and some of the very best among the reactionary ones." By this he meant me.

＊

The reverberations of the Spanish Civil War lived for a long time, even after 1936 when Soviet Army men and writers, returning from Spain, were sent to prison. In Moscow in 1936 many families adopted Spanish children— orphans. In this way the boy who shared my desk at school got a "little Spanish brother," and everyone envied him. We all wore Spanish hats with tassels and knew the expression "*No pasarán!*" At a large New Year's party, arranged at Voroshilov's dacha, the guests of honor were two Spanish girls—Charita and Luli. They sang Spanish and Russian songs to a piano accompaniment, and everyone wanted to give them presents.

Later the "Spanish children" grew up, became Soviet citizens; but they didn't forget their native tongue and longed to return to their fatherland. I knew many of them at the university. José García and Eloina Lantarón became historians. All of them had to get used to Russian frosts, to *valenki* (knee-high felt boots) and fur caps—poor unhappy birds of passage. . . .

When Franco allowed them to return, they rushed back to their mother country. But to live and work there, with their "Soviet past," proved to be difficult; many begged to return to the U.S.S.R., where their life was not an easy one either. Their glamorous halo had faded away long ago.

Feelings toward the Spanish War changed together with the change of generations. I saw this illustrated vividly in a certain Moscow family. The father had perished in Spain, where he had been in command, under a false name, of one of the international brigades. He was a true romantic: a Hungarian who came to Russia as a prisoner of war in 1914. After the Revolution he remained in the U.S.S.R., wrote lively, witty stories, directed, in the twenties, a young people's left-wing theater, married a Russian woman, and soon became a well-known Soviet writer. They lived well; his daughter attended one of Moscow's best schools and longed to go on the stage.

As soon as war broke out in Spain, he dropped everything and went there, where "people were fighting for the Revolution"—something he missed in Moscow. His nature craved danger; he was brave, and in Spain soon became a general. He was killed quite by chance. His wife and daughter continued getting letters from him for six months after his death. The letters traveled by slow wartime mail through many countries.

He wrote beautiful letters home about the war. War was his calling. Tamara, his daughter, with whom he had always been very close, grew up on these letters. To her, her father was the embodiment of everything that was best and brightest in this world.

She entered the Theatrical Institute and would have become a stage director, but when World War II broke out she announced to her mother her decision to go to the front as a nurse. Her mother was in a dreadful state, but she remained adamant. She couldn't help it—the romantic memory of her father called her to face mortal dangers.

Tamara spent all four years of the war at the front, doing whatever was most needed—working as an army nurse, or as a Party worker, or organizing concerts for the soldiers in times of temporary calm. At the front she married an officer. They had a "war wedding" in a dugout. Later they returned to Moscow, and Tamara gave birth to a son, who grew up to be my son's friend. Tamara and I became friends, too.

Our sons were almost of the same age. They had no desire to go to Vietnam or the Congo to "defend the Revolution" and would have considered any such volunteers as out of their minds. Stasik knew French well and was studying Spanish. He wrote fairly good short stories. He was learning to speak Spanish because he wanted to become a journalist and someday go to Spain to find out all he could about his grandfather. As for his stories, they were either about love or about the "generation gap."

He considered his own parents hopelessly old-fashioned, especially his father, a colonel, who liked to admonish him in a truly military fashion and demanded absolute obedience. The boy refused to accept such "front-page editorials," as he called his father's admonitions, refused to obey, and soon left his home altogether, so as not to live in "such a narrow middle-class atmosphere."

For a while he shared a room with a comrade of his, in which, instead of furniture, they had just two mattresses on the floor, and on one of the walls a large portrait of Ernest Hemingway. It was not easy to become a hippie in Moscow: a place to live could not be found, and the police would soon return the "vagrant" to his parents' home, where he was registered. But Stasik was not a hippie. On the contrary, he was very careful about his appearance, and his shirts and trousers were made for him by his friend, the famous Slava Zaitsev. It was just that Stasik did not wish to reconcile himself with his parents' "backwardness and naïve Party line."

Slava Zaitsev—a designer of clothes, well known now in Paris, London, and the United States—belonged to the same generation as my son and Stasik, a generation for which no ideals of any kind were worth a war.

Instead of military exploits Slava Zaitsev had longed since childhood for fine clothes. He was born in a basement, into a *dvornik's* (janitor's) family, and grew up in a basement. Later his father was killed at the front, his mother died, and he was left an orphan. A kind woman—also a *dvornik* by profession—brought him up. Like all *dvorniki*, she, too, lived in a basement. Where, under such conditions, did the boy get his ideas about beautiful clothes? But then, Gorky, too, while still living in "the lower depths," dreamed of beauty. Slava could have become an engineer, a soldier—

there were many careers open to a young man—but all he wanted was to design beautiful clothes for others.

On graduating from the Institute of Art, he soon drew attention to himself with his models of everyday, simple, comfortable clothing. He was invited to work in a clothes factory, where fat, conservative women designers met him as an enemy, having instantly sensed in him a dangerous rival. But Slava Zaitsev's models continued to be exhibited, continued to win prizes, and foreign correspondents came seeking interviews with him. They were able to talk with the famous young designer anywhere but in his home. To show Slava Zaitsev's home to foreigners was out of the question. With his young wife and baby, he occupied a tiny cubicle, the walls of which he himself had painted in different colors, one of them black. On this black wall he pinned up sketches of his new creations. After a basement this wasn't too bad, and Slava had no idea how famous designers lived in the West. Perhaps by now he has his own apartment?

Military feats of fathers and grandfathers were a thing of the past. The new generation wants to live in freedom and beauty. It does not want to *kill*.

＊

Unforgettable Zhukovka! What a strange collection of people this settlement on the outskirts of Moscow, unified by "Platform Zhukovka," where on Sunday evening, by the one-track railway line, in expectation of the electric train, its whole diverse population would find itself gathered.

The old village of Zhukovka was the nucleus. It had a sickly kolkhoz, but most of its population commuted daily to factories in the vicinity of Moscow. In summer log huts without plumbing—a privy in the vegetable garden—would be rented to university professors, literary critics, movie directors, poets—to those among them who hadn't yet earned a dacha for themselves, and probably never would.

In 1946 the government rewarded the inventors of the atom bomb and of the first cyclotron with gifts of dachas, built in a pine grove near "Platform Zhukovka." Thus came into existence dachas of both secret and openly acknowledged scientists, all of them officially belonging to the Academy of Sciences. The location was convenient and attractive, and these two-storied dachas, built at government expense, sprang up like mushrooms. A few years later sputnik-inventors were added to the atom-splitters and, judging by the rapidly growing number of dachas, Soviet science was making big strides. After a while, widows began selling dachas to other categories of Soviet rich, so that among physicists, chemists, and mathematicians now appeared the cellist Mstislav Rostropovich and the composer Dmitri Shostakovich.

At last, with the passing of 1953, after much talk about curtailing the ever-distending government apparatus, it transpired that the apparatus had distended even more and that there were not enough summer dachas to go around. So three more settlements were built, consisting of small standard wooden cottages with heating, each settlement surrounded by a communal fence. Some of the dachas were given to widows and pensioners, me and my children among them.

We spent every summer there. But ten years later, when my children grew up, I announced that we had no further need for a dacha. This created a furor. "We have never had anyone giving up a dacha," I was told by an official from the Council of Ministers. "People beg for them! What do you think you are doing? You're giving the impression that you have chosen this way of expressing your protest against the new government." (Khrushchev had just been dethroned.) "When we deem it necessary to do so, we shall take your dacha from you. Until then continue to use it and don't raise the question again." So we stayed on.

The three sections of Zhukovka—the village, the "academicians," and the "Council of Ministers"—led entirely different and separate lives.

In the village there was a common everyday general store, in which produce was sold. In summer a long queue always stood on the main road outside the store. For some incomprehensible considerations of their own, the police would not permit a village market to be organized.

On the "Council of Ministers'" territory there were several stores, supplied with the best provisions. To prevent the villagers from buying there, the administration of the dacha settlement prepared passes, which were issued to all dachniks. In order to enforce this, they had to place special guards at every gate—there were not less than five gates—to check the passes of all those who, with purses and bags, were going to the stores; and if a pass was not presented, turn the person away. All these guards were village women. After spending their appointed time at the gates, they would go into the stores and buy grain and sugar for their village people, at the same time damning the "accursed Sovmin (Council of Ministers)." The wives of academicians, or their cooks, were the chief sufferers from this system of passes. They, too, were supposed to get passes, which, for some reason or other, were not issued to them until the end of the summer. The wives of academicians, however, were stubborn and persevering, for they, too, had to prepare dinner, and near the gates and the stores loud, squealing arguments would often break out. . . .

On holidays passions grew red-hot; then the village youths, with a few drinks tucked under their belts, would start a fight with the Sovmin youth in the movies, where all social groups met. And on peaceful summer mornings, while waiting for the morning train to Moscow, elegant girl interpreters in cotton dresses would stand at one end of the platform, while the ministerial ladies, in silks, would occupy the other.

As everywhere else, my life in Zhukovka was paradoxical. I knew none of the Sovmin crowd. My personal friends in summer lived in the village proper. A little later I got to know some of the "academicians."

One day my Katie brought by the hand a little girl with fiery red hair, her new friend. Then appeared a boy, Yura, a friend of theirs, with his white dog, a spitz. Since then— all of ten years by now—those three have remained inseparable, and redheaded Tonya Zalessky's parents became our dear friends. These elderly, respectable people, who had two married sons and several grandchildren, were amazingly young in spirit. Every Sunday in winter we went on skis into the beautiful neighboring woods, an oddly assorted group of children and sixty-year-old friends of the Zalesskys, all of them jolly, rollicking fellows like themselves. This noisy crowd, having worked up in the frost bright red cheeks and sound appetites, would all roll into our house, or into the unheated kitchen of the Zalesskys, ransack the supplies— sandwiches, chopped meat, sausages—fry eggs, and drink a bottle of cognac. Tonya's parents and their friends were inventors who had won many prizes and decorations, but without any publicity in the press. Their inventions were State secrets. This did not prevent them from being full of fun and loving poetry, music, sports, and crossword puzzles. Having satisfied our hunger, we would all go to the station, and in the train on our way back Semyon Alexandrovich Zalessky would read aloud to us poems by Selvinsky, Pasternak, and Yevtushenko.

In summer at their dacha they had badminton and ping-pong, at which our two little girls and Yura would play with the grownups. The children at an early age became interested in mathematics, physics, chemistry, astronomy; they read the same books, studied English. The girls were not yet fifteen when I saw them carrying a learned biography of Einstein, later a university textbook on physics. When they didn't understand something, they would ask Semyon Alexandrovich, who was always glad to explain. Yura knew more than the girls; his grandfather was a Nobel Prize

Laureate in Chemistry. The family was apt to spoil the high-strung boy, who was talented and extremely well read for his age.

His other grandfather had "invented" something so hush-hush that one couldn't even mention it. He lived in one of those new cities that were not even shown on the map and had no address except a postbox, and Yura would say, "Grandpa and Grandma have gone back to their box." There Grandpa would test his "inventions," which were instantly recorded on all seismographs the world over. But the U.S.S.R., of course, pretended that no one knew anything about it.

To Katie's and Tonya's enthusiasm for physics, sports, and dogs was now added a passion for horseback riding, which they indulged in at a riding school. The two girls made a solemn oath never to marry and to dedicate their lives to physics, sports, and the collection of books. Tonya even wrote to her father a signed pledge to this effect, which he, chuckling to himself, locked in a drawer of his writing desk. My Katie didn't quite dare venture that far.

In the last few years the appearance at our dacha of Brajesh Singh, of black Bertha, and of frequent Indian guests created an agitation in the Zhukovka settlement. The Sovmin ladies pulled long faces every time they saw Bertha and her daughter strolling along the walks and going into the stores. To make it even worse, Bertha spoke English to her child. They didn't see Brajesh because he was in no condition to go out, but they stared in astonishment at the women in saris who came to visit him.

The "academicians" stopped calling on us after once seeing an Indian Embassy car in front of our house.

"I don't want to have to write a deposition against myself tomorrow," Semyon Alexandrovich told me sadly. If he did not, "someone else" would, but this he refrained from saying.

Yura's and Tonya's parents were not allowed to meet for-

eigners without special permission. The reason for such senseless rules was known only to those who made them. But
nobody knew these nameless individuals who, contrary to
Soviet laws and the Soviet Constitution, dictated to Soviet
citizens what kind of lives they should lead.

Tonya Zalessky's parents, and their merry contemporaries,
had retained in their hearts their youthful romantic Communism of the twenties, which they refused to disavow.
Their Communism was not so much the theory of Marx
and Lenin as a memory of their own early postrevolutionary
days, with a hungry but gay student life, a memory of the
stage appearances of Mayakovsky and the Meyerhold
Theater, of free debates on politics and art, and an ever-
present hope for a "World Revolution." Now, I suppose,
their chief hope was for a gradual rapprochement of the two
sections of the world, split into Communism and Capitalism. Having put their faith in Communism during their
student years, they were loath to part with the "sins of their
youth."

But their two sons, both engineers, looked upon everything in a very different way: they considered their parents
old-fashioned. As for Tonya, Yura, and my Katie, they will
not seriously study Marxism-Leninism, which, in their eyes,
is hopelessly out of date. Having acquired at an early age
the habit of objective, mathematical thought, these youngsters will doubtless never divide mankind into classes and
parties, but rather into those who believe in the theory of
Relativity and those who don't; they already know that the
language which mankind—and the whole Universe for that
matter—will eventually have in common will be the language of mathematical formulas.

❋

The Lvovs, husband and wife, were both astronomers.

I couldn't conceal my profound admiration for that quick,

graceful, elegant Lydia Yulyevna. She not only carried on fascinating work, editing scientific publications on astronomy, but found time to do all the household shopping, take care of a small grandson, nurse her sick mother-in-law, and in the evening accompany her son, a student, to the movies.

The family lived in a small old wooden house that from the outside looked like an ordinary log hut, a real monument to old-time Moscow. Inside, with great trouble, laboring with their own hands, they had installed modern conveniences—gas, heating, a bathroom. Old Russian furniture, pictures, silver decorated the house. In what lovely porcelain cups tea would be served in the drawing room, which also served as a study and bedroom for the hosts. Around this small round table, of an evening, the entire hard-working family would gather together: the two astronomers with their son, a physicist, and their daughter and son-in-law, both of them painters.

No one here ever mentioned Communism. For these people, whose ancestors had been artists and physicists, serving science and working for the progress of mankind, it just didn't exist. The revolution had brought poverty, confinement, and humiliation into the lives of these hereditary Russian intellectuals. But they continued to do their work, ignoring, despising this absurd regime, these uneducated rulers, preserving in everything their human dignity, and anxious only that their children, like themselves, should continue to serve Progress.

Above the narrow sofa, on which Lydia Yulyevna's son slept, there hung a rickety shelf, laden with books; above her daughter's bed, a silver crucifix, inherited from a grandmother. Everywhere on the walls lovely water colors painted by Lydia Yulyevna's father in the Crimea. At the round table nobody discussed politics; politics were neither liked nor talked about in this house. The conversation would be about the small grandson, about new movies, new books.

On one of her fingers Lydia Yulyevna wore an enormous sapphire from India, a gift from her first mother-in-law. Long ago, in her youth, when Lydia Yulyevna had just started working at the Pulkovo Observatory, she had met the famous Indian astronomer Chandrasekhar, and afterward had always wanted to have a look at India. In this house India was loved and understood, and maybe that was why I always felt so at home in it. But Lydia Yulyevna to this day has been unable to go anywhere, except to East Germany and Bulgaria.

She had small, strong, unmanicured hands. With those hands she did all the housework. The sapphire ring, and another with a large agate, never seemed in the way, having become an integral part of her hands. I used to visit her in winter in her cold dacha, when she lived there with her grandson. She lit the boiler, brought in the firewood, prepared meals, did the washing, bathed the little boy, all of this to free her daughter of such chores, so she could graduate from the Art Institute. But no one freed Lydia Yulyevna of her work. Only more of it was piled upon her shoulders, and she managed it all, always remaining calm, elegant, and attractive.

What secret strength helped her to flutter about all day on her quick, light feet? She was not religious in the strictly accepted sense of the word—she had too much of the astronomer's rational eye on the Universe. But perhaps it was this profound knowledge that had convinced her of the existence of sources of energy unknown to others?

To me Lydia Yulyevna exemplified true refinement of the spirit, purified of worldly sediments and smog, of everything that corrodes and soils human existence. She never reviled anyone, never hated anyone—she had no need for such emotions, her whole day being filled with positive work. She could not afford wasting any time on gossip and protests. Her life, as a result, was rich and fruitful. Even a brief meet-

ing with her always brought me a calm assurance of the ultimate strength of goodness and creativity.

❋

A bit like her, in some ways, was Vera, whose classmate I had
been for ten years. We had known each other even before
that because our mothers had been friends. In Vera's family
were preserved the traditions of the Russian intelligentsia—
not of noble but of middle-class stock—which carried enlightenment from the capitals to remote villages, to the
people. Her parents had been village teachers in the so-called
"people's schools." Their lives had been selfless, poor, pur-
poseful. They had never known any affluence and had never
enjoyed even simple luxuries. Their riches and treasures
were all of the spirit, and these they passed on in full to
their children.

In appearance Vera was the exact opposite of Lydia
Yulyevna's refined elegance. She wore a braid around her
head—the habitual hairdo of fair-haired village women in
Russia. Her smile was shy, her gray eyes immense, clear, intelligent, and sad. Why, then, did these two women seem
alike to me?

The answer lay in the fact that Vera, too, stood for purity
of the soul, decency, truth. And it was to such higher types
that I, sinful weakling, had to turn for help and support in
order to cleanse my spirit and gather some of their strength.

Vera was a biologist. Genetics were her specialty. This had
made her life difficult, for in 1948 genetics had been obliged
to face a Party prohibition of the chromosome theory. An
immense section of this science was declared forbidden. Was
this an inquisition of the Middle Ages? A trial of Galileo?
The burning of Giordano Bruno? No one was burned at
the stake, but the "all-knowing Party" had declared the
Mendel-Morgan theory a *heresy*, and heresies had no right
to exist in the U.S.S.R.

Nevertheless, this "heresy" continued to live underground, scientists continuing to experiment under the pretense of studying other subjects. At times experiments had to be carried on at home, in some communal kitchen or in the only room in which the whole family lived. Many of Vera's colleagues did exactly this. It only served to strengthen their perseverance.

When after several years the chromosome theory was "rehabilitated," it turned out that the years had not been wasted. In the Institute of Genetics, reinstated only in the sixties, the work of Vera and her colleagues found its rightful place.

When in 1956 Vera was sent to a conference in Paris, she learned French in four months and was able to read her report and answer all questions in French. She had her own system of quick application in everything: how to learn grammar quickly; how to learn to type quickly; how to prepare anything at an accelerated pace when time was scarce; how to handle a card index swiftly and scientifically.

At home she lived alone with her aging father, whom she fed, nursed, and adored. On his account she had declined a six-month trip to England; it was impossible at the time to find a woman in Moscow who would do the housework and "baby-sit." She was offered a very advantageous job in Cuba, Fidel Castro having suddenly decided to organize an Institute of Genetics and place himself at the head of it. Counting on their fraternal help, he invited scientists from many Socialist countries. The living conditions offered amounted to luxury. Vera was even invited to bring her father, but she only laughed. Cuba was not for her. To move to another regime in which the dictator could place himself at the head of an Institute of Genetics was contrary to all her principles.

She and her father lived in two small, spotlessly clean rooms in which, except for a large collection of records and a record player, there were no objects of luxury. No bathtub either. No elevator, no telephone, although she lived in the heart of Moscow. The kitchen was tiny and window-less.

Vera earned a good deal, but money in the Soviet economy didn't amount to much. She had little hope of obtaining a telephone, and no hope at all of getting an apartment, not being a Party member. A Party activist, spending half of his time at meetings and in a regional committee, would always be first on the long list of people waiting for separate modern apartments with a telephone. A prominent scientist who was not of the Party, like Vera, would always be last on such lists. She knew this and didn't complain. Nor did she go begging—this was not in keeping with her character.

But how nice it was in her home, such cleanliness every-where! Potted plants flourishing abundantly on a sunlit window sill, a gay strip of blue sky in the large windows—warmth and friendliness breathing in every corner of this home, plain almost to the point of asceticism.

In her tiny room she had two tables laden with books and letters. She received letters from her colleagues in Paris, from other cities in Russia, for she was already a recognized authority in her line of work. The walls of her room were hung with pictures painted by young artists, those whose works were not allowed to be exhibited: new symbolists, impressionists, somewhat on the lines of Vrubel, with very bright colors and fluent composition. Such pictures will never be publicly shown in the U.S.S.R. until some drastic changes take place not only in art but in the life of the whole country, not until Russia finally gets out of the grim dead end she is in at present. Vera understood this well. That is why young artists had chosen the walls of her room as the most appropriate place for their works.

Manuscripts were also brought to her, not by writers but by people who only aspired to write. Her evaluations and criticism were severe, but her judgments were believed. People loved her.

Shortly before my departure from Moscow she told me

about a young research worker, an American, who had appeared in her Institute and had won everyone's affection by his simple and gay nature. Doubtless she would have gone to France again with pleasure to see her colleagues there, and would also have liked to go to England if it hadn't been for her sick father. Everywhere abroad her work would have been valued according to its merits. But in the ranks of those eligible to obtain visas for trips abroad Vera, who held no Party card, would always be the last in line—and Lydia Yulyevna, too.

＊

Boris Andreyevich and Anna Andreyevna were born in Tsaritsyn on the Volga and went on calling it that, although it had been first renamed Stalingrad and then Volgograd.

This unhealthy passion to change the names of cities and streets was typical of the general instability of Soviet life. Perm had been changed to Molotov, then back to Perm. There had been a town called Trotsk in the Urals, but they had to give it back its old prerevolutionary name. In Moscow the famous Vozdvizhenka Street became the Street of the Comintern; but after the latter had been abolished it became known as Kalinin Prospect. In Leningrad the famous Nevsky Prospect was finally given back its name, but for a long time it had been known as the Prospect of the 25th of October. . . .

The Vladimirovs, brother and sister, had been born into the family of a Russian doctor and his wife, an Italian singer, who had founded a School of Music in Tsaritsyn. They looked Italian—dark eyes, dark hair, dark complexions. In their childhood the boy had played the violin, the girl had played the piano. Anna Andreyevna finished at the Conservatory, but her brother had been lured by politics and at the age of seventeen, having given up the violin and his school, became a commissar in the Red Army.

After the Civil War he became a Party worker in Transcaucasia, where he busied himself with publishing, cultural
work, and art. His mother and sister joined him in Tiflis,
quickly became used to the sharp southern cooking, and fell
completely in love with Georgia, where the family spent
the best years of their lives. Georgian actors, writers, artists
visited their home; they organized musical evenings. The
twenties were years of freedom in art. The young "Commissar" knew and understood this particular milieu and he
himself acted in movies, not disdaining to take the part of
a chieftain of a band of anarchists—the famous Makhno—
something that no Party worker of later years would have
ever dared to do.

In those faraway days the following scene was also possible: Boris Andreyevich one day entered the office of
Ordzhonikidze, who then directed the Party in Transcaucasia, and found a woman in a dusty traveling cloak, her
arms crossed on her breast, kneeling in front of Ordzhonikidze and making an impassioned speech. This was the writer
Marietta Shaginyan, who had run in straight from the road
to implore Ordzhonikidze to protect an innocent engineer
on a big construction project who had been accused of sabo-
tage. Her plea helped the man. In those days such things
were still possible.

Early in the thirties the Vladimirovs moved to Moscow.
Boris Andreyevich, together with Alexander Fadeyev and
Leopold Averbach, became a member of the management
of RAPP (Organization of Proletarian Writers), and one of
the leading literary and movie critics. He often saw Gorky
and met my father.

He told me how upset Gorky had been about the Party's
unexpected decision to do away with the grouping of writers
according to the nature of their work. In spite of frequent
visits paid him by Stalin, Voroshilov, and others, Gorky's
opinion on the matter was ignored and he had been advised
of the accomplished fact. He was obliged to accept the

honorary role of "Patriarch of Soviet Literature," with which
the Party had honored him, although he drastically disagreed with its decisions to abolish the different group-
ings and establish "Socialist realism" as the only style for
all writers. He had had no choice but to halfheartedly deliver his official address to the First Congress of Writers,
which took place in 1934, marking the complete subjugation of literature to the Party.

After this event Boris Andreyevich quit the Union of
Writers and went to the north to work on a construction project. He saw clearly that affairs had taken a dangerous turn
and that art, as such, had been done away with. Fadeyev,
his old colleague at RAPP, was able to adapt himself to
the new trend, and after Gorky's death became the head of
the Union of Writers. In 1937 he helped send many a "proletarian writer" to his death, including his old comrade
Averbach. Boris Andreyevich was excluded from the Party
and, relieved of his work, sat waiting for his arrest.

The arrest never came. But there was no work either. To
rise to the surface and draw attention to oneself was dangerous. So, upon his return to Moscow from the north, Boris
Andreyevich sat at home, making hand-dyed batiks—he
had excellent taste. He lived in this way until war broke out,
when his engineering experience came in handy and he built
bomb shelters.

After the war he returned to the movie industry, working
as an editor of scripts. The scripts were written by members of the Union of Writers, still headed at that time by
Fadeyev, a fact that caused Boris Andreyevich considerable
anxiety. In 1948, when the Party embarked on a campaign
against "cosmopolitans in art," Boris Andreyevich was relieved of his job, accused of being both a "cosmopolitan and
an antipatriot." His "guilt" had consisted in rejecting scripts
of no merit, written under orders and depicting as the truth
the lie displayed about Soviet life.

Once more Boris Andreyevich turned to dyeing batiks,

and repairing watches and lamps in expectation of an arrest.

But at last times changed. After the Twentieth Congress Boris Andreyevich returned to literature and the arts, became once more a member of the Union of Writers, and was reinstated in the Party. Those "proletarian writers" who had managed to survive—and they were few—returned from prison. As for Fadeyev, he shot himself at his dacha in Peredelkino, lying in bed, with Stalin's picture on the night table beside him. "Sashka's own conscience did him in, I'm not sorry for him," Boris Andreyevich said when he heard of the suicide.

It was at this time that I met the Vladimirovs. Boris Andreyevich was then screening O. Henry's *Cabbages and Kings.* Slowly the family was returning to life, but health, strength, and years had been irretrievably lost.

Boris Andreyevich had remained a Communist, though by no means of the irreconcilable type he had been in his youth. It was with profound pessimism that he now looked to the future of art, of the country, of the Party. At the Union of Writers, whose meetings he had begun to attend again, he found no one of "his kind." He could not bring himself to agree with either the liberal hopes of the idealists or the noisy vociferations of leftist poets. As in the past, the management of the Union looked at him askance. From the point of view of creativity Boris Andreyevich considered the Union a hopeless organization. He looked with the same hopelessness upon the efforts of the Institute of World Literature—the organization I was working in—to write a history of Soviet literature.

There were profound reasons for his pessimism, which ran counter to the then prevailing rosy expectations. In 1956 the Institute undertook to re-establish the "true history of Soviet literature." Andrei Sinyavsky was entrusted with writing an article on Pasternak's poetry. But by 1966 Sinyavsky was in prison, Pasternak dead, having been excluded from the Union of Writers prior to his death, and an order was issued for the three volumes of *The History of Soviet Literature* already published to be re-examined and revised. . . .

Boris Andreyevich lived with his son, his daughter-in-law, and his granddaughter in a communal apartment. Both father and son were excellent cooks, and so was Anna Andreyevna, Boris Andreyevich's sister. In this charming family, with which I had become close friends, I was taught to cook. Most of my culinary knowledge came out of that crowded little communal kitchen. Everyone in it officiated with a white apron around him. No one could prepare better coffee, better salad, a better punch than Boris Andreyevich. How difficult it was to choose a piece of cheese that would please these gourmets! What a delicious sauce—a *spécialité de la maison*—the brother and sister would concoct for the herring, carefully grating ingredients for it. And what an incomparable Georgian *satzivi* and *lobio* would be prepared there on the occasion of family birthdays. And finally—to the fury of their neighbors in the apartment— what wonderful aromas would fill that narrow kitchen with its ceiling blackened by soot.

In this family I learned far more than just the art of cooking.

The stories I heard here were in themselves an education. Boris Andreyevich had seen Trotsky in 1924 when the latter had come to the Caucasus to rest; he had known Kirov and Ordzhonikidze in his Civil War days and during his work in Tiflis. He had talked with Stalin about literature and films, had shown Mikoyan the construction of the electric power station in the north, where he had been working at the time. He knew the history of the Party and its leaders inside out, from personal experience, not from textbooks. He really should have written his memoirs, but he knew too well the habits of the Writers' Union: his manuscript would not only never be published but might one day mysteriously disappear from his desk. . . .

We used to go to recitals at the Conservatory. Brother and sister had not touched the violin and the piano for years, but their taste in music was impeccable. At the Tiflis Conservatory Anna Andreyevna had been the pupil of Paliashvili. Both had spent their lives in the world of art, had known Eisenstein, Babel, Bagritsky. Intrinsically artistic themselves, their friends were members of the intelligentsia of the arts. Many of them had been arrested, many had perished; some had returned alive. All my older friends of the last years, who belonged to the latter category, I had met through the Vladimirov family. And it was through them that I learned all over again the history of my country, of the Party, of the Revolution and the Civil War, the kind of history which for fifty years now official Soviet historians have been unable to write.

*

Venerable old ladies sometimes invited me for a cup of tea and a chat. I like old people, just as I like old trees: in their shadow there is freshness and peace, one admires them, and around them everything is so calm.

Martha Lazarevna lived with her grown-up son in one room because they had no other. The son was a talented engineer, who had received, together with a group of colleagues, the Lenin Prize of the "secret" kind, never mentioned in the press. He and his mother had the right to two rooms—more than that they were not entitled to—but they disliked the idea of moving from the center of Moscow to the suburbs. They much preferred the quiet of their one big room with a cupboard full of books as a partition, to modern apartment houses with low ceilings and walls that let every noise come through.

If the truth be told, they had another reason for their refusal to leave this communal apartment, in which six housewives gathered in the kitchen and a long line formed outside the toilet, and the reason was this: Martha Lazarevna had been born and bred in this apartment, which had formerly belonged to her father. It had been an immense apartment. After the Revolution a family had been assigned to every room, leaving the owners with only one. A long and difficult life had been lived among these walls, and it was hard to tear oneself away from them.

Martha Lazarevna took in translations of technical works in English. Her son Vitaly—a mathematician, physicist, and engineer—collected books on art and phonograph records. This is what they spent all their money on, although they might have bought themselves a car or a TV set. They succeeded in obtaining rare foreign editions of surrealists, recordings of American folk songs—the "black market" in Moscow supplied anything one wanted, yet in a regular shop one couldn't find a new American book on Picasso.

Of a trip abroad they could never even dream, although Vitaly worked in an Institute that often sent its members "beyond the border." There were four reasons for this: first, Vitaly was a Jew; second, he was unmarried; third, he spoke good English; fourth, he was not a Party member. From the point of view of those who granted exit visas it was about the worst possible combination. They preferred sending out those who depended on the Party, on an interpreter, on their family, which had to remain in the U.S.S.R. as hostages.

Mother and son were exceptionally close. It was so pleasant having tea with them at their small round table in the middle of the room, with bookshelves full of books all around one and a serene bronze Buddha squinting down from a tall antique bureau. Gentleness and calm emanated from the inhabitants of this room, who had humbly accepted life in one room, with a communal kitchen and their own door as a coat-and-hat rack, with the necessity of traveling to work every day for an hour and a half by train, with the knowledge that there was no escape from this life and never would be—accepting it all with open hearts, simply because it was Fate.

Perhaps this family accepted Fate with such calm because a real miracle had happened to Martha Lazarevna's brother. But that was an instance of a lucky break.

He was already a middle-aged man and had been working in one of the State ministries in Moscow when in 1941 he took a rifle and joined the militia to defend Moscow. A hundred percent civilian and intellectual, he was immediately surrounded and taken prisoner. After that there had been no news of him, and his family had considered him dead, all the more so since it seemed hardly possible for a Jew to survive in a German prison. And yet, twelve years later, in 1953, he reappeared alive and unhurt, and what's more, from the wrong direction—from the East, out of Siberia. I met him at Martha Lazarevna's. The "Miracle" was tall and looked young for his sixty years, and there was a merry twinkle in his eyes. He was back now at his former job in the State ministry and spoke only jokingly of his "adventures," pleasantly rolling his r's as he did so.

He spoke fluent French, and this had saved him: when he was captured he had succeeded in convincing the Germans that he was French. In Germany he had worked for more than three years in a factory, as hundreds of other Russian prisoners had done. Then came liberation. . . .

But for Soviet prisoners of war "liberation" meant being loaded into closed cars, like so many head of cattle, and dispatched, without even a chance, straight to Siberia, there to continue their hard labor. Instead of a German munitions factory he now found himself in Siberian forests cutting timber, guarded by Soviet "watchdogs" instead of German ones. To write home, just to tell his family that he was alive, was against the rules: those who had survived imprisonment in Germany were considered criminals for having survived.

Like my friend Marina and her husband Nathan, this

man belonged to those who returned spiritually annealed, purified, made enduring, like a diamond. These people, full of humor and tolerance, brought back with them no bitterness, no rancor. As a rule they preferred not to recall the difficult years. If they spoke of them at all, it was to remember some outstanding personality they had met among the sufferers, or to recall either acts of kindness and courage or some amusing incidents.

I remember one elderly woman, a translator of Spanish classics. She was arrested and sent to a women's concentration camp in Kazakhstan, in all probability accused solely of having traveled abroad with her husband. Upon her return from Kazakhstan in 1954 she used to say that "hard work and simple food" had improved her health. Once again she took up translations. Her husband had died and she, an old solitary woman, was given a room in one of the new buildings that had mushroomed during the past years around Moscow—all of them standard five-story buildings without elevators or telephones. Her immediate neighbors were young men, also returned from concentration camps. All of them, although they were former thieves, treated "Granny" very well. Still, on the days when she got her pay, she had to lock her door, as those men would pester her for something "just to buy a half-pint with." Nor would they leave her alone, kneeling outside her room, imploring her, until finally she would slip them a three-ruble note under the door. Her friends in town were horrified. "And you are not afraid?" they would ask. "Why, those men might kill you!" But she would only laugh: "They are good lads. *Out there,* you know, I was among such people. *After that I'm afraid of nothing. . . .*"

I found this attitude in others who had returned: *After what they had seen,* nothing could frighten them. Now they just enjoyed every moment of life as no one else could.

In the home of Vitaly and Martha Lazarevna we often listened to records. Vitaly liked modern jazz as much as he did classical music. He would listen to it with that concentration typical of mathematicians. Music engenders in them images, rhythms, figures, and then suddenly they find some unexpected solution. A mathematical mind is different from the minds of ordinary men. Not for nothing did priests in ancient days engage in mathematics and astronomy—there is, in mathematics, something of the nature of religious officiation. Although centuries have gone by, the mathematical process of thought hasn't changed. In the mind of a mathematician, dealing with eternal categories, such a trifling matter as the fall of a government or of a prime minister simply does not arouse interest.

I have noticed more than once, when in the company of mathematicians, that they don't say much, only what is essential. Idle chatter irritates them. Lies also. What could be more beautiful than objective truth? Truth that has evolved, grown in depth through the efforts of many generations, many centuries, many countries. Truth which mathematicians in India, Japan, Russia, England understand without interpreters. "If a message from another civilization in the Universe ever reaches us, it will most certainly first be understood by mathematicians, for it will be couched in mathematical terms," as my friend used to say.

In the company of mathematicians I had had occasion to hear the name of Alexander Yesenin-Volpin, the poet, who gave a philosophy course at Moscow University on mathematical logic. The talent and originality of this man were recognized by everyone but the police. He was arrested more than once, for he was always protesting against injustice. But since the charges were never grave enough for a prison sentence, he was more often locked up in a psychiatric hospital. There were a few of these run specially by the police. If the man thus caught happened to be perfectly sane and there was no reason to detain him in such an institution, they would render a diagnosis that sounded something like "subjective idealism." This was no anecdote, this was the truth! People who had been in these hospitals spoke of this diagnosis. In Martha Lazarevna's home Alik Volpin was loved, his amazing talents were appreciated, and no "sicknesses" were ever observed in him.

The last time I visited Martha Lazarevna, Alexander Yesenin-Volpin had been arrested again and we talked about him a great deal. I learned then how he had tried to bring his case to the highest judicial courts, hoping to obtain an open trial against bureaucrats and the police. Needless to say, nothing came of it. The trial was never held.

Yet Alik was not transgressing in any way. On the contrary, he was trying to uphold and activate Soviet law and the Soviet Constitution. It was for this, apparently, that the police declared him mentally unbalanced and sent him to be treated for "subjective idealism."

*

Among my brightest memories are tea-sessions in the kitchen of the famous tragedienne Fanny Nevskaya; I used to call on her with my son, whom she dearly loved. She was a lonely woman. Her sister came from Paris to live with her, and the old women lived in a modest two-room apartment.

Many years before, the sister had gone abroad with her husband. There was a brother, too, who lived somewhere in Rumania. The sister's husband, a professor, had died, and the lonely widow decided to return to her fatherland. She knew that Fanny had become a famous actress of the Soviet stage and screen, and she had visualized a large house, a villa out of town, several automobiles, jewelry—she hadn't been in Russia for forty years.

Fanny didn't want to disillusion her sister, yet she longed to share her solitude with her. She therefore sent her an official invitation and the necessary documents.

Upon arrival, the sister found these two small rooms with a tiny kitchen, without servants, without a dining room, without silverware or crystal. No villa either, no car, no chauffeur. But in the streets taxis would stop when they saw the famous actress—the drivers liked giving her a lift. The movie audiences thought of Fanny Nevskaya as a "comic old woman," little guessing that she was about as comic as Charlie Chaplin when he called forth laughter and tears. Salesgirls adored Fanny Nevskaya, and she, buying some cheese, would "act up" for their benefit. She was always given the goods without having to wait in line.

By Moscow standards a separate two-room apartment for a single woman was the height of luxury, even if that woman happened to be an actress famous throughout the land. Only her sister was horrified by this. Fanny herself was totally indifferent to the fact that she had no servants, not even a fine dress. She was above such things.

In the movies she made audiences laugh. In the theater —in Dostoevsky's *The Gambler*—the profound tragedy of her acting shook her audiences, and shivers would run down the spectator's spine.

Among her devoted friends were Boris Pasternak, Anna Akhmatova, Galina Ulanova, all of them true artists. Their photos stood on her table, with loving inscriptions from equals to an equal.

She was a real person. You couldn't just gossip with her, or lie to her. With her you spoke as if you were at confession. And she always said straight to your face what she thought. To a certain Moscow woman journalist, who wrote "command" articles on the "inconsistencies of Capitalism" and "Communist decency," she once said, "Tanka, you are nothing but a little bitch!"

She always saw the amusing side of things and was very witty. But then she would also confess, "Sometimes, when I think how awful everything is, I want to run out into the street and howl! Just that—howl! For there are no words to express how we live!"

The last time I saw her was in the hospital, when I went

there to see Brajesh. She was strolling about, portly and immense, in hospital pajamas that looked more like a convict's outfit. Patients looked over their shoulders at her, giggling: the famous comedienne! Fanny told me about Mikhail Bulgakov's novel *The Master and Margarita,* which had recently appeared in the magazine *Moskva.* She referred to the novel as a satire of genius.

"Would you like me to introduce you to Singh?" I asked. Fanny remained silent for a long time, trying to remember something. Finally, in her bass voice she slowly pronounced, " 'Apple a day keeps a doctor away.' That's all I remember in English, my dear," she added, as usual combining sadness with laughter.

Her taste leaned toward the grotesque; it was her style. Few people understood her, afraid of her sharp candor, not understanding her exaggerated jokes. As for herself, she simply "lived" in art, seeing everywhere around her grotesque caricatures of Truth, Goodness, Honesty, Love, Justice. She would render into words what she saw, creating her own images on the spot. Frightened middle-class minds would shy away from her in horror. It must be admitted, however, that this was precisely what she wanted. And no one knew how much tenderness there was in that heart, and how children, whom one could not fool, would respond to a caress from her.

The hospital hardly had time to deliver all the telegrams she received—it happened to be her seventieth birthday and congratulations came from everywhere. No important government nabob in this government-run hospital had ever received so many congratulations. She answered every single one of them. People dissuaded her, suggesting a general "Thank you" through the press to "all persons and organizations"; but she said she just couldn't do that. "I'm not some cabinet minister to thank people through a newspaper," she would say, and sent telegrams to everyone who had wished her well.

In the hospital I told her the whole story about Brajesh and me. Brajesh was already hopelessly ill at the time. When he died, she called me up on the telephone. I remember that low voice of hers, hollow now and stifled, full of pain. Few of those who hadn't known Brajesh personally spoke to me like that in those days, although there were many friends around me.

❊

We all loved our school—it gave us a supply of knowledge for life and a stock of friendships and attachments. Several years ago I had a reunion at my home of twelve of my classmates—all of them by then doctors, teachers, engineers, translators, lawyers. Everyone in our class of 1943 had been able to enter the university and other institutions of higher learning—during the war this wasn't difficult. In our class no one remained without a higher education, not even the most backward pupils. It became much harder for our children to get admitted to colleges, especially girls. Boards of admission gave open preference to boys—something that had never happened in our day.

How unexpected the destinies of some of my classmates!

The girl who had been tops in sports, who couldn't even sew on a button, ended up a respectable family woman, a model mother and housewife, who made her children's clothes, even their overcoats. She also became an excellent cook. Together with her husband she made all the repairs in their home—actually they could have built themselves a whole house with their own hands, had they been given the chance to do so. When they first got married, they went to live in East Germany, as Lena's husband was serving in the army at the time. She told me that she would remain forever grateful to the kind German woman whose house they rented and who taught her to do housework. Our former school champion gave birth to a child and might have perished through her ignorance of practical matters that had never been taught her in her childhood. Under the guidance of the German woman she attended to the baby and the kitchen, and she told me how all of a sudden her whole attitude toward Germans underwent a change. Yet Lena had been among the most implacable and aggressive in our class! She returned home so changed, so softened, that one could hardly recognize her. Actually we met again many years later. Lena by then had become a "chocolate engineer," designing machinery for candy factories. She hadn't lost her independence, but it was strange to hear her discussing how best to hang wallpaper. At school she could only discuss Mayakovsky.

One of our most talented classmates, whose future had seemed to promise brilliant, unusual prospects, became a teacher of English. The girl who had been almost at the bottom of the class had become a successful biologist and was finishing her thesis. A boy who had absolutely nothing outstanding about him became a first-class lawyer; while the boy who had been gifted in every way turned out to be an average journalist.

On the day I left Moscow I gave all my best books on India to the daughter of my former classmate Misha. Misha and I had become fast friends at school when we were eight years old; but later life separated us, and we met again as grownups, because Misha never forgot any of his class-mates and school friends. Misha, in the meantime, had become a builder of stadiums, embankments, and bridges, whereas in his school days he had wanted to be a philolo-gist and a historian. He was constructing a new stadium in Luzhniki, a new embankment on the Moskva River, and he was tunneling passages under Moscow streets.

He told me how "unexpectedly" such projects sprang into being. One day Khrushchev was driving with a Party leader and grew irritated because the street was jammed and people were slow in crossing it. The decision was made on the spot: here there would be an underground passage!

The fate of the New Arbat (one of the chief thoroughfares of Moscow) had been decided in more or less the same way, without taking the real need of the people into consideration. To break a way through old streets and alleyways for this new Moscow avenue, one had to tear down many good solid structures built at the beginning of the century. Residents were moved out into the suburbs. They protested and were promised faithfully that they would be the first to get new apartments on the New Arbat, in many-storied skyscrapers. But when the skyscrapers had been erected, the government changed its mind and assigned them to various official institutions. Instead of a modern residential section in the heart of the city, a bureaucratic avenue had been conjured up. Misha said that when old houses were being wrecked in Molchanovka, all the workers were in despair, for everybody knew that such houses would never again be built and that to wreck them was an act of vandalism.

Misha lived in one room with his wife, two children, and his grandmother. If only he could have built himself a house, what a beautifully planned house it would have been! But he had only his single room to work with. In square footage it was all that the norm prescribed, and there was no hope of getting anything else.

Misha, however, found a way of reconstructing his room. It was an old-fashioned room with a very high ceiling, so he turned it into a duplex apartment, and the children lived on the newly created "entresol." Such reconstructions were permissible after many long arguments with the commissions that issued the permits and tried never to permit even minor improvements. At the same time buildings for governmental departments and offices were springing up like mushrooms after a good rain.

How many bronze monuments on granite pedestals Misha had to erect on the squares of Moscow! Here to the "great Chekist" Dzerzhinsky, there to the "great poet" Taras Shevchenko. He had to carry out a variety of building projects. At one time he had as a project a big iron fence around a cathedral. But the most needed and useful of all his constructions was undoubtedly that mezzanine floor in his room.

My old school friend Alya had three daughters and a husband who was an engineer. She worked with publishers, editing books on history, economics, the art of the East, although she had graduated from the university majoring, as I had done, in the history of the United States; it wasn't always possible to find work according to one's specialty. Alya was happy to be working in one of the best publishing offices in Moscow.

At school she had been a pale, thin little girl who, physically, seemed to be the weakest in our class. She was endowed, however, with an immense strength of spirit. She got married when she was still a student, and together with her husband went to the construction site of a big electric power station. To a city dweller, who loved the Conservatory, the poems of Gumilyov, and Olyosha's prose, life suddenly showed its frightening side, crude and ugly. Most of the workers at the site were prisoners. The climate was fierce, food almost lacking. Alya used to write me how she had to learn everything over again, how difficult it was to free oneself of an "intellectual's prejudices." But she had the gift of perceiving the good and kind sides in people who appeared uncouth and rude. As a result, she didn't despair. During the years spent at that construction site she became a mature, intelligent, profound human being.

She returned to Moscow a few years later looking so well that one could hardly recognize her. In their small, two-room apartment, she and her husband occupied one room, their three daughters the other. On Alya's desk one invariably found some manuscript or galley proofs—somehow she managed to spend every free moment at work. Yet she also had to buy provisions, feed the children, make regular trips to her office. How she managed also to read new books, visit exhibitions, see new Italian and Polish films, was beyond my comprehension. But Alya said that she could never stop working, for that would be a spiritual death. She preferred the physical exhaustion of strenuous overwork to the spiritual death of idleness. Even at the construction project, when her children had just been born, she had found work to do, either at the library or in publishing a local newspaper.

Long ago, in our school days, we loved to take walks in spring around the Kremlin—Alya, Lena, and I. We strolled about and talked of our uncomplicated problems, of books, of art. In later life we had growing children and grown-up problems, we had no time for such carefree walks under the linden trees of the embankment. But we continued to love one another, and Alya became a close friend of my children.

Her eldest daughter chose a hard profession: she was to teach children with defective hearing and speech. For this one required immense patience and love—but that was just the soul-quality of Alya, her children, her family.

Alya told me how in their publishing office, at the insistence of all the employees, Alexander Solzhenitsyn had once been invited to come and give a talk on literature. "That man," said Alya, "gives one the impression of absolute truthfulness. I have never before heard anyone speak as he does—so simply, so naturally, with such strength, and so convincingly. Honesty itself seems to be breathing in him. He never compromises. If you could have seen how he held his audience, although he is not at all an orator in the ordinary sense of the word. But then everybody knows that he writes only the truth. He speaks it, too. And that is the most difficult thing to do these days. A truly glorious deed!"

❋

There was one small family, consisting of two members only, in whose company I was always happy.

Liza's husband was a disabled veteran. Needless to say, they lived in one small room in a communal apartment. Half of their room was taken up by a large low divan. But at their small square table, on which Liza would place coffee, cheese, and a simple salad, there was such warmth and homeyness.

Their large window with its wide, old-fashioned sill served as a larder. Here, together with pots of flowers, one found milk bottles, pots of soup, cheese curds, butter. On a shelf there were some fine books on art. Liza had graduated from the university but wasn't working, as the care she had to give her sick husband took up all her time. Kostya had gone to war as a student. He was wounded—a nerve was severed—and one leg withered as a result. He had great trouble in walking with the aid of a cane. Kostya was a critic, a connoisseur of poetry and ancient Russian art. They had some splendid old icons in the room, and also some new, stylized works by a young artist.

Kostya was a very sick man. His condition worsened steadily. It was hard for him to work. His pension as a war invalid was not enough to live on, and so he went on working, writing.

Liza's true call in life was to comfort others. She was just a sweet, lovely woman, but how much was expressed in that "just"! She had no "socially useful" activity, maybe because she might have considered such activity useless. But her kindness, which she generously gave to others, was indeed socially useful, for Liza was like a ray of sunshine, like a shining light in one's soul, and nothing helps people more than that.

In this consists a pastor's work. Every intelligent, real priest finds the proper words to bring courage to him who despairs. It is the same in all religions. But there are certain people who, without knowing it, spend all their lives doing this pastor's work among others, consoling, helping, advising; or else, just taking a friend's hand in silence and looking deep into his eyes, *save* him from fear, errors, and despair. There are many such people in this world, more than there are such priests, for priests very often, like Pharisees, replace with rituals the living word of the heart. But the power of the spirit and of love finds its way to other hearts through any obstacles.

"Is it true?" was all Liza had asked over the phone on that day of my departure for India. She couldn't believe that I was actually leaving. After that she fell silent for a while.

Sweet, wise woman, what went through her mind, in her heart, during those moments? Did she get an inkling of what my destiny was to be?

*

I first made the acquaintance of Andrei Sinyavsky, the critic and connoisseur of literature, in the Institute of World Literature. When I joined the Institute, Andrei, who was a bit older than I and also a university graduate, was already known as one of the most talented workers in the Section of Soviet Literature. He wrote about Gorky, Bagritsky, Khlebnikov, about the wartime poets and the poetry of the first years of the Revolution. There was in his articles the professional master's touch, with a sharp style and a striking individuality.

Andrei spoke very well. At the meetings of the Section of Soviet Literature we often discussed the new works of our members. More often than not there was little to be said about them, and people spoke merely for the sake of formality. Andrei, however, who had a shy manner, spoke little and exclusively to the point. Sometimes there would come an expressive gesture of his narrow white hand. Soft fair hair would fall over his forehead, and he would brush it back.

His expressive face with its large features and big beard

could not be called handsome—a real village peasant. But there was intelligence in the forehead, gentleness in the eyes, and thought shone in this beautiful, inspired face.

He had let his beard grow when he started going north in the summer, where he and Masha, his wife, spent their holidays, descending the river in a boat to distant villages, with knapsacks as their sole baggage. All northern peasants wore beards. That was why Andrei had grown a beard, too; otherwise the peasants would have refused to talk with a "mere kid."

They took photographs of village architecture, collected peasant costumes, embroideries, utensils—everything they could find in the region, which to this day has preserved the customs and handicrafts of northern Russia. Andrei and Masha really knew Russian antiquity; their home was full of original northern handiworks made of bone and Karelian birch. In the north they also collected old icons, which Masha used to restore. They also had brought from there old books in Church Slavonic. Their room was decorated with a big sixteenth-century icon of Saint George on horseback, cleaned and restored by Masha. The icon was shown at the exhibition of northern art in the Tretyakov Gallery. The Sinyavskys had found it in a barn, lying forgotten—an old painted plank.

Masha, a specialist in ancient Russian art, could not find work easily. Besides, her character forbade her to conform with the official point of view, and without such conformity work was unobtainable. Masha, therefore, took to making sketches for young artists who, in small studios, were re-creating ancient Russian art, working in bone, wood, metal, making ornaments, beads, earrings, bracelets, based on northern Russian patterns.

Andrei had inherited from his mother a strong religious feeling. In him this innate, pure, poetical religiousness lived side by side with a sharp critical mind, which mercilessly analyzed everything: a poet's art, the subtle nuances of a word, his own feelings and emotions. Andrei was a severe critic, first and foremost of himself, of his own weaknesses and sins. In the sincere conviction that "I am but inconsequential dust," in a profound humility toward the Almighty, lies the whole essence of true religious consciousness. This humility was a part of Mahatma Gandhi, who raised India to her feet, deeply convinced that everything he had done had been the carrying out of God's will. All truly religious people think in this way.

About himself Andrei always spoke with a disparaging smile, and with no mercy, as one can see from his *Thoughts Unaware.** Such books repel those who are afraid of looking into themselves, preferring instead to pretend to be beautiful and noble. Yet it is in this same merciless vein that Gandhi wrote his autobiography. Again we find here the resemblance between two deeply religious people, who "analyze sin" and ardently desire to purify themselves through penitence and the disclosure of truth.

But also how equally sharp was Andrei's feeling for everything that was beautiful. His analysis of the poetry of Pasternak, Akhmatova, Bagritsky was graceful and convincing. In the works of new poets Sinyavsky instantly recognized promising qualities and annoying weaknesses. No one ever penetrated as deeply as he had into Yevtushenko's dualistic creations. His derision was stinging: in five minutes he had been able to prove that the poet Anatoli Safronov was, after all, no poet at all. This was something for which "famous" Soviet writers could not forgive Andrei.

About Akhmatova Andrei wrote with true inspiration. He disclosed with exactitude wherein lay the social importance of such profoundly intimate poems. How beautifully he explained Pasternak—how important would become a currant leaf, rain, a thunderstorm, an interior. And how sharply

---

* Published in the United States as "Thought Unaware," *The New Leader,* New York, July 19, 1965. TRANS. NOTE.

and sensitively he understood Isaac Babel, that grotesque, derisive, and sorrowful artist.

Andrei Sinyavsky was not only a critic, he was a talented writer as well. Satire, the grotesque, were his favorite ways of expressing himself. In his novel *Lyubimov*,* Soviet provincial life was presented to the reader in hyperboles, resembling those of Saltykov-Shchedrin and Gogol. *Lyubimov* was at once *The History of the Town of Glupov* and *Dead Souls*, seen through the story of a small Soviet town.

His novella, *The Trial Begins*, written in 1956, strangely anticipated Sinyavsky's own inevitable arrest ten years later, although it spoke of things of the past, which were not supposed to happen again in the U.S.S.R. But they did. And all those interrogators, Chekists, informers, spies, so vividly described by Sinyavsky's pen, had risen again to the surface of Soviet society, tightly encircling a man until only one road was left open to him: prison. The man had but one fault: he was a writer.

Sinyavsky's short stories—"Icicle," "Pkhents," "Graphomaniacs"—were fantastic, but their hyperboles stemmed from actual life in Moscow apartments, where life itself reminded one of a nightmare, far exceeding any literary fantasies.

The article "On Socialist Realism" disclosed the conditions in which Soviet power had placed art and literature, conditions in which creativity simply had to stifle and die, or else turn into its own opposite—the official glorification of the rulers, the way Russian classicism had done under the eighteenth-century empresses. Sinyavsky is a philosopher. His reflections about the fate of art in Soviet society are based on deep study and knowledge.

Andrei is a versatile man. As a lark, he wrote (with a co-author) a book on Picasso's works, and even here showed

---

* Published in the United States as *The Makepeace Experiment*, New York, Pantheon Books, 1965. Trans. note.

a shrewd analysis of art. Andrei always loved in art all that
was grotesque and exaggerated. How many times I had
heard my friends in the U.S.S.R. saying, "Would it be possible to express our crazy, abnormal, modern life in sedate
classical images? Everything is so grotesque, people are
standing on their heads, instead of faces they have dogs'
muzzles, everything has turned into a nightmarish parody!"
It seems to me that Andrei Sinyavsky's works—his novels,
novellas, short stories—stemmed from such a point of view.

At his trial they came out with "quotations" instead of
evidence—every image a caricature—and on this the court
built its case and gave its verdict.

Andrei himself was a peaceful soul, spoke quietly; his
Russian was beautiful, one just had to sit and listen to it. He
loved Masha, loved his son. A quiet, gentle man. Yet what
crimes did they not accuse him of at the trial—anti-Semitism, pornography, participation in mythical underground
organizations! The judge, Smirnov, came to our Institute and
for two whole hours tried to convince us that there was "a
Social Revolutionary smell" about it all; but he had nothing
to substantiate his accusations with, outside of those same
grotesque quotations.

Andrei used to call on me sometimes, and we would sit in
our kitchen. He always gazed at the little church in the
yard and would ask only for a cup of coffee. "How peaceful
it is in your home," he would say, "how good! And your
children are quiet, it's a pleasure to be with them." My home
to him must have been a pleasant change after the "communal hell" in which he was obliged to live.

For several years he had lived in the country sixty miles
from Moscow, in a hut with a large stove and no plumbing.
From there he used to come to meetings at the Institute,
always wearing a blue beret, a warm red scarf, and extra-
thick boots—the mud was knee-deep in the country.

It was not surprising that Andrei had such a strong influence over all those with whom he was friendly, all those

who came close to him. Shy by nature, he had the tired face of a man who worked at night and didn't get sufficient sleep. Andrei did work whole nights through in a basement, which Masha had transformed into his study. The life in their communal apartment was replete with bickering, with the mutual hatreds of poor, disillusioned people; Hoffmann's caricatures and masks paled before this degrading communal living. In order to create, one had to escape to the basement.

Sinyavsky's novels, stories, and novellas were not published in the U.S.S.R. because in the U.S.S.R. satires on everyday life were inadmissible. Mikhail Bulgakov was not published for twenty-eight years. Zoshchenko was destroyed by official criticism. Sinyavsky was published abroad, and immediately became a "political criminal."

They made him a political criminal at the trial. His caricatures had frightened the Party activists at the Institute in which he had worked far more than a hydrogen bomb might have done; this for the simple reason that for centuries in Russia people had been afraid of a truthful word.

Sinyavsky, the writer, had merely laughed, mocked, exaggerated everything that was dense and stupid, but nowhere had he called for the overthrow of the Soviet regime. Nonetheless, the trial accused the author of "anti-Soviet activities" and condemned him to seven years of hard labor in concentration camps. The same happened to his friend Yuli Daniel. Neither of them acknowledged the crime they had been accused of, nor could they have done so: they were writers, aesthetes, artists, critics, and not political activists.

Nevertheless, they are now in a concentration camp. From there Andrei continues to write letters about literature to his friends and family. Nothing can crush his creative spirit, and his profound religious feeling only serves to strengthen him in his heavy trials and tribulations. He has a small son left at home.

These conditions cannot continue for long. One of these days you will return home, Andrei, to your son and friends, and your place in the concentration camp barracks shall be taken by those who condemned you. The same has happened more than once in Russia's history, which in itself resembles a sad and weird grotesque.

＊

I was lucky: I managed to escape from that cage.

But my classmates, my university comrades, the girls 1 knew, my friends of childhood, my recent acquaintances are still behind those bars: all those from whom I had at least once a warm, unforgettable word—at least once.

I know how difficult it is for them; I also know that at present there is nothing in the U.S.S.R. that holds a promise of a better and freer life. Perhaps just the contrary. We cannot write to each other, we cannot call each other up. The habits of the Soviet police are too well known to us all, and their methods haven't changed much. The police are merely biding their time, knowing full well that their time will come; they will then show what they are capable of doing. Stalinism was "repealed" fourteen years ago, but the system has remained the same, no one has dared change the basis on which Soviet ideology and power have been built. A Moscow journalist once said to me—this was still in Khrushchev's days, before the Sinyavsky trial: "All this liberalism is only for a while. The apparatus, created and trained by Stalin, has only been temporarily 'switched off'—you know, the way one pulls an electric plug out of its socket. But the machinery itself is intact. Just plug it in and it will work again. . . ."

And because the nature of the Soviet police is well known, it is better for me not to seek contacts with my friends or my children. For them it could only become a source of danger. . . .

Neither my children nor the majority of my friends will be granted permission to go abroad even as tourists. None of them could afford a tourist trip anyway. All I can do is live in hope of a change in the future, when citizens of the U.S.S.R. will perhaps be given the right to travel freely. It is a right so intrinsic in the free world that people here don't even suspect that one can exist without it.

It is then, when free travel becomes the right of Soviet citizens, too, that we shall see each other again. As for the present, in spite of the silence, of the lack of contact, I know that they understand me, that they won't forget me, and that they, too, will wait for the chance to meet again.

Then, Bertha will at last be able to see with her own eyes the frescoes and sculptures of Africa, about which now she has only read in books. Alyosha and Sanya will go to Berlin, where Alyosha was born, and to Paris, where his parents had lived, and will come to the States to hear the Philadelphia Symphony Orchestra. The Leningrad bibliophile will visit his friends in France and in Rome, from whom at present he receives letters only once in a long while. Tamara and her son Stasik will travel all over the roads of Spain and will find the place where Tamara's father perished during the Civil War—by then Stasik will be speaking Spanish fluently. The Lvovs, husband and wife, will be able to accept the invitations of their friends, the astronomers, and how wonderful it will be for them to see all the great observatories of the world. My friends of the literary world will at last have the chance to meet those about whom at present they can only write—the German, Spanish, and American writers; at present this privilege is enjoyed solely by Yevtushenko and Voznesensky. Vera will then meet the geneticists of England, France, and the United States. Vitaly will be "permitted" to meet his colleagues abroad, even though he does not belong to the Party, and will refuse to leave his wife as a hostage in Moscow: they will be able to go together. Fanny Nevskaya will see the best actors of

Europe and America, and they, in turn, will learn of her great tragicomic talent; and she will make taxi drivers in Paris laugh, just as she does at present in Moscow. Alya with her husband and three daughters will visit her aunt in Detroit, and all the children will play noisily together.

As for Andrei Sinyavsky, he will meet the many readers of his books, both in Russian and in translation, and will get to know his publishers. And he will write a new book, perhaps something like "One Day in the Life of Andrei Donatovich," about the life of writers in post-Stalin camps.

I am an optimist. I firmly believe that we shall meet again. . . .

Destiny

In the middle of April I learned that on the twenty-first I could fly to the United States. It seemed so strange for everything to come about so quickly after so long a period of indecision.

During those days I found time to walk all over Fribourg, visit several times the Cathedral of St. Nicholas, go for boat rides on the Murtensee, and take a stroll along the shores of Lake Neuchâtel; have a look at Castle Gruyère, visit Zurich and Bern, Montreux and Vevey. Near Vevey I saw, in the distance, the villa of Charlie Chaplin, that great actor and humanitarian of modern times. How often Soviet movie authorities had invited him to visit the U.S.S.R., but he had invariably given them the same answer: "Why is the U.S.S.R. the only country in which my latest films are not shown?" Those who had invited him had been obliged to admit that they had seen *Limelight* and *The King in New York* somewhere in Hong Kong, Rome, or London.

At this same time Emmanuel and Louba d'Astier, my only European acquaintances, came to Fribourg. We met in the home of their niece.

It was a noisy, excited party, at which Russian, French,

and English were spoken all at the same time. The drawing room was packed with people. It was impossible to answer a question because immediately it would be forgotten and another asked in its place; everyone there was so anxious to ask me as many questions as they could. One thing, however, became clear: d'Astier had arrived with his own plans for me.

They consisted of talking me out of going to the United States ("You'll just get out of one prison into another"); of delaying the publication of my book by a whole year ("At present it will arouse a violent reaction on the part of the Soviet Government"); and, in general, of inducing me to remain in Switzerland ("You can depend on my niece's hospitality"). I thanked him for the offer of hospitality, but explained that I was anxious to publish my book first of all, and that everything was already arranged about my American visa; as for the reactions of the Soviet Government, I really cared nothing about them, as I was cutting myself loose from both that government and the U.S.S.R.

In Switzerland I felt a sympathy toward me on the part of those I had met, and I was sure I could have found plenty of good friends there. But to remain silent for another forty years could have been achieved just as well in the U.S.S.R. Switzerland offered refuge, but stipulated that all those who benefited by it should not get involved in any way in politics. I could never have explained while there why I was cutting myself off forever from the Communist world. This was unacceptable to me.

Somehow, I fancied my destiny as being different.

❄

Since my departure from Moscow I had often thought about destiny. The peaceful banks of the Ganges and the quiet days in Switzerland disposed one toward thought. I felt that I myself was incapable of fully understanding, as yet, the immense changes that were taking place in my life.

Go to meet destiny halfway and destiny will come to your assistance. This I had known for a long time. But my life in the U.S.S.R. had been so hopelessly lacking in any glimmer of light that it seemed nothing could ever lead me out of its narrow defile.

I myself took the decisive step in Delhi. No one helped, no one gave advice, and no one knew what I was doing. But I believe that all our thoughts and acts are in God's hands. And I know that without this Providential assistance, which had come to me as an inspiration and an immutable decision, I would never have had the strength to take that step.

The Lord is my light and my salvation; whom shall I fear?

The Lord is my shepherd; I shall not want. . . .

Be of good courage, and he shall strengthen your heart, all ye that hope in the Lord.

During this difficult time nothing helped me as much as this religious feeling. It was my support in everything I met with.

A religious feeling awakens in a moment of crisis, when a man's inner life is suddenly brought to an edge. To different people it means different things, and my explanation of it is perforce as individual as my life.

People are born with different predilections. Some have mathematical abilities; others are unable to think abstractly beyond x and y. Some have a musical ear, which hears all the nuances of a sound, memorizes complex musical phrases, discerns the various themes in an immense symphony orchestration. Others cannot distinguish a tune, cannot sing the simplest little song, cannot take a step in time with music, yet they live happily without it and do not suffer. Some react sharply to color, are unable to live in a room painted in cold or harsh colors. Others cannot distinguish between green and brown; to them trees, flowers, all of nature are like a black-and-white photograph. Yet such people can have lives spiritually rich and interesting in many ways.

A sense of religion is something one is born with, like a musical ear. One can develop it, cultivate it, enrich it, but if one hasn't got its seed to begin with, no powers of the intellect, no sophistication of "evidence" can awaken it. A man can live a long, noble life, doing a lot for others, yet never have this feeling, this sensation. A man can even go to church every morning, repeating prayers, and think that he has faith, yet it will be nothing but a mental juggling, or a habit nurtured since childhood. The heart remains silent.

All the great religions of the earth have a high moral teaching in common. All such religions demand that man should not kill; should not steal; should do good; that he should not harm others if he does not want them to harm him. Nor should he strive after glory and riches, for they are temporal. Spirit alone is eternal. Set your mind on that. Preserve a pure heart.

Far more people on earth live by these commandments, by this eternal truth, than is commonly supposed. Eternal truths have not vanished from the face of a modernized planet, as one might sometimes suppose they have. Fortunately for us all, the eternal is indestructible.

Many have been taught all this since childhood. For many these have been incontrovertible truths absorbed with their mother's milk; they have never known any others. But for those who, like myself, have been brought up in atheism, eternal truth discloses itself in unexpected and unusual ways; and then only an inborn religious sense can be of help.

It was passed on to me by my two grandmothers, who were deeply and truly religious. But until I had experienced it myself, I knew not that I had it, just as a man cannot know that he has a musical ear until he has heard a melody.

The melody of a religious feeling is the music of life it-self. To those who do not hear it I could not explain what it sounds like—let them stop reading right here. If the spark isn't smoldering somewhere inside one, no efforts can ever bring it into existence. Water cannot catch fire. But if there is a smoldering within one's heart, then sooner or later, under certain conditions, it is bound to burst into a bright flame.

That, in all probability, was what happened to me.

I remember well the spring and summer of 1961 in Mos-cow. I was thirty-five then, my children were at school, I had already had time to see a thing or two in life. As a child I hadn't enjoyed robust health. Every year at school I used to miss half of my classes. Now I had a too rapid heartbeat, frequent colds and bronchitis, incomprehensible neuralgic pains around the heart. I was melancholy, irrita-ble, inclined toward hopeless pessimism; more than once I had contemplated suicide; I was afraid of dark rooms, of the dead, of thunderstorms; of uncouth men, of hooligans in the streets and drunks. My own life appeared to me as very dark, dull, and without a future. I didn't know how to enjoy myself, nor how to meditate. I was tormented by an inner anxiety, which nothing seemed able to quell. I had no interest in religious services, in religious books or icons—they meant nothing to me. But even at that time I already knew a few people of my own age who were re-ligious. I used to think of them with astonishment and re-spect.

And then came the spring. That year for some reason I felt its coming in every drop of my blood. Nature began to awaken, the first streamlets started running in the gutters along Moscow sidewalks. The reflections of sunshine in the windows of streetcars, trolley-buses, automobiles, were blind-ing. After a long cold winter, spring comes to Moscow slowly and with difficulty. Sometimes at the end of February the sky would suddenly sparkle a vivid blue, while the earth still lay locked in frost. "The wind brought from afar a hint of the song of spring. Somewhere a strip broke out of a bright deep sky. . . ." These verses by Alexander Blok, whom I have always loved, resounded with the song of spring louder than usual. Something had happened to me: an extraordinarily sharp sense of life had suddenly sprung up.

It had been an ordinary spring, an ordinary year, with no unusual events in my life or around me. But the joy itself of living, hearing, seeing, drinking that spring air still frosty in the evening; of walking along the streets, watching the re-awakening of life—all this yearly happiness, so ordinary, so unnoticed before and unappreciated, suddenly hit my eyes and my heart. It seemed to fill me to the brim.

In March the snow started melting into streams. In April the earth peeked through the snow, small fields were disclosed and grew dry, branches were heavy with sap, the first pussy willows came into bloom. During the day the sun burned hot and bright, the first dust streaked the asphalt, but toward evening small puddles got a coating of ice. The air became fresh, even frosty, and a young crescent of moon would silver in the mauve sky.

Then came the month of May with its bird cherries, lilacs, lilies of the valley, its intoxication, which is so momentary and withers away all too soon. But that year everything was different. The summer waxed generous with warm showers under bright rainbows, the rustle of leaves under rain, the smell of mushrooms and strawberries.

Life's richness and plenty pressed upon me on every side. Never until then had I liked the rain, but now, after a good drenching under a downpour on the streets of Moscow, I felt happy. Why? What made me so happy? I don't know. In my room I threw open the door onto my balcony and gazed at the slanted rain falling on the tall poplars, on the little church in the yard; and the sun began to shine through the rain, opening a wide expanse across the Moskva River right over to the Vorobyov Hills. For almost ten years I had been looking at this from my window. Why of a sudden had it become so alive?

For the first time I myself was happy to be alive. Happy that I could hear, see, feel all this indescribable beauty around me—this rain, this emerald grass in the yard, that embankment and that river. I couldn't understand what was happening to me; I was still as numb as a fish, not knowing the *words*, not knowing the *tongue*, in which I could express my feeling.

Once during those days, in a conversation with Andrei Sinyavsky, we touched on the subject of suicide. He said: "A suicide only thinks that he is killing himself. He is killing only his body, and the soul after that languishes, for God alone can take the soul. God gives life and takes it. A suicide infringes on the laws of life. That is why suicide is a dreadful sin, which frees one of nothing, but only adds suffering to the soul."

We were sitting on a small bench, not far from the Kropotkin Gate. I don't know how we came upon such a subject. But that conversation was a revelation, because it expressed something new to me, something that I came to feel fully and understand only fairly recently.

No one has the right to destroy or take life, neither his own, nor that of any other man, nor of any living creature. It's not we who give life, and it's not for us to take it. *Thou shalt not kill* is the basis of man's behavior on earth. Life is eternal, enormous, generous as that rainbow, that rain, as this lovely spring. To make an attempt on life is a great crime. To help it in every way is a great happiness. To feel oneself a minute particle of the great life that spreads from this earth to the farthermost star, to rejoice in it, to bless and thank it, that is what constitutes a religious feeling. Religion means a binding. If a man does not feel himself a part of the Universe, and does not hear its pulse, he is not religious. But once he has heard that pulse, he will be hearing it always. Every day his life will replenish itself from this inexhaustible source, eternal and powerful as the sun.

I looked for the word that could express this new sensation, and found it in the Psalms of David. Since then I have known nothing that better expressed the Higher, Eternal Life, immense, filling the whole Universe, to which my small life belonged like a tiny speck of dust.

David sang, his heart wide open and throbbing like a drawn string. His words were a living authentic flame, uncooled by the intellect, unflooded by the cold waters of philosophy. He rejoiced in the life around him and saw God in it; implored Him for help when his strength was at an ebb; disclosed to Him his weaknesses, errors, sins; repented of his own imperfections, his insignificance, sensing himself to be but a mote in the great Wisdom of the Universe. And he endlessly thanked and extolled God, who had given man all the wealth of the world around him, a helping Hand in times of stress, and the light of Truth in his soul.

Nowhere have I found words more powerful than those in the Psalms. Their fervid poetry cleanses one, gives one strength, brings hope in moments of darkness. Makes one look critically into oneself, convict oneself, and wash one's heart clean with one's own tears. It is the ever-burning fire of love, of gratitude, humility, and truth.

Now I began to read Tolstoy and Dostoevsky in a different way. What a profound meaning revealed itself in *The Possessed*, in the teachings of Starets Zosima. Tolstoy became closer to me, and I understood now why.

In the spring of 1962 I was baptized in an Orthodox church in Moscow, because I wanted to be in communion with those who believed. I felt this need with all my heart; dogmas meant little to me. Through friends I had the good fortune of meeting one of the best priests in Moscow. He is no longer among the living, and since then I have never met anyone who conducted a religious service more simply and with a greater earnestness of feeling, who spoke with his parishioners the way Father Nikolai used to do.

He was severe and didn't conceal it. He spoke of life in simple everyday terms, without sanctimoniousness, with no anxiety to exonerate a mistake under any circumstance, without an effort of any kind to make a deal with his conscience. If you didn't like it, you could leave. Go to another, who would find justifications for your sins, who would forgive and cleanse your conscience of torments. Father Nikolai never did this. His eyes were piercing. He was stern as truth itself, which does not tolerate any wiles. In this lay his grace and his great help to others. One could not escape him.

The Moscow Church authorities disapproved of him. When he died, they wouldn't even allow him to be buried near the little church beside the Donskoy Cathedral, where he had served. He obviously did not bow his head before those in power. He understood perfectly well that in becoming baptized I was breaking the rules of the Party, that it was dangerous both for me and for him, and for that reason he didn't write my name in the church's register.

I shall never forget our first conversation in the empty church, after the service. I felt nervous, never having spoken to a priest before. From my friends I knew that Father Nikolai was natural, that it was easy to speak to him, and that he always had long talks with those he was to baptize.

An elderly man approached me with a quick step and a face like Pavlov's, Sechenov's, Pirogov's, the great Russian scientists. A face at once plain and intelligent, full of inner strength. He pressed my hand with vigor, like that of an old acquaintance, sat down on a bench near a wall, crossed his legs, and invited me to sit beside him. I grew confused because his manner was so *ordinary*. He asked me about my children, my work, and suddenly I found myself telling him everything, without realizing that this was confession. At last I admitted my ignorance as to how one should talk to a priest, and asked him to forgive me for it. He smiled: "As with any ordinary human being." It was said seriously, penetratingly. Yet all the same, when he stretched out his hand for a usual handshake, I kissed it, in obedience to some impulse. He smiled again. His face was reserved and severe; a smile in it was worth a great deal. . . .

On the day of my christening he was agitated. Seating himself on a bench and making me sit beside him, he said, "When a grown person gets baptized, life may undergo drastic changes. Sometimes for the worse, both in his personal life and in general. Think again, so as not to be sorry later." I replied that I had already thought a lot and was afraid of nothing. He glanced at me with a half-smile almost of amusement: "You know, only the chosen do not fear!"

He baptized me under the name of Photina, saying that this was the original Greek form of my Russian name.

After the christening I asked him if I could put in the church plate, as an expression of gratitude, the rings and earrings I had brought with me (I had little money at the time). But Father Nikolai's reply was firm: "No. The church has means. You came to us yourself—that's far more important."

There was such dignity in his words and in his whole manner. He spoke little, but what he said was weighty and convincing, without any effort to attract through amiability and softness, without lavishing smiles. When he spoke, it was about life on earth with all its confusions and worries, not about life beyond.

Nikolai Alexandrovich Golubtsov knew life well. He had become a priest after thirty years of life as a layman. His profession was gardening. I do not know what had pushed him to take the cloth at an adult age, why he followed in the steps of his two brothers, both of them priests. Undoubtedly, it must have been brought on by some mighty impulse. The impression he made on all those who knew him was indelible.

He baptized me, gave me a prayer book, taught me the simplest prayer, taught me how to behave in church and what to do. He brought me into communion with millions of believers on earth.

After a service a long line of his congregation would queue up to have a talk with him. He spoke to each one, listening attentively to any complaints. One time I stood in such a line for an hour and a half, for in front of me was a young couple who apparently were having matrimonial troubles. Father Nikolai had a weak heart. He had had two attacks, after which he had continued with the services, standing afterward for hours talking to his parishioners. It was his third attack that brought death.

After this I ceased going to church. No one said the liturgy the way he did, no one spoke to people as he did. Always there would appear that hypocritical, mundane side of the Church, not the real feeling. "Exhibition! Nothing but an exhibition!" Father Nikolai once said harshly to a woman who was kneeling piously, and refused to talk to her. He must have known something about her.

There was no exhibitionism whatsoever about the way he served. The church was small, without a choir—only a few nuns read prayers. The last time I was there was in June 1963, after the Trinity, on Whitmonday, when the entire church was still decorated with birch branches, and freshly mown grass was strewn on the floor. A long line stood waiting for Father Nikolai's blessing, and he spoke to every single man and woman.

Again he asked me about my health, my children, what worries I had at home. Then, after a brief pause, he suddenly asked, "And you—are you alone at present? Is there anyone at your side?" Confused by the directness of the question, I only shook my head. "Don't hurry," he said. "You always hurry too much. That's why you have so many reverses on the personal front. Wait, do not hurry, your faraway prince will be coming soon. . . ." And he smiled strangely, turning slightly away.

I was not astonished by either the turn his words had taken or by the archaic expression he had used. A "faraway prince" was so far from my consciousness and my whole mode of life that I didn't take it seriously. Yet every word said by Father Nikolai should have been taken seriously. Two months later Brajesh Singh arrived in Moscow; and in October—when Father Nikolai was no more—all the lucky chances and coincidences combined to make us meet and draw us together. The rest is already known. Father Nikolai never threw his words idly to the wind.

During that last talk I remember so well his big strong hand, a gardener's hand, a worker's, placed on my head. As always, his vestments were without gold and silver. He usually officiated in a plain black cassock, and in summer in a light one. When he went out into the street, he changed into an ordinary suit with a plain raincoat. Often people waited for him in the yard outside the church, and there again he would stand and talk for a long time.

In September 1963 he died.

Since then much has changed in my general outlook and in me.

The bad and the good, as taught me in my childhood, changed places. The heroics of wars and revolutions lost all meaning, and men I had been taught to consider as great crumbled in my eyes. The authority of brute force ceased to exist, even if it cloaked itself in the highest ideals. The best people now were the quiet, kind, sincere, and truthful, the unnoticed and unknown, instead of the rock-hewn heroes of suppressions and victories. The lies and bigotry of political and Party life became unbearable. Any secret, any underground activity and thoughts that had to be kept under lock and key, were repulsive; any violence against human beings, animals, or life in any form, inadmissible. People filled with ambitions and envy, self-enamored posturers, cold cynics, and snobs became far more terrifying than crude physical dangers, which for me had ceased to exist. I was no longer afraid of death, darkness, physical violence; but a man who lies, even with the best of intentions and for the highest cause, frightens me so that I feel like taking to my heels.

I became healthy, I now enjoyed being alive. At present I am in much better physical condition than I was twenty years ago. The great happiness of contemplating nature and listening to it was disclosed to me. In the past I ran by in a hurry, although I had lived far more in the country than in town. I had simply been blind. My attitude toward children, the sick, and the aged underwent a change. I began to feel any physical pain or injury inflicted on others as if it were my own pain. Tears shed by others brought tears to my eyes. I learned to weep and laugh with my whole being. My heart was thrown open now, which previously had been compressed and jammed. The beauty of nature, colors, sounds, shapes, became brighter and richer. It was as if I had suddenly gained my sight and my hearing, as if I had stepped out of an underground tunnel into cool fresh air.

Since then I have been in many churches, seen many religious services. There is a grandeur about the fraternal prayers of the Moslem under the open sky, in large squares in front of mosques: they recognize no idols, no representations of the Most High. The religious worship of the Hindus is diverse and multiform, from the adoration of a monkey god to the contemplation of the live flames of a fire. The waves of an organ in a Catholic cathedral resound like rain and thunder. The peaceful lights of tapers in small chapels, open at any time of the day or night, warm the heart. All that is necessary is to have a heart open to goodness and truth. This alone is real, and for it one needs not the gold and glitter of temples and vestments; the most detailed rituals do not help it.

I have witnessed real faith and genuine sincerity in the holy places of many different religions, and in every case my heart responded to them. I will be entering many more churches and holy places and see a good deal more, I'm sure; but to me the best church of all is the sky's starry dome above. The whole of nature is my temple, and so are my room and my small heart, as long as it is alive and beating.

> I will extol thee, O Lord; for thou hast lifted me up, and hast not made my foes to rejoice over me.
>
> O Lord my God, I cried unto thee, and thou hast healed me.
>
> O Lord, thou has brought up my soul from the grave: thou hast kept me alive, that I should not go down to the pit. . . .
>
> Thou hast turned for me my mourning into dancing: thou hast put off my sackcloth, and girded me with gladness;
>
> To the end that my glory may sing praise to thee, and not be silent. O Lord my God, I will give thanks unto thee for ever.

I have acquired strength, which helps me to perceive the truth, take fewer erroneous steps, and correct those that have been taken. This sensation of oneness with nature, with all-embracing life, with the Universal Mind, fills me with gladness, reverence, humility, and happiness. I feel infinitely sorry for those who turn away from this eternal source, this powerful impulse, just as one feels sorry for the deaf, the blind, for paupers and cripples. But to argue with them would be useless.

And although just now it had been hard and painful to think of my friends, my children, with whom I have parted for a very long time, yet never before had I felt with such clarity and forcefulness how right I had been in doing what I had done. It was what I had to do. I couldn't have acted in any other way. And the realization that this was indeed so made me feel free, buoyant, and lighthearted.

I knew that my life and destiny were in the hands of the Most High.

III. THE NEW WORLD

On Another Continent

It HAD BEEN a cold and rainy morning in Zurich. Now the weather had cleared and beneath us lay the blue, sparkling Atlantic, separating two continents—the Old World from the New.

The blue ocean, an eloquent boundary between those two worlds, to me was my own boundary, which we were crossing with amazing swiftness. The hours had to be put back; we were flying west.

This flight was so unlike the one over the Hindu Kush into India! The sparkling surface of the ocean below was not only space, it was also time: my new life into which I was stepping. I wasn't anxious about anything in particular. It was as if I were being reborn, as if I were becoming a different human being, yet remaining myself—this I also knew. I would have liked us to have gone on flying for hours, giving me plenty of time to think about it all. But everything in this modern world moves at such an accelerated pace: no time at all to stop and think.

How very small the world was. One realized this when viewing it from the great height at which our jet was traveling. So helplessly small, all these oceans, continents, the

"Old" world and the "New"—with no land in sight, with only spacious clouds below and overhead the sparkling sky drenched in blinding sunshine, one could clearly perceive how conventional and nearsighted was man's mental outlook.

The luncheon menu was brought. I thought I would try lobster; I had never tasted it before. In Russia, after the Revolution, oysters and lobsters had gone out of circulation. Only my old nurse used to tell me sometimes how "in St. Petersburg one used to serve them in the old days."

The lunch was plentiful. Alan Schwartz had a martini first, then some wine, ending up with a cognac. I drank two glasses of tea with aspirin. I felt a splitting headache in the offing— everything was happening so quickly.

An impending interview with the press lay in wait for me at the New York airport. I would have to stand behind a microphone and say something. This, like the lobster, was my first experience of the kind. How much was there still ahead of me to be done "for the first time"? The idea of a "speech at a microphone" made me laugh; in Moscow this was done by all "arriving VIP's": prime ministers, cabinet ministers, kings, presidents. What did I need with such things? Was it for this that I was coming here?

My day starts with the morning. I never plan ahead. Therefore, I never try to foresee, nor would I know how to go about it. Others are more able in this respect; they try to explain and be helpful, like Kennan, for instance, whose letter I was now rereading:

. . . An unpleasant test awaits you: a meeting with the press at the airport in New York [sentence written in Russian in the original]. I wish I could spare you this ordeal. I cannot.

. . . There will inevitably be troubles and difficulties in this country; but some of us will do all we can to help you; and I think there will also be pleasures and satisfactions for you in our life here.

. . . Your problem of adjustment to a life outside your native

country is a difficult one; for the shadow of your relationship
to your father will always tend to follow you wherever you go,
and you will have to have greater courage, greater patience,
greater faith than most people have [to overcome it]. . . .*

Later—weeks and months later—I had many occasions to
remember those words, but at the time their meaning didn't
sink in. It seemed to me that I had cut myself off from my
past once and for all, and nothing here could ever remind
me of it. Didn't this ocean beneath me, which we had almost
crossed by now, confirm that much?

Already I could see the first islands and headlands of
America. Alan looked down and said, "In a moment you'll
see a small island—Nantucket—where my family and I go
every summer. Next August you must visit us there. Okay?
There, look!"

"Okay," I said.

The ocean with its islands suddenly began to slant—our
jet was making a turn.

Of course I shall visit the Schwartzes on Nantucket! My
second invitation! The first had been to the Kennan farm in
Pennsylvania. I felt happy and lighthearted. Difficulties, did
they say? My whole life so far had consisted of difficulties
and abnormalities. It couldn't be any worse from now on.

The strip of land below was Long Island. That was where
we would land. How splendid that the airport had been
named "Kennedy"—it was nice that America met her newcomers with that name. Alan, meanwhile, was saying that my
written statement would be given to the press, that at present
all I needed to say was a few words, mentioning that there
would be a press conference soon, at which I would be able
to answer all questions.

All right: "Alan, don't worry, everything will be all right!"
I could see that he was nervous. The press, my statement,
difficulties—none of these people seemed to understand how
at ease and happy I felt. They had all crossed the Atlantic

* Letter of April 16, 1967.

many times, had traveled over half of the world; nothing could surprise them. They could not grasp what it was like to have always lived under a heavy yoke and suddenly to find oneself able to fly out free, like a bird. They did not value the freedom in which they had been born and bred, for no one values the air he breathes every day. This charming young Schwartz, still almost a boy, how could he have known what it meant to live all one's life in Russia and then be able to leave? Kennan knew, he understood everything; that was why he felt anxious. But I, at that moment, couldn't stop to think of "difficulties." I felt so happy and well.

The microphone and the reporters waited for us at the bottom of the ramp. I ran down, stepping as on air.

"Hello! I'm happy to be here!" I said, expressing what was in my heart.

All right, go ahead, take my picture, take notes, write anything you want about me. I know that at present you don't understand me. But someday, maybe, you will know what it's like to be able really to say to the world what one thinks.

✳

From Kennedy Airport we drove to the home of Mr. Stuart H. Johnson on Long Island. He was the father of Priscilla Johnson, the translator of my book, who had invited me to stay with them upon my arrival.

My first impression of America was of the magnificent Long Island highways. After that tiny, homey Switzerland, everything here appeared immense, spacious, vast, reminding one of Russia. This was the strangest thing of all, something I had least expected. The vastness of the flat landscape under a sky which that day was overcast, the litter strewn all over the place (in Switzerland one never saw so much as the minutest scrap of paper). A lot of fat men and women with Slavic features. Maybe this was just my own personal impression—I am forever seeking likenesses, not differences.

No, there was something more than just that here: an informality, a naturalness and simplicity of manner so like ours. In Switzerland I had seen good, unconstrained manners. In India it had been politeness and respect, full of ceremony and manners. But Americans paid no attention to ceremony and manners, just like Russians. But only how much freer, how unrestrained they were, and how they loved to smile!

The second thing I noticed on our way to Locust Valley was the number of women driving cars. I am a driver from way back, I love good roads and good automobiles; and I noticed at once how many new cars were on the roads. But it was the variety of feminine types at the wheel that struck me: pretty young girls, still almost children; smartly dressed women; many Negroes, young and old; women in furs and extraordinary big hats, like shrubs in bloom—and finally gray-haired women, for whom in the U.S.S.R. the only possible vehicle would have been a wheelchair, driving cars expertly and with a certain dash, smoking a cigarette and chatting with a companion.

"A woman's health is the nation's health." This was said by some sociologist back in the nineteenth century. These women behind the wheel, apparently the owners of the cars, looked charming, with their hair either cut short or long and flowing, their bright, slightly vulgar ornaments. No uniformity in style here, every woman looking the way she pleased. Many had two or three children with them, and dresses on hangers in the back of the car to avoid mussing them up in suitcases. The good health, the freedom and independence of this young nation presented themselves graphically before my eyes during that hour's ride.

In the U.S.S.R. so many men had perished in wars and revolutions that the majority of the population now consisted of women. That's why the majority of doctors, teachers, salespeople were women. Over there women performed some of the heaviest work ordinarily done by men. But then, did they look the least bit like these women here? An unfortunate

woman taxicab driver in Moscow, who was forced to work
in a cab pool only because she had returned from the war as a
driver and there was no other work to be had, cursed
her hellish labors, which sooner or later were bound to ruin
her health. Outside of a few famous movie actresses, no
women in the U.S.S.R. owned automobiles.

We came to a stop in front of a white wooden, two-storied
house with black shutters, and were met at the door by Mr.
Johnson, rosy-cheeked and blue-eyed, and of course with a
broad smile on his face. He looked about sixty, although he
was actually seventy-four. It will take me some time to
accustom myself to how young Americans look for their age.
This, too, is a sign of good health.

As we went up to the second floor, this house amazed me
by its old-fashioned appearance. It turned out that Americans
love everything that looks to them like an antique. In the
U.S.S.R. we thought of all houses in the U.S.A. as being of
concrete and glass, either skyscrapers or flat-roofed, one-
storied, ranch-style houses. And when I saw lively wallpaper
everywhere, starched, ruffled curtains at small windows,
"Richelieu" runners on the bureau and colorful porcelain
figurines, I felt as if I were watching a play by Ostrovsky on
the stage of the Maly Theater in Moscow. Well, it only went
to prove that I hadn't studied the United States sufficiently
at the university, that I didn't know much. All that day, and
again at night lying with closed eyes in a squeaky wooden
bed, I couldn't get over my amazement: a Victorian interior
was the last thing I had expected to find in the United States
of America.

I spent my first month and a half in this house; in the end
I grew accustomed to its old-fashioned comfort. I grew attached to my kindhearted host, too. The library, with its
open fireplace, where Mr. Johnson always had his evening
martinis, where the shelves carried Chekhov, Tolstoy, and
Dostoevsky in English and pictures of Mr. Johnson's late
wife stood on small rickety tables, was my chosen refuge. It

was so very cozy near the fireplace; Mr. Johnson would tell
stories of the First World War and would show with pride a
collection of books and drawings by Winston Churchill. In
the dining room, of an evening, we always ate by candlelight
—a lovely American custom. The embroideries under glass
on the walls and the lace doilies, their angles sticking out
in different directions, no longer aroused my curiosity. The
house was run according to rules established by its hostess,
recently deceased, and the housekeeper, Maria, a neat little
German woman, saw to it that they were strictly adhered to.
Those dinners, with flowers and candles invariably on the
table, were like the performance of a ritual. I found in it a
kind of soothing charm, for the world outside was showering
me daily with new surprises.

The first ordeal, which awaited me a few days after my
arrival, was a press conference at the Plaza Hotel in New
York. I must admit, though, that, totally lacking in any idea
of what lay in store for me, I treated the whole matter rather
offhandedly, completely forgetting the TV cameras, placed
somewhere far away, and concentrating all my attention on
finding the proper English words for my answers. That was
why, I think, everything passed off successfully; judging by
all reports, I had been "very poised." Actually, I just didn't
realize that I was being watched on TV even in Europe. This
sense of unreality had been increased by the difference in
time, to which I hadn't quite got adjusted yet, and also by
the fact that electric lights were used unrestrainedly throughout the day, so that in the end one lost all sense of day and
night.

I felt just as lighthearted and happy as on my first day,
I wanted to smile all the time and think of nothing. Everyone
congratulated me on my success; that same evening I looked
in astonishment at myself on TV, my own voice sounding
like that of a stranger.

The reporters and photographers let us go at last, after
we got stuck in the same elevator at the Plaza in which

Khrushchev had got stuck during his visit here. New York in the evening, under the rain and flooded with lights, reminded me of Moscow in the evening—all large cities are alike at night.

The first ordeal about which Kennan had written was over. Such a pity that the Kennans had gone to Africa, then to Europe, and we wouldn't be seeing each other until August.

Before their departure Mr. and Mrs. Kennan had come to Locust Valley. It had been a warm spring day, we had walked in the beautiful neglected park; somehow, we hadn't felt like talking business. Anyway, everything was moving along surprisingly successfully. Kennan, however, warned me again of possible future troubles; he was afraid of some unexpected disillusionment. He spoke of his country with great love and pain. He wanted me to understand it:

. . . You simply cannot judge our society as a whole. You must discriminate. It is not really a unified society but a great battlefield, on which are fought out issues that have meaning for all of humanity. The outward aspect of it will often repel you—it repels us. But don't forget the many of us who are struggling, as best we can, against all this ugliness and error. We are in a sense your brothers and sisters; and you must look at us as such—with sympathy for our difficulties.*

Annelise by nature was very calm. She reminded me so of my Moscow friend Marina—small, firm, collected. Annelise, a Norwegian, had the rather severe features of a northerner, with blue eyes. A yellow spring suit on her svelte figure, a large ring on her hand, she held herself with dignity, wasting no smiles. Everything seemed calm about her; I could see without being told that she would understand much and would give good advice. She was not a university professor, nor a writer, nor a historian; she was just a woman. And that is best of all. . . .

The invitation to spend the summer on their farm in Pennsylvania was given me again. There was one other

* Extract from letter of April 22, 1967.

member of the family I had to meet—their daughter Joan, who, with her husband and two sons, lived in Princeton.

But for the time being I was still to remain on Long Island, with the Johnson family. We had to start working on the translation of *Twenty Letters* and see how it would go. Everything seemed so easy, and I couldn't quite understand why Kennan was worried. The days and weeks that followed, however, showed that all his warnings had not been groundless. He knew all too well the Soviet Union and its possible reactions. He knew his own country even better. And one more thing: he knew human nature and feared that the intoxication of these few days of happiness might result in a painful hangover.

Confusion

THE DAY AFTER the press conference at the Plaza
I felt tired and worn out; it had been too much of a strain.
I sat in Mr. Johnson's living room, watching in astonishment
how every half-hour mail was brought in, baskets of flowers,
more mail, then baskets again. I started out by reading every
letter I got, then I just took to looking through a few; in the
end I hadn't the strength to go on.

"Welcome to America." "We hope you will find peace and
happiness here." "Do not despair, your children will be with
you!" "May God bless you!" "We came here forty years ago
and now this is our country. You will find many friends. Your
children will understand. God bless you!"

This flood of mail continued to pour in throughout the
whole time I spent at the Johnsons.

There were letters of another nature, too: "Go back home,
Red dog!" "America is not for a Red plague and for Stalin's
family!" "Our cat is better than you, she takes care of her
children!" "You don't know how to speak English, go back to
Russia!" . . .

But of this kind there were few, about three to a hundred
that wished me well.

I hadn't expected such a reaction to what I had done and said. At first I was surprised. Then I began to weep over every kind, sweet note I received. Still later, I grew desperate. I wasn't accustomed to being noticed, to being the center of attention; I was unaccustomed to having thousands of unknown people thinking about my life and destiny, speaking, writing about me—people who from now on would be curious about my every step, from whom I would be unable to hide anywhere.

Who did they think I was? Dozens of invitations came from colleges and universities to "lecture," "give a talk," "answer questions" about the Soviet Union. More from various religious organizations to come and tell them about "my experience and how I found God"—and again, to participate in special religious programs on the radio and TV. To visit a women's club and tell them about Soviet women. Invitations to attend religious services—Russian Orthodox, Roman Catholic, Baptist, Presbyterian, Quaker, services in a Temple of All Religions, in a Vedanta ashram on the West Coast. And all this in the spirit of friendly hospitality and of sincere sympathy, with an immense desire to know how people lived in the U.S.S.R., since it had made me reject Communism, reject my country, and leave my children behind.

At the press conference I thought I had explained everything I could. I knew I would be writing a second book, in which I intended to say all I could about life in the U.S.S.R. and why I would never return there. But the thought of turning into an itinerant lecturer on "Soviet problems," appearing at large gatherings, made me shudder. On the other hand, to talk on television about religious experiences seemed like a profanation of the profoundest essence of one's soul. To talk about politics, to tell about life in the U.S.S.R., would have been a form of self-advertising; besides, such talks should be given by a historian, a professional lecturer, and not by a woman to whom politics had never been the foremost factor in her life.

I categorically refused all such invitations. To address an audience had always been difficult for me—this was the reason for my not teaching at Moscow University. I wished to remain myself in this country, where social life was active, free, abundant. To be a lecturer, a sociologist, was not my métier. But I knew that with my refusals I was violating something very essential in this country's customs and habits. In fencing myself off from public auditoriums, I was unwittingly hurting the feelings of all these people, who believed in me and were opening to me their hospitable doors.

Under the influence of these letters, this interest in me, these "friendly embraces," I suddenly felt I didn't have the strength to live up to what I myself had done. I was incapable of responding to all these calls and accolades. I was too weak for such a role. I had taken upon myself something that was too heavy a burden for my weak shoulders, something that in the end would crush me. It was as if I had stepped out on a stage in front of a huge audience in an immense opera-theater and found that I had no voice to sing with.

> The rumble dies. I come on stage.
> Leaning against the entry,
> I search a far-off echo
> For my future.
>
> The gloom of night is beamed at me,
> A thousand binoculars lined up.
> If it be possible, Abba, Father,
> Take away this cup from me.

This is from "Hamlet," one of the poems written by Pasternak's Doctor Zhivago.*

To add to my confusion, about this same time I received a letter from my son, which had reached New York via Switzerland. It was like a knife thrust straight into my heart.

* Editors' translation.

My son had been shaken by our telephone conversation; he had understood that I would not return, and it was then that he wrote this letter. My decision not to return was dreadful to him for another reason, too: we had always spoken as mature equals; now he felt himself betrayed, forsaken— himself and Katie and Helen. He couldn't get over the fact that I hadn't given them even an inkling of a warning, and that they had had to suffer such an unexpected shock. As usual, he didn't touch on any possible political motivations; our personal relationship was far more important to him, and the bitterness of his words was sincere:

. . . When we spoke on the telephone and I heard all you had to say, I was so lost that I was unable to answer you coherently. It took me several days to think it all over, for things are not at all as simple as you seem to think. . . .

You may rest assured that your words on "tourism" were fully understood, and I have no intention of inducing you to return, especially after our talk. . . .

You must admit that after what you have done, your advice from afar to take courage, to stick together, not to lose heart, and not let go of Katie, was, to say the least, strange. After all, we have many close friends here, who will always give us good advice, and not only good advice but real help. I consider that by your action you have cut yourself off from us and, therefore, please allow us to live as we see fit. . . .

I want to emphasize once again that I do not take it upon my- self to judge your actions; but since we have endured fairly stoically what you have done, I hope that from now on we shall be allowed to arrange our own lives *ourselves*. . . .

Try to think deeply about this, and try to understand us, too.

Joseph

April 14, 1967

For me every line implied more than it actually said.

I knew my son, I could see the three of them in our kitchen, with endless telephone calls, questions from ac- quaintances, and the necessity, at the same time, to work and get ready for their exams—not one of the three had ever been lazy; they were used to hard work. I could be calm on this point. There would be no outbursts of hysteria, drunkenness; they wouldn't throw up their studies and become dropouts. No, such things could never happen there. But between the lines there was so much distress and pain that I felt shattered:

". . . Since the day you called, Katie has not been herself. She is suffering far more than we. . . ."

I wept. I couldn't stop weeping. I wanted to go far away, beg God's forgiveness for my sin against my children. I wanted to go back to that monastery in Switzerland, anywhere, anywhere—just to hide from all this hospitality, this curiosity, from people who thought that everything was simple and easy for me!

My new friends became alarmed. Not for nothing had Kennan warned me. In my despair I wrote him—he was then in Africa, in Johannesburg. His answer came soon enough. As always, he endeavored to look above and ahead of events:

. . . (and above all) you should not permit it to shake your confidence in yourself. . . . You, in doing what you did in Delhi, followed the deepest needs of your own nature. Had you gone back to the U.S.S.R. at that time, you would have gone back not only as an enemy of the system but in a sense as an enemy of yourself. All this would have done your son no good, either. . . .

. . . dear Svetlana, even in the face of this greatest sorrow, be confident that in some way of which probably neither you nor I are now able to conceive, all this courage and faith will be vindicated—and for him as well.*

＊

The whole of May in Locust Valley was spent in a state of harassment and dismay. It prevented not only work on the translation but the possibility of any quiet, sober thought.

* Extract from letter of May 11, 1967.

Newsmen came to the door, took pictures of the house from a helicopter, "spied" from behind bushes when Mr. Johnson and I took the dogs for a walk. A bus belonging to an Italian television company remained parked for a long time near the house, ending up with an interview with the gardener, a Pole. Two good fat Hungarian brothers, private security men, who had escaped from Hungary in 1956 after the Soviet Army invaded their country, took turns on duty in the kitchen, completely unbalancing the tidy housekeeper and the cook. Priscilla's sister took me shopping. Next day we found our picture in the papers, trying on shoes in a shop. Interviews were demanded from me, from Priscilla, from her husband, from Maria. The local police kept a car on duty near the house twenty-four hours a day. There was no need for this, but the police feared possible incidents.

Apparently the Soviet Embassy was not planning to kidnap the defector. Moscow simply didn't know yet what to do.

So far they had merely demanded of Andrei Voznesensky, who was visiting New York at the time, that he publicly condemn my action. Voznesensky did not do it. Poets and students listened to him, as he read poems about people being brothers, about nations wanting friendship and peace, about all governments standing in their way. (For this he was not allowed to return to the United States that summer.)

Letters continued to arrive every day. Archbishop John of San Francisco sent an autographed copy of his book. Professor S. K. Majumdar sent his lectures on Yoga. Unknown Russians congratulated me on the Orthodox Easter. Unknown Catholics wrote about the miracles of Garabandal and Fatima. They all sent me their blessings, invariably ending with: "We are praying for you and your children." I wept over these letters, feeling that I lacked the strength to be a "famous public figure."

No one helped me to answer the numerous letters. I had no secretary. Priscilla tried to help, but it was impossible, for she would then have been unable to translate the book.

She was in just as much confusion as I was. Being hurried and unable to weigh everything properly, I consented to have the book serialized in newspapers and magazines two weeks before the date of publication. I was told that with my permission one or two chapters would appear in their entirety, which would whet the public's appetite for the book. I agreed to this, although it seemed to me rather vulgar to publish in a newspaper a book concerning family affairs.

My children were both born in May—my daughter on the fourth, my son on the twenty-second—and I sent them short congratulatory telegrams. I kept the receipts. But from later interviews given by my son, I understood that the postal authorities in Moscow had never delivered those telegrams.

I spent most of my time in Priscilla's room, which had been assigned to me, or in the living room downstairs. I didn't feel like taking walks, accompanied by security men in plain clothes. I had had enough of that sort of thing in Switzerland and had hoped that here it wouldn't be necessary.

There were many Russian books in the house. People continued to send me books through the mail; thus the first "possession" I acquired in America was a library, collected in this way. I was finally able to read everything Andrei Sinyavsky had written in his brilliant literary style. In Moscow, nothing of his that had been published abroad was ever shown even to us, his colleagues at the Institute. We were made to condemn him without knowing what for! His courage helped me to nerve myself to a certain degree. When I thought of Andrei in a concentration camp, I felt I had no right to complain, that I must thank Providence for giving me freedom and independence instead of a prison. But the trouble with human beings brought up in a cage is that they do not know what freedom is and have to get trained into it, gradually. One cannot give a starving man a large meal right off the bat: it will kill him.

Little by little, my hospitable hosts, their friendliness and simple approach, the concern and sympathy of my new friends, and, last but not least, spring itself brought me back to my senses, back to life. Like Columbus, I began to "discover America," first through the home life of those whose guest I happened to be during my first half-year or so. At Moscow University I had already studied the political life and history of this country, and at present these aspects didn't attract me much. I had always felt that family life was more significant in getting to know a country and its society as a whole. The first home I became familiar with on the American continent was the Johnson home.

Seventy-four-year-old Mr. Johnson, who played tennis every day with three neighbors—all of them his contemporaries—and who in the evening would drink a martini with me, was "my President" of this country. He was the embodiment of its sound health, humor, good nature, hospitality, simplicity, and naturalness. He used to turn into a joke the presence of the police car on duty outside his house. One day, with a sly wink, he suggested that we "run away." We got into his Chevrolet, and for a long time he drove around the pretty sites of Locust Valley, Oyster Bay, Mill Neck; then took me to the ocean, enjoying our "escapade" like a small boy. At home he had trouble in climbing the stairs, for he was stiff in both knees, but he assured me that on the tennis court he found them more flexible. He enjoyed going to the post office every day—his own postbox could not contain all my mail. These trips amused him. His house was thronged with unknown people, much to the servants' displeasure; but when the day of my departure came, he said his house would now become empty and dull once more.

His youngest son was a teacher in New York. He came on Sundays, bringing his three small children with him, skillfully handling the youngest, who was only two years old. Not far from the house there was a neglected playground with swings, where the grandchildren now played. I used to sit with them there near a sandbox, while the children "baked" sand cakes, or else helped them onto the shaky swings, and it seemed as if I had known for a long time this good-natured teacher and his children, fair-haired and as chubby as cherubs. The playground reminded me of my own childhood; in general, the whole of this neglected estate, with its empty stables, overgrown lawns, discarded lawn mower, reminded me somehow of the untended fields and meadows around Moscow. The fat young teacher would tell me about his children, his school; about his childhood and adolescence on this estate, how he had played near the pond, where to this day one found the half-ruined house of Johnson grandfathers and great-grandfathers. The old homestead stood dilapidated, its paneless windows open to all weather. It threatened to crumble at any moment, but the family was reluctant to have it torn down; Mr. Johnson preferred to wait until it had died a quiet death of its own.

The teacher saw that I was troubled, and I confessed: "Yes, it's as if I were watching life here as on a screen. I look at it, I like it, but I have a feeling that I cannot get onto that screen. And I'm afraid I will never be able to."

"No, no, that'll pass," he would say, trying to make me believe in my own strength. "It'll pass! I understand. I know how painful it must be thinking of your children. But believe me, you will find many friends here!"

He brought me from New York Brahms' First Piano Concerto, fixed the record player in the living room, and we listened to music in silence, each one buried in his own thoughts. We listened to Mozart, Schumann, to the preludes of Bach. He did his best to cheer me up. He bought me Ravi Shankar's improvisations on a sitar; looked everywhere for a certain song of Nat King Cole's I was anxious to find.

The eldest Johnson daughter, Priscilla's sister, lived not far away with her husband, a doctor, and her teen-aged children. In her yellow slacks, she looked as graceful as a young girl. Her house was modern, its simplicity elegant and cozy. There was always a smile on her lips—a natural smile, nothing artificial about it. It's a magnificent quality in women here not to burden you with their problems and worries, although each of them must have worries and troubles of her own. She used to take me shopping. Later she bought me some dresses and a few other things on her own—it was best for me not to show myself in public.

She hovered about like a butterfly. One could never have guessed that she was over forty. Her manner was friendly, and she never asked questions. This, at the time, was perhaps the kindest thing that could be done to me—not to ask.

I went twice to New York to visit Alan Schwartz and his wife, Paula. There we were instantly photographed by a reporter, just as we were getting into the elevator. Paula looked about eighteen, although she was thirty. A graceful young woman who handled expertly her two boys—two little devils—her household, and her young husband, from whom the boys had obviously inherited their exuberance.

At last I succeeded in meeting Ashok, Suresh Singh's son —that same Ashok who lived in Seattle with his Dutch wife and worked for the Boeing Company. We had called each other up, then he had written me a letter, finally he flew out to Long Island.

He turned out to be a charming young man, with all the politeness of the East and the freedom and naturalness of the West. We spent all day near the open fireplace in Mr. Johnson's living room, talking about his parents and Kalakankar, about the possibility of building a hospital there.

When it had become known in Mr. Johnson's household that an "Indian relation" was coming to see me, Maria asked what he would eat, then tactfully tried to find out whether he would sit on the floor and wear a turban and beard. The handsome, well-mannered young man charmed her. He praised her pastries, had friendly chats with her and the cook, finally took snapshots of them and of everyone else in the house. When he had left, Maria said, "That's a real gentleman!"

Sometime toward the end of May I woke up one night in my "Victorian" bed; a fresh predawn breeze was blowing in at the window. Somewhere dogs were barking. There was a smell of cold, dew-drenched grass. And drowning it all, giving one no time to breathe, tangling all one's thoughts, there poured in at the window the intoxicating scent of lilacs. Lilies of the valley in the grass; lilies of the valley everywhere in the house. And outside, near the house, lilac bushes in bloom, like immense mauve haystacks.

No, this was not a Moscow suburb, not Zhukovka—although it might well have been; there, too, at this time there would be lilies of the valley, lilacs, the barking of dogs in the night. . . .

In this strange year of 1967, which had begun near the Ganges, spring had met me three times, as though in compensation for all the sorrows and losses.

First it had come in India at the end of February, and its coming had been hard to perceive. As in "winter," roses and gladiolus continued to bloom, at night the same chirping of cicadas. But one fine day, among the dark rough foliage of mango trees appeared little brushes of flowers; this had indicated the arrival of spring.

And instantly, with lightning speed, everything around us had begun to be covered with blossoms—every little shrub, every little branch. In the evergreen treetops new leaves came out and old ones fell to the ground. And not in the fall, as in the north, but in the spring, dry leaves would rustle on the terrace, blown into piles by the wind. There had been no awakening of nature, as in northern climes, for life here flowed smoothly, eternally, like the Ganges, never falling asleep in winter. The renewal would come in the middle of summer after the monsoon rains. Spring in India had run its course like a fleet-footed maiden, her bracelets tinkling, hot summer breathing at her very heels like a scorched desert.

The second spring had come in Switzerland at the end of March. There that familiar renewal of life was in evidence all around. But in small, peaceful Switzerland even this was a sedate affair, calm and assured. Spring arrived without hurry, unafraid of the last snows which had covered the purple violets and the snowdrops. It knew that it would have its way. And indeed, in less than half a day the snow melted, the sun grew warm, and, as though nothing untoward had happened, forsythia displayed itself in festive yellow, and hyacinths pushed their way through the ground. In the morning, again dark clouds might cover the sky, and again at night winds might howl, but with another morning, skies would be sparkling once more, a vivid blue. And it was such joy to experience this unalterable rotation of nature. With it, involuntarily, came a renewal of one's soul.

When I left Switzerland in April, spring was in full swing. On my last ride to Zurich the roads saw me off with the pink of wild cherries, the blossom of almonds, and the white froth of apple blossom. This was Switzerland's last farewell to me—a presage, I felt, of a successful journey. Like signposts, those blossoming trees remained in my memory. And my memory of the sweet little country remains filled with the flourish of spring.

But on Long Island, in late April, it was still cold; no leaves on the trees, no flowers anywhere. Only toward the middle of May did spring come with a suddenness and brightness that took one's breath away.

The American spring is like the country itself: abundant, rich, flowing over you like a full tide. That particular year it had been retarded by a cold April. But then, after several delays, everything suddenly began burgeoning at once, almost noisily. There was an unreal, dreamlike quality about it.

Azaleas were suddenly ablaze. White dogwoods stood like brides in the wood—these trees of all colors were new to me; one does not meet them in Europe, and dogwood cannot even be transplanted to other continents. White and pink magnolias, yellowish rhododendrons, all of them lived happily side by side with our ordinary lilacs and lilies of the valley—the Russian symbols of spring. The only thing missing was the bird cherry. I only knew its Russian name—*cheryomukha*—and no one here knew what it was called in English.

Everywhere, the wide world over, spring was flourishing, filled with blossoms and fragrance.

> *... spring was spring even in town. ... Full of joy were the plants, birds, insects, and children. But people—mature grown people—never ceased deceiving and tormenting themselves and others. They considered as sacred and important not this spring morning, not the beauty of God's world, given for the benefit of all creatures—a beauty that disposed one to peace, harmony, and love—; sacred and important to them was that which they themselves had invented to dominate one another.*

This was how Leo Tolstoy began his novel *Resurrection*. An old English edition of the book, in a red morocco-leather binding, stood on Mr. Johnson's bookshelf.

A Stifling Summer

EARLY IN JUNE everyone left Locust Valley. Priscilla went to Atlanta, Georgia, to her husband, where she would be working on the translation. Unfortunately, we never had an opportunity of looking through it together. Since then we haven't seen each other.

In the meantime, I had had the opportunity of meeting Joan Kennan, and now I went to their farm. Later, Joan and Larry would be going to Tonga, small islands in the Pacific Ocean, to work there in the Peace Corps. They were a handsome young couple, and I was glad to spend two months with them.

We rode through the green fields and hillocks of Pennsylvania. The radio in the car announced the news of the war between Egypt and Israel, which had just begun. This was my last trip with the two Hungarian brothers; on the farm I was not to have any security men. The two fatties mercilessly filled the car with thick cigar smoke, listening to the radio all the way. In my suitcase lay their farewell gift: a ball-point pen with an inscription: "To Svetlana. Use with happiness. Al and George."

The green farming country of Pennsylvania looked rich

and fertile, a bit like the Ukraine and the Kuban, except for the most important thing, which still remains in the U.S.S.R.: a "village." The white and dark-red houses of the farmers looked like comfortable modern cottages, a car parked in front of each house. Here and there engine-driven mowers were cutting the grass. There were no hedges or fences around the houses. To me this was a pleasing sight: people didn't fence themselves in, didn't lead secret lives and had nothing to hide. Garden furniture stood on lawns outside the houses, or on porches looking out on the road. It created the impression that people trusted each other. Fences made of crossbars could be seen in some places, but they were for the cattle.

Quite unexpectedly, the large Kennan house turned out to be much like an old-time country home of a Russian *pomeshchik* (landowner). Particularly the side of the house which should have been considered its main entrance, with a wide flight of stone stairs, stone vases for flowers, a porch with columns. But people entered from the other side, which was typically American and led straight into a living room and kitchen. The same strange but harmonious mixture of styles was to be found inside the house. The Kennans had brought from Russia old engravings, pictures, porcelain, small Fedoskino lacquered tables. There was even a large photograph of the Kremlin Embankment, at the sight of which I couldn't help shuddering, thinking to myself, "Not again those Kremlin walls!"

Joan and Larry explained that the house had been built at the beginning of the nineteenth century and later done over by someone who had come from Russia. Hence its resemblance to Russian architecture. But that former owner had been a Jew, a merchant; that's why at the side of every door a mezuzah had been inserted—a small tube, about the size of one's little finger, in which lay a slip of paper with a sacred text. Joan used to say it was thanks to this that the house was such a happy one for their family: the mezuzah protected all entrances from evil men.

Like a cat in a new place, I went through the whole house on that first day, looking, almost sniffing at every stick of furniture, every corner. The house was well lived in, cozy, especially the rockers everywhere, wooden or upholstered. The place was at once European, American, Russian, with the addition of those mezuzoth. All this I liked, because I always preferred a mixture of different traditions to any single one.

There was something special about every room. I found Norwegian figurines and an engraving of Kristiansand, where Annelise Kennan's parents lived. A bearskin lay near the fireplace in the living room. In every room there was something from Russia—a small box, a *matryoshka* (a nest of painted wooden dolls fitting one inside the other), a small table. And everywhere a great many Russian books.

The large study on the third floor was full of sunshine, reflected in squares on the yellow parquet floor. The study itself was rather empty, and this was the most wonderful part of it. One wall was covered with bookshelves painted white (exactly the same kind of white shelves I had left in my apartment in Moscow), full of books, Russian newspapers and journals. Material on Russia and newspaper clippings were kept in folders. The huge plain wooden table —light, with no drawers—was so convenient for work, it seemed to invite one to settle down. Of course near the window there was the inevitable rocker, an old, hard one, polished by time. There was also a card index here and a floor lamp. Just pace the room from corner to corner, think, and then write. It was George Kennan's favorite place to work. An old-fashioned typewriter stood on a support made of plain boards, nailed together by the professor himself. Joan said that her father found relaxation in all kinds of work needed on the farm. But farming itself interested no one in the family. Next door lived a tenant farmer who took care of the land.

Toward evening the three of us sat on the steps of the back porch. In front of us, beyond a small lawn, lay a wavy, pale-green field of wheat, and beyond it a small grove. With no American buildings in sight, the landscape looked singularly like something in central Russia.

The back porch was the family's favorite spot for evening talks. Here we spent every evening of that stifling summer, with its many downpours and electric storms, with fireflies hovering among the fir trees.

There was something melancholy, something very Russian, about this place. The impression was enhanced by the music from the movie *Doctor Zhivago,* which Joan loved to play on the record player. The theme of Lara and the Varykino winter was really very moving, changing at times into a waltz, at others into just a memory, which turned your heart inside out. . . .

Fortunately we listened to other music, too—folk songs by Joan Baez, Judy Collins, Pete Seeger, and Mitch Miller's chorus. We also listened to Grieg, Bach—Joan always played the records while dinner was being cooked and we were in the kitchen or drinking cocktails on the back porch.

There were no servants here. At the kitchen stove each one of us prepared what he liked. I once made a real curry, Joan made pancakes on Sundays, and Larry, in the yard, would prepare steaks every evening on a charcoal grill. How many different sauces we would invent! Even the Georgian *chakhokhbili,* made of chicken and tomatoes, was enjoyed by everyone. After dinner Joan and I would wash the dishes, putting a record on extra loud, so as to hear it clearly above the noise of running water.

We spent half the day in the kitchen. Here the morning was started with coffee at a long wooden table near the window. The table stood with its narrow end to the window and benches on either side—just as in my kitchen in Mos-

cow. Here the children were fed. Dinner would be served
on the veranda, protected by screens, for grownups only;
the children would be in bed by then. There would be
lighted candles on the table, and we would sit there in the
semidarkness, while in the grass and in the air outside fireflies kept twinkling.

How easy and unconstrained I felt with my young hosts,
both of them ten years younger than I was. They didn't have
my life experience of pain and traumas, but they had the
maturity of people brought up in a strong, close family—
something which here, apparently, had been passed on from
generation to generation. That was why they took care of
me as if I were a younger sister. Everything spoke of this,
starting with my room upstairs, which was simple, without
Victorian furniture and ruffles at the window, but very comfortable at the same time. Joan knew that for the time being
it was best for me not to appear in shops. She, therefore,
chose for me summer dresses, lingerie, canvas sneakers, a
bathing suit, cosmetics. No one had fussed over me so much
for a long time. Every purchase had been carefully thought
out and filled some need of mine. Larry bought me blue
jeans, without which one couldn't live on a farm; and seeing
how I stored my needles and thread in a box that had held
Swiss chocolates, he one day brought me a small sewing kit.
These were not just ordinary friends; we lived so well together those two months that they became like a brother
and sister.

Joan was an unusually lovely woman—tall, long-legged,
svelte, with the natural grace of a doe. This naturalness was
her chief charm. She looked a bit like Katharine Hepburn
in her youth, that same delicate form which yet held in itself
something very strong and sad. Her smile was always slightly
melancholy, for no reason at all. I would often ask her if
she felt ill or was tired, or had something happened? No,
she would assure me that she felt perfectly well and happy,
while calmly hanging out the laundry to dry, or ironing, or

preparing the children's meal. I sometimes found myself unable to take my eyes off her. She always wore shorts in the morning, and would change into some sweet graceful dress in the evening. This young woman knew how to run a house, and I often wished she could have been the hostess of a big house so as not to have to attend to the cooking and washing, but only entertain many guests, all of whom would admire her and take delight in her company. Her life, however, was full of cares, and added to them, there was I. Every day she would bring my enormous mail, which used to drive me into utter despair.

I needed not three lawyers, not literary agents and publishers, but one good efficient secretary. This I did not have. As before, 95 percent of my letters were written with sympathy and understanding. Many responded to my article, "To Boris Leonidovich Pasternak." They understood what had prompted me to write it. By now I had acquired many friends in different countries through this correspondence. One day I received a letter from Mrs. Singh in London, where she lived with her twenty-eight-year-old son. I was happy to get news of Brajesh's only son.

On the Kennan farm all the agricultural work was done by the tenant farmer and his family, who lived in a neighboring house. On the very day of my arrival I saw a red sports car stop near the garage. A young woman stepped out, wearing white shorts and a fashionable hairdo.

"Probably someone for you, Joan?" I asked, certain that it must be a friend.

"That's Juanita, the farmer's wife," Joan replied.

I kept silent. . . .

A farmer's wife? And that was her car? She looked like some famous Soviet movie actress, only the latter wouldn't have owned such a swanky automobile! And the farmer's house was in no way inferior to the houses of famous Soviet academicians. . . .

Soon after that I became friends with Juanita. Her whole

family worked from morning to night. Electricity ran the machines that milked thirty cows; in the large barn Juanita's eight-year-old son had grown the finest young pigs in the neighborhood. Every morning would start with the mooing of cows, the bellowing of a bull, and the squeals of piglets in the barn. All the milk was sold—this was part of the farmer's income; the family spent all their days in the fields. They cut the grass, stacked the hay; later they reaped corn and then wheat. Everything was done with machines. Behind the barn there was a whole array of agricultural machinery. Later in the summer, when Kennan's son and nephew arrived, they would help with the work in the fields.

Juanita only rolled her eyes when I asked her how she found time to do everything. She had four children. One had to manage, and the whole family helped.

She often asked me how they farmed in the U.S.S.R., whether they had machinery and who owned the land. I explained that in the U.S.S.R. all the land, its produce, and the income therefrom belonged to the State; that the peasants owned nothing but their houses and a small kitchen garden. They got paid for their work in the kolkhoz with money and produce, but payments depended on the kolkhoz's output. The kolkhoz, in turn, depended on State regulations and could not decide for itself what was most advantageous to grow. Peasants were deprived of all initiative and interest. Young men migrated to the cities. The villages were left with old men and invalids, and every fall the cities had to send thousands of students and State employees to gather the harvests. No one was interested in working, knowing that no matter how much he worked, everything would go to the State. That was the reason why a village in the U.S.S.R. did not look like Juanita's home, but rather like something that might have been seen in Pennsylvania perhaps over a hundred years ago.

Juanita would only shake her head.

One day she remarked: "Maybe we don't value what

we've got. We're always griping about life being more difficult and expensive."

And I replied: "If you could only get a glimpse of a village
in the north of the U.S.S.R., or in India, you would know
how much you have here!"

Juanita, her husband and children looked tired toward
evening but happy. After work, having changed and washed,
they would settle down around the television. Joan's children
would run over there, as the Kennans had no TV set. When
television had presented an interview with Khrushchev in
his retirement, everyone had gone over to Juanita's house to
watch it.

Sometimes the farmer's family would show a colored
movie film they had taken: the children playing or riding
on ponies, the arrival of relatives for a visit.

And this was a farmer! A farmer! I kept repeating to myself. In the U.S.S.R. they claimed that stories of such living
conditions were nothing but propaganda, but here I was
seeing them with my own eyes. Poor unhappy Russia! How
rich and prosperous you, too, could have been, if your peasant had been allowed to till the soil with joy, and for his own
benefit!

I recalled the words of the Soviet writer Vladimir Solou-
khin: "Work in the fields brings joy. When the peasant is
deprived of this joy, his work becomes meaningless to him."

The harvest was good that summer. There had been many
thundershowers; in the daytime the sun had been hot. We
ate fresh corn every day. Joan's boys and the farmer's children became sunburned and looked healthy. We all went
swimming in a small pond, where Larry had constructed a
float. Larry worked all day—he could do anything. The family was getting ready for their approaching departure to the
Pacific. They had already sold their house in Princeton.

In both their characters there was a strong strain of romanticism; and Joan, in addition, had a great need to help
others. She finished a course in nursing, in preparation for

her work on that distant island. Neither of them was afraid of the forthcoming change from every conceivable comfort to a primitive life. They kept repeating that "the climate would be a healthy one for the children." True, there might be some tropical and intestinal diseases, but they were taking some medicine with them. Looking at them, I said to myself that this active couple would get lost nowhere. And their two young rascals would only become healthier from swimming every day among coral reefs. Joan's melancholy smile did not denote a weakness of any kind, and her blue eyes would sometimes sparkle with such brightness and strength that I actually did feel like a "younger sister."

In that sultry summer full of thunderstorms I was not given long to enjoy the peace of this sweet family. All too soon a storm broke over my own head.

✳

It took Moscow a long time to recover from its shock and decide what to do about the "defector." I could see it all, how they consulted one another, the Party, and the secret police, "solved the problem" with the Central Committee.

On June 25 at a UN press conference, Premier Kosygin declared: "Alliluyeva is a morally unstable person and she's a sick person and we can only pity those who wish to use her for any political aims or . . . [to] discredit the Soviet country."

We were at supper when the radio broadcast the press conference. Lighted candles stood on the table and our glasses were filled with red wine. I could hear from the Premier's tone that he was restraining himself—he wanted so to express himself in a ruder way. The interpreter translated, and in his rendition the words had a politer, a more decent sound. Even so, Joan and Larry burst out laughing. We drank some wine. I didn't give those words much significance. But one should never forget that the Party had its apparatus, and now this "computer," into which an idea had been inserted, would start working. It was only the first shot from the heavy artillery.

During the next month I learned from the press many new things about myself. It transpired that all my life I had been under the care of psychiatrists; that I was unusually oversexed; that I wore the diamonds of the Romanovs, ate from their gold plates, and lived in the Kremlin in a former Romanov palace; that I had been present in 1939 at the signing of the pact with Ribbentrop—incidentally, already an adult at the time. That my father consulted me on every political move, I ran his house, and without me not a single decision had been taken. That I had gone to Switzerland to collect the money deposited in Swiss banks by my father. American and European newspapers wrote all this, and the clippings were sent to me by unknown people. One reader added the copy of her written protest to the paper.

The *Ladies' Home Journal* and *McCall's* magazine wrote that Brajesh Singh had converted me to Hinduism and vegetarianism, and that I daily visited the temple of Shiva (an ancient phallic cult), performing religious rituals, including daily bathing in the "sacred Ganges."

Moscow's *Literary Gazette* wrote that all my life I had been "an hysterical paranoiac"; and Pimen, the Metropolitan of Moscow, said, "I know nothing about Alliluyeva's christening; she is not a Christian, she is interested in all religions at once." This bishop had been interviewed by a correspondent of a London paper, Victor Louis, who was a Soviet citizen.

After that the government of the U.S.S.R. permitted Victor Louis to interview my children, to photograph every room in my apartment, moving the furniture at will, to remove family photographs locked in my desk, take a copy of my manuscript and sell it to London papers with his own commentary. (Copies of the manuscript of *Twenty Letters* still remained in the U.S.S.R., in the hands of friends, and by that time it had been read by many people in Moscow.)

In a short time the London *Daily Express* began publishing the photos stolen from my desk under the heading, "Stalin's Secret Albums," together with comments by Victor Louis. In them names, dates, facts were all mixed up. Victor Louis had shaken a strange cocktail out of these photographs (that could be of interest to no one), his own text, and quotations from my manuscript. All of this was also published by *Stern*, a journal in Hamburg, as "Svetlana's Memoirs." In London, in Italy, Germany, Belgium, and Spain, the publishing of *Twenty Letters*, which had been planned for the end of October, was threatened: everywhere Victor Louis offered publishers his version instead of mine.

In Hamburg he told newsmen that he had received the photographs and manuscript in Moscow "from Alliluyeva's family," although my children had never known of the manuscript's existence and there was no copy of it in my home. The photographs locked in my desk they might have given, of course, but only under orders from the government. The *New York Times*, the Washington *Post*, the London *Times* openly called Victor Louis a "well-known agent of the KGB (Soviet Secret Police)."

In the middle of July Alan Schwartz came to the farm. One could hardly recognize him, he looked so pale and had lost so much weight. We had gone to court everywhere in Europe, protecting our copyrights. It had become absolutely necessary to publish immediately at least two hundred copies of the Russian text, in order to protect the copyright. Harper & Row now decided to move forward the publication date to the beginning of October. But a new obstacle arose: Moscow brought pressure to bear on the American Ambassador, on the State Department, on many influential Americans, to "postpone the publication of Alliluyeva's book, as its appearance on the eve of the Fiftieth Anniversary of the October Revolution might be harmful to Soviet-American relations." But the publishers refused to comply.

Apparently Moscow was counting on the whole world losing interest in my book, if it first had a chance of reading Victor Louis' version with photographs. Besides, his version and commentaries developed the chief points of Moscow's propaganda: "A crazy nymphomaniac, and her father's closest assistant." My innocent infatuation with Kapler was blown up into a "passionate affair with orgies." The "kisses smelling of tobacco," which my father used to give me in my childhood, were turned into a sensational headline: "My Father Was a Good Man."

Since in my manuscript, written four years earlier, there was no mention of any intention to leave the U.S.S.R., Moscow took it upon itself to explain this by other means. Enzo Biaggi, an Italian correspondent close to the Communists, was offered a chance of interviewing my children, my niece—my brother Jacob's daughter—and a few so-called "friends," specially picked for the occasion. For needless to say, Western correspondents would never have been allowed anywhere near my real friends in Russia. And so these "friends" merely repeated that "after her father's death and after the Twentieth Congress she had felt very unhappy. Her old acquaintances had left her. Her former glamour had faded. So she decided on an escape abroad as the sole way out of the dismal situation, hoping that through the publication of her manuscript she would draw some of the lost attention back to herself." Enzo Biaggi didn't hesitate to interview even Kapler and his present wife. My son was repeatedly questioned as to "how many more husbands there had been." I can only be proud of the dignity and self-control with which the poor boy endured these trials.

By contrast, Gulya, my niece, who had also been interviewed, told a lot of incredible tales about Brajesh Singh, whom she had never seen.

I must say one thing about Enzo Biaggi: in his articles he maintained a decent tone. Victor Louis, on the other hand, lied unblushingly: he referred to an interview with my aunt, Anna Redens, who had been dead for a long time; quoted conversations with my former husbands, although from the text it was clearly evident that he hadn't even met them. He placed Yuri Zhdanov in Odessa University instead of Rostov. Morozov he turned into a "specialist on Germany," a country which had never occupied his attention. And yet people believed Victor Louis.

I knew and I felt that lies spread about me in all countries would be believed sooner than anything I might say or write, because this was a psychological factor in social behavior. My father's name is too odious, and I am living under its shadow. Society's reactions have their own "laws of motion," which are cleverly taken advantage of by experienced and cynical journalists.

Suresh Singh wrote my lawyers in alarm, having learned from the newspapers that I had "suffered a bad nervous breakdown and was laid up in a hospital." He hadn't written to me for over a month. So I wrote and told him that I was perfectly well. Later it transpired that the Indian Communist Hajra Begum, who had been extremely amiable with me in Moscow and Allahabad, was now spreading the rumor that I had been locked up in an insane asylum.

I knew that one couldn't react to a lie with all one's heart —it would be destructive; I knew that from now on I would have to meet with slander and detraction all my life. A free press was like a double-edged sword: everyone wrote what he wanted. To spend my life denying all the falsehoods spoken about me was not worthwhile. My friends said: "Don't react. Forget it. Get used to it as to an inevitable annoyance." I knew that they were right. But the change from total silence in the U.S.S.R. to the world of the free word was so great that I felt as if all my poor bones were cracking as I turned the sharp corner.

Fortunately I do not suffer from a stung ego. And it is my greatest fortune that every new day, every fresh morning, the flowers, the trees, the kind people around me with all their warmth, swiftly restored a hundredfold whatever spiritual strength had been spent on reading filthy little articles.

One day, when there was no one left on the farm but seventeen-year-old Christopher Kennan, the smaller children, and the girl baby-sitter, I called them all out onto the veranda, where on a window sill stood a small charcoal grill on which meat was always roasted. The grill contained fresh coals. I asked Christopher to bring me the liquid used to make them burn better. The children looked on with great curiosity.

I said, "Christopher! You are all present here to witness a solemn moment. I am burning my Soviet passport in answer to lies and calumny."

With that I threw the passport on the burning coals. Christopher opened his eyes wide. The passport flared up brightly. The farmer's children were looking in through the window screen. We were surrounded by children, all of them watching in silence. When it was over, I carried out the handful of ashes and blew on them. The wind carried them off. . . .

Joan and Larry had left with their Peace Corps. In the middle of August George Kennan returned from Europe, looking thin and anxious. He had been assailed on all sides with letters, telegrams, demands for the publication of *Twenty Letters* to be postponed. He was suffering for me. I could see that. He had foreseen it all and had warned me about it in the spring.

The time had come to leave the farm for New York, where a second press conference was to be held. Something had to be said in answer to this widely deployed campaign.

Freedom is a priceless gift.

One has to pay dearly for it.

Encounters and Business Matters

MY COMPARATIVELY QUIET seclusion in Pennsylvania came to an end.

September and October were spent in a constant flurry of moving to new places, making new acquaintances. This would have been interesting and pleasant, if my existence had not been poisoned by two circumstances: constant concern about being seen by newsmen in the streets and in shops, and the ever-growing campaign against the book and its author, which spread like circles on water.

In order to protect the copyright, two hundred copies of the Russian edition were brought out in London. Shortly after, the first reviews appeared, some praising the book to the point of absurdity, comparing its style with Tolstoy, Turgenev, Chekhov, Pasternak all in one, others calling the book a pathetic effort at convincing the reader that "her father was a good man." . . .

On the fifteenth of August, on Long Island, in the home of Evan Thomas, a vice president of Harper & Row, I met with the representatives of the magazines and newspapers that had acquired the rights of serialization: about fifteen in all, from Europe, the Americas, and Asia. They wished

to know everything about the manuscript, thoroughly confused by Moscow's propaganda and no longer certain *what*
they had bought. For two hours I answered their questions.
We sat in a circle on a beautiful green lawn.

If only they could have known how fascinated I was to
see these people from another world, all of them curious and
friendly! But they could not have guessed this, completely
absorbed as they were by their own wonder. How they eyed
me at first! I don't know what they had expected to find—
a proverbial Russian *baba* in bast shoes, or a dark-haired
Georgian with a mustache and a pipe in her mouth, like my
father? Whatever it was, after two hours they warmed up
to me. The conversation was unconstrained and interesting.
They could not guess, of course, how much I would have
liked to continue talking to them for a few more hours, ask
them questions, go to a restaurant with them, have a long
heart-to-heart talk with every single one. If only they could
have understood what a yearning for the outside world is
experienced by all of us, the cloistered and incarcerated of
the Soviets!

I would like Joyce Eggenton of England, Bertil Torekull
of Sweden, Sakari Määttänen of Finland, Atsuhiko Kawa-
bata of Japan, Gershon Yaacobson of Israel, George Veni-
zelos of Greece, and Alberto da Cunha of Brazil to know
how glad I was to meet them.

To the Western mind Russia is a paradox. My whole life
consisted of paradoxes. And until this has been fully understood, nothing will ever be clear. All that has happened and
is still happening in the U.S.S.R. is accepted and compre-
hended by the West with difficulty. Sometime during World
War II Walter Lippmann said of Russia that "it was the
most Eastern country in Europe and the most Western in
Asia." I may not be quoting his words exactly, but I understand their meaning. A Russia with democracy retarded a
hundred years, with a revolution that has turned into the

most reactionary counterrevolution of the twentieth century, and a Russia which by some miracle has preserved in its innermost depths the embryo and ferment of freedom, independence, and universal brotherhood—is that not a paradox?

From the questions I was being asked and the way I was being ogled, I felt that these representatives of the free press both believed and did not believe me. Nonetheless, after that meeting most of their magazines and newspapers came out with friendly reports of the interview, in many ways refuting the falsehoods of Victor Louis and giving my explanations their due.

After this meeting, I left for Nantucket—that same small island which Alan Schwartz had pointed out to me from the jet on our flight from Zurich. Now I was going to spend two weeks there with the Schwartz family.

Nantucket was all subdued colors: gray, overcast skies, yellow dunes, purple heather in the marshes, and, of course, the ocean, changing every day, every hour. Inconstant, capricious, at times gray, at others blue, and then again black with the white froth of rage. One never grew tired of contemplating that difficult, changeable temperament. But in Russia we were accustomed to difficult, changeable temperaments. Perhaps that was why all Russians loved the sea so, although Russia itself was a vast land of fields, meadows, and forests. Russia's yearning for the sea is a psychological and historical factor. All Russian fairy tales, legends, folklore were full of tales of the sea—the blue sea. The poetry of Pushkin, Lermontov, Pasternak, the prose of Tolstoy, Chekhov, Gorky, all spoke of the same thing: to reach the blue sea, to feel in one's heart its expanse, its freedom, see its glitter in the sun, enjoy it to the full and dissolve in it:

Farewell, free element! For the last time you roll your blue waves before me and shimmer in your proud beauty. . . .

Full of your memories, I shall carry into the forests and the silent wildernesses your crags, your creeks, and the glitter and the shadow and the murmur of your waves.*

Pushkin, the great poet and captive, talked to the sea. Pasternak listened to it. Gorky said: "The sea laughed."

The sea is an element—the element of freedom—and this is what captivates the heart! We Russians are all the same; we long for freedom, which has not yet come to Russia, and express our love for it through our love of the sea.

On Nantucket that August I met the Japanese artist Naoko Matsubara, the German artist Fritz Eichenberg, the American illustrator Joan Walsh Anglund, the editor of children's books Margaret MacElderry, the publishers Storer Lunt and Cass Canfield. At times it seemed as if, instead of Nantucket, Massachusetts, I was back at Koktebel in the Crimea, a small seaside village in the U.S.S.R., where writers, artists, poets from all over the country gather together, and, just like those here, crawl the beaches on all fours in search of small pebbles and shells. Later these collections are taken north, to Moscow and Leningrad, where the colorful pebbles and small pieces of glass thoroughly polished by the sea are kept in small boxes to remind one of the sea, the sun. The little stones are set in rings and bracelets, made into beads, for the Koktebel carnelian and jasper are symbols of the Element Freedom.

Such were the thoughts that passed through my head on Nantucket to the sound of rain, sitting beside an open fire, a martini glass in my hand. If one could only bring our people from Koktebel here and let them mingle on the ocean beach with their counterparts from Nantucket! Robert Lowell and Andrei Voznesensky were a thousand times right: governments *prevent* people and poets from understanding one another. "All of us poets, American and Russian, form a united *nation of poets*. How wonderful if we poets could

---

* "To the Sea," in *Pushkin*, introduced and edited by John Fennell, Baltimore, Penguin Books, 1964.

have our capital on wheels, a train, in which we could wander through the world, like Gypsies!" This exclamation escaped Voznesensky when he was in the United States in the spring of 1967. Nantucket in Massachusetts and Koktebel in the Crimea are the "Gypsy capitals" of poets.

While on Nantucket, I received two letters from Joan Kennan from the Tonga Islands in the Pacific. She sent me snapshots—the boys standing near some coral reef, the main street of Nukualofa looking like a village. But Joan and Larry were not losing heart; there was a great deal of work to be done, the natives were friendly, and the Peace Corps could help them in many ways.

In September I moved from the "Gypsy Capital of Poets" back to Long Island, this time to Bridgehampton, where Eleanor Friede had a summer house. She was the widow of an Estonian who had come from Russia, a writer and a publisher. On a wall in the living room hung a portrait of Emperor Nicholas II, which Eleanor wanted to remove on my account. I assured her that the portrait did not disturb me in the least and begged her not to change anything in her sweet house on the dunes.

The small one-storied cottage, right on the ocean, was full of gifts of the sea, collected throughout the years: shells, stones, polished pieces of wood, so unexpectedly expressive that they looked like sculptures.

Dear Eleanor, we, too, collect the "gifts" of our Black Sea; we adore and value such collections—you would have seen many similar ones had you been able to come to the Black Sea coast. We would have shown you the marvelous deserted beach at Pitsunda, which looks like your beach here. One can walk it for hours, collecting knotty pieces of wood.

On the Bridgehampton beach Eleanor pointed out Truman Capote's house. He has been well known in the U.S.S.R. for a long time, but I'm no hunter after celebrities and, may Truman Capote forgive me, did not try to meet him on the beach.

Upon my arrival, the Atlantic had been blue and docile. Then it grew darker, became covered with white crests, and roared the whole night through. A strong wind was blowing, we shut all the windows. The ocean, doubtless, was angered by our puny spirit and shallow-water disposition. . . .

Those first few days in Eleanor's house were a blissful rest. But a cruel shock followed. On the tenth of September the serialization of *Twenty Letters* was to start in newspapers and magazines. Upon opening the first installment in the *New York Times* I almost fainted. There, on the page in front of me, were those family photographs, the same that had been taken out of my desk in Moscow last summer, brought to the West and sold there by Victor Louis. But how did they get here, mixed up with the digest, instead of an excerpt from my book, instead of the one or two complete chapters, to which I had given my consent in May?

It was too late to ask questions. There was only time to ask the *New York Times* to place in the very next issue a note under the headlines to the effect that "The photographs were neither supplied nor approved by the author."

The headlines were dreadful: "In the next installment: 'My First Love.'" "In the next: 'How My Mother Killed Herself.'" "Beria Ruled My Father." Nowhere in my book were there any such titles or headlines; it therefore stood to reason that they should not have been given as coming from me. The text accompanying the photographs picked up the inaccuracies I had seen in the London *Daily Express*. All those photographs had no direct connection with the book, and the idea of illustrating it with them would never have crossed my mind. I took part in none of it—I was absent like a dead classic, like Balzac.

It was useless sending a denial to the *New York Times* and *Life*. Some of those photographs, obtained from unknown sources, were falsifications: The fat woman with cropped hair and an emaciated child looking like a plucked chicken were not my mother and I. A picture of a friend of mine with her children was presented as a picture of me. In a family group our governess was called my mother. My protest was published in *Life* magazine among the "Letters to the Editor" section—and how many people would take the trouble to read that small print?

My only consolation came a few days later when I held in my hands the first copies of *Twenty Letters to a Friend*, published by Harper & Row in the Russian original and in its English translation. I spent a week in Bedford Village near New York as a guest of my publisher, Cass Canfield, and his wife, Jane Canfield. It was here that I was given my book. A German translation, published by Fritz Molden in Vienna, was also lying on my table. Seeing the book published at last gave me enormous satisfaction. Only six months earlier I had been in India. The publication of the book had then seemed an unrealizable dream, a fantasy—and now here it was in my hands. It was no less than a miracle!

Shortly after that I left for New York, as a television interview had been arranged for the second of October, the official publication date. I thought that the conversation would be about the book, that I would have an opportunity of explaining that I had had nothing to do with the serializations and the "stolen photographs." I was hoping that this interview would give me a chance to reply to some of the misunderstandings in reviews, which had arisen from the fact that historical memoirs had been expected, whereas the book was actually about a family's private history.

But the questions I was asked had nothing to do with my book. The interview was a torture. I sat immobile in an armchair under blinding lights, a microphone round my neck, my face covered with a thick layer of make-up for colored transmission, unable to see the clock and figure out how long I could take in answering each question; also, having no idea how many more questions there would be. I was at a complete loss. Sweat was pouring down the cheeks of Paul Niven, the TV interviewer—he, too, was nervous, and his nervousness transmitted itself to me.

After the television interview came a new flood of letters. For me this was again an exciting contact with Americans, with Russians who had lived here for a long time, and with those who had left the U.S.S.R. after the Second World War. For the most part, the letters expressed sympathy and an extraordinarily keen understanding of what I had wanted to express in my book. Many had already bought and read it. Unprejudiced readers accepted my book for what it was: a family chronicle with no pretensions to historical generalizations. And, having read it from this point of view, they understood why I would never return to the Communist world. They wished me happiness in this country, about which they wrote with affection and even rapture, expressing hope that I would understand it, not be frightened by unpleasant external aspects, and would come to accept this country as my home.

I remained in New York until the end of October, living in Brooklyn in a cozy old house, the guest of my lawyer, Maurice Greenbaum, and his dear wife. The house stood on an elevation on Highland Boulevard, trees grew all around, and the view of the bay and distant Kennedy Airport was lovely. It reminded me somewhat of the view of Moscow from the Vorobyov Hills, with its panorama of the entire city. The tall young poplars in front of the kitchen windows and the veranda were exactly like the poplars in the small yard of our apartment house in Moscow. . . . When we went out for a walk in the evening, I would suddenly stop and say, "What does this view remind me of?" My companions would laugh: "We know what you are going to say." I could not help it—too much in this country reminded me of what I had left behind in Russia. I do not know if this was due to my instinctive search for likenesses, rather than differences, or whether there actually were so many parallels. Anyway, when in the morning we settled down at the small table in the kitchen for our coffee, and the poplars outside would quiver in the wind, I could do nothing but sit there and smile. It was a pleasant likeness. No nostalgia about it. On the contrary, it seemed to enliven and warm my heart.

The point lay not in the poplars, of course. It so happened that I first entered into American life "through the family table in the kitchen." This was not the first house in which I had sat at such a table. And everywhere I found the same homey atmosphere of informality, mutual trust, and simplicity. I was glad not to have spent my first six months in hotels, for then I would have felt like a tourist. In this way, everywhere I was made to feel at home.

In that small Brooklyn house I was assigned the room of my hosts' niece, a twenty-two-year-old student. Debbie had the same open expression on her round dimpled face, the same soft brown eyes as my Katie: the expression of a kind, gay child, prepared to be affectionate at any moment. But in spite of a childlike appearance, Debbie had a grown-up heart. One could discuss anything with her. She understood everything. We spoke of her future work either in television or the movies; I told her about my children. She was studying art, literature; she had spent a year in Greece and was ecstatic about that country. Debbie played for me her favorite Greek records, we went shopping together. She would cut my hair, as Joan had done on the farm in summer, and, like Joan, she protected me in every way.

I met her friends: two students—a Greek and an Irishman —who had spent the summer traveling through Canada and the United States on a student tour. There was also a young girl from Israel, a pianist, who had come to New York to study with a famous teacher. It was a pleasant evening when these young people gathered round the table. Almost all of them were of the same age as my son and daughter. I think that's why I found it so easy and absorbing to be with them.

And how many countries they had already seen! To think that my son was never given permission to go as a tourist even to Yugoslavia.

Looking at them now, I couldn't help thinking that international borders had been invented by dull-witted people. Here was a new generation for whom national borders had no meaning. They were the same everywhere—these young people here, the Indian students I knew in Moscow, and a boy I met in Switzerland. If one could get them together, they would understand each other without words. All of them looked at the world with wide-open eyes.

Prejudices and traditions did not interest them. They treated me simply, saying nothing significant or profound, showing no curiosity. This was wonderful! From those young lips I never heard a single commonplace about my past, my father, about what awaited me in the West. They treated me as a friend, simply, naturally, as they would have treated anyone else. And it was this that made their company so worthwhile.

On Nantucket I had met teen-agers, who were younger—their ages from twelve to sixteen. There was an innocence and freshness about them, and that delicious clarity of a young mind's outlook on serious matters. Clarity and truth. A girl called Kathy had golden fingers and excellent taste. She embroidered very well and engraved designs on bone. What's more, she was charming. Her brother, Nicholas, took me for a ride in their motorboat at night, anxious to show me the bay, the sleeping boats with lonely lights attached to buoys, the quiet oily black waters, in which the stars lay reflected. Thank you, Nicholas. That boat ride through the sleeping harbor I shall not forget.

If you only knew what pleasure you gave me, whose children were so far beyond the ocean, "twenty-seven lands away" as they say in Russian fairy tales, behind seven locks. Neither Kathy nor Nicholas, nor Joan Anglund's children could guess how happy I was to be with them. I saw in them

my own Katie, Joseph, Helen, and all the young people of
their age back in Moscow. What difference that they spoke
another tongue? The same locks of hair falling over their
eyes; the same intolerance of commonplaces, of establish-
ments. The same yearning for freedom. The same giftedness,
the same unquenchable thirst for truth: "You grownups
can't fool us: we understand everything!"

I kept thinking, if by some miracle my children could
have found themselves over here—on Nantucket, in Brooklyn, in New York—they would only need five minutes to
start feeling in their element, like fish let loose in a free
ocean.

I also met other people during this time.

A telephone conversation with Alexander Fyodorovich
Kerensky. He was ill and told me that he had read *Twenty
Letters,* had watched my television interview, and was in
agreement with much of what I had said. It wasn't a long
conversation, but a good one, full of warmth. It seemed
strange, somehow, that this man, who had experienced the
tragic fate of a political failure with an honest soul, should
have found something of interest for himself in me and my
book. I thought of his sad destiny, a man who had kept his
love of life, his optimism, his dignity, who might have been
the Prime Minister of a new democratic Russia. The Provi-
sional Government had a better understanding than the
Bolsheviks of the historical problems and needs of that immense, disorderly, peasant country. It knew what the country
needed. Lenin's proletarian revolution took place prema-
turely. It had been premature, historically groundless and
unjustifiable. It was from this that all the sorry results had
stemmed. After fifty years it was impossible not to recognize
this fact.

On the eighteenth of October I met Alexandra Lvovna
Tolstoy. She was very sweet and friendly. But I doubt that
she could have fully grasped how excited I had been on
my way to Valley Cottage, New York. To me this was a

meeting with a whole epoch. I had been several times to Leo Tolstoy's house in Yasnaya Polyana, and I knew about the life, views, and creative works of that colossus, whose novels to this day stand as unsurpassed models of perfection in the Russian language, in their simplicity of style and their way of thought. The name of Leo Tolstoy meant too much to me. I was so excited at the prospect of meeting his living daughter that I simply cannot recall what she and I talked about. There was a dinner with Russian borsch, buckwheat kasha, real rye bread, vodka and herring. Alexandra Tolstoy had been giving much help to those who did not wish to return to the U.S.S.R. Even the priest in the church on her farm was a former Soviet scientist, a chemist. But above all else in importance was the fact that Alexandra Tolstoy was alive, in good health, living in America, a citizen of the United States; that she was used to this country and had grown to love it, like hundreds of other immigrants. Her lectures and books about Tolstoy and Russia have been of great importance. Many times efforts had been made to entice her back to the U.S.S.R., but she had always refused to receive the "messengers of truce." And that is magnificent!

Is there anyone one cannot find in America? Georgians and Ukrainians, Germans and Italians, Armenians and Irish, Serbs and Poles. Alexander Fyodorovich Kerensky adores New York, loves to walk its streets. Alexandra Tolstoy lives on a farm, in a very special colony, somewhat reminiscent of Yasnaya Polyana. Everyone can settle his life here as he wishes. Many unknown people wrote me about this, telling me of their own lives, hoping that I, too, would get to feel at home here. "The American way of life" consists of complete freedom offered to every newcomer to settle his life in accordance with his tastes. As a result, such a blending of cultures and nationalities is to be found nowhere else— except perhaps in Russia.

All of this staggers one so that at first one feels almost dizzy. New York City is unique in this world, inimitable, unreproduceable. At first it crushes and frightens one. Then slowly, as one's eyes get accustomed to it, one begins to grasp its details. What a motley crowd! What a play of colors on women with skins of every shade. But one must remember their various origins, the different countries they or their ancestors had come from, and instantly one tries to imagine the lives of every passer-by.

At first I felt crushed by Manhattan. The narrow streets of Greenwich Village—the section in which long-haired hippies roam—are impossibly dirty and grim. Debbie and I went to a small café there. It was dirty, tasteless, and uncomfortable. No air in it at all; I wondered how people could breathe there. True, they all smoked something, replacing oxygen with narcotics, which had already reached deadly doses and effects. I preferred old-fashioned Brooklyn, where boulevards and parks still reminded one of European cities and people looked normal, healthy, as most Americans do. Hippies are nothing but froth, nothing but trash in the streets of large cities. They are not the face of the land.

One finds the face of America in small towns or on farms —it is the epitome of health. All those women, heavy-set and thick-boned to my amazement, so many of whom spend five to six hours with ease at the wheels of their cars; the old men who play tennis; the apple-cheeked children and teenagers who gobble their fill; the students, jolly and eager for knowledge—none of them are interested in narcotics. They are clean and tidy, with no beards, no long dirty hair, no filthy bare heels. All of this is not necessary in order to think, or to disapprove of the acts of one's government. From the Americans I met in my first six months I heard plenty of criticism of their country and its politics. At times they were so merciless that they seemed to deny their own worth.

Like favored, spoiled children, on whom parents had lavished an overmeasure of candy and gifts, they revile those same bewildered parents, their homes, their families, the walls in which they grew up, forgetting that no one in the whole wide world lives as they do. They even try to claim that "socialism is a good thing!" and that "America, in her own way, is gradually moving toward socialism."

It is most fortunate for them that in this they are mistaken. If they could only experience one year of life under Socialism, which they seem to fancy so much after getting but a glimpse of it on a two-week tour of the U.S.S.R., they would stop forever calling on their country to "move closer to Socialism." And maybe only then would they understand why people leave their country, their children, their friends, as I have done, to escape from Socialism. And only then, I fear, would they stop asking me: "What was it that actually prompted you to leave the U.S.S.R.? And is it possible that your children can't come to visit you?"

You are naïve, but that's all right. Born and bred in this opulent, generous, hospitable land, you could not think in any other way. And I am happy to be with you. I am so tired of grim, suspicious, frightened men and women, who talk in whispers, who conceal and hide things, who believe no one—not even themselves; tired of distrustful malice, pessimism, deceit and self-deception, of enforced double-facedness that has become second nature to all those who live in the Communist world. Yes, I definitely prefer the rosy-cheeked, blue-eyed guilelessness of America to the premature physical and spiritual decay of the "average Soviet man," trained to lie from his very diapers, who from his earliest school days knows that one cannot say aloud what one thinks. But do not try to convince us, who have left Russia, that Russia has achieved great progress in the last fifty years. When it comes to "progress," kindly allow us to know better.

About this "progress," a lot had been written daily that year, for it was the "jubilee autumn" of the Bolshevik Revolution. It was funny and sad. One felt like leaving New York for some quiet spot, where the radio and TV would busy themselves with local topics. And I accepted with pleasure an invitation to a small town in New England—Bristol, Rhode Island. I was to be a guest in yet another American home, belonging to a lady who had served for twenty years in the U.S. Army and was now a colonel in retirement. She lived alone; she had a large house, in which she was going to let me have the second floor. No one there but us two, her dog, and two favorite cats.

How fine! Bristol on the bay, close to the ocean, to Newport: a beautiful spot for walks. I shall continue my discovery of America. But let me do it my way, the way that suits me best. Don't ask of me or expect historical and political articles and formulations. Let me remain myself in this country. This is the only thing I ask of Freedom. All I want in this free land is to assert for myself that which I have attained with such trouble and sacrifice—the right to be a free individual.

Boomerang

During October all the principal reviews of *Twenty Letters* appeared in the United States and in Europe.

From this unusual defector, on the eve of the Fiftieth Anniversary of October 1917, people had expected some supernatural "revelations about the secrets of the Kremlin." A family chronicle just could not satisfy at such a moment. As a result, the author was qualified as "a devoted daughter, defending her father," who "threw the blame for all the crimes on the villain, Beria." I was called "the Devil's awkward advocate," "the blind Kremlin princess," who had seen nothing beyond the Kremlin walls, who knew not the history of her country, nor the sufferings of its people. . . .

True, not everyone spoke in this way. My best readers turned out to be women. Family and human relationships meant something to them, disclosing history and an epoch. I felt so happy when I read in their letters that the deepest impression had been made by my mother's fate, and that of her sister Anna. . . .

But it was something else that turned out to be the strangest and most important.

When I wrote *Twenty Letters,* I wanted to free my memory of the past, free my own self of my childhood memories. All of it came pouring forth in a lyrical flow, which I could not stop and later felt incapable of altering and revising. I wrote it, and I forgot it. It seemed to me that I had "shelved" my own past, which I never wanted to touch again. I wanted to live in the present, think in the present, and not fuss with memories.

But now, all of a sudden, like a boomerang, my past came flying back at me. From all the countries of the world my own words were rushing at me. Words that had been pronounced quietly, intimately, in "letters to a friend," had turned into a loud, strident scream. They acquired a new tone when repeated by others in newspapers, magazines, in quotations from reviews. Torn out of the general context of the "letters," words and lines sounded *different,* although they were my own. I had no intention of disavowing them. Written four years earlier to a friend who knew how to read between the lines, these words, flung into a wide-open, wild, greedy world, which often could not or did not wish to understand, were flying back at me with a different sound, a distorted meaning. . . .

The "returning boomerang" hit me every day, causing sharp pain. I thought and thought about my book all over again. Every time the boomerang hit it made me think of how the immense free world was reading my book, reading about all the things that had happened so long ago and which I had so wanted to forget.

I found out that it was not easy to get away from one's past: it ran after one, caught up with one, like the shadow of a cloud blown across the sky.

During that fall, when all the papers were writing about Russia, about the Revolution which had reached its fiftieth birthday, about Communism, about Lenin and Stalin, I was made to fall back again in thought to my father. How I would have liked to escape this!

＊

In my *Twenty Letters* I wanted, first and foremost, to tell the story of our unusual family and its sufferings, of its members and the relations among them which developed in such a tragic way. For me, the author, my father was not the principal hero of the story. But he was the center, with a black circle drawn around it, within which everything perished or was destroyed; he *was* the stem around which our life circled. In my story my mother was the heroine, the luminous creative being doomed to destruction, who perished because it was impossible for her to live within that "black circle"—and with her death the family fell apart, everything that had been bright was extinguished, annihilated, until gradually complete darkness set in. And in it, as before, my father was the center; having driven away or destroyed those who were closest to him, he remained in that gloomy void completely alone.

I described my father as I had seen him at home in the family. Children, servants, relatives saw him and knew his human qualities and weaknesses, his inner contradictions, and at the same time his narrow single mindedness, his inflexibility. These traits in his character were the physical foundation on which his political—and human—biography developed and grew. To those who saw him from the outside, only his exterior, historical biography became manifest, a monstrous accumulation of at times inexplicable facts, which brought many to the same conclusion: this man was psychologically not normal—witness the frightful results of his rule.

To explain everything in this way—as madness—is the easiest and simplest thing, but it isn't true, and it isn't an explanation.

The more I thought of my father, especially after his death, even when I was still in the U.S.S.R., the more I was made to think of him again outside Russia while reading much that

I had not known before—often plausible, at times absurd—
one thing stood out clearly in my mind: in order to explain
one had to start from the very beginning, with the innate
physical and psychological traits, to which was later added a
conscious fixity of purpose in given situations. I would never
undertake to "explain" what motivated all my father's actions,
simply because I do not possess the psychological genius of
Dostoevsky, who knew how to "penetrate" into another man's
soul and "examine it from within."

To tell the truth, I have no great wish to "examine" this
grim soul "from within." I am not attracted to it.

But I can see what an immense interest in Stalin's personality exists in the free world, and I understand that
my *Twenty Letters* could not fully satisfy it. His portrait
there was not drawn in full. Therefore, at the risk of being
repetitious, I want to speak in greater detail about his nature
and uncommon life experience. Perhaps it will help to open
the eyes of those who are still blinded by the pseudo great-
ness of his so-called "achievements." On the other hand, I
might possibly be able to prove the unlikelihood of some
assertions, based on an absence of knowledge.

My father's health, on the whole, was strong. At seventy-
three acute sclerosis and high blood pressure brought on a
stroke, but his heart, lungs, liver were in excellent condition.
He used to say that in his youth he had had tuberculosis, a
poor digestion, that he had lost his teeth at an early age,
that his arm, injured in his childhood, often hurt him. But
in general he was in good health. The dry Siberian frosts
proved to be easily borne by this southerner, and in the
second half of his life his health kept growing stronger.
Under no circumstances could one call him a neurotic; rather,
powerful self-control was part of his nature.

He was neither hot-tempered, nor openhearted, nor emo-
tional, nor sentimental; in other words, he lacked all that
was characteristic of a typically Georgian temperament.
Georgians are impulsive, kind, easily shedding tears when

moved by compassion or happiness, or when enraptured by beauty. Aesthetic feelings, music, poetry, plastic art, play a great role in their lives. They go into ecstasies at the sight of a beautiful woman and take pleasure in acting the chivalrous knight to a lady. Devotion to the family, to friends, even to the relatives of friends, is of utmost importance to them. They are tender with children, having a special fondness for their sons; they respect old age, they respect death. Nowhere are wakes as sumptuous as in Georgia: they treat the entire street, so that the deceased may be kindly remembered; and every year thereafter they drink wine around the grave. The hospitality in Georgia, and the trust shown by Georgians to strangers, have nothing to equal them anywhere: their house is open, their heart is open, come in and be a friend. . . .

The openheartedness and trust of Georgians irritated my father. "Fools! Georgians are fools!" he would say in anger, when during his trip through Georgia in 1952 he was met on the roads by entire villages. He couldn't bring himself to have a good talk with those sincere peasants—maybe he was already afraid of everything. He refused to accept their offerings, their greetings, and, turning the car around, would leave them behind.

Typical, hundred percent Georgians were Ordzhonikidze, Yenukidze, Svanidze—all the above-mentioned qualities were theirs. But not my father. In him everything was the other way round, and cold calculation, dissimulation, a sober, cynical realism became stronger in him with the years.

Sometimes he told me about his childhood. Fights, coarseness were not unusual in the poor, half-literate family, in which the head of the household drank. The mother would beat the boy, her husband would beat her. But the boy loved his mother and defended her—one day he threw a knife at his father. The father rushed after him, screaming, and neighbors hid the boy. Both his parents were of peasant stock; the height of attainment for the father had been to work as a cobbler in a factory. The mother had more fantasy and ambition—she wanted to make of her only son a priest, thus raising herself from the lower depths in which her life was spent. She was truly and deeply religious, and having become a widow at an early age, she worked her fingers to the bone in order to give her son an education.

The son was an ordinary village boy, who fought, played naughty tricks. One day he dropped a brick down a chimney into an open hearth, frightening and burning the owners of the house. At school he liked arithmetic above all else, later mathematics. He drew a little. In his old age he still remembered Greek.

His ambition, his aspiration to attain greater heights, to raise himself above others, must have come to him from his mother. Perhaps that was the reason for his being among the best pupils in the parochial school in Gori. In the Tiflis Seminary he no longer figured among the top students, and he dropped out of the seminary without finishing it. A church education was the only systematic education my father ever had.

I am convinced that the parochial schools in which he spent more than ten years played an immense role, setting my father's character for the rest of his life, strengthening and intensifying inborn traits.

My father never had any feeling for religion. In a young man who had never for a moment believed in the Spirit, in God, endless prayers and enforced religious training could have brought out only contrary results: extreme skepticism of everything "heavenly," of everything "sublime." The result was total materialism, the cynical realism of an "earthy," "sober," practical, and low view of life. Instead of a "spiritual outlook," he evolved something very different: a close acquaintance with hypocrisy, bigotry, double-facedness, typical of a goodly number among the clergy, who only believe externally—in other words, do not believe at all. And as this youth did not possess the purity of heart and sincere religious feelings of his illiterate mother, at nineteen he found himself prepared for a "service" that was very different from the one she had wanted for him.

He joined the revolutionary movement of Transcaucasia with this "moral training" and not as an idealistic dreamer of a beautiful future, like my mother's parents, the Alliluyevs; not as an enthusiastic writer like Gorky, who described in romantic hyperboles the coming Revolution, the coming Liberty; nor as an educated Westernized theoretician like Plekhanov, Lenin, Trotsky, and Bukharin. High Ideals, with capital letters, made little sense to the sober youth with a practical outlook on life. He chose the way of a revolutionary because in him burned the cold flame of protest against society, in which he himself was at the bottom of the ladder and was supposed to remain there all his life. He wanted infinitely more, and there was no other road open to him but that of revolution.

He believed not in ideals but only in men's realistic political struggles. Nor did he romanticize people: there were the strong, who were needed; equals, who were in the way; and the weak, who were of no use to anyone. From his experiences at the seminary he had come to the conclusion that men were intolerant, coarse, deceiving their flocks in order to hold them in obedience; that they intrigued, lied, and as a rule possessed numerous faults and very few virtues.

In addition to this fundamental philosophy of life, he had a poor man's thwarted ambition, which was strong enough to move mountains out of his way, and the poor man's patience, that knew from childhood that he had to work long and hard to earn a holiday. What's more, there lay in him a firm conviction that the precept about using any means to attain an end produced far greater results than lofty ideals ever could. And, having started as a rank-and-file Party organizer, still almost unknown at the time of the seizure of power in October 1917, he had by the time he was sixty attained everything that the poor Georgian boy had once upon a time dreamed of. He alone ruled Russia, and the whole world knew of him.

True, his mother, who lived to see his glory, said to him before dying, "All the same, it's a pity you didn't become a priest!" Her dream had not come true. Perhaps the illiterate old woman had sensed that all his life her son had been aided not by God but by someone very different. She herself remained what she had always been: honest, poor, religious.

And my father, too, fundamentally remained what he had been the day he walked out of the seminary. Nothing was added to his character; only its basic traits had developed to the utmost degree. Ever since those early days the political game, with all its change of moods, its ruthlessness and guile, had dominated his life. Politics pushed all other human interests into the background, and it remained that way all his life. Rivals and adversaries were done away with. The country and the Party recognized him as the sole supreme authority. Everything around him grew silent, seemingly reconciled to the situation. Even beyond the borders of Russia there were those who burned incense at his feet. He should have been happy, he should have lived and enjoyed a full life, he should have loved everyone and everything around him. But he could not; he was incapable of rejoicing over the harvest he had reaped. Spiritually drained, with all human attachments forgotten, stalked by fear, which in the last few years grew into a genuine persecution mania, his nerves of steel at last gave way. Yet his mania was no sick fancy; he knew that he was hated, and he knew why. Finally, cut off by his power, his glory, his semiparalyzed consciousness, from life and people, he sent them from his deathbed what he could: a look full of terror and rage, and a threatening gesture of his hand. . . .

When I was a child, my father was in his sixth decade. When I grew up, he entered his seventh and last decade. What I was able to observe was the culmination of a lifetime.

By then there was hardly anyone left who knew and understood him well. But after his death, when my aunts returned home, their postprison stories explained a lot to me. Now no one was afraid to speak. From all sides I heard tales, one more terrifying and implausible than the other.

I shall give here only one example of how a myth is born. My brother Vasily, as I have already said, died in 1962, an alcoholic, but many simple people, who imagined the life of our family in their own way, refused to believe that he was dead. They insisted on their own version: Vasily had gone to China and was in command of the Chinese Air Force. They refused to believe me. Even to his children, who had been at his funeral, they would say, "Oh, come off it, *we know*. Someone else was lying in that coffin. We understand —you are unable to tell the truth."

It was the same where my father was concerned. The story that he had killed my mother seemed more plausible to many than the truth about her suicide, and they continued not to believe the truth. He had driven my mother to suicide by being what he was. If she could have lived through that moment of intense strain, she might have found sufficient strength in herself to leave him, as she had wanted to do more than once. By driving her to this extreme, he was, of course, indirectly her murderer. He always killed people "indirectly": all those millions whom he had sent to their death at the hands of his agents. He himself would turn away and forget about them, never giving a thought to how they had perished.

Many people today find it easier to think of him as a coarse physical monster. Actually, he was a moral and spiritual monster. This is far more terrifying. But it's the truth.

I heard, when I was still in the U.S.S.R., all kinds of stories about how my father had "killed people in moments of temporary insanity." Repeatedly people tried to make me confirm one highly improbable story about Stalin walking at his dacha—this was in winter—and seeing footprints in the snow. Calling a guard, he asked whose footprints they were. The guard did not know—he was seeing them for the first time. Stalin then drew out his revolver and shot the guard on the spot, remarking that the man "wasn't guarding him properly." No matter how many times I tried to prove that this story was out of keeping with my father's character, people did not believe me and tried to convince me that the story was true.

The fact, however, remains that my father was capable of flaring up, of flying into a temper, and using rude language. He slapped my face twice on an occasion when he lost his temper. He hit Vasily once, when Vasily was still a small boy. Such short outbursts were sufficient to cool him down. Vasily was far more unrestrained: he beat his wives as drunken peasants do in a village; he was capable of hitting his adjutants, his chauffeurs, any subordinates, even policemen in the street—in those days everything was forgiven him. Later, all of it cropped up again as evidence against him. But my father's grossness was limited, in essence, to his tongue.

I once saw how, having completely lost his temper, he grabbed the telephone with both hands and flung it against the wall; the telephone had been giving a busy signal and he had been in a hurry to put a call through. My nurse said that my father had once thrown a boiled chicken out of a casement window in our apartment in the Kremlin. This was way back in the years when there were ration cards for food and famine reigned in the country—it must have been 1929 or 1930. (It happened in the same small apartment in which Henri Barbusse had interviewed my father, and which he later described.) Mama had nothing for dinner but this chicken, but my father was fed up with the same "menu." For the rest of her life my nurse was unable to get over "such valuable food being thrown away." It was a case of temper, of choler, but not of temporary insanity. My father was far too cold-blooded a man for fits of temporary insanity or Othello-like passions.

His sphere of human relations was always very limited. He gave himself fully to political interests and emotions, leaving too little room for everything else a man lives by.

Any tenderness and love remembered from his childhood days was personified in his mother, whom in his own way he loved and respected all his life. But he was so removed from her, both geographically and in spirit, that he knew not how to make his feelings felt by her as something real; they simply never reached her, getting lost in those vast distances between them. There had been a time when on her own shoulders she had pulled him out onto the highway, doing everything for him that was possible under the circumstances. She had taken in washing—she had no other skills, there was nothing else she knew how to do. I doubt that in later years he ever repaid her in any way for all her efforts and cares. My mother had tried to persuade her to come and live with us in Moscow, but the old woman refused. She had never left Georgia, had never seen any city outside of Tiflis. In the last years of her life the Georgian Government arranged for her to move to Tiflis, supplying her with a modest minimum for her needs. They settled her in the former viceregal palace, where she occupied a small dark room— probably a former wardrobe room—and slept there on a plain iron cot. The artist Brodsky made a lovely pencil portrait of her. A young Georgian woman, a connoisseur of the stage and theater, told me: "When I was a schoolgirl, I often dropped in to see her, just to have a chat. That old woman could converse with anyone. She had immense dignity and a natural intelligence. Being with her was an experience. . . ."

From time to time she would send her son in Moscow some nut jam, which she had made. One day she sent him a blanket she had made with her own hands out of light Caucasian wool. How could he respond? He did not know what to do, nor did he know how to do it.

Everyone to whom he had ever been attached, for whom he had ever felt any affection, had been connected in his consciousness with his mother. His first wife bore her name— Catherine. This quiet, pretty girl had pleased the mother, and at the mother's insistence the marriage had been solemnized in church. But the mother had not been the only one to arrange this marriage; the bride was the sister of the Georgian Bolshevik Alexander Svanidze, and weddings, as well as other family festivities, were always taken advantage of by the political underground for its meetings. Shortly after the wedding my father left; then he was sent into exile to Siberia; and the young woman soon died, leaving a little boy, Jacob, who inherited her quiet disposition. The boy was brought up and educated by his aunts. My father forgot all about him. He was irritated by Jacob's sudden arrival in Moscow; and it was then that my mother and all the Alliluyevs took upon themselves the boy's care.

In my father's case, his marriage to my mother had probably also been dictated by considerations of convenience. He had known the Alliluyev family for twenty years. They were old, devoted friends, who had taken care of him, had sent him parcels in Siberia. Olga Alliluyeva, his future mother-in-law, had a warm spot for him, and perhaps this had reminded him of his mother's love. But Olga was not happy about her daughter's marriage; she made every effort to talk my mother out of it, calling her a "fool." She, personally, had had a taste of being married to a revolutionary. She thought of her life as having been "wrecked." In her heart she could never reconcile herself to my mother's marriage. She believed my mother to be profoundly unhappy, and her suicide the result of "all this foolishness."

My father's family life with my mother lasted only fourteen years. During that period (1918-1932) he was absorbed in internal Party struggles, in the intricate process of seizing power, and stood remote from everything else. Mother had created the home; she was the center of friendship and human relations: it was part of her nature to create, to give, to spread warmth. All the relatives clustered around her—the Svanidzes and Alliluyevs. My father's old Party comrades loved her; she organized an interesting life for us children. My father took all this for granted. He considered her his devoted friend, and he was sorely in need of devoted friends. But he neither understood nor sensed that she was a young thinking human being, that to her independence was absolutely necessary, and that she had her own opinions. She argued with him, made objections; she considered herself his *equal*, and this went against his purely Oriental approach to women and to a wife. It only served to irritate him. And when, after her death, he realized at last the full extent of her independence, her protest, her challenge, it only served to harden him. He wanted no equals. Equals argued, got in the way, objected, while he wanted blind devotion and absolute submission to his will.

He loved me while I was still a child, a schoolgirl—I amused him. "Funny how much you look like my mother. She, too, was redheaded, covered with freckles!" he would say, this doubtless being the main source of his tenderness for me. In my childhood I had been the recipient of the greatest tenderness he had ever been capable of. Later, when I developed my own tastes and interests, he cooled off considerably. In 1938 he gave me the first copy issued of *A Brief History of the CPSU*, inscribed by him, and commanded me to read it. I never got around to reading it—it bored me so; and when he found this out, he grew very angry. He wanted me to make a study of the Party's history —his version of it.

About this same time someone suggested that I send him my signed photograph for his birthday. His reaction took everyone by surprise. He sent the picture back to me with an angry letter. "You have an insolent expression on your face," he wrote with a blue pencil in that pointed handwriting of his. "Before, there used to be modesty there and that was attractive." In that gay photograph of a schoolgirl with a Pioneer's red tie and a grin from ear to ear, he thought he saw a challenge, an independence. It had given him something in the nature of an electric shock, and he called it "insolence." He would have preferred lowered eyes, a look of obedience—what he called "modesty."

How often he used to speak about this modesty! "Modesty embellishes a Bolshevik." In everyone he wanted to find lowered eyes and silent acquiescence.

He could not tolerate a personal opinion in others. That was the reason for his becoming so irritated about my enthusiasm for literature, my choice of friends, my first marriage. He wanted me to be friends with Gorky's granddaughters and not with unknown girls at school. Gorky's eldest granddaughter actually was one of my friends for a long time. While we were at school together she used to come with me to our dacha and, in summer, to Sochi on the Black Sea. But I had a larger number of interests in common with other girls, and at the university I formed a quite different circle of friends. My father was furious that my first husband had been a Jew. He had wanted me to marry Zhdanov's son. Five years later this came true, but by then Andrei Zhdanov, the father, had died, having lost my father's confidence; so now this marriage of mine was of little interest to him. But when, two years later, I left the Zhdanovs, he again became irritated—he saw in my action too much self-assertion.

As a schoolgirl I had been a good student, and this brought out his affection and interest in me. He was forever scolding my brother for his ignorance. But when we grew up, his attitude switched. After the war he said to me more than once, "If you say to Vaska, 'Vaska, go jump in the fire,' he'll jump without giving it another thought. But you—oh no! You'll start thinking. Oh, you diplomat! Always thinking, never giving an immediate answer!"

He was not mistaken. My brother was ready to throw himself into fire or water at a word of command from his father. This was what our father wanted. And his contemptuous "diplomat" and equally scornful "you'll start *thinking*" were the qualities which, in his eyes, did not suit a woman, qualities which he did not wish to see in me.

True, outside of this willingness to obey any order, he never saw anything worthwhile in my brother. Altogether, he was cold and distant with both his sons. He lacked all sentimental or tender feelings toward them. He was probably disappointed in them, as later he was to be disappointed in me: not one of us would carry on his work. Jacob was honest, quiet, without ambition, and my father saw no sense in this; all the more so since, for all his quietness, Jacob was not submissive, he would never "jump into the fire."

To my father the fact that Jacob had become a prisoner of war was nothing but a "disgrace" before the whole world. In the U.S.S.R. the news was kept under cover both during the war and after, although the press in the rest of the world was writing about it. And when a foreign correspondent officially asked for information on the subject, my father said that ". . . in Hitler's camps there are no Russian prisoners of war, only Russian traitors, and we shall do away with them when the war is over." About Jacob he said, "I have no son called Jacob."

According to evidence given by Thomas Cushing, who had been a prisoner with Jacob in Sachsenhausen, Jacob was deeply crushed by these words, which were quoted to the prisoners over the radio. According to many others, he had always behaved as an officer should, defending the actions of his country and its army. But that day he went in search of death, and perished by throwing himself on electrified barbed wire.

I am inclined to believe this version of his death more than any other I have heard. The details are of no importance; without doubt, Jacob must have realized at once that this was not Nazi propaganda but his father's actual words. . . .

During the war my brother Vasily served first on the Air Force General Staff. Starting with the spring of 1943 he commanded an Air Force regiment, then a division, then a corps on the Western front. His career was swift and unusual. After the war his corps was stationed near Berlin. Service in the Army of Occupation bored him, and he flew to Moscow in July 1947 to "fix" himself up with a transfer to the capital. He succeeded with the help of such patrons as Beria and Bulganin. Marshals and generals feared him, knowing that he had gotten out of his way Marshal A. A. Novikov, whose attitude toward him had been critical. Novikov, as a result, had landed in prison. Vasily, on the other hand, having, with my father's approval, been placed in command of all the Air Force of the Moscow Military District, could not resist the pleasure of seizing Novikov's empty dacha, to which he brought from East Germany his family and his lavish loot. I flew with him then to Germany for ten days, to see his wife, who had given birth to a baby girl; and I returned in the same "private plane," full of "trophies" for Vasily's dacha.

This, my first encounter with Europe, was a depressing one. During a week of touring in a car from Rostock-Warnemünde through Berlin, Dresden, and Leipzig to Jena and Weimar, I saw nothing but war ruins and frightened, silent people. But the house of the former owner of a bicycle workshop in a small place called Kyritz, in which my brother lived at the time, testified to the high standard of living in Hitler's Germany. . . .

Vasily was transferred to Moscow, and for a while my father was pleased to hear his son being praised as "very capable." But pretty soon he became convinced that alcoholism had destroyed the thirty-year-old general, and in 1952 he was obliged to discharge Vasily from his high military post. His sons had not brought any glory to his name, either in the army or in politics.

His eight grandchildren aroused no interest in him. There had been a time when he had liked playing with children. But by now he had so far removed himself from all those who had been close that they, in turn, had ceased being interested in him. Vasily knew that his children had been brought up in fear and would probably start howling, so he never took them to see their grandfather. My children and Jacob's little girl my father saw about twice and was pleased with them because they were gay and well behaved. But for him those two visits sufficed—he would have just as much enjoyed the children of strangers.

At one time in his youth he had been fond of fishing, hunting, and he had loved dogs. In his Siberian exile he had had a dog called "Tishka," also known as "Tikhon Stepanich," with whom he liked to go hunting in the taiga, or else he would simply talk to the dog. At times he would reminisce about this "Tikhon Stepanich." But to have a dog in the house now was something he no longer wanted. With the years he had lost the habit of friendly contacts and attachments, and he probably blamed other people, myself among them, for so seldom coming to see him. But he could never have admitted, even to himself, that he had created this void around himself with his own hands. In the end he was surrounded solely by the silently "devoted" Chekists, their eyes lowered in fear, and "modest" accomplices, ready to "throw themselves into the fire without giving it a thought."

Human feelings in him were replaced by political considerations. He knew and sensed the political game, its shades, its nuances. He was completely absorbed by it. And since, for many years, his sole concern had been to seize, hold, and strengthen his power in the Party—and in the country—everything else in him had given way to this one aim.

I believe that my mother's death, which he had taken as a personal betrayal, deprived his soul of the last vestiges of human warmth. He was now free of her moderating and, by the same token, impeding presence. His skeptical, harsh judgment of men only hardened; this came naturally to his unsentimental nature.

I don't think he ever actually moved away from it during those fourteen years when Mama had stood by his side. But the force with which it broke through after her death is well known. Kirov's murder followed, and the destruction of the former opposition, the trials and executions of his Party comrades, his companions of the Revolution, the arrest of millions of people who had nothing to do with Party struggles. In 1937 he did not hesitate to destroy his relatives: the three Svanidzes, Redens, Yenukidze (my mother's godfather). A suspicion of personal disloyalty to him was far more dangerous for relatives than for strangers. With relatives he became even more implacable.

The same thing happened in 1948 with my aunts. He considered that they harmed him personally by "knowing too much and talking too much." Nothing stopped him from arresting two elderly widows, who had already suffered sufficiently and whose health was poor. There is no doubt that he remembered how close they had been to all that had happened in our family, that they knew everything about Mama's suicide and the letter she had written before her death. Doubtless he had not forgotten, either, the talk he had had with Yevgenia Alliluyeva in August 1941 at the beginning of the war, when he had urged her to flee with her children to the Urals. She told me of this conversation later.

"I had never seen Joseph so crushed and in such confusion," was the way she described it. "I came to him, thinking I would find support, hoping to get some encouragement. Novgorod, the city of my birth, had just been surrendered to the Germans and I was in a panic. I was even more frightened when I found he was almost in a panic himself! He said, "Things are very, very bad! Get yourself evacuated. One can't stay in Moscow.' I left completely lost; I thought: this was the end."

He remembered this and didn't want others to know about it. And so Yevgenia Alliluyeva got ten years of solitary confinement, from which only my father's death released her six years later. True, my aunts were inclined to blame Beria for the arrests which had fallen upon our family. They stuck to this opinion, basing it on the fact that Beria had had encounters and scores to settle with Svanidze, Redens, with all the old Georgian Bolsheviks who, in the days when they were still in Georgia, had stood in the way of his obtaining the post of First Secretary of the Central Committee of Georgia. Yevgenia Alliluyeva maintained that, as far as she was concerned, Beria could not forgive her a personal insult. Having a sharp tongue, she had once, in a large company, in my father's presence, made fun of the crude way in which he made advances to women. Beria had felt foolish, everyone had laughed, and this he had remembered.

There is no doubt about Beria's having had a close connection with our family long before he became head of the Soviet Secret Police in 1938; and that, whenever possible, he had added fuel to the fire by submitting to my father trumped-up evidence against those whom he himself wanted to destroy. But, of course, no one but my father could have sanctioned the execution of Redens and Svanidze, the arrest of other relatives. Such power Beria did not possess.

In a system of terror and secret reprisals, men like Yagoda, Yezhov, Agranov, Beria were indispensable to my father, and he always found them with an unerring instinct. Without this system, the Soviet Government could never have felt secure: Lenin had Dzerzhinsky for the same purpose. Without Chekists the collectivization and the liquidation of the opposition could never have been achieved. Neither did the Ministry of Foreign Affairs forgo their services: behind every ambassador there always stood a secret emissary. True, a

violent end lay waiting for all these bosses of the secret police, for they really did "know too much." Thus Yagoda,
Yezhov, Agranov (directly involved in Kirov's assassination)
were done away with. By some miracle Beria escaped. He
was extremely sly and knew how to play on my father's weaknesses, flattering him in every way he could. This had helped.
Yagoda had protested the atrocities during the enforcement
of collectivization and paid for it with his life.

Beria was fully aware that his own life was in constant
danger. It was he who had actually handled the renewal of
arrests in 1948, the "Leningrad Affair," massacre of former
prisoners of war, persecution of the "cosmopolitans" and
doctors, reprisals against any freedom of thought in the armed
forces, against foreign Communist parties. He had also carried
out the abominable liquidation of whole army units, at times
very large ones, who, during the swift German advance
into the Ukraine and Byelorussia, had found themselves
cut off from their own lines, and who later, against frightful
odds, had found their way back. It was Beria, too, who had
executed the eviction and resettlement by force of entire
nationalities: the Volga Germans; the Tatars, the Bulgars,
the Karaims from the Crimea; the Chechen-Ingush, the
Kabardians, and the Balkars from the Caucasus. He "knew
too much." And that was why he had been unable to conceal
his joy at my father's death.

The ax fell upon him, nevertheless. He was hurriedly
executed by the new government, together with his assistants—Kobulov, Merkulov, Dekanozov, and a little later,
Abakumov. He not only "knew too much," he knew what to
do with it, and might have used his knowledge against the
new leaders. All the archives had been in his hands.

Beria's "trial" was staged in the same hurried, secret, law-
less way, without any evidence or proof, in which all trials
had been conducted by the secret police, his subordinate
organization for fifteen years. General A. A. Vishnevsky,
Chief Surgeon of the Soviet Army, told me that Beria, after

his arrest, had been kept for a few days in the basement of the General Staff Building in Moscow, and had been shot there ten minutes after the sentence was pronounced.

Everything had tended to indicate my father's complete trust in Beria and his dependence on him, but of this one could never be quite sure. I shall never forget how startled I had been by something my father said in 1941 during the first days of the war. I was visiting Beria's wife at their dacha. My father had always encouraged my friendship with her. I was talked into staying the night. Next morning my father suddenly called up in a fury. Using unprintable words, he shouted, "Come back at once! I don't trust Beria!" I left completely baffled. My father never referred to the incident again, and for ten more years I remained friends with Beria's wife and son, who, in contrast to Beria himself, were nice people. My father was never able to trust fully even those who were totally submissive to his will—such was his nature. Too many atrocities had been committed with and through the chiefs of the secret police for the memory of it all to warrant a peaceful sleep.

My father was intolerant in his relationships with people, unbending in the political demands he made of them and of the Party, even though Bukharin once referred to his "mastery of administering the right political dose at the right time."* I don't know whether it was to confirm or refute this that Bukharin's trial and execution took place—they exceeded all doses. Bukharin had been a tolerant, tractable, subtle politician; he thought that my father was capable of conceding a point, that the Party might yet make him submit to the will of the majority. In what a dreadfully tragic way life proved the contrary!

In contrast to Bukharin, my father could never agree to a gradual rapprochement of Socialism and the peasantry. He

* In Russian Bukharin's phrase was *"genialny dozirovshchik,"* according to Boris Nikolaevskii, *Power and the Soviet Elite*, New York, Praeger, 1965, p. 135.

chose what was closer to his nature: a sharp break, with the aid of violence, the liquidation of a whole social group of the well-to-do peasantry—the so-called kulaks—virulent castigation, suppression. This lack of compromise, this inflexibility, this inability to agree with an opposing opinion even if it was obviously a good one, I also attribute to his experiences at the seminary, where students had been imbued with fanaticism and intolerance. And, of course, this intolerance was only strengthened by an inadequate education, which my father never supplemented in later years.

He had never had so much as a taste of European democratic civilization, of its traditional freedom of thought. Liberal Georgian noblemen of the nineteenth century, who had received through French a Western education, who had been close to Pushkin and the Decembrists, had been democratic and progressive. In the twentieth century the "Leader of the World Proletariat" established his power not with the help of advanced, educated classes but through the ignorance of millions who had been separated for centuries from Western democracy, had believed blindly in the wisdom of their "father" the Czar, and had distrusted everyone who "didn't speak their native tongue."

My father fully understood that in Russia this was of help to him, that advanced, educated intellectuals would not lend him their support. He did not belong to them, and they did not consider him as their own. But all the semiliterate, semiblind peasants and workers, to whom his power offered a chance of becoming engineers, Party bureaucrats, generals, state ministers, ambassadors (speaking only Russian), those who had "tended calves" in their youth, like M. Suslov, but who now ran the Central Committee of the Communist Party, to all these he became for a long time "their very own." They sincerely believed that the executed Social Revolutionaries, the exiled Trotsky, the liquidated opposition, and the marshals who had been shot had all been "lackeys of imperialism," that Lenin and Stalin, together, had organized the October Revolution, and that Stalin was "leading us along Lenin's way."

Not everyone in Russia rejected Stalinism. On the day of my father's death there were those who rejoiced, but there were also those who wept in all sincerity. At my father's coffin I saw Marshal Rokossovsky standing, his uniform drenched in tears. Togliatti, on the other hand, sat there completely calm.

The mass psychosis, born of the "purges," when children turned against their mothers and schoolchildren "caught spies," came as a psychological answer to what was being fed them from above, an answer based on ignorance.

Ignorance is the worst of evils, said Goethe, the enlightener and encyclopedist. When ignorance comes to power, encouraging ignorance and basing itself on ignorance, then historical monsters such as Hitlerism, Stalinism, Maoism are born. . . .

Soviet Russia in the twenties had at her disposal educated Marxists in the Party, educated diplomats, a free art, a free economic policy (NEP), a free peasantry. Russia wanted to become Westernized, to learn democracy. I have no intention here of idealizing the twenties as a counterweight to the thirties, for terror as a means of retaining power already existed under Lenin. Already they had shot and destroyed the Social Revolutionaries, the political party which, under the conditions existing in Russia, had been one of the most realistic. Already Lenin had laid the foundation of a totalitarian regime, based on suppression and terror. But in the twenties the country had not been fenced in. Everything had been streamlined toward joining the world and taking from outside the fruits of civilization. With the coming of the "Era of Stalinism" the country sank into a chauvinistic boasting about everything "ours": "our nation," "our this," "our that," and all "Western influence" was declared harmful, pernicious.

My father made up for his poor education only in the field of technical knowledge. Everything concerning industrialization, armament, interested him—he considered it of importance. He knew the essentials about tractors, tanks, airplanes, cannons, automobiles; he amazed high government officials, builders, and foreign generals with his questions and knowledge. In this lay his "sober" approach. But he never acquired any knowledge about modern history, philosophy, contemporary social thought, and remained therefore to the very end of his days a dogmatic and, in essence, an uneducated man.

On one occasion he came close to admitting it himself. It was in Gorky's apartment in Moscow, in those days of the early thirties when my father had sought Gorky's support in getting the sympathy of writers. Among the guests were Alexei Tolstoy, other writers, a few scientists—Gorky's usual circle. Everyone sat round a table, discussing some new discovery in science, and when my father was asked his opinion, he said, "Well, you know, I'm a bit backward in such matters," in this way avoiding a direct answer. The atmosphere was completely informal; they were drinking wine; and the young physicist Fyodor Fyodorovich Wolkenstein, Alexei Tolstoy's stepson, suddenly made a pun: "In that case let's drink to the health of *Otstalin!*" ("*otstaly*" in Russian means "backward"). For a moment dead silence reigned in the room. But my father "swallowed" the joke, raised his glass, and the toast was drunk.

He had a certain acquaintance with languages, dating back to his seminary days when he had studied Latin and Greek. He could read Georgian but used to say that he had largely forgotten the language. He knew Russian well in its simpler, conversational form; therefore, in Russian he could not be an eloquent orator or writer, lacking synonyms, nuances, depths. With the help of a dictionary he could make out a simple German text. This he considered sufficient to enter, in 1950, into a discussion about the theory of linguistics and condemn, "from a Marxist position," the School of Marr, the world-renowned linguist. The only people who profited by it were Marr's enemies, who were subsidized by the "Wise Leader."

The same thing happened with the theory of Mendel-Morgan on genetics, when my father gave his support to Trofim Lysenko, flattered by the false "practical conclusions" of that climber, who played cunningly on my father's weakness for everything "practical." I recall how in 1948 Yuri Zhdanov, who was then working in the Central Committee's Department of Science, came out against Lysenko, who, in turn, was instantly defended by my father. "Now genetics are finished!" said Yuri at the time. In obedience to Party discipline, Yuri Zhdanov had to "acknowledge his errors" and write a repentant letter to Stalin, which was published in *Pravda*. And then he was made to present the refutation of the chromosome theory "from a Marxist position."

It was in my father's nature to simplify, to reduce things to a practical level, to a peasant's good sense and mother wit. It was not a simplicity reached as a result of great knowledge, refinement of taste, a simplicity that comes after immense and complicated work to people who know much. This was simplification by a man who did not know, who did not want to know, the complex many-facedness of life, knowledge, art.

Russia had known Mikhail Lomonosov, a fisherman's son from the White Sea, who in the eighteenth century came on foot to Moscow in search of knowledge, who went looking for knowledge in all the universities of Europe, becoming in the end a great Russian scientist, member of the Academy, co-founder of Moscow University, and correspondent of the French Encyclopedists. Russia had known Chaliapin, had known Gorky—my father's contemporaries—who had raised themselves from the lower depths to the heights of European culture and who took pride in that culture and not in a peasant's practical sense. In all these people there had been a bright inner light that had drawn them to beauty. My father was moved by a very different impulse, which whispered in his ear that much could be attained by making use of backwardness. . . .

My mother's absence only served to free my father, for she had been the restraining center in our home. Needless to say, she was not, and could never have been, happy with him. But it must be said, too, that for my father she had been too complicated, too refined, too demanding a woman. He had been pleased to find in her a good housewife, to see that his children were kept in good order, but on top of that her aspirations, her personal opinions, her spirit of independence irritated him. To have in his own home a modern, thinking woman, who stood up for her point of view on life, appeared to him as something unnatural. True enough, he quite often expressed himself in favor of the equality of women, when mass labor had to be encouraged. Such sayings of his as "Women in the kolkhozes are a great power!" decorated all village clubs. But at home he expressed himself very differently.

When Vasily had told him that he had divorced his first wife because there "was nothing one could talk about with her," my father roared with laughter: "Look at him, so he wants a woman with ideas! Hah! We have known that kind: herrings with ideas—skin and bones!" This happened in my presence; but immediately after this outburst, father and son started an obscene discussion and I took my leave. In general my father never expressed any interest or sympathy toward educated women; he couldn't stand the governesses whom Mother brought into the house. In his life my mother had been the exception, because she had succeeded in growing spiritually and developing intellectually after her marriage, transforming herself from a naïve schoolgirl into a mature, intelligent human being; my father had not contributed to this in any way. The level of his demands on women was far simpler.

My aunts told me that during one of his Siberian exiles

he had lived with a local peasant woman and that their son was still living somewhere—he had received a slight education and had no pretensions to the big name. Altogether, my father had a purely peasant's outlook on many things—a narrow practicality, a distrust of erudition. In latter years he would often say to the police commandant of his household, "You should all be fired, you know nothing from nothing! A simple peasant woman could cook better than you and run a household more efficiently!" And I think that the round-faced, pug-nosed Valechka, who was his housekeeper his last eighteen years, completely fitted his ideal of a woman in a home: she was corpulent, neat, served at table deftly, and never joined in any conversations. Nothing could be more unlikely than the story spread in the West about "Stalin's third wife" —the mythical Rosa Kaganovich. Aside from the fact that I never saw any "Rosa" in the Kaganovich family, the idea that this legendary Rosa, an intellectual woman (according to the Western version, a doctor), and above all a Jewess, could have captured my father's fancy shows how totally ignorant people were of his true nature; such a possibility was absolutely excluded from his life. In general, according to my aunts, he paid little attention to women, not going beyond expressing his approval of the singer Davydova, a performer of Russian folk songs. He never reacted to aggressive women who tried to arouse his interest.

Oddly enough, in the West they stubbornly tried to relate us to the Kaganovich family. To my astonishment, I learned from the German magazine *Stern* that I had been married to "Kaganovich's son"—to my astonishment inasmuch as Kaganovich had no son. I actually had been friends with his daughter, and the adopted boy in the family was ten years younger than I; he, when he grew up, married a girl student of his own age.

When my father spoke to Vasily about "herrings with ideas," he had had in mind independent, politically-minded women of the first years of the Revolution, who had gradually vanished from the scene in the U.S.S.R. of the thirties. At that time the measure of what a woman could attain in the land of Socialism was represented by the tractor-driver Pasha Angelina, the beet-harvester Maria Demchenko, the cotton-picker Mamlakat Nakhangova, the aviatrix Valentina Grizodubova. (The Minister of Culture Furtseva, introduced into the Politburo by Khrushchev after my father's death, only goes to prove that in the U.S.S.R. the social type of politically-thinking women had been done away with for a long time.) In conformity with the prototype of the "heroines of labor," Soviet art created in the thirties a new type of movie star: the place of elegant Lyubov Orlova, very English in appearance, was taken by Marina Ladynina, a swineherd in a kerchief, and the monumental Tamara Makarova with her "heavy Russian beauty."

There is no doubt that this thoroughly conformed with the tastes of the "Great Leader," who viewed every new film. He had a utilitarian approach to art, and the exaggerated "window-dressing" films like *The Tractor Drivers* and *The Swineherd and the Shepherd* he approved of, remarking without any pretensions, "Pyryev [the director] certainly knows how to present the joy of kolkhoz labor." As a result, Pyryev's wife, Marina Ladynina, totally lacking in talent, became the leading Soviet movie star.

In his rare meetings with writers, actors, scientists, my father liked to appear interested and well informed, which often created an impression. If the visitors came to his dacha, he would display old-fashioned courtesy to the ladies by presenting them with a freshly cut rose or a magnificent branch of lilac. He was gallant with the wives of well-known aircraft designers, the wives of marshals, whenever it was necessary to express friendliness to the husbands. But in his ordinary, everyday life he showed no inclination toward any kind of politeness, or any evidence of aesthetic feeling.

At home, when at table with his usual circle of "companions in arms," he always spoke the coarse language of

workingmen, often using obscene words. Until the very
outbreak of war he came regularly to dinner accompanied by
the Politburo. They came to the dacha, too, always without their wives. They all copied him, trying to appear
ascetics with no family ties, and with no other interests but
that of the "Party's great cause." At these all-male, round-
the-table gatherings, I alone could have been a restraining
element, but my presence never prevented him from cracking coarse peasant jokes and telling coarse peasant stories.
Sometimes I had to leave the room and stay away. On such
occasions, after about an hour he would suddenly notice
my absence and someone would come to fetch me. "The
hostess," the emissary would say, "is invited to the table."
When my father was in a good mood, he would greet me
with, "Comrade Hostess! Why have you left us poor un-
enlightened creatures without giving us some orientation?
Now we don't know where to go! Lead us! Show us the way!"
(This was intended as a parody on existing official glorifica-
tions such as "Comrade Stalin leads us along Lenin's way!")
This particular joke went on for years until I grew up.

On days when he was out of sorts he would say rudely
in front of everybody, "Now get out, I'm busy!" Often, and
also in front of others, he would criticize my appearance,
my clothes, reducing me, a teen-ager, to tears with such re-
marks as, "Why do you wear that tight-fitting sweater? You
are a grown girl now, wear something loose!" After this all
I could do was leave the room.

As a matter of fact, he would just as readily, and without
the least embarrassment, offend an adult. Once, shortly before Andrei Zhdanov's death, knowing that the man suffered
from recurrent heart attacks, my father, angered by Zhdanov's silence at table, suddenly turned on him viciously:
"Look at him, sitting there like Christ, as if nothing was of
any concern to him! There—looking at me now as if he were
Christ!" Zhdanov grew pale, beads of perspiration stood out
on his forehead. I was afraid he might have an attack and

gave him a glass of water. This happened in the fall of 1947 at one of my father's dachas on the Black Sea, where all of them used to come regularly to see him.

About this same time I remember Poskrebyshev telling my father who would be present at dinner that evening and naming, among others, Alexei Kuznetsov (the Leningrad Secretary). My father didn't object in any way. But when his guests had arrived and handsome young Kuznetsov approached him with a smile, my father suddenly drew back his hand, saying coldly, "I didn't summon you." Kuznetsov turned grim and seemed to shrink. He was, of course, obliged to leave. The "Leningrad Affair" must have been brewing already; for soon after he was removed from his post, later arrested. He was shot in prison.

During the last few years those round-the-table gatherings at Sochi and at Kuntsevo were large and drunken. I witnessed several of them and always had to retire in a hurry. My father did not drink much; but it gave him pleasure to see others eating and drinking their fill, and as usual in Russia on such occasions, the guests would soon get thoroughly inebriated. One day, however, my father did have too much to drink and sang folk songs with Smirnov, the Minister of Public Health, who could barely stand on his feet but was, nonetheless, in a seventh heaven of rapture. With great difficulty they finally got the Minister quieted, put in a car, and taken home.

Usually toward the end of dinner the personal bodyguards would step in, each "custodian" dragging away his drunken "charge." These merrymaking leaders amused themselves with coarse practical jokes, the victims being mostly Poskrebyshev and Mikoyan. As for Beria, he would just incite my father and the others. My father sat at the table, puffing at his pipe and watching without participating directly in the "fun," while a tomato would be slipped onto a chair. When the victim sat on it, there would be loud roars of laughter. A spoonful of salt might be dropped into a glass of wine, or vodka mixed into the wine. Apparently Mikoyan and Poskrebyshev, whom my father always called the "Chief," were the most patient and submissive. The "Chief," more often than not, would be carried home dead drunk, after having lain for some time in a bathroom, vomiting. Beria, too, would often go home in this condition, although no one ever dared slide a tomato under him. My father called him the "Prosecutor."

Sometimes my father made fun of Beria, repeating the same old joke while directly addressing the "Prosecutor," who would never have taken it from anyone else. The joke was about a Chekist and a professor who lived in the same apartment. One day the professor, irritated by his neighbor's ignorance, exclaimed, "Oh you! You don't even know *who* wrote *Yevgeny Onegin!*" The Chekist felt insulted (because he really did not know). Soon afterward he arrested the professor, boasting to his friends: "I got him to confess it! *He was the author!*"

A rather grim joke, and usually no one laughed. . . .

In summer the leaders indulged in the same amusements out of doors. At my father's dacha there was a small shallow pond, into which the "Chief" was sometimes pushed to the accompaniment of raucous laughter. Later, under some pretext or another, the personal guards drained that pond, afraid one of the leaders might get drowned. All this reminded one of Peter the Great's imperial pranks with boyars. Needless to say, nothing of the sort had ever happened in my mother's day, when guests arrived with their wives, and the spirit of debauchery was absent. Even before the war get-togethers of this kind did not take place. It was in later years that I witnessed them several times, and I knew that such amusements, in the narrow circle of my father's closest "comrades in arms," had become habitual, the same thing repeating itself over and over again.

All of this was so unlike the gay round-the-table gatherings in Georgia, identical there in both town and country:

they would amuse themselves by competing in refinements of oratory, in long toasts to friendship and love, to the beautiful and eternal; there would be some lovely singing in three or four voices, mostly without accompaniment; and when one grew tired of eating, drinking, and singing, one would dance a little, then return to the table once more. To get drunk and use bad language at table was inadmissible.

In the postwar years there was hardly room on Soviet screens and in Soviet paintings for the immensely long tables that appeared on them, loaded with a Flemish abundance of food, on which miners, workers, and peasants feasted. This was as far removed from reality as a dream. But how was my father to know? To his table fish was brought from special ponds, pheasants and baby lambs from special nurseries; there would be Georgian wines of special vintage, and fresh fruit flown from the south by plane. He knew not how many transports at government expense were needed in order to supply his table, nor did he know where the food came from. The women serving him received strict instructions: if, for instance, he asked, "Where are these cherries from?" they were to answer, "From the base, Comrade Stalin." This would infuriate him and he would ask angrily, "Where is this town, Base?" but he never got an answer. Although he himself ate and drank sparingly, the abundance of his repasts was famous. And he took it for granted that art was "truthfully reflecting the improvements in living conditions" when he saw the same abundance on a movie screen.

I have no idea if my father knew that the "base" existed mainly as a place where special doctors chemically analyzed for poison every scrap of food that went to his kitchens. Formal written records saying, "No poisonous elements found," with official seals attached and signed by a responsible specialist in poisons, were attached to every loaf of bread, every package of meat or fruit. Sometimes Dr. Dyakov would appear in our Kremlin apartment with his test tubes and take samples of the air in our rooms. Inasmuch as we lived there, and the servants who cleaned the rooms remained alive, everything must have been in order. But all the same, it was the doctor's duty to come from time to time, "take a sample," and make out a written report.

My father did not know how much his dinners, dachas, and "poison tests" cost, for the simple reason that he never paid for anything. All his living expenses were footed by the State. His own monthly wages came in envelopes from the Central Committee of the CPSU, from the Defense Ministry, from the Council of Ministers and other institutions of which he was either an honorary or a symbolic member. He would put these envelopes away, without looking at them, into drawers in his desk. The desk was in his apartment in the Kremlin. Later everything was transported to his dacha, where he had a similar desk at which he never worked. The drawers were full of sealed envelopes of money, which, when the drawers became too full, would be taken away somewhere. When my father died, all this money instantly vanished.

Valechka, my father's housekeeper, asked me once, soon after his death, whether the money kept in the desk had been given to me or any other relative. But I had no idea where that money was. Valechka then swore and summed up the situation briefly: "The scum must have stolen it!" I don't know whom she had in mind: the bodyguards of the secret police, who had been running the house during the last days and hours, or the Great Socialist State. . . .

Twelve years later a cashier in the savings bank, where I used to receive my pension, told me in strict confidence that in another bank there was a savings account (she gave me its number) in my father's name, obviously deposited there by his secretary, to which the heirs—that is, the grandchildren and I—had a legal right. Through a notary public we sent in an official request for payment, and each one of us was handed two or three hundred rubles. The money had been deposited in the bank in 1947 at the time of the first monetary reform, and since then the original sum had dwindled to less than one-tenth its original size, as a result of several monetary transactions. The kind cashier had wanted to help us. Breaking all rules, she told me about the money, which came in very handy at the time for all of us. But evidently, on the day of my father's death, the generals of the secret police had taken good care of their own families. As for my father, he had never thought of his children, his grandchildren, of making a will. He lived above material interests at the expense of the State.

In art, outside of pure propaganda, satire and humor appealed to him most. In them his own skepticism and sarcasm found an outlet. He often reread Gogol and the early works of Chekhov; together with Zhdanov he would sometimes take from the shelf Saltykov-Shchedrin, in order to quote something from *The History of the Town of Glupov*. But these two men alone were permitted to do this—Soviet satirists were strictly forbidden to "defame our reality." Saltykov, senator and nobleman, who had written a biting satire on Russia in the nineteenth century, had become inadmissible in our day and age.

In the U.S.S.R. Charlie Chaplin was "allowed" to appear in his old silent movies, and in *City Lights* and *Modern Times*. At his dacha my father would often look at these films again, delighted by how "cleverly they made fun of work on an assembly line under Capitalism." But the revealing and indicting *Great Dictator*, with Chaplin's own impassioned speech defending Jews against Fascism, was never shown in the Soviet Union. Soviet satire remained fed on Mikhalkov's toothless fables. The great tragicomic actress Faina Ranevskaya had to tumble head over heels down the stairs, which made my father laugh till tears streamed down his cheeks, and the director of that film received rewards. . . .

My father did not care for poetical and deeply psychological art. I never saw him reading any poetry—nothing beyond the Georgian *Knight in the Tiger's Skin* by Rustaveli, the translations of which he considered himself expert enough to judge. I never saw on his desk either Tolstoy or Turgenev. Yet about Dostoevsky he once said to me that he was a "great psychologist." Unfortunately I did not ask him what he had in mind—the profound social psychology of *The Possessed* or the analysis of human behavior in *Crime and Punishment.*

No doubt, he found in Dostoevsky something deeply personal, of which he preferred not to talk or give any explanation. Officially at that time Dostoevsky was considered a totally "reactionary" writer.

I think that my father also found something personal in his favorite opera, *Boris Godunov,* which in his last years he often went to see, usually sitting alone in his box. But once he took me with him, and I felt shivers down my spine during Boris' monologue and the recitative plaint of the Fool in Christ's Name. To glance over my shoulder at my father would have been too frightening—maybe he, too, at that moment had "bloodstained little boys before his eyes"? Why of all operas did he constantly choose this one, when in general his tastes tended toward what was gay, the folk story of *Sadko* or *Snegurochka* (*The Snow Maiden*)? We also went to see *Ivan Susanin,* but only for the sake of the scene in the forest, after which my father would go home.

This forest scene is very dramatic. Ivan Susanin, an old Russian peasant, leads the Polish Army into a dense winter forest near Smolensk, into its very heart, from which there is no way out. He is killed, but the Polish Army also remains there forever, frozen to death. After this scene my father used to leave, never remaining for the next act with its lovely ballet—a mazurka and a polonaise. What did he find in this destruction of Poles in a forest? Perhaps it reminded him of the ten thousand Polish officers, prisoners of war, secretly shot by the Soviets in the Katyn woods near Smolensk in 1940?

In the last years my father reread Gorky, yet he spoke of

him with irritation. Long ago, when he had wished to be in Gorky's good graces, he had inscribed in Gorky's "The Maiden and Death": "This thing is stronger than Goethe's Faust. J. Stalin."

I don't know if Gorky had been flattered by this exaggerated praise of his rather mediocre short poem, but I can say with certainty that nothing in art was further away from my father's understanding than a glorification of woman and love. Gorky wrote a great deal, with sincerity and depth, about love and women. They played an important part in his life and in his mental outlook. My father was indifferent to it all. But since it had been with difficulty that Gorky had been induced to return to the U.S.S.R. from abroad and it was important to draw him to the side of the Party, my father had not hesitated to pay a compliment over which later connoisseurs of Soviet literature puzzled a great deal, breaking their heads to find some explanation for such an inscription; but no matter from what angle one may look at it, Goethe had nothing to do with it. . . .

There had never been such a prostitution of art as the exhibition in 1949, arranged in honor of my father's seventieth birthday. The immense exhibition in the halls of the Tretyakov Gallery featured one subject only: Stalin. From every canvas the same face looked at you, sometimes in the shape of a Georgian lad, his eyes raised to heaven, or as a gray-haired general in a Russian Imperial uniform with epaulets. Armenian artists gave the face an Armenian look, the Uzbeks made it look Uzbek; in one picture there was even a certain resemblance to Mao Tse-tung—they were represented sitting together in identical semimilitary tunics and with an identical expression on their faces.

Stalin would be represented on various festive occasions seated among red-cheeked women and children stretching out their arms to him, every inch a kindly, gray-whiskered grandpa; or else, at the head of the Politburo, a group of national heroes with dark, bold brows, himself like some miraculous Russian legendary knight, broad-shouldered and powerful. All of this pseudo folk art was based on obsequiousness, in an effort to gratify at all costs the "Leader's" tastes, while the "Leader" himself did his best to gratify some of the least attractive traditions of the people, whose support he needed. It should be said here, however, that my father never saw a single one of those pictures, fortunately for their creators; but the jury saw to the prizes, which were distributed among the "best."

Time and again my father tried to appeal to the "simple people" and their "national ways," loading his speeches with folksy sayings, wearing his trousers tucked inside his boots, the way Russian workers had done before the Revolution. This created an impression in the Soviet Union's semi-lower-middle class, which he had brought to power in the Party, in the State apparatus, in the police force, in the official ideology. He would also appeal to the most reactionary Russian failings—to anti-Semitism and to marauding during the war. He officially allowed the armed forces to loot the conquered countries of Europe.

"We'll show them how to gut people!" he would say malevolently of the Germans—those same Germans with whom he had wanted so to be in a long, solid alliance. He had not guessed or foreseen that the pact of 1939, which he had considered the outcome of his own great cunning, would be broken by an enemy more cunning than himself. This was the real reason for his deep depression at the start of the war. It was his immense political miscalculation. Even after the war was over he was in the habit of repeating, "Ech, together with the Germans we would have been invincible!"

But he never admitted his mistakes. To do so would have been contrary to his nature. He considered himself infallible and, whatever happened, never had any doubts in his righteousness. He considered his political flair unmatchable.

"So they thought they could fool Stalin? Just look at them, it's Stalin they tried to fool!" he would say, speaking of himself in the third person, as if he were standing aside and watching while certain miserable misguided people tried to lead him by the nose. It never occurred to him that he might fool himself; to the end of his days he was on the alert for those who might treacherously outwit him. This, indeed, had become a mania.

I don't believe he ever suffered any pangs of conscience; I don't think he ever experienced them. But he was not happy, either, having reached the ultimate in his desires by killing many, crushing others, and being admired by some.

There was neither happiness nor peace in him. He went on building dacha after dacha near the Black Sea—in New Athos, in Sukhumi, on Lake Ritsa, and even higher up in the Caucasus Mountains. There were not enough old Imperial palaces in the Crimea, all of which were now at his disposal; so he built new dachas near Yalta. I never saw all these new houses, by then I no longer accompanied him to the south; neither did I see the new house on Lake Valdai, near Novgorod.

According to his former interpreter, Vladimir Pavlov, elected a member of the Central Committee at the Nineteenth Congress, my father at the end of 1952 had twice asked the new membership of the Committee to sanction his retirement. Every member, as one, said that it was impossible. Had he actually expected any other answer from that unanimous chorus? Or was he suspicious of some one man who might be aspiring to replace him? And did he really want to retire? The whole story brings to mind Ivan the Terrible, who on a couple of occasions retired to a monastery, claiming to be too old and tired to reign and ordering his boyars to elect from their midst a new Czar. The boyars, needless to say, afraid that anyone whom they might elect would instantly lose his head, each time begged him on their knees not to forsake them, to go on reigning over them.

As for the Politburo, to the very last day, as always, they

came to my father to discuss affairs, and he never let anything slip out of his hands; although he already knew he was a sick man and had stopped smoking. He had dismissed his former secretary, Poskrebyshev, had his old guard, Vlasik, arrested; he even arrested his old doctor, afraid of everyone and everything; but he had still refused to give up his place. . . . He was his own "victim"—victim of that terrible thirst for power with which tyrants are born. It burned him from within, driving him all his life toward a false, tragic dead end, down the long road on which everything living had been destroyed by him. In the end he attained an inner emptiness, which he did not wish to reveal either to himself or to others. And in this lay his end.

Looking at him and his whole life now as through inverted binoculars, I feel how far removed it all is from me. And I rejoice in the lightness of my heart, in this unaccustomed inner liberation. It's as if, after a long painful illness, one awoke in the early morning, opened the window, and breathing in the air full of sunlight, felt: "O Lord, what bliss— I'm well!"

Jubilee

The MERRITT PARKWAY ran through Connecticut from hill to hill. It was a clear day late in October. The cool sky was blue. And as far as the eye could see, woods of yellow and fiery red lay stretched to the very horizon. A "golden autumn," as they say in Russia . . .

It was good to go to New England and leave New York behind, where in this "jubilee" year much would be written and said about the Fiftieth Anniversary of the October Revolution. Not a single newspaper, magazine, or television program would omit mentioning the Revolution's "achievements." A jubilee is a jubilee: it is customary to speak only of success. Everywhere there would be talk of sputniks and lovely Soviet ballerinas. Art Buchwald had already cracked a joke about it all: "In the United States a society has been founded for the Protection of the Celebrations of the 50th Anniversary of the October Revolution."

For me this was the first autumn without the obligatory official festivities of November 7. It's a dull feast that fails to touch the hearts of millions of people in the U.S.S.R. No one rejoices over it, yet there's no place to hide from it, either. And one could well imagine what would be going on there in this particular year!

I spent a month and a half in Bristol, Rhode Island, with Ruth Briggs, Colonel in retirement. The Colonel had light-blue eyes and a blond braid, which she wore Russian style, wound round her head. She was probably over fifty, but I no longer ventured to judge anyone's age in this country. She looked young, moved about swiftly all day on high heels, smoking a cigarette and laughing gaily. The Colonel was active, full of the joy of life, and left me no time for meditation.

From the very first day we busied ourselves in her big garden with a view of the cold expanse of Narragansett Bay. We started by freeing a dogwood of ivy that had almost strangled the poor tree. For half a day we crept about on our knees, cutting away and sawing the roots; after that I climbed a ladder, and with scissors in my hand cut away the vines that clung to the branches. The Colonel got her hands all scratched but was very pleased; the liberated tree came to life with a gay rustle of leaves. I thought my back would break, but not so the Colonel, who went about blithely, as if she had done no work at all. In the evening we settled down in the living room near a TV set, lit a fire; beside us the other "members of the family" lay stretched out on a rug: an airedale terrier and two black tomcats. Ruth brought two small "TV tables," lit a cigarette, and mixed two strong martinis on cracked ice.

From then on this became our evening ritual. Only the TV and the tobacco smoke bothered me in this house; everything else was pleasant. The Colonel was gay and good-natured; the airedale and the two cats accepted me. One of the tomcats had an admixture of Burmese blood and with it, I felt, a definite idea of caste, for he treated me as the maharajas and maharanees had in India, with a polite and patient disdain. The other cat, a fat Frenchman with a white waistcoat and cuffs, was a real gentleman. He would ask

politely to have the door opened and would then go for
walks with me in the garden, rubbing against my leg and
purring. The airedale, a faithful friend, understood everything, looked one straight in the eye, and sometimes went
upstairs to my part of the house to sleep.

I worked in the Colonel's garden, enjoying the cool breezes
and the smell of apples. Every day apples fell from big apple
trees. We gathered them in baskets and took them to be
turned into cider. We then weeded all the flowers for the
winter. During November snow fell several times, and I
would say to myself, Well, so here comes winter! But not
at all. The snow did not stay on the ground.

We used to go to the bay for walks along the shore, taking
the dog with us. There was a picnic area there under some
trees, with tables and benches from which one could watch
the sunset. We also drove over to Newport for walks along
the ocean, where tides rolled in over the rocky shore. The
Atlantic breathed deeply and rhythmically, sea gulls flew
over our heads. The ebbing tides disclosed rocks covered
with seaweeds.

Walking around Bristol, I came across plants and grasses
I had known in the vicinity of Moscow, and one day I
could hardly believe my eyes when I saw on the side of the
road some sweet white clover. How wonderful to find here
this sweet-smelling meadow plant, which, after it is mowed
in summer, in Russia adds such fragrance to the hay. But
from the very first day of my arrival I found that the trees in
this country were special: round, rich in branches, with unusually fresh foliage; like people, they were able to grow and
breathe here freely.

On the thirty-first of October exactly a year had gone by
since the death of Brajesh Singh. Only the year before on
this date I was still in Moscow, sitting in my apartment and
never dreaming that I would ever tread New England soil.

How incredibly one's life is apt to change. Here, on this
day, there was a gay children's festival—Halloween. In the

evening children went about ringing at doors, and when they came to ours I carried out candy and cookies. The children wore amusing masks. More or less the same thing was doubtless happening in Kalakankar; in India priests and children are treated in memory of the dead, and all of them are free to enter a house. It was on this day, too, that we sent a notice to the press, announcing that part of the money from the publication of *Twenty Letters* would go to build a hospital in India. Two children's homes—one in France, the other in Switzerland—would benefit by it, as well as Russian émigré newspapers and magazines in the United States, and the Tolstoy Foundation.

From Kalakankar to Bristol, Rhode Island, came a long telegram from Suresh and all the inhabitants of the village. In Bristol, on Sundays, telegrams were delivered through the drugstore, where a telephone was located. At once the town discovered my whereabouts, and newsmen rushed to Ruth Briggs' house. But the Colonel repulsed the attack with ease, and in the end we got away with just a short notice in the newspaper and a picture of her house.

In general the people of Bristol showed no curiosity about me, and this was delightful. I went to the post office to pick up Colonel Briggs' mail, took walks in the streets. In New York, after all the television interviews, this would have been impossible. I began driving the Colonel's big Chevrolet through the quiet streets and along the bay, getting used with difficulty to the automatic transmission. One local lady questioned me at length about the fate of the Russian Imperial family, about which I knew hardly anything at all. She said, "I seem to know more about Russia than you do!"

The dentist, to whom I was obliged to go, talked so much about Pasternak and *Doctor Zhivago* that he could hardly do any work: we wasted all our time talking. After that we had dinner with him and his family. This dentist lived better than any academician in Moscow. The nearby home of a professor from Brown University could not be compared to anything by Moscow standards; such a house had never been dreamed of over there even by ministers of state.

There were at the time four postgraduate students from the U.S.S.R. working on their doctorates at Brown University —four young engineers: a Lithuanian, a Ukrainian, an Armenian, and a Russian. An interview with them appeared in the papers, and I was glad to read that they had said, "A lot in the United States reminds us of our country." So it wasn't just my imagination that had been haunting me from the day of my arrival. It must be true, since these young men and I had not talked it over or seen each other. I know how careful Soviet citizens have to be abroad when they are being interviewed; for the slightest slip of the tongue they would be thoroughly "grilled" by the Party organization for being "politically immature." But in everything these young men had said one could discern their admiration and sincere sympathy for the United States and the people they had met. A man not completely stuffed with official propaganda, whose eyes and ears are open, cannot fail to discern the friendliness of this country and respond in kind. . . .

But things of a different nature had also been happening. Back in September I received an unexpected letter from a woman employee of the Soviet Embassy in Washington, whom I had known slightly in Moscow. She wrote that she would like to meet me, offering me her services in case I wished to write a letter or send a parcel to my children. All of a sudden she had remembered me, although I had been in this country for six months; all of a sudden she felt deeply distressed over my loneliness in the U.S.A., where she herself in "two years had been unable to make friends with anyone." She wrote: "I often think of you in the evening. Is there a single person here with whom you could talk? I know Americans, they are indifferent to the lives of others, uninterested." This did not surprise me; serving as she did in the embassy, she was not permitted to make friends. Also, it was possible that she had no ability to arouse sympathy in

those she met. Her offer to meet me and have a talk was
sheer hypocrisy: we had never been friends in Moscow. She
was a typical employee of a Soviet Embassy, who, having
bought herself enough stuff to last her for a few years, was
preparing to go home. There was no doubt in my mind that
this unexpected letter had been dictated by her superiors.
I answered that I was in no need of her services and that for
a "heart-to-heart talk" I had a sufficient number of friends
among Americans. . . .

*

On November 7 and 8 the entire Communist world bent
backwards trying to convince itself and others of its achievements and superiority.

For me these days were always poisoned by the memory
of my mother's death. This was the thirty-fifth year since she
had left us.

I remember the very first parade I ever saw on Red
Square, in 1932—Mama had taken me to it. I was six and
a half years old and my childish impressions were vivid.
Next day our governess told Vasily and me to write and
describe what we had seen. I wrote, "Uncle Voroshilov rode
a horse." My eleven-year-old brother made fun of me, saying that the proper way to describe it was, "Tovarishch
Voroshilov pranced on his steed." In the end he reduced me
to tears and Mama laughed. She had looked into our nursery
for a moment, wearing a bright-colored bathrobe, and had
then left. We never saw her again.

My brother must have had the makings of a capable
editor: he noticed at once that I underestimated the political
importance of events and simplified a historical moment.
Apparently this quality in me has stuck the rest of my life.
To me Voroshilov always remained an "uncle." I had no
reason for raising him to a higher level. I might add that
all those other "uncles," who used to appear around my

father like a lot of mute performers on a stage, never rose in my eyes to the status of political leaders, which, in essence, they never had been.

I knew their families, their children; I knew how they lived. There was nothing attractive about their lives and I was never close to any of them. Their wives, who had been my mother's friends, treasured a memory of her as of a human being of great spiritual purity, who had performed a heroic action. Catherine Voroshilov, Paulina Molotov, Dora Andreyev, Maria Kaganovich, Zina Ordzhonikidze always spoke of her with immense admiration; in their eyes she had grown into a symbol of truth, of independence of spirit—something that was beyond their own strength. They led the life of Soviet grandees, of illustrious ladies of that new class created in Soviet Russia by the Revolution after the old aristocracy had been done away with. They could only follow their husbands, former workers and peasants now transformed into Soviet lords. Zinaida Zhdanov, my second husband's mother, spoke of my mother as being a "sick woman"; but she had never even seen her and was merely repeating the Party's official line.

The young generation in these families sometimes succeeded in raising themselves sufficiently to cast a critical eye upon their parents and the cause they had espoused. They were helped in this by their education, by the university, by their knowledge of foreign languages—by all the things their parents lacked.

"Uncle" Voroshilov was one of the oldest and most illustrious grandees of the Revolution, one of the few surviving old commanders of the First Cavalry Army, famous during the Civil War. He and Marshal Budyonny. The reason for their survival lay in their political inactivity. Budyonny now busied himself with horse breeding and lived very simply. But Voroshilov loved splendor.

His dacha near Moscow was about the largest and most sumptuous in existence. My father alone was in the habit of giving to museums the numerous gifts sent by workers to their leaders. The houses and dachas belonging to Voroshilov, Mikoyan, and Molotov were crammed with fine rugs, gold and silver Caucasian weapons, valuable porcelain. After the Second World War a flood of gifts began arriving from other, especially fraternal Socialist countries and from China. Jade vases, carved ivory, Indian silks, Persian rugs, handicrafts from Yugoslavia, Bulgaria, Czechoslovakia. It was hard to imagine valuables that did not decorate the abodes of these "veterans of the Revolution." Gifts continued to arrive at their homes, symbolizing the "fraternal solidarity of the working classes." The medieval custom of vassals paying tribute to their overlord had been resuscitated. Voroshilov, being an old cavalryman, received horses; he never gave up riding at his dacha. Neither did Mikoyan. Their dachas had become luxurious estates with fine grounds, hothouses, stables, all of it maintained and further developed at government expense. On the whole, all the "leaders" had the same sources of income; the difference in the way their properties looked depended solely on the taste of the hostess and the partialities of the host.

Voroshilov was dashing in appearance even after he was sixty: at his dacha he wore white flannels and walked with the light step of an old officer. Mikoyan, too, had a youthful and dashing appearance. He kept his diet and weight under strict control.

Mikoyan and his wife had been deeply impressed and influenced by their first visit to America. In many ways it had shaped their way of life and had given a more modern aspect to their home. But Voroshilov remained forever within the narrow scope of a cavalryman's outlook. Ukrainian folk songs, which he sang well, remained for him the ultimate in art. Extremely poor portraits of all the members of his family—the work of Alexander Gerasimov, "court academician of art"—decorated the walls of his dacha. Voroshilov never refused to pose; portraits of other "leaders" had to be made with their photographs as models.

A great deal depended on the wives. Catherine Voroshilov liked portraits; the other wives cared nothing about art. And, of course, payments to the "court academician of art" for his creations were made by the State. Catherine Voroshilov in her youth had been a worker and a Party activist. Now she had grown into a fat Soviet lady, dedicating herself to the study of the Party's history. For many years she worked in the highest Party school, where Zinaida Zhdanov also pegged away. The standing joke was that together they served as "visual aids to learning the history of the CPSU."

At family dinners Voroshilov liked to make speeches, using any pretext and blending them with whatever happened to be the political situation of the moment. The habit of expressing themselves authoritatively during family meals in their dachas had become customary with some of the "leaders." Even with only his wife, family, and some old acquaintance like myself present, Voroshilov would pronounce a toast, standing up with a glass in his hand; while his son, daughter-in-law, and grandchildren lowered their eyes and sighed with boredom.

N. M. Shvernik, who became President of the U.S.S.R. after Kalinin's death, also indulged in such performances at Sunday dinners. Personally I witnessed this strange custom only in these two houses; most people behaved in a normal way in their homes.

Voroshilov's big, three-storied dacha, with its immense library, was burned to the ground after the war through the carelessness of a small grandson, who had been playing with fire near a New Year's tree. But the dacha was soon rebuilt as large as ever. Only the library was irrevocably lost.

Voroshilov, Molotov, Kaganovich, Mikoyan, all had the same libraries as the one in my father's apartment in the Kremlin. In accordance with a standing regulation, all newly published books were sent to these people by the publishers. Needless to say, no one paid for the books. The most valuable items in these private collections were the unique Soviet publications of the twenties and thirties, completely withdrawn from circulation after the purges of 1937 and '38. Of course, no one could withdraw anything from these private libraries, and so literature of aesthetic value, the works of authors who had later been arrested and had perished, still stood on those shelves. Along with them were Party publications reflecting struggles among its various factions and trends—Trotsky, Bukharin—publications that had vanished leaving no trace in public libraries; and finally, every important periodical published in the U.S.S.R. since the first postrevolutionary years could be found in these private collections, enjoyed chiefly by the young generation in the family.

Voroshilov's library was burned. The government decided to confiscate my father's, disposing of it at its discretion. Kaganovich and Molotov, after being kicked out of the Politburo and the Kremlin, were permitted to retain their libraries as their personal property. They sold the most valuable and rare items, taking the rest with them from the Kremlin to their new modest dwellings. In the U.S.S.R. the State twists the law whichever way it wants, including laws governing private property. In Mikoyan's family the library has been apportioned among his sons, who enjoy making use of it.

Ashkhen Mikoyan was a quiet, attractive woman, an excellent housewife. At their dacha one found her seated in front of the house on a well-mowed lawn, airing in the sun Caucasian woolen blankets, pillows, rugs, winter clothes. With four surviving sons—one having been killed during the war —and a whole gang of nephews and nieces who came from Armenia every summer, she was kept very busy. She usually wore the same modest little housecoat and carried a dustcloth in her hand. Ashkhen had no wish to be either an "illustrious lady" or a connoisseur of the Party's history. . . .

America impressed her with the rationality of its way of life, and upon her return home she renovated the bathrooms and kitchens in her different residences, modeling them after what she had seen over there. Their old apartment in the Kremlin was the simplest of these State dwellings, and Ashkhen grieved when all the "leaders" were offered State residences on the Lenin Hills, with walls upholstered in silk, with expensive wooden paneling, marble mantels, and massive furniture. She continued to prefer her dacha, where she could shake out her pillows on the lawn. She was a warmhearted, simple, sweet person, and some inner sense had helped her to remain that way to the end of her days, without becoming a "Soviet lady."

When Mikoyan went to Cuba, she had been gravely ill. I visited her at her dacha. She was lying on a couch, flatly refusing to be moved to their Moscow home. Here in the country she was surrounded by the same paneled walls with Gobelin tapestries, Dutch-tile floors, carved oak furniture, left by the prerevolutionary owners of the place. In this house very little had been acquired by the new hosts. This probably was what she liked about it. While Mikoyan was having his meeting with Castro, Ashkhen died.

A democratic attitude and a simplicity of relationship were preserved in this family. But one must not forget the vast sums spent by the State on the maintenance of numerous relatives, four married sons, many grandchildren; on footing bills for their travel expenses, automobiles, apartments. . . .

Mikoyan's sons had a flair for sophistication. The Voroshilov portraits by Academician Gerasimov would have been thrown out by them. And often, when Mikoyan went to formal banquets or on official trips abroad, he had to borrow fine socks and ties from his sons.

The existence in Moscow of special "closed" stores was carefully concealed from Mikoyan, who for many years had been Minister of Commerce; yet his daughters-in-law frequented these stores, buying in them imported goods for his sons. The Minister took it for granted that "distributors," who had existed during the war and in other days of rationing, had long since disappeared, together with the ration-card system. But the Moscow "aristocracy" and the Ministry of Commerce itself knew better. A few selected people were admitted into the restricted section of GUM (the big department store on Red Square), where they could purchase, without being crushed or having to wait in line, Yugoslav shoes, English sweaters, and French perfume. Nothing was said to Mikoyan about this for fear that he might order the clandestine trade closed: Soviet diplomats going abroad would then be unable to get properly outfitted to represent "with dignity" the Soviet Union in foreign lands.

Before my departure for India Mrs. Kassirova, who knew all the ins and outs of MID (Ministry of Foreign Affairs), took me to this "closed section." There I bought myself an English summer coat, which I am still wearing today in Princeton. My white Yugoslav pumps, which, after my interview with the press on Long Island, were described in all the papers, had been bought not in New York but in Moscow, thanks to a salesgirl I knew, who hid them for me under a counter. Mikoyan, however, thought that the import trade in the U.S.S.R. was "expanding every year."

He believed all the figures submitted to him. At Mikoyan's dacha, even in winter, fresh green vegetables from his own hothouses were always served. Helping me to some, he once said, "In the U.S.S.R. people haven't got the habit of eating green vegetables." To which I told him that everyone loved green vegetables but couldn't buy them anywhere.

"What are you saying!" exclaimed Mikoyan. "This year we sold twice as many green vegetables to the people as in any previous year!"

Molotov's apartment in town and his dacha were distinguished by good taste and luxurious furniture (by Soviet standards, of course). Molotov's wife was always the best-dressed of all the government ladies. Our own dull government apartment in the Kremlin could not compare with Molotov's home, which was far more lavish than any other such residence.

Molotov's wife had also been a factory worker in her youth, had worn a red kerchief, and had been a Party activist. Later she had been placed at the head of the Soviet perfume industry. After visiting Paris, Berlin, America, she forgot her proletarian past, having become the first lady of Moscow, hostess at diplomatic receptions at her own dacha and in other official residences. Her home was run in grand style. Her only daughter was given an excellent education—English, French, German, music, and a special teacher of gymnastics. Paulina Molotov had once been a member of the Central Committee; she was also Minister of Fisheries, a deputy to the Supreme Soviet, member of the jury at the House of Models, and member of all kinds of societies and institutions. Then she suddenly began to suffer from inexplicable ailments, for which there seemed to be no treatment. She went to Europe—to Berlin, to Karlovy Vary.

When she was arrested in 1949, everybody thought that physically she would be unable to bear it. For four years even her daughter did not know where she was, and everyone considered Paulina Molotov dead. When, immediately after my father's death, she was brought back from her exile in Kazakhstan, it was almost impossible to believe that she was still alive. But she, laughing, said that "severe conditions had improved her health." And indeed, she looked better than before, and all her "mysterious ailments" had vanished.

Human destinies undergo some amazing changes in the U.S.S.R., and the reactions of individuals to them were at times amazing, too.

There is no doubt that Paulina Molotov had been arrested with the consent—and perhaps on the explicit order—of my father, who considered that, being Jewish, she was "mixed up with Zionists and was spying on Molotov." She knew this perfectly well but insisted on blaming her misfortunes on Beria. She told me that she had "danced with joy like a madwoman" when she heard of his arrest. No one had resisted the Twentieth Congress and Khrushchev's new direction more than Kaganovich and Molotov. As for Molotov's wife, she was even more vehement about it. Kaganovich and Molotov considered Khrushchev their personal enemy, because he had ousted them from the government and had recommended their expulsion from the Party. When Kosygin came to power, they instantly sent in a demand for reinstatement in the Party, which was refused. After that they grew incensed at the whole world and began singing praises to the "memory of the great Stalin."

I saw Molotov after Khrushchev had been replaced by Kosygin. He looked old and wizened, living as a pensioner in a small apartment. As usual, he spoke little, only backing with yeses what others said. In the past I had heard him yessing my father. Now he was yessing his wife. She, on the other hand, was full of energy and battle cries.

She had not been excluded from the Party and now attended Party meetings in a candy factory, as she had done in her youth. When I arrived, the family was gathered round the dinner table. Paulina said to me, "Your father was a genius. He destroyed the Fifth Column in our country, and when war broke out, the Party and the people were as one. Now there's no revolutionary spirit left, only opportunism. See what the Italian Communists are doing! It's a disgrace! They have all been scared out of their wits by this fear of war. There's only one hope left—China. There alone the spirit of revolution still survives!"

Molotov kept nodding his head and yessing. Their daughter and son-in-law sat in silence, with eyes glued to their plates. They belonged to another generation and felt embarrassed by such talk. The older Molotovs were like the fossils of dinosaurs, petrified and preserved in glaciers. Paulina Molotov crumbled diced garlic into the borsch, assuring us that "Stalin always ate it this way." Later she reviled the laundry service, complaining of having to do the washing all over again; then she inveighed against Khrushchev: she could never forgive him for expelling her husband from the Party. But she had forgiven my father for destroying millions of human beings. She called that "destroying a Fifth Column."

After this visit I no longer wondered how the Molotovs could have liked it in Mongolia, where he had been ambassador for some time. There, in that backward satellite country, they had found the political obscurity they cherished so, among barbaric nomads who had leaped from a tribal state straight into Socialism. More than once Paulina Molotov mentioned the "healthy spirit" of the Mongolian Republic. When I left the Molotovs, I felt as if I had come out of a paleontological museum.

Fortunately such visits in my life were rare. I used to call on Paulina Molotov because she had been on friendly terms with my mother, and there were so few people left who remembered Mama.

I never saw how Kaganovich—that other pensioner—lived after his downfall. But I had been in the Kaganovich home several times in the old days when he was still an all-powerful member of the Politburo. His pretty daughter and her husband were both architects, nice young people who led an independent life. Actually it was the younger couple that I used to go to see.

Kaganovich, of course, was also one of the old Soviet grandees. The same big dacha, the same large library, the same level of education as Voroshilov's, the same kind of wife as Molotov's, who had once worked in the textile industry and later clothed a crowd of relatives at government expense. Like all these other households, this one, too, had an officer of the secret police attached to it, in command of a detachment of guards; it also had the same "tail"—a second car that always followed the leader's personal limousine (to "ride on the tail" was what the Chekists called this line of duty). The Kaganoviches, like the rest, had also owned an armored Packard with green bulletproof glass in its windows.

But a sense of humor can exist anywhere, and the "Kremlin children" had their own jokes. A line of State Packards rushing at full speed down the Arbat toward the Kremlin, sirens blowing, was known as "a dog's wedding." In the vernacular of the secret police, homes of Politburo members were known as "objects." The children, therefore, used to say, "The subject has gone to the object."

Kaganovich's home lacked Voroshilov's expansiveness, Molotov's refinement and taste, the democratic rationality of Mikoyan. It was the home of a rich parvenu, full of ugly, expensive objects and palm trees in buckets standing in various corners. Kaganovich himself was loud and coarse. He looked like a very fat landowner. He was considered a good organizer of industry and transportation, which at one time he had headed. But his administrative activity in the capital, apart from the construction of the subway, was closely linked with the destruction of cultural and historical landmarks. No one knew why the Chudov Monastery had to be pulled down, and the "Red Porch" in the Kremlin, the Cathedral of Christ the Saviour, the Sukharev Tower, the Iberian Gate and Chapel. And why the green parklike ring of boulevards encircling the city had to be transformed into a "sea of asphalt." A Palace of the Soviets was supposed to rise in place of the Cathedral of Christ the Saviour but was never built, although its blueprints had been drawn under Kaganovich, who had personally sanctioned the so-called "Plan for the Reconstruction of Moscow."

All Party leaders without exception were preoccupied with this "reconstruction" of the capital. It was in the spirit of the Party. Architects tried in vain to talk Khrushchev out of building the Palace of Congresses next to the old Kremlin cathedrals, as this would disfigure the general view of the

Kremlin. Khrushchev refused to listen. Now, behind the Kremlin walls, rises a white modern building that looks like a huge department store, with the golden dome of the Belfry of Ivan the Great absurdly perched on top of it. Young people call this Palace of Congresses a "*stilyaga* among boyars."

Kaganovich, however, tried hard to take an interest in art. One of his relatives was a violinist, and for this reason his children sometimes took him to recitals. One day I was in the same box with him at a recital given by Yehudi Menuhin in Moscow. The recital was a real feast of art: Menuhin and Oistrakh played Bach's Concerto for Two Violins. It was a beautiful, harmonious performance. Suddenly Kaganovich turned to me and winked: "See how *our* boy is beating the American?" To him it was a contest, a kind of horse race.

The mode of life of those who had become "leaders" at a later date differed slightly from that of the old-timers. Beria rose to the highest pinnacle in a very short time and, of course, being a member of the Politburo, had all the advantages of State lavishness. But an artistic taste is ingrained in Georgians, and his house looked elegantly modern.

One must give his hostess—the charming and beautiful Nina—her due. When still not quite seventeen, she had lived in her native Mingrelian village. Upon hearing that Lavrenti Beria, Head of the GPU of Georgia, had arrived, she went to plead with him for her brother's release—he had been arrested. Beria had arrived in a special train. Nina entered his car, and never again saw her native village. She was carried off, her beauty having caught the police boss' fancy. He locked her up in a compartment. That was how she became his wife.

But Georgian women are loyal wives. Although Nina sometimes cried and complained to me about her unhappy, humiliating life, she would never have admitted it to anyone else. She had studied and had become an agricultural chemist who might have worked successfully in the fields and gardens of Georgia. This is what she had longed to do. But it was impossible. Her husband had brought her to Moscow, which she hated. She continued to play the part of wife and hostess, although she had long ceased being either. There was, however, no way out. She gave all her attention to her only son and attained excellent results: he received a good education, knew German and English, and became one of the first missile engineers in the country, who built the first guided missiles. He was gentle-mannered and agreeable, like his mother. Together they presented a sharp contrast to Beria, a born executioner and zealot, to whom the GPU was a vocation.

It was unpleasant meeting him even in his own home. On Sundays at his dacha he amused himself by shooting at a target with various firearms. In the evening a movie would be viewed, his son translating what was being said in American and German films. Then Beria would suddenly go away, no one knew where. It was difficult finding a subject of conversation with this man, who was rude and constantly used bad language.

Beria lived in the dacha that had formerly belonged to Vlas Chubar, a well-known Ukrainian Bolshevik, arrested in 1937. Houses also have their own destinies. All superior dachas, originally built at government expense by good architects, were "inherited" by the next owner. Molotov lived in Yagoda's former dacha, Zhdanov in Rudzutak's. In 1933 we moved into Bukharin's apartment in the Kremlin. The souls of former owners seemed to linger within those walls. Beria's family was arrested in 1953 in the same dacha in which Chubar had been arrested in 1937. Khrushchev took possession of Molotov's dacha after the latter had been expelled from the Party, although Khrushchev already owned a dacha of his own. This house of Molotov's was not a lucky one: in 1964 Khrushchev was forced to part with the big estate, where he had already had time to do away with the magnificent roses and plant corn in their place.

Who knows, maybe Mikoyan was so successful and invulnerable in his political career because he never aimed at anything larger than the house that had been assigned to him in 1919, whose old aspect he had preserved. . . .

Beria's dacha was sumptuous, immense. The big white house stood among tall spruces. The furniture, the wallpaper, the lamps had all been made to the architect's designs—the same architect, Miron Merzhanov, who at one time used to build my father's dachas, until the day in 1949 when he was sent to prison and never returned. Nina made the house seem cozier, being herself a sweet and cozy person. There was a movie-projection room in the house, but then such rooms existed in all the "leaders'" dachas. They were enjoyed by the younger generation, who preferred looking at foreign films in order to get some practice in foreign languages. I'm sure I'm not mistaken in saying that German, American, English, and French movies were, in this particular set, the chief source of information about the outside world. All other sources—books, newspapers, magazines—were unavailable. Young people took a keen interest in everything that could give them some fresh knowledge.

In Beria's house, however, one could always find English and German books, and foreign magazines. Nina had a quiet, tidy German woman living in the house, who had brought up her boy and whom Nina had saved from exile during the war. When the son got married and granddaughters appeared, Nina spent a great deal of her time with them. She had no life of her own, and could not have had one with such a husband. But she always behaved with the greatest dignity.

Shortly after Beria had been arrested and shot in June 1953, the Central Committee issued a long secret document about his crimes. The reading of this paper at Party meetings took more than three hours. In addition to "international spying for the imperialists," of which Beria had been accused, more than half of this secret letter was devoted to Beria's "amoral aspect." The party officials handling the affair must have taken pleasure in poking through the dirty linen of an enemy no longer dangerous, and no Party meeting had ever been as fascinating as this one: the descriptions of the fallen "leader's" love life were given in minute detail. One thing, however, remained unclear: of what was the Central Committee trying to convince the Party ranks? All this filth had nothing to do with politics, nor with internal strife in the Party. The document explained nothing and convinced one of nothing, except perhaps that the hypocrites in the Central Committee had exposed their own foul natures.

After 1953 Beria's wife and son were exiled from Moscow to the Urals. A few years later Nina asked permission to live and work in Georgia; she might at last have returned to her native village and occupied herself with agricultural chemistry. But her request was turned down. Actually, this beautiful, unhappy woman, whose life had been ruined by despotism, is living in exile, although no accusations of any kind have ever been leveled at her.

The lives of Malenkov, Andreyev, Zhdanov, comparatively young "leaders," in appearance were less extravagant and more democratic. Their democratic spirit, however, was relative: they simply didn't try to become Soviet nobles. But with the prevailing living conditions in the Soviet Union, they still stood on unattainable Olympian heights, living on a level of luxury of which ordinary Soviet citizens could not even dream.

I used to visit these families, as I knew the younger generation of about my own age. Possibly the young people determined the whole mode of life in these homes. Zhdanov's son was a chemist, always surrounded by friends from the university. Andreyev's daughter was a biochemist, her hus-

band an architect, her brother an aircraft designer, his wife
an expert on art. Malenkov's daughter was an architect. In
the summer they all played tennis, rode aquaplanes on the
river (water skiing came into fashion later); in winter they
skied. They celebrated the birthdays of children and grandchildren, went gathering mushrooms in the woods, tried
never to miss good concerts at the Conservatory. To a certain
degree their elders must have lent an ear, adapted themselves to the views and tastes of their children.

Malenkov's family was probably the most intellectual of
this "high-level" lot. He was an electrical engineer by education; his wife, for many years, had been the Director of the
Institute of Energetics, one of the most advanced technical
schools in Moscow. Their two sons and daughter were
brought up like any other children in an intellectual milieu,
without any emphasis on attaining the luxurious status of a
grandee. No one here posed for his portrait. No Persian rugs,
no Chinese jade or gilt weapons were collected here. Their
house was simple; there were no cheap porcelain knickknacks; nor were there any pretensions to being a "summer
palace."

Malenkov's two sons studied in a special school where
they were taught in English. Their mother's brother, a
teacher, lived with them, helping them with their studies.
In summer the family planted flowers and took care of the
vegetable garden. At table the conversation was always general and of interest to both children and parents. The boys
published their own wall-newspaper, just as we had done
in our childhood long ago.

No wonder that Malenkov was clearly the most reasonable
and sagacious member of the Politburo, and the youngest
member to boot. The program for the development of light
industry, submitted by him in March 1953, found an instant
response; it was a crying need of the whole country. He instantly won popularity, and this was his undoing. Chased out
of the government, he left for Kazakhstan and is probably

still there, working as director of a small electric-power station. He never once came to Moscow to seek favor, nor did he ever beg forgiveness. This annoyed the Politburo, who continued to persecute him in Kazakhstan, flinging accusations at him, including demagogism. Malenkov's "demagogism" consisted in his standing in line for bread like the rest of the population in the small town he lived in. This was regarded as an "insolent challenge" to the government.

Yet for Malenkov and his family this change in their lives was not the tragedy it was for Molotov and Kaganovich, to whom existence outside the government orbit, outside the pale of power, spelled total ruin. The Malenkovs simply returned to the kind of ordinary life for which their education had prepared them, and the giving up of great expectations didn't cause them much pain. It was enforced pensioners like Kaganovich, Molotov, and now Khrushchev who quickly disintegrated spiritually and physically, because to them life without power over other human lives became senseless.

A somewhat special fate was that of Zhdanov. I knew his family better than any other, his only son, Yuri, having been my husband for two years. I had then lived in their home. This was after the death of Andrei Zhdanov himself.

He had been the son of an inspector of public schools. In his early youth he had dreamed of becoming an agriculturist. He loved flowers and gardens. Besides him in the family there had been three sisters. All the children had been educated at home. Their mother had belonged to the nobility; she had been an accomplished pianist, a graduate of the Moscow Conservatory.

Zhdanov's three sisters were older than their brother. They became passionately attached to the cause of enlightening the masses. No one in the family had thought of Marxism before the Revolution. The sisters became teachers; and when the First World War broke out, two of them joined the army as volunteers and drove army trucks. For women in those days this was an unheard-of display of independence. They worked as drivers most of their lives after the Revolution, never had families of their own, and whenever possible carried on with their educational work. The eldest sister remained a teacher. She had a son and grandsons, but she left her husband and was the head of her own family. She hardly ever came to Moscow.

Andrei Zhdanov had been a student at the Petrovsko-Razumovskoye Agricultural Academy in Moscow at the time of the First World War. When the Revolution broke out, he became a Bolshevik, this being a general enthusiasm at the time. Like many other weak people who had taken upon themselves something contrary to their nature, he became conscientious and dogmatic, trying to alter and outsmart himself. I knew Zhdanov as a sick man with a heart ailment, on the whole pleasant and good-natured. That in the history of Soviet art his name should have become associated with the dismal streak of repressions and persecutions in 1946-1948 was the result of the man's zeal in carrying out the will of others, in this case my father's.

I doubt that my father ever went into the fine points of Akhmatova's poems, of Prokofiev's and Shostakovich's music, of Zoshchenko's satires. He never "got around" to detail. Zhdanov, on the other hand, was considered someone who "understood the problems of art" and was therefore delegated to "put things in order." So Zhdanov made a speech at the First Congress of Writers, announcing that "Soviet literature was richer in political ideas than any other literature in the world." He denounced Akhmatova's poems as too intimate, Zoshchenko's stories as too "filled with psychology." Thumbing a tune on the piano, he would teach composers how to write music "for the people." He once said to a movie director, whose film had been rejected, "Why do you present Soviet reality in black and white and life in some distant past in color? Does this mean that our life is dull and gray?"

Whenever it was necessary, Zhdanov was ordered to make pronouncements on foreign policy, on the history of philosophy, on the international labor movement. In the end, everyone grew to hate him as an executive aide, Stalin's possible "heir" in the Party.

Yet actually he never had any pretensions to such a role. He had exclaimed on several occasions, "Let me not outlive him!" (meaning my father). He lacked the ambition to fight for power; he would have given it up voluntarily, and gladly.

At home he had always been under the thumb of women— his sisters, his wife. Life in his family centered around its only son, the son's friends, the son's interests. They used to have amusing, gay, young parties. Yuri's friends from school and from the university came to his house without thinking of his father's "high position." Here many were helped whose parents had suffered during the years 1937-1938; here friendship didn't end because of political persecutions. There were no angry or cruel individuals in this family, but a narrow outlook, dogmatism, and something very fanatical revealed themselves in many ways.

It's true that Zhdanov viewed art from the bigoted and puritanical points of view prevalent in the Party. Zhdanov's wife once expressed them admirably in one of her unforgettable aphorisms: "Ilya Ehrenburg loves Paris so because there are naked women there." Creative imagination in music, art, films was as alien to him as higher mathematics. But taking the bit between his teeth, he would rush into combat to prove himself more Catholic than the Pope, to "prove" Tito's wickedness and the uselessness of idealistic philosophy in all centuries. Maybe he was trying to stamp out the remnants of idealism in himself.

Long ago, at the very start of his activities in the Party, he had administered the Gorky Region (formerly Nizhni Novgorod on the Volga), where the first Soviet automobile factory was then being built. Those were the best years of his political career. From there he was summoned to Leningrad, immediately after Kirov's assassination, introduced into the Central Committee, and told to speak to the Congress of Writers. Such a wide scope of activities was too great for this weak man with a weak heart. He clung to my father as a child clings to an adult's hand, trying desperately to appear grown-up himself. As a result, Zhdanov has left of himself an ugly memory as of a *Derzhimorda* (a policeman in Gogol's *Inspector General*).

All in all, the ten highest families in the land led more or less the same kind of life, dull and colorless. Their children endeavored to get away from it as soon as they could and lead their own lives. Almost none of the "Kremlin children" followed in the political footsteps of their fathers. Olga Ulyanova, Lenin's niece, became a chemist; so did Frunze's daughter. Kaganovich's daughter is an architect, Voroshilov's son an engineer, three of Mikoyan's five sons and Andreyev's son are airplane designers, Zhdanov's son a chemist, Kuibyshev's son and Malenkov's daughter architects; while Shvernik's daughter is a television technician. All of them are intellectuals with a good education who have moved far ahead of their fathers in their outlook on life and culture. Only Jacob Sverdlov's son, Andrei, went into politics and became a professional Chekist, ardently "fighting the remnants of Trotskyism," and especially concerned with the "trend of thought" in the younger generation, many of whom he has sent to prison.

Almost every family—Molotov's, Voroshilov's, Mikoyan's—had its victims in the purges: if not relatives, then friends. Mikoyan's youngest son married the daughter of Alexei Kuznetsov, leader of the Leningrad Party, when the latter had already been removed from his post and was awaiting arrest. At his daughter's wedding he appeared thin and depressed. Soon after the wedding, Kuznetsov and his wife were arrested, and Alla Kuznetsov remained in the Mikoyan family, where she was treated as a real daughter by the family. The parents of Voroshilov's daughter-in-law were arrested, and only with great trouble, through Voroshilov's own inter-vention, was the verdict in their case softened from concen-tration camps to exile. In every one of these families the members were afraid of saying what they really thought. They lived as quietly as possible, brought up their children, and kept silent.

Strictly speaking, the Politburo's role in governing the country consisted in nothing else. As a recompense, its mem-bers remained alive and invulnerable, quietly growing old and fat in their dachas. Every single one of them, from Beria with his secret police to Malenkov and Mikoyan, who busied themselves with economics, did nothing but say "yes."

True, they engaged in another, secret activity, which never rose to the surface and only seldom betrayed its presence through some overt sign: the leaders intrigued one against the other, trying to push their colleagues out of their way and gain the position of favorite. But in doing so they were very careful, each one afraid of losing his own head while trying to push the other onto the scaffold. Only after my father's death did all this come storming to the surface.

Until March 1953 one could always see Malenkov and Beria walking arm in arm. They always moved as a couple, and as such used to come to my father at his dacha, in ap-pearance the closest of pals. This friendship, so obvious to everyone, must have been based on their joint dealing in some debatable matters. The interrelationships inside the Politburo were complicated, involved, and reciprocally spiteful. In the Zhdanov home Malenkov was never referred to in any other way than "Malanya," on account of his round, womanish face—Malanya, or Malashka, being a common name among Russian peasant women.

Zhdanov was, in a sense, at the opposite pole from Malen-kov and Beria. Everyone, without exception, feared the latter. In point of fact, Molotov had been virtually removed from affairs since the arrest of his wife in 1949. No one gave Kag-anovich, Voroshilov, Andreyev, Shvernik any serious consideration. Mikoyan somehow managed to live in peace with them all. . . .

But when, after my father's death, Beria had almost jumped into his place, everyone turned against him with amazing unanimity. In June 1953 Malenkov did not support his "old crony"; the whole Politburo as one threw Beria out and had him arrested. With my father dead, Beria was left with only one support, that of the secret police and its regiments. Marshals and generals of the regular army supported the Politburo, and on the day of Beria's arrest armored tanks were moved into the streets of Moscow, in fear of the MVD's (Ministry of the Interior's) troops. No one could understand what was happening. The police in the streets kept asking the soldiers in the tanks, "What is this? Maneuvers? Then take the circuit route around the city—you are ruining the pavement!"

No one came to Beria's support, everyone now being as afraid of him as they had been of my father. The government's secret archives were in his hands, and this didn't suit the members of the Politburo at all. Even such collaborators as General I. A. Serov, who had worked closely with him in the MGB (Ministry of State Security) and the secret service, preferred supporting the government. This was not surprising in a land where secret plots and palace upheavals were the sole means of unseating those in power, there being nothing else to resort to in a society devoid of democratic procedures of any kind.

Under Khrushchev nothing changed in the Politburo's behavior. "New times arrived, new names arose," wrote Yevtushenko. New names rose on the political horizon—and still keep on rising—but the system, the social order, remained the same. And the mode of life of the new "ten families" remained, on the whole, the same as that of the old ones.

Under my father's rule Khrushchev had been quiet and had kept his mouth shut. But when he came to power, he became talkative, ambitious, intolerant, and quite unexpectedly began to display a pattern of dictatorial behavior. I hardly knew his family and never visited their home, but this change in the man's whole nature was striking.

In the whole history of Khrushchev's rise and fall, the fate of his son-in-law, Alexei Adzhubei, was extremely characteristic. In it, as in a drop of water, lay reflected the whole order of life in the U.S.S.R., ugly and antidemocratic to its very core.

Alyosha Adzhubei had been a promising student, who was preparing himself to become a journalist. I knew his mother well, the best dressmaker in Moscow, who dressed all the ladies in the "ten top families." She was a really talented person, and a good deal of her artistic sense and energy had been passed on to her only beloved son. Alyosha married Khrushchev's daughter in 1949, when they were both still students. Nothing at the time had presaged his future flights and falls. He had graduated and could have lived like all journalists, talented and otherwise, within the cabals of editors and censors and the Party's plans and disciplines.

But luck was with him: with the coming of Khrushchev to power, he was quickly pushed to the top, all the more so since he was truly talented and bright. I felt a liking for him because I loved and respected his mother. She had dignity, despising profoundly the government ladies, her customers. She had spent a life of hard labor; she had come from the provinces to Moscow and had acquired popularity through her beautiful workmanship. She wanted to see the same qualities in her son. Upon entering the family of the all-powerful Premier, she stopped working in her atelier, sewing only occasionally for Nina Petrovna Khrushchev and for her daughter-in-law, who both implored her to do so. She had no other contacts with the Khrushchev family, nor did she seek any. She moved into her own apartment, next to her son's, who always displayed toward her a touching solicitude.

He had become the Chief Editor of *Izvestia*, the principal

Moscow newspaper, and gave that paper a new breath of life, making it as interesting as was possible within the framework of "Soviet reality." The circulation rose at once. He turned the paper into an evening organ, re-equipped the editorial office, reorganized the entire apparatus, helped his journalists to find living quarters, knowing all too well what poverty means and under what conditions ordinary newsmen were obliged to live. The whole staff of *Izvestia* simply worshiped him. Everything could have been perfect—but man never has enough. . . .

During the eleven years of Khrushchev's rule, Alyosha became an important political figure. One could no longer just call him up at his office. Having a chat with Adzhubei almost amounted to having a chat with the government. Alyosha went abroad with his father-in-law, headed Khrushchev's Press Bureau; people began fawning on him, seeking his patronage, hoping to obtain favors.

Then suddenly one day everything crashed: Khrushchev was deposed. The talented editor was no longer allowed to run the paper as before. In an exact analogy to his father-in-law's situation, Adzhubei was accused of all the deadly sins and was subjected to a long public reprimand in front of assembled Party members, a reprimand that amounted to abuse, accusing him, among other things, of alcoholism, although he drank no more than anyone else and also behaved like everyone else. He was kicked off the newspaper and the circulation instantly fell, while the paper itself reverted to the dull gray rag it had previously been.

Now he works as editor of a small magazine. His mother is probably again dressing her prominent Moscow customers. The antique Spanish mantilla and high comb, which her son had brought her from Cuba, remained as relics of the eleven years spent at the "very top." It's quite possible that she does not regret them. . . .

A new Premier, a new First Secretary of the Party, a new set of "ten families," a new Politburo, which, as be-

fore, has authority over no one. New lords of a new class
of Soviet aristocracy, risen from workers and peasants. These
men never had, and never could have had, any other criterion
of power than that of the lord of the manor. Each one of
them could have no other ideal than to become himself a
lord of a manor, could have no other range of vision than
"in my home village."

For fifty years now society in the U.S.S.R. has been living
under the law of caste and privilege, having in essence installed a caste system, which India has done away with.
The Party here is the priestly caste; the army, the warrior
caste; and the strength and power of this society rest upon
the shoulders of millions and millions of workers, fooled by
"priests" and cowed by arms.

In the Indian village in which I spent two months, they
had criticized their government, had had a choice of seven
candidates during elections, representing seven different
parties. The U.S.S.R. is fifty years behind India, starting from
that "unforgettable" day in 1917 when power was seized by a
small group of Bolsheviks, who became the sole ruling
Party. "Let us catch up and outdistance India with its par-
liamentary democracy!"—that's the kind of slogan missing
among the official Commandments of Communism, given
every year to the people by the "priests" and "pharisees" of
the Central Committee, gathered in their "temple" on the
Old Square in Moscow. . . .

Every year on the seventh of November, the members of
the Politburo, their wives, children, and grandchildren
betake themselves to Red Square to look at the parade,
some of them standing on the Mausoleum, others beside it.
They all freeze, catch chills, and are sick for a long time
afterward. On the eve of this celebration it is obligatory to
be present at a solemn lecture about this yearly anniversary,
after which a grand concert is given. From year to year one
hears the same praises sung; the man held in greatest re-

spect that year by the Politburo delivers the report. The lecture itself, however, is written beforehand in the Central Committee, where all slogans for the event have been sanctioned in advance, too.

On Red Square these slogans are shouted by someone from the Moscow Committee who has the loudest voice. He reads them from a piece of paper, raising his hand with every new slogan in the direction of the demonstrators, who respond with a meager "Hurrah!" Actually, they do not have to shout at all, for the loudspeakers set up in the square shout the "Hurrahs" for them. The sounds of popular jubilation, like those of authorized songs and marches, have also been recorded in advance. And so the radio from Red Square and the Mausoleum—that Holy of Holies of Communism—carries throughout the world more "canned" cries than the actual voices of those marching in the parade. After all, there is always the possibility of some unpredictable human being suddenly shouting something not officially authorized: like *"Down!"* instead of "Hurrah!" For this reason the loudspeakers shout with all their might and no one can possibly outshout them.

That was how it was the first time my mother took me to the parade. That's what happened again and again during the next thirty-five years, under Stalin, under Khrushchev, after Khrushchev. The same is happening today in Moscow on Red Square, in Leningrad, in all the Soviet republics, in all Socialist capitals. As always, the Politburo stands on the Mausoleum, their wives, children, and grandchildren beneath them, close to the Holy of Holies. At a distance, moving from one foot to another, stands the Diplomatic Corps, freezing. Still farther off, the well-ordered ranks of the bureaucracy, State ministers, generals, members of the Central Committee and the Party apparatus, with their wives, children, and grandchildren, creating an impression of a jubilant crowd. Movie cameras diligently take pictures of this farce every year. The shots remain standard. Only on the Mausoleum new faces appear, and in the square new cannons. . . .

The crowds, carrying paper flowers and red transparent portraits, are hurriedly pushed through the square, through lines of guards in civilian clothes, standing in a formation resembling the teeth of a comb: Pass through these teeth, keep moving, hurry up!

Behind the tribune, next to the Kremlin wall, rifles are stacked—just in case. . . .

I have had a taste of everything. I have stood near the Mausoleum among the select. I have stood farther away among lesser beings. I have marched with other university students of my year through those "teeth" along the square, waving to those on the Mausoleum. I have walked as an adult, waving to no one. Later I stopped attending altogether, stopped walking or standing. I have seen it all many times on the Moscow television, knowing exactly every word that would be said by the marshal opening or receiving the parade. Long ago "Uncle" Voroshilov had ridden a horse—ridden it well. So had Budyonny. But Bulganin had trouble in riding—he had to go through lengthy training in a riding academy, and still remained in constant fear of falling off his horse. Later the chiefs adopted the Western custom of passing along the lines of soldiers in open cars, standing up and saluting.

As for the crowds, they had to gather in the streets at seven in the morning and wait for hours, moving slowly through Moscow, only to pass quickly through Red Square to the strict, hurrying commands of "Keep moving!" Later they would return their paper flowers and red transparent portraits to be checked according to lists; only after all this could people at last go home to rest and get drunk after their long walk in the cold. They did not care what the marshal had to say. They knew that it was the same every year, that nothing had changed in the country. Only every year new faces appeared on that barbarous, Pharaonic sanctuary of World Communism—the Mausoleum.

They say that the idea of preserving Lenin's body forever in the Mausoleum belonged to my father. Lenin's entire family had protested against it, and Krupskaya, his widow, had refused to visit the "sanctuary." I understand Krupskaya: the whole idea of the Mausoleum always seemed absurd to me—the age of holy relics has gone by. When my father's body was placed in the Mausoleum next to Lenin's, I was invited, with a chosen few, to visit it, and the horror of this unnatural "peering into a grave" remained to haunt me for a long time. I therefore considered it natural when my father's body, after many trials, was finally laid to rest in the ground, though the government, in doing this, had wished to stress the move as a reduction from "sainthood" to the ranks of sinful mortals unworthy of resting in a "Pharaoh's" tomb.

Today Communists of all countries believe that the "sanctuary," cleansed of the transgressor, is again shedding a bright new light over the earth. And this will be believed for a long time to come by crowds of pilgrims who come there to worship from all ends of the U.S.S.R. and from other countries: crowds of blind slaves, who are in need of sarcophagi, pyramids, and a Pharaonic rule instead of freedom.

How happy I am not to be there any more.

＊

In this unusual year, instead of the usual "October festivities" I celebrated the American feast of Thanksgiving. It is the thanksgiving of the first pilgrims to land on American soil, a celebration of their first harvest, of fall abundance and rest after hard labor. This is my feast. I am a pilgrim, I reached this promised land; behind me lie difficult months and the whole of my paradoxical life. In the end all anxieties are stilled. So let us sit down around the Thanksgiving table.

From early morning Ruth and I cooked the turkey, prepared the potatoes and pumpkin for a puree. We decorated the table with fruit and nuts. Our guests were the Professor from Brown University and his wife. American food is plentiful; it may not be as refined as French and Chinese cooking, but it is good food, of which one does not like to leave any scraps. It's not for nothing that those first pilgrims came to this continent. And how much more appropriate is this fall Thanksgiving to a generous Nature than the dubious worship of Pharaonic sarcophagi.

I had much to thank this country for, which gave me a helping hand at a difficult moment in my life. I was received, helped, in spite of a chorus of traducers that sounded loudly and in unison. After Moscow's attacks, after the sensation caused by my book, after all the things I had read about myself in the press and in reviews, I came to Bristol with nerves frayed, unable to sleep at night. Colonel Briggs, with the military discipline of her household, the march of her heels, and the sound of her gay laughter, put my whole being into order.

I owe a debt of gratitude to Colonel Briggs, to the little town of Bristol, to the charming Governor Chaffee of Rhode Island, to the whole of this immense country, on whose shores the waves of Destiny had set me—just as they had those first pilgrims.

It was with all my heart that I celebrated here my first feast of Thanksgiving. What a marvelous substitute for the state-run Fifty-Year Jubilee of the October Revolution!

The Journey's End

THE YEAR of travels and of a Gypsy's nomad life
was approaching its end. In all my life I had not seen so
many new countries—Asia, Europe, America. The time had
come to stow away my bags and try to return to a settled
life.

But what life? What kind was it to be? And what actually
am I?

I did not leave Soviet Russia in order to continue to be
the "Dictator's Daughter." In that capacity I could have just
as well gone to Georgia and lived there among those who
still worship the memory of the "Great Georgian." On second
thoughts, I would not have had to go anywhere: the Soviet
Government was invoking that memory more and more.

In the fall of 1967 Moscow suddenly changed its tactics
toward me: it made me an indirect offer to return home.
For this purpose they arranged a televised interview between
my son and the German magazine *Stern*. The interview was
staged in my apartment, in which my children were still
living. My son announced: "If Mama should wish to return
now, there would be no punishment." A twenty-two-year-old
student could not have made such a statement on his own

initiative; there can be no doubt that he had been instructed to do so. By way of a reply I sent a brief notice to the German paper *Christ und Welt*, explaining how interviews with foreign correspondents were "organized" in the Soviet Union and describing the briefing I received from Molotov before my interview with William Randolph Hearst, Jr. in 1955.

The world, though, is full of kind people. A musician from Israel, who had been giving concerts in West Germany and had there seen the interview with my son, wrote to tell me that my children had looked strained and unnatural, and that the whole performance bore the earmarks of a badly staged show. That it had been just that—a show—I had never had any doubts, but I was grateful to this stranger for confirming it.

I, of course, knew that I would never go back.

While still in Bristol, I had the unexpected happiness of getting a note from my friend Marina, who was then visiting her cousin in Italy. Her letter had reached me, although it had been addressed simply in care of *Life* magazine. We called up the number in Italy which she had given, and lo and behold! there was Marina's voice.

She told me what I needed to hear most: "Don't worry about the children. They are all right. We all love you, we remember you. We know we won't be seeing you for a long time. But we all love you!" How I longed to hear just such words! Except for my telephone conversation with Bertha when I was in Switzerland, I hadn't heard from any friends since last December.

"We remember you and we love you." Those were the words I needed to hear.

My dear Marina, fearless little woman so full of joy and energy. Looking at her, who would have said that she was closing on sixty? And who could have guessed that seventeen of those years had been spent in prison, concentration camps, and exile?

Marina had been through the mill all right. She had been saved by her happy disposition, her optimism, her profound faith in the ultimate triumph of truth. Long ago, when I was still in Moscow, she told me how she had twice lost and found her daughter; she was a wonderful raconteur and at the time had been thinking of writing about those episodes. But such a manuscript would have ended "in a drawer"; publishers of Soviet magazines do not care for that kind of story.

When Marina was arrested in 1938, she had still been a young woman, and her daughter—an only child—had been five. When war broke out, Marina was spending a "term" in a concentration camp. At first she had been made to fell trees and saw them into logs, but later, thanks to her previous experience as a surgical nurse, she was given work in the camp's hospital. News from the outside world leaked through to prisoners with difficulty, yet somehow Marina heard that children were being evacuated from Leningrad during the blockade and famine. But how was she to find out if her little girl was alive and what had happened to her?

Marina's basic assumption was that "good people were to be found everywhere." And it was perhaps because of her complete faith in this that she was fortunate in always finding everywhere good people who did lend her a helping hand. In some incredible roundabout way she managed to send a tracer to an institution in Leningrad that handled the evacuation of children. After a long time she got an answer: the little girl had been evacuated to a children's home in a village in the faraway Altai region in eastern Siberia near the Mongolian and Chinese borders. Marina's concentration camp was located somewhere in the Urals, more than two thousand miles away from that Altai village. Upon receipt of the news Marina began begging the man in charge of the hospital to let her go in search of her child, whom she proposed bringing back to the concentration camp, to the hospital, where she could be properly taken care of after the privations she must have suffered. Such a request was in itself incredible and unheard of; but such was the trust people had in Marina—and this must have been based on her faith in people's kindness—that her chief let her go for two weeks, supplying her with an official traveling permit from the hospital.

The frail little woman was allowed to go free for two weeks solely on the strength of her "word." This was in 1944. War was on: railway stations blacked out, no trains running on schedule. "I came out into darkness and chaos," Marina used to say. "I couldn't grasp what was going on around me. After all, I had been arrested in peacetime. Leningrad then had been full of life. And all my life until then I, too, had lived well, knowing no troubles. Now I found myself in some strange hell. In my knapsack I had bread and small bottles of alcohol instead of money. I had been told that this, especially the alcohol, would be of help everywhere. Personally, I could think of nothing but my yearning to see my child, who was eleven years old by then. I carried the address of the Altai village with me. And God's help was with me, too."

Marina changed trains many times, paying people with either alcohol or bread, imploring, explaining the purpose of her voyage. There were no railway tickets to be had, all the trains were army transports, carrying wounded and evacués— but people helped, and eventually she reached the Altai.

She still had some distance to cover on foot, hitchhiking, trying to catch a truck going her way, or a horse and cart, or failing that, just going on walking. She plodded along, paying with alcohol or bread whenever she got a lift. Night caught her on the road and she slept, hidden behind a large rock. In the morning she walked on again.

Reaching the village at last, she found the children's home, but she could not recognize her child: the difference between a five- and an eleven-year-old was great. And all the children there looked emaciated, hungry. She was led up to a thin, morose girl, who showed no interest at seeing her. The child's skin was covered with sores, her tangled hair was full of lice. Marina could find no words to say to her. . . .

She had to leave the very next day. The directress of the home commandeered a truck for her, and that same evening arranged a "supper" in honor of the happy mother. Marina had not seen such an abundance of food in six years, which amazed her, as kasha (gruel) was the only thing the children were given to eat. Her small daughter literally threw herself on the food and as a result fell ill of dysentery the next day, running a high temperature. This time Marina had to travel with a sick child; she could not wait, her "leave" was fast drawing to an end.

Again she caught trucks or carts, implored stationmasters, carried the sick girl in her arms. At times her child lost consciousness. But again kind people would help, giving up their seats in crammed cars.

Marina overcame it all. She brought her child to the concentration camp, nursed her back to health in the camp's hospital. After her "term" had been served, they returned to Leningrad together. The girl finished school, entered the university, got married. But in 1948 Marina was arrested again: she had broken a standing regulation and had lived in Leningrad, where, as a former inmate of a concentration camp, she was not supposed to live. And again she was separated from her daughter, this time for seven years.

When at last Marina returned from her Kazakhstan exile, she found herself the grandmother of two boys.

I know that Marina worries about me now, as she would have done about her own daughter; perhaps even more. . . .

Why does she love me so much? What made her divorce me so completely in her mind from the surroundings in which I had been brought up? The answer lies in the fact that those who have suffered a great deal acquire a wide range of vision; their attitude toward others, and toward life in general, is wise, mature, and humane.

*

I haven't tried to correspond with either my friends or my children: in the U.S.S.R. I am considered a political criminal; any contact with me would be dangerous and prejudicial.

When speaking to Marina from Bristol, I repeated several times that I would not return. But she understood this without my telling her. I couldn't say much about myself. As always, making no plans for the future, I had but a vague idea what my new life was going to be like. I only knew one thing: I would not return to the U.S.S.R. Sometimes in my dreams I would see Moscow streets, or the rooms in my apartment, and I would wake up in a cold sweat. To me this was the worst of nightmares.

Outside of a few rare exceptions, I met in America with nothing but prodigious friendliness. Letters beginning with "Welcome to America" still continued to arrive. I received invitations from many people in different cities, in different states, to come and stay with them as their guest. I was invited to lecture to various audiences about the U.S.S.R., about myself, about women and family life in the Soviet Union, about my father. They all wanted to know what had made me turn my back on Communism and my country. I could have accepted most of those invitations, could have traveled all over the United States and made new friends. But I did not want to do it.

I did not, and I still do not, want to become a lecturer, a historian, a biographer of my father, a "traveling sociologist." I do not want any more television interviews, or interviews of any kind. The best way of conversing with the public— and the one that suits me best—is by being a writer. I wanted to comment on all the questions I had been asked in both kind and unkind letters. It is in this way that I am willing to say everything I know.

During the previous summer, when George Kennan had returned to his farm from Norway, I had discussed with him the outline for my next book, which had been gradually shaping itself in my mind. I could have written the book in India, in Switzerland, in any country, for that matter, in which I might have found myself upon leaving the U.S.S.R. But now its framework, its subject had become clear: the story of the year that had so totally altered my life. During the fall I had spoken of it to Cass Canfield, Senior Editor of Harper & Row. But then it was still only a project. Now I had to find a "quiet haven" in which I could settle down to a normal life, and work.

The decision was reached to try to "take root" in Princeton, New Jersey, that small university town to which scholars come from all over the world. Princeton is an international town; its inhabitants are accustomed to newcomers and are not curious about anyone or anything.

I had seen the town once in summer and another time in the fall. There was something cozy and old-fashioned about it. Beautiful old trees lined the streets, giving them the appearance of drives in a park. I simply have to talk to trees, I could not live without it. Life in Princeton was quiet. People bought their food in the same stores, their medicine in the same pharmacy. There is only one post office, one main street, one "central" square—Palmer Square—with a bronze tiger in it, symbol of Princeton and its university. Many students stroll the streets, but they are without beards, without long, unwashed, uncombed hair. Princeton is rather conservative, but evidently the hippie influence is reaching it, too.

Kennan and I walked through an autumn wood near his Institute, made a tour of the college campus, looked into the university chapel, leaving outside his black poodle, who followed us everywhere. No one paid the slightest attention to us, and this was the best thing I could have wished for.

In Princeton I wanted to continue the mode of life I had

followed in Moscow the last fifteen years: no servants, no regular household help, all of which made one so dependent on others. But I could not help wondering whether freedom and independence could be easily achieved in a new country, in which the whole way of life was so different and where every well-known person lived under the public's eye.

The public! There really is no such thing in the Soviet Union. There is no public opinion, no public information, no public reactions. The public is in a state of total paralysis; it's as though it were sunk in a lethargic sleep, not reacting in any way even to world affairs, not to mention the lives of private individuals. I came to the free world from a world of silence and lethargy. Now I had to get accustomed to something I found very difficult: this new sensation of life as on a stage, on which the curtain was permanently raised. In a certain sense this was a good thing: I had no secrets, nothing to hide; and I had had enough of those eternal Soviet "mysteries," those high walls, closed-in fences, those gloomy dens inhabited by indifferent, comatose bears. . . .

I was anxious to meet new people; I knew I would easily find many who shared my views. During this half-year I had moved within a narrow circle. I hardly knew anyone outside of it, moving endlessly as I had from place to place. I wanted to get to know this country not by traveling as a tourist, but from within, through many, many "kitchen tables." In sum, what I wanted more than anything else was to remain myself under completely different conditions.

I was afraid of nothing, I was sure everything would be easy and good. Never before in my life had I been so sure of having done the right thing. Previously, uncertainty about my own abilities and possibilities had haunted me. It had always been too easy for me to believe that everything I did was wrong, done badly. An inner shyness, an inner entrammelment, stood between me and other people, between me and an audience. More often than not I would have an urge to find a place to escape to, shutting the door behind me. All this was the psychological outcome of many years of life under a heavy weight, the result of an education in an unnatural family, the result of a long existence in a society that was silent and enslaved. In the Soviet Union there are many such people, oppressed and spiritually paralyzed.

Since leaving Moscow, and after living in India and here, I have become another person. My friends in Moscow would never believe that I could feel so completely free and at ease among strangers. I find it impossible to explain what this feeling of inner freedom, which now fills me, is like. No one in the Soviet Union knows anything like this sensation, and neither did I. Now I could not live even a single day without it. All small daily worries and details retreat into the background. Fatigue, a bad mood, indisposition, can dim a bright day, it's true; but the light of freedom, this inner freedom, goes on shining from within, from the heart. To experience it one has to have gone through all that I have been through. . . .

Early in December I moved my books and bags into the house I had rented for a year in Princeton. During the past month I had acquired a fairly large library, consisting of Russian and English books received by mail from readers and authors whom I didn't know. Books and the most indispensable clothes were all that I brought with me. But the owner of the house had rented it to me fully equipped and furnished.

The house, with its splendid library, was the home of a big New York publisher, recently deceased. His widow, Dorothy Commins, a professional musician, said to me: "We built this house ten years ago to work in, not to entertain guests."

The large living room had been arranged for home recitals; the circle of Mrs. Commins' friends belonged to the musical world, her son played the violin, her grandchildren also took part in concerts. Mrs. Commins left at my disposal a large collection of records and a first-rate record player. She treated me not as a future tenant, but as a friend who, exhausted after many hardships, had at last found a peaceful abode. She did everything possible to make me feel at home in her house, leaving me every conceivable household implement, with a wonderful foresight about everything I might be in need of. And indeed, I could have lived here for a whole year, working and without ever giving a thought to any purchases.

Mrs. Commins knew what work meant. In the living room stood a large oak table on which her husband had worked over manuscripts. She herself had recently published a collection of lullabies from all over the world, having spent several years in collecting the texts and musical scores. In Princeton she had pupils ranging from children to students and professors—she was an excellent piano teacher. Now she was planning to leave for a year to collect children's songs and musical games of different nations in thirteen countries of the East and West. She was no longer young and looked fragile, but she was starting off intrepidly on this long voyage, certain of finding everywhere friends who would help her.

In Mrs. Commins' house there were numerous books, musical scores and records, fine engravings and water colors on the walls, old silver and bronze, heavy furniture, and an excellent grand piano. Blessed peace and quiet reigned in this house, whose masters had loved to work and had cherished peace and quiet. In all the homes I visited I was always accepted as a friend: the Johnsons, Kennans, Canfields, Greenbaums, Schwartzes, Eleanor Friede, Ruth Briggs, Dorothy Commins. Everywhere I had felt surrounded by the warmth of a good home. Does not the face of America consist precisely in this—a land of pilgrims, exiles, discoverers of new worlds? The crux of the matter lies not just in hospitality, of which there had always been plenty in Russia until she fenced herself in from the rest of the world; of far greater importance is that in America the right is reserved for everyone to live the way he wants, always remaining himself wherever he may be.

Before leaving, Dorothy Commins had me meet some of her friends, wanting to be sure I was not left without help and someone to look after me.

There was Armand Borell, who had just begun taking piano lessons from her. He was a Swiss mathematician and had lived with his family in Princeton for many years. He owned an immense collection of classical music and folk songs, and I found in him the same contemplative approach to music I had known so well in Moscow mathematicians. Incidentally, Armand knew many of them personally and liked them, having a profound regard for Professor Gelfand of the Moscow University. At home his wife, his daughters, and he spoke French. Gaby was an excellent cook, and the two daughters, aged twelve and fourteen, were coquettish and graceful as only French girls of that age can be.

Dr. Edward Kendall, the Nobel Prize Laureate who discovered cortisone, liked to come and sit in Mrs. Commins' living room near the open fire. He was eighty years old but, like everyone else in this country, looked younger: clear blue eyes, a lively mind, a long ascetic life full of research work that went on day after day, hour after hour, sometimes resulting in a discovery.

Margot Einstein is a sculptor. Her small Madonna stands on Mrs. Commins' grand piano in the living room: a sad little figure, hiding her baby in her lap. There is something sad in Margot, too—a small, shy person, but easy to talk to, who understands what you want to say even before you have said it. The studio in her house is full of her works, small, graceful, full of mood.

In the home of Frank and Peggy Taplin there was chamber music almost every evening. Their two daughters—large girls with soft brown eyes and loose hair—looked so much like my Katie. I often found my children in the students I met here, and this was pleasant. Not sad at all. It comforted me.

There was also Louis Fischer, who had spent fourteen years as a correspondent in the U.S.S.R., whose sons had attended a Moscow school, and who had written a good deal about Soviet politics and life. Now he was a professor, a historian, and a writer. India had played a big role in his life. He knew that country well and loved it: in this we instantly found a great link in common.

I also got to know Professor Robert Tucker of Princeton University. His wife is a Russian from Moscow. For many years they had been made to suffer, waiting for the Soviet Government to grant Zhenya a visa to join her husband. Only since 1953 have marriages with foreigners been permitted in the U.S.S.R. Now Zhenya teaches Russian at Princeton.

Dorothy Commins need not worry; I will not be left without help here. The Kennans live five minutes away—it was Annelise who helped me find and rent this house.

In the middle of December I began receiving Christmas cards. This was my first Christmas; in the U.S.S.R. one only celebrates the New Year. But then, when you come to think of it, the New Year actually starts not on the first of January but on the date when, after the shortest, darkest day of the year, the sun "moves toward summer," and every new day after that adds unto itself a new minute. With this lengthening of days one's soul grows lighter, too.

So here was another feast for me. The wife of my Vienna publisher sent me decorations and candles for a Christmas tree. I shall remain at home, light the tree and listen to Christmas carols, sung from house to house by children. I shall remain alone, at home. I will like it better than being a guest in someone else's house. As I sit in this, my new living room, Christmas cards stand all around me, almost two hundred of them. Most of them came from Americans I have never seen, filled with warm greetings, wishes for happiness in the New Year and in this country, blessings. Others came from Germany, Switzerland, England, Australia, Canada, South America, Sweden, from people who knew and understood that I would never return to the U.S.S.R., and from people who had read *Twenty Letters*. I shed tears over many of these cards, such warmth seemed to flow to me from strangers from all over the world. This would never have been believed in the U.S.S.R.; as a result of half a century of Soviet rule people have been weaned from a belief in human kindness.

✻

On the nineteenth of December, 1967, at a small table in the restaurant of the Princeton Inn, sat Annelise Kennan, Louis Fischer, and I.

"Think of it!" I said. "Only one year ago today, I was leaving Moscow. What a blizzard was raging! My son saw me off at the airport late at night. Could anyone have imagined that I would settle down in Princeton and would be sitting here with you at this table?"

"Let us drink then to this *year of freedom!*" Louis Fischer said.

And we all three raised our glasses.

Acknowledgments

The Russian manuscript of this book has been thoroughly typed twice by Leokadija Maciunas, who in the process gave some useful editorial suggestions. Virginia Fiabane and Alberta Howard of the Princeton University library helped with the technical work.

The manuscript was read in Russian by George Kennan, Louis Fischer, Professor Robert Tucker and Mrs. Tucker, and Professor Richard Burgi. Mr. Kennan kindly allowed me to quote from his letters to me. Ambassador Chester Bowles permitted me to use the original text of my statement to the U.S. Embassy in Delhi, and gave some details of the situation caused by my coming there.

Rev. George Florovsky, Professor at Princeton University, and Mrs. Florovsky also read the manuscript, as did Archbishop John of San Francisco, who has given me constant encouragement since I came to this country.

The first part of the manuscript was read by Milovan Djilas, at the time a guest in Princeton. It was also read by Arkady Belinkov, a writer from Moscow, and Mrs. Belinkov, who chose to live in the United States.

Edmund Wilson read the manuscript in Russian. Paul Chavchavadze, before he made the translation, suggested some useful additions. I'm grateful to him for his beautiful translation in which the intonation of the Russian original is so perfectly reproduced.

The Russian text was carefully edited by Paul Olferiev, who also read the proofs of the Russian edition.

The English translation was read by a friend and neighbor, Dorothy H. Smith, and by my lawyer and friend, Alan U. Schwartz.

Mr. and Mrs. Cass Canfield read the translated version; the text was carefully edited by Frances Lindley and Richard E. Passmore. To read the proofs with them was a pleasure for me.

I am glad to express my deep gratitude to all these people for valuable suggestions and, most of all, for their friendly attitude. Of course, the responsibility for this book is mine only.

SVETLANA ALLILUYEVA